PROGRAMMING
VERTEX AND PIXEL SHADERS

WOLFGANG ENGEL

CHARLES RIVER MEDIA
Boston, Massachusetts

Publisher: Jenifer Niles
Cover Design: Tyler Creative
Cover Images: Copyright YAGER Development GmbH 2004

CHARLES RIVER MEDIA
25 Thomson Place
Boston, Massachusetts 02210
617-757-7900
617-757-7969 (FAX)
crm.info@thomson.com
www.charlesriver.com

This book is printed on acid-free paper.

Wolfgang Engel. *Programming Vertex and Pixel Shaders.*
ISBN: 1-58450-349-1

All brand names and product names mentioned in this book are trademarks or service marks of their respective companies. Any omission or misuse (of any kind) of service marks or trademarks should not be regarded as intent to infringe on the property of others. The publisher recognizes and respects all marks used by companies, manufacturers, and developers as a means to distinguish their products.

Library of Congress Cataloging-in-Publication Data
Engel, Wolfgang F.
  Programming vertex and pixel shaders / Wolfgang Engel.— 1st ed.
     p. cm.
  Includes bibliographical references and index.
  ISBN 1-58450-349-1 (pbk. : alk. paper)
  1. Computer games—Programming. 2. Three-dimensional display systems. I. Title.
  QA76.76.C672E58 2004
  794.8'16693—dc22
                              2004015282

Printed in the United States of America
06 7 6 5 4 3 2

PROGRAMMING
VERTEX AND PIXEL SHADERS

Contents

Acknowledgments

This book could not have been completed without the help of many people.

I would especially like to thank the technical reviewers of this book, Naty Hoffman and Lutz Latta (EA).

Additionally, I would like to thank Tom Forsyth (RAD GameTools) for helping me improve my knowledge on hardware specific quirks, Sim Dietrich (NVIDIA) for discussing aspects of shadow maps and for helping me to find out the capabilities of the NVIDIA GeForce 6800, Jason Mitchell (ATI) for answering my numerous questions regarding the *Rendering with Natural Light* demo, Gary King (NVIDIA) for proofreading the first draft of the first four chapters, which were afterwards rewritten with his comments in mind, Tzu-Chien Chiu (XGI) for examining Chapters 12-15 thoroughly and asking me the right questions, and all the students of the Advanced Rendering course at Gameversity (*www.gameversity.com*), especially Krystian Orzechowski, Juan Rufes, Robert Lewis, Ionut Costica, and Richard Geary.

I have to thank Philipp Schellbach, the technical director of Yager Development, for allowing me to use screenshots of one of my favorite games (*http://www.yager.de/en/project.html*) for the cover design of this book.

Additionally, I would like to thank Ken Hurley, Mark Dochtermann, Paul Keet, Matt Rusch, Andy Karn, Patrick Ghiocel, and Marvin Gouw for having a great time while working on the DX8 renderer of *Medal of Honour Pacific Assault* at EA LA.

Furthermore, I would like to thank Jenifer Niles and Dave Pallai for their patience with me, and the good time I had during our dinner at GDC 2004.

My special thanks goes to my wife, Katja, and our daughters, Anna and Emma, who had to spend many evenings and weekends during the last two years without me, and to my parents who gave me a wonderful and warm childhood.

Wolfgang F. Engel (*wolf@shaderx.com*)

I

Introduction

Until the advent of shader-capable hardware in 2001, graphics accelerators used a fixed-function graphics pipeline implemented in hardware. Specific graphics algorithms were "fixed" into the graphics chip, and the quality and availability of these algorithms differed on graphics cards depending upon the hardware vendor. This made it quite challenging to create a game that looked the same on different graphics cards while being visually unique.

It was a huge improvement to the visual quality of games when graphics cards with programming interfaces to their graphics-processing unit (GPU) became available. This step was influenced by a software package named Photorealistic Render-Man(tm) from Pixar Animation Studios, which had existed for more than a decade prior. Pixar's use of RenderMan in the development of feature films such as *Toy Story*, *A Bug's Life*, and *Finding Nemo* has resulted in a level of photorealistic and non-photorealistic graphics that has amazed audiences worldwide.

Today, the graphics card is programmed in assembly or in one of the high-level languages like the High-Level Shading Language (HLSL) provided by the DirectX SDK or the OpenGL shading language (GLSL). However, a relatively modest subset of the RenderMan shading language can be used on hardware via a new high-level language compiler from ATI, named ASHLI (Advanced Shading Language Interface), which is still in development.

This fundamental change from fixed-function to programmable graphics hardware offers a whole new level of opportunities for real-time graphics programmers. Shaders not only enable you to create unique games, but they also allow you to be far more creative than in times past.

1 Introduction

What You Will Learn

This book covers DirectX vertex and pixel shader programming with the High-Level Shading Language (HLSL) compiler provided with the DirectX SDK. We start from scratch, so you don't need any previous knowledge of shader programming. We will deal with the following topics:

- Writing and compiling HLSL shaders
- Tools of the trade
- Simple and advanced lighting algorithms
- Environment mapping
- High-Dynamic range lighting
- Projective textures
- Shadow maps
- Shadow volumes
- Displacement maps
- First steps to geometry images
- Shaders as part of a graphics engine

What You Need to Know and Equipment Requirements

You need a basic understanding of the math typically used in a game engine, and you need an intermediate understanding of the Direct3D API. It helps to know how to apply transformations and how to set a texture, filter a texture, and combine different values in the multitexturing unit. If additional support is needed, it is recommended that you work through an introductory level book first.

Your development system should consist of the following hardware and software:

- DirectX 9 System Development Kit (SDK)
- Windows XP Professional with the newest service pack (Windows XP Home does not support debug runtimes)
- At least Visual C++.NET 2002 (the DirectX shader debugger requires this)
- At least 512 MB of RAM
- At least 500 MB of free space on your hard drive
- A Pentium IV/ATHLON with more than 1.5 GHZ
- A graphics card that supports pixel shader Version 2 or 3

The most important requirement is the graphics card. To receive real-time visual feedback from the examples, your graphics card should support pixel shader Version 2 at the least. The examples in Chapters 26 and 27 require a graphics card that supports pixel shader Version 3.

If you do not have such a graphics card, the DirectX reference rasterizer (REF) will take over, and the examples will run very slowly, but most of them will run fast enough for you to see what is going on. Because the REF will be installed only with the DirectX 9 SDK (or newer), the SDK must always be installed first to test the example programs.

The source code of the examples will be updated for upcoming graphics cards. Watch for updates on www.wolfgang-engel.info *and* charlesriver.com

How This Book Is Organized

This book leads you through the fundamentals of setting up the DirectX runtime and the shader debugger to a more advanced level of implementing lighting models, shadow maps, etc. Therefore, it is best to work through the book one step at a time.

Our roadmap for the next couple of sections looks like this:

- Set up the working environment and the tools
- Shaders in the Direct3D graphics pipeline
- Shader support in software and hardware
- Fundamentals of HLSL shader programming

Then we will look at examples that use HLSL shaders. These examples will get more complicated as the book progresses into advanced rendering techniques.

Let's start by setting up our working environment and tools.

Tools of the Trade

All the tools we use throughout this book are provided with the DirectX SDK and the Visual C++.NET package. To be able to program HLSL shaders, we need to check if the following tools are installed and configured correctly:

- HLSL compiler (fxc.exe) to compile HLSL shaders
- Visual C++.NET integrated development environment (IDE)
- Shader Debugger to debug shaders

The Visual C++.NET IDE needs to be installed before the DirectX SDK so the SDK installer can set the paths for the include, exe, and library files of the SDK, and install the debugger into the existing .NET installation.

The HLSL compiler is located in the utility directory of the DirectX SDK installation. On many computers, this is the following directory:

```
D:\DX90SDK\Utilities
```

To integrate the HLSL compiler into your development environment, the Visual C++.NET IDE needs to know where to find it and how to call it.

HLSL Compiler

The High-Level Shading Language is a C-like language with extensions for graphics. (See the upcoming Chapter 3 "HLSL Shader Programming" for more information.) It is designed to build an assembly program from the HLSL source code.

The compiler (fxc.exe) can be invoked by calling the D3DXCompileShader*() functions from within the source code of your application or by calling fxc.exe from inside the integrated development environment (IDE).

To use the compiler within the Visual C++.NET integrated development environment (IDE), an *.exe path must be added to the list of Executable files directories in the Tools > Options > VC++ Directories dialog box as shown in Figure 1.1.

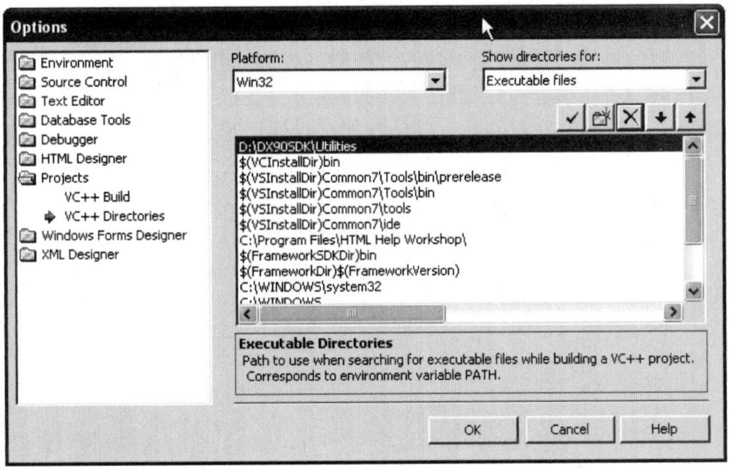

FIGURE 1.1   *The Options dialog of Visual C++.NET.*

To be able to use the HLSL compiler with a specific file in the Solution Explorer of the Visual C++.NET IDE, we need to set up a Custom Build Step in the IDE. This is done by right-clicking on the shader file in the solution explorer of the IDE. From the resulting pop-up menu, choose Property Pages. Your computer screen should now look similar to Figure 1.2.

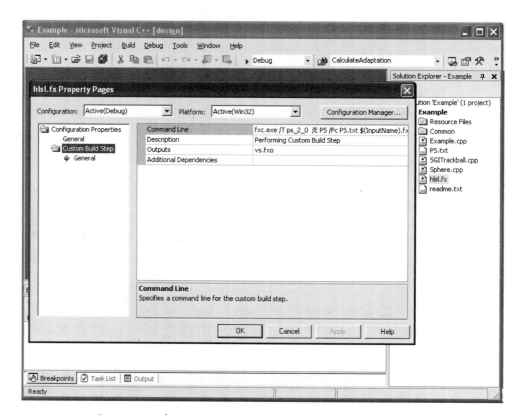

FIGURE 1.2   *Integrating the HLSL compiler into the Visual C++.NET IDE.*

Having the compiler integrated with the IDE can be convenient in the development process, because you can learn from the disassembled output or provide pre-compiled code with the shipping application.

The command-line options are summarized in Table 1.1.

Table 1.1 HLSL Compiler Command-Line Options

Option	Description
-T target	Compile target (default: vs_2_0; special: fx_2_0)
-E name	Entrypoint name (default: main)
-Od	Disable optimizations
-Vd	Disable validation
-Zi	Enable debugging information
-Zpr	Pack matrices in row-major order
-Zpc	Pack matrices in column-major order
-Fo file	Output object file
-Fc file	Output listing of generated code
-Fh file	Output header containing generated code
-D id=text	Define macro
-nologo	Suppress copyright message

Most of these options will be explained in more detail in the upcoming HLSL shader programming chapter. An example of a command line can look like this:

```
fxc.exe  /T ps_2_0     /E PSProjTexture /Fc $(InputName).txt  \
$(InputName).fx
compiler compile Target Entrypoint      output assembly       \
input file
$(InputName).fx
```

This command line is typed into the entry field named Command Line in the Property Pages Box. The second entry field expects a descriptive sentence that will be shown in the output window to identify the custom compile step. The entry field labeled Output stores the name of the output file.

Because there can be many shaders in one effect file, there is the special target command, fx_2_0, to dump all shaders in an effect file into one text file.

```
fxc.exe /T fx_2_0 /Fc $(InputName).txt "$(InputName).fx"
```

Being able to see the generated assembly code not only allows you to optimize code on the HLSL level, but it also shows you which calculations that happen per vertex in the vertex shader could be moved into the application layer and executed per object.

After having provided all necessary data, the dialog box can be closed and the HLSL compiler can be invoked by right-clicking on the shader file that holds the shader source code (in this example, CookTorrance.fx) and then clicking Compile.

Visual C++.NET Shader Debugger

A shader debugger is provided for Visual C++.NET and higher. The installation of the shader debugger is an option in the DirectX 9 SDK installation routine, which is selected by default. Figure 1.3 shows the dialog box that enables you to install the shader debugger.

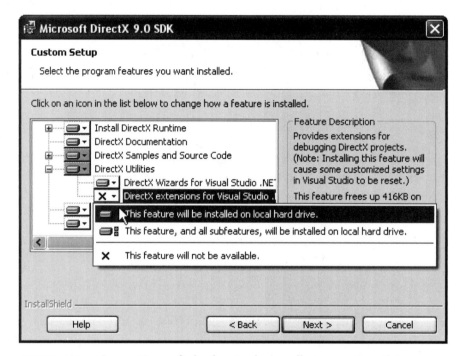

FIGURE 1.3 *Custom Setup dialog box in the installation routine of the DirectX 9 SDK.*

The shader debugger will be installed if DirectX extensions for Visual Studio.NET is selected. Furthermore, to debug shaders, the Use Debug Version of Direct3D and Enable Shader Debugging checkboxes in the configuration panel of the DirectX runtime need to be marked as shown in Figure 1.4.

This Properties box can be found in Windows XP at Start>Control Panel >DirectX.

With the debug runtime switched on and set to the highest level, we can move on to the following section, which deals with the compilation and debugging process of shaders.

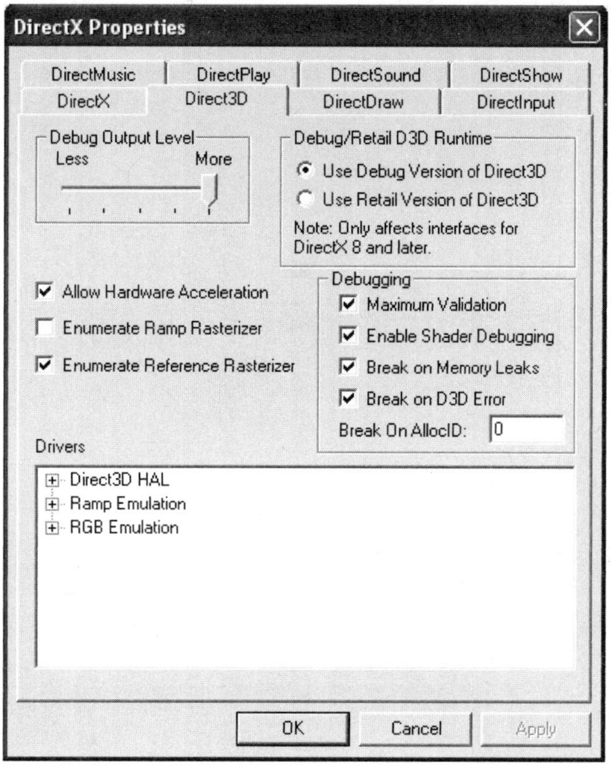

FIGURE 1.4 *The Direct3D Properties box.*

Compile and Debug a Shader

Compiling and debugging an HLSL shader-driven application is shown step-by-step in the following screenshots. These screenshots were created with the first example program of this book, which can be found in Chapter 4 - Ambient\Ambient on the companion CD-ROM.

ON THE CD

Compiling an HLSL Shader in the IDE

To compile an HLSL shader from inside the Visual C++.NET IDE, right-click on the shader file in the solution explorer and then click on Compile as shown in Figure 1.5.

The output of the HLSL compiler is shown in Figure 1.6. The most important output of the HLSL compiler are warnings and error messages together with line numbers that help you to track down bugs. In Figure 1.6, you can see that an assembly output of the compiled HLSL code is stored in PS.txt.

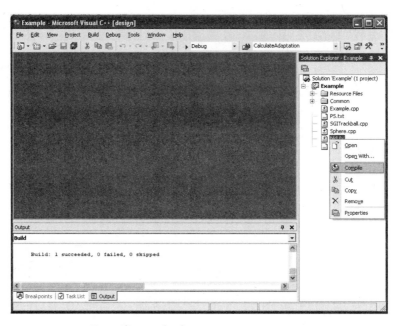

FIGURE 1.5   *Compiling a shader.*

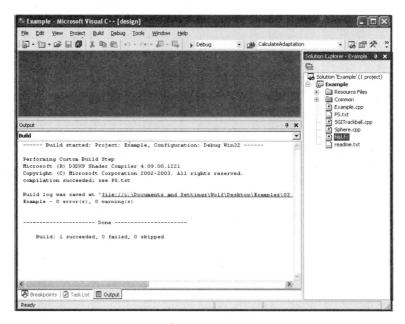

FIGURE 1.6   *HLSL compiler output.*

Debugging a Shader

During the compilation process, you may need to locate a bug. The Visual C++.NET shader debugger will aid you in this. To debug a shader, you need to do the following:

ON THE CD

- Launch Visual C++.NET and click Open Solution (try Chapter 4 - Ambient\ Ambient).
- Confirm that the shaders are compiled with debug information by setting the flags D3DXSHADER_DEBUG | D3DXSHADER_SKIPOPTIMIZATION. If you exceed instruction slot limits when running unoptimized, there is an additional flag you can choose. D3DXSHADER_FORCE_VS_SOFTWARE_NOOPT (or D3DXSHADER_FORCE_PS_ SOFTWARE_NOOPT) forces the compiler to compile against the next higher available software target. Because software shader models do not have instruction slot limits, this flag ensures that unoptimized shaders do not have this problem. This flag still does the other things that the skip optimization flag does, such as preventing instruction reordering and dead code elimination.
- Set a breakpoint in the vertex shader or the pixel shader.
- Launch the application with Visual C++.NET IDE with Debug > Direct3D > Start D3D.
- Select the reference rasterizer as the default driver by pressing F2.
- Shader assembly can be viewed under Debug > Window > Disassembly.
- Render targets can be viewed under Debug > Direct3D > RenderTarget.

If you only want to debug vertex shaders, it is enough to select SOFTWARE_VP from the Vertex Processing drop-down menu of the Direct3D Properties dialog box in the example programs or to provide the software vertex processing flag D3DDEV-TYPE_SW as the device type to the CreateDevice() function.

Figure 1.7 shows how to set debug breakpoints and how to invoke the shader debugger:

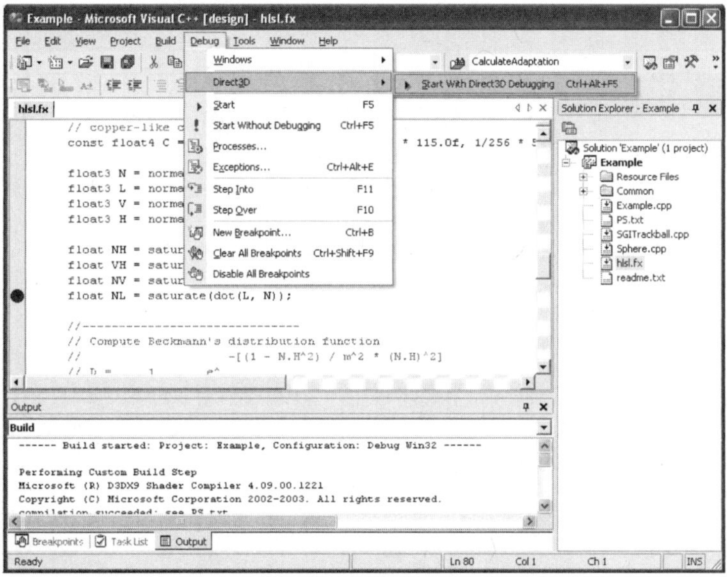

FIGURE 1.7 *Set debug breakpoints.*

The shader debugger can be used in the same way as the Visual C++.NET debugger. You can see values of variables by hovering over the variable with your mouse pointer, as seen in Figure 1.8.

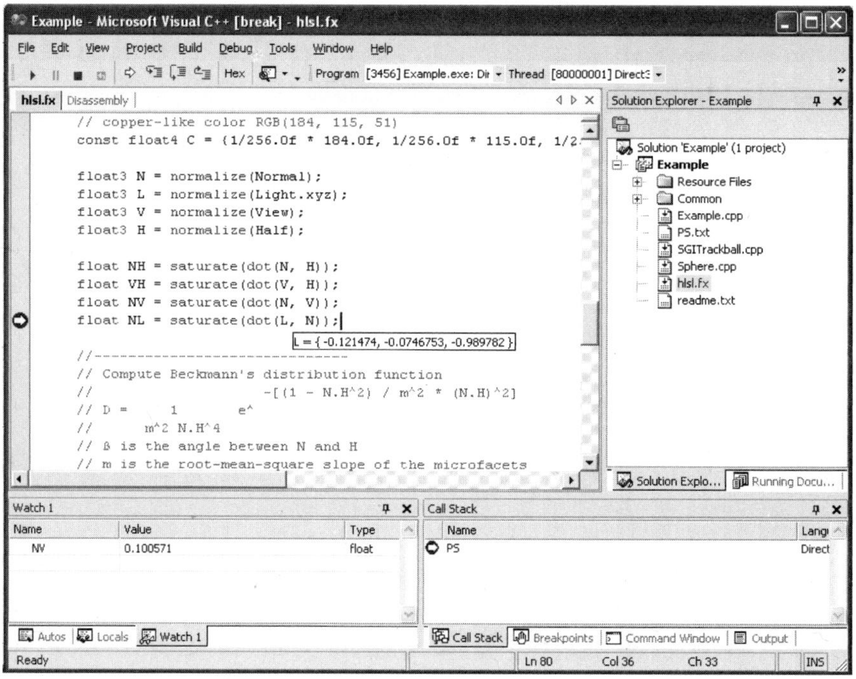

FIGURE 1.8   *See values of variables.*

Variables can be added to the watch list by right-clicking the variable and then clicking Add Watch. This is a convenient way to keep track of variable data.

To inspect the assembly of an HLSL shader, click on Window > Disassembly. Figure 1.9 shows a screenshot from an HLSL shader with assembly source.

With the shader paused at the breakpoint, you can hold the mouse over individual registers to see the contents or drag and drop a register into the watch window to look at the contents.

Additionally, you can set a breakpoint that will only stop the application if a certain condition is met; for example, after some number of vertices have been processed or only if a certain normal vector value is seen. This is called a conditional breakpoint. Here is an example of how to set one:

- Right click on the breakpoint and select Properties, as shown in Figure 1.10.

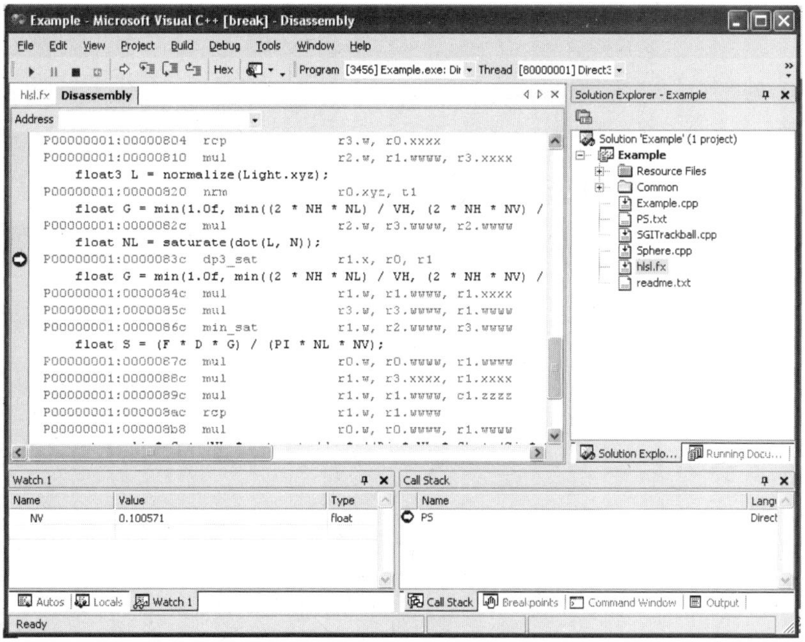

FIGURE 1.9 *Disassembly output of an HLSL shader.*

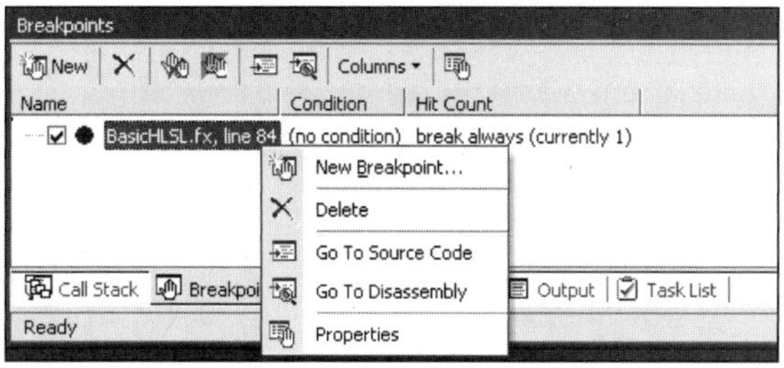

FIGURE 1.10 *Properties of a breakpoint.*

- Click on Condition in the Breakpoint Properties dialog box shown in Figure 1.11.
- In the text box on the Breakpoint Condition dialog box, enter an expression that evaluates to a Boolean result.

The debugger will break if the condition is true. This way conditional breakpoints offer a powerful method for fine-tuning the debugging process.

It is even possible to set pixel area breakpoints by specifying the x and y value of the pixel that should be inspected. To get to the dialog box that allows this, choose Debug > New Breakpoint and then click on the Data tab.

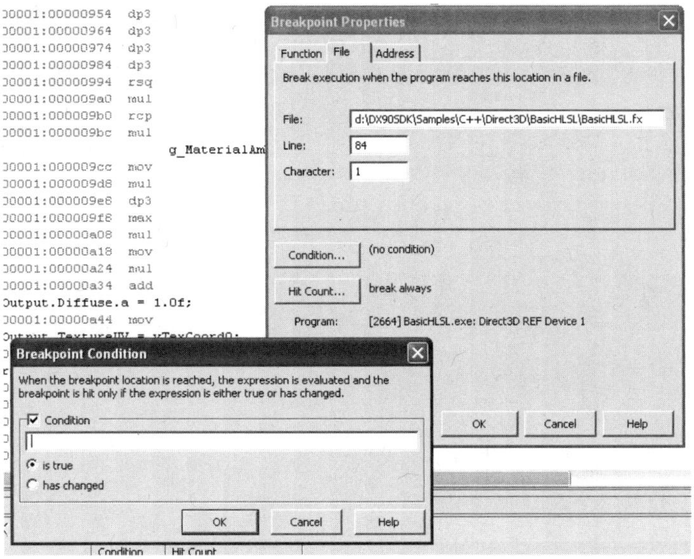

FIGURE 1.11   *Conditions of a breakpoint.*

Although there are numerous other features supported by the shader debugger and the HLSL compiler, these are the most important to get started. Furthermore, there are many more tools that help to make writing shaders as simple as possible. The following section presents the most common tools at the time of this writing.

Other Recommended Tools

The following sections describe other tools that simplify the shader writing process.

ATI RenderMonkey

At the time of this writing the shader integrated development environment of choice is ATI's RenderMonkey™. It offers all the tools necessary for rapid prototyping of shaders, as seen in Figure 1.12. Additionally, you can export DirectX effect files from the program, create a dialog box for the artist, and use the native XML format used by RenderMonkey for developing your own shader file format.

RenderMonkey helps to create assembly for DirectX 9's High-Level Shader Language shaders. It additionally supports the OpenGL Shading Language (GLSL) and provides an SDK to integrate it better into the production flow of a game development team. RenderMonkey can be downloaded from *www.ati.com/developer/ tools.html*.

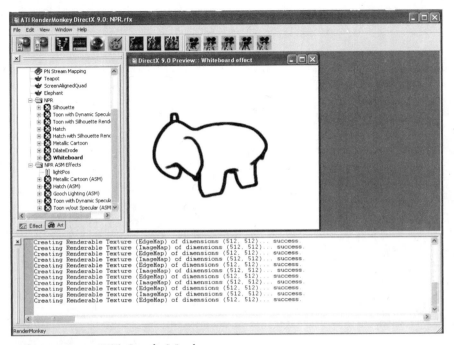

FIGURE 1.12   *ATI's RenderMonkey.*

NVIDIA's FX Composer

Another great shader integrated development environment is FX Composer™ by
NVIDIA (*developer.nvidia.com*). It offers several ways to optimize shaders specifically
for NVIDIA graphics cards. Additionally, at the time of this writing it already supports the latest available shader versions (vs_3_0 and ps_3_0).

Figure 1.13 shows, in the upper-left corner, the dialog that lets you choose the
shader. Each picture shows a preview of the shader. To see how the geometry is
processed by FX Composer, a view control that shows the content of the scenegraph
is available. FX Composer offers the ability to define a very flexible dialog box to offer
artists the ability to tweak properties of the shader.

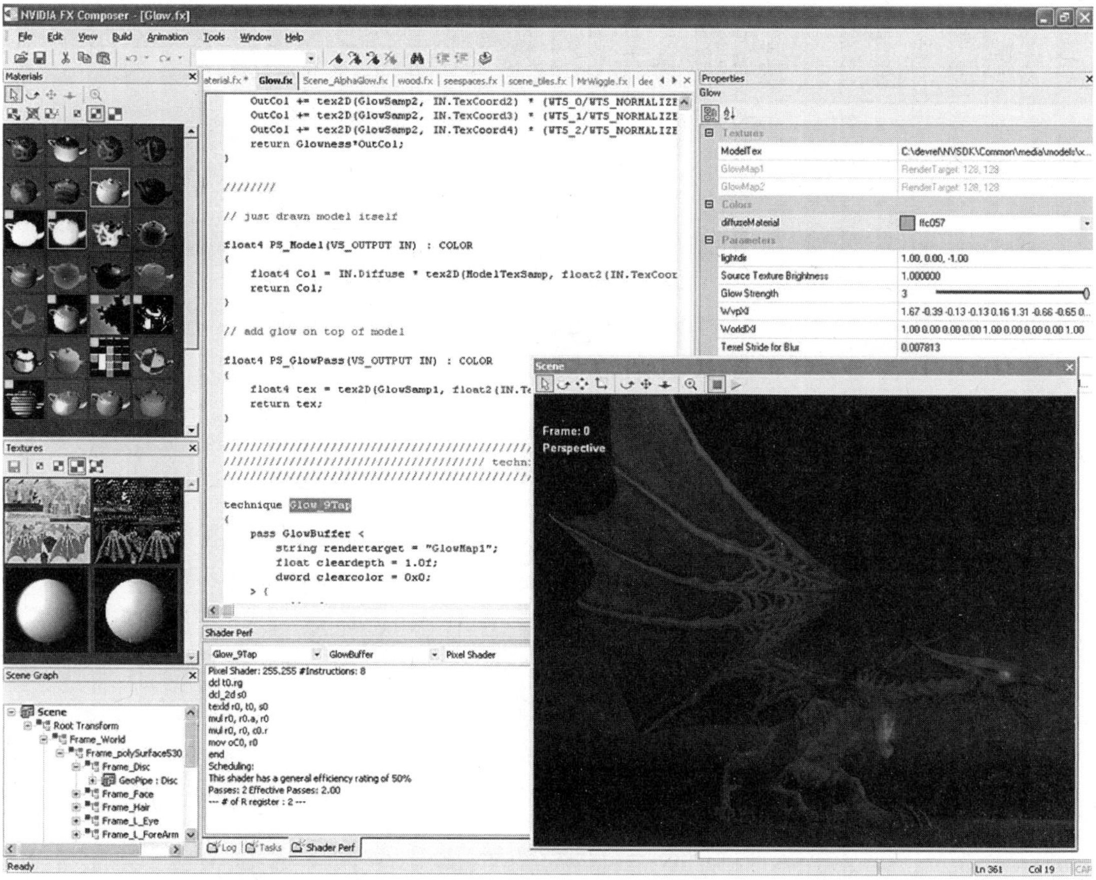

FIGURE 1.13 *NVIDIA's FX composer.*

2 Direct3D Pipeline

Having integrated the tools that are necessary to start shader development, we now need to examine the Direct3D graphics pipeline to understand the capabilities offered by vertex and pixel shaders. The Direct3D graphics pipeline shown in Figure 2.1 outlines the order of the graphics operations that manipulate the input data in a way that leads to the illusion of 3D graphics. Please note that this outline follows a more didactical concept than actually reflecting a software or hardware implementation. It is targeted to the programmer who wants to use this pipeline but not implement it.

Seeing the tasks of the shader stages in the Direct3D pipeline aids in understanding what the stages above and below the vertex shader and pixel shader stages expect from these stages, and it helps to show how vertex and pixel shaders can be used to influence these stages.

Direct3D Pipeline

The following diagram divides the Direct3D pipeline stages into groups that tessellate, operate on vertices, and operate on pixels.

In the first group, vertices are tessellated. DirectX 9 supports two types of higher-order primitives, or patches, that are tessellated. These are referred to as N-patches and Rect/Tri patches.

The next series of stages covers operations that are performed on the vertices provided by the first stage. There are two different ways of processing vertices:

- The fixed-function, *Transform & Lighting* (T&L) pipeline, in which as the name implies, the functionality is essentially fixed.
- *Vertex shaders*, the new mechanism to operate on vertices first introduced in DirectX 8.

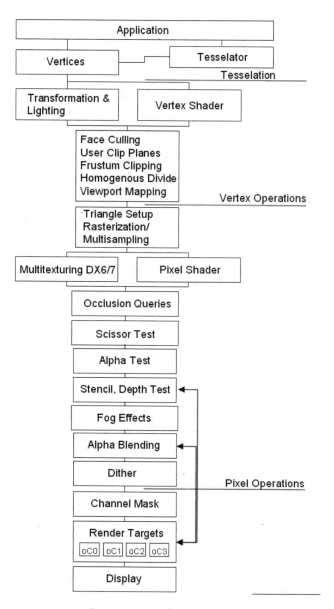

FIGURE 2.1   *Direct3D pipeline.*

The vertex shader reads, for example, one untransformed vertex, transforms the vertex, and writes the resulting transformed vertex to its output registers. It can manipulate all the data sent to it via the vertex buffer. The data layout of a vertex buffer is usually outlined by a vertex structure. Such a structure might look like the following:

```
struct Vertex
{
    D3DXVECTOR3 Position;
    D3DXVECTOR3 Normal;
    D3DXVECTOR2 TexCoord;
    D3DXVECTOR3 Tangent;
};
```

In this case, the position data, a normal, a texture coordinate, and a tangent are sent to the vertex shader. The vertex shader can manipulate each and send the result to the following pipeline stages. To manipulate this data, the hardware unit that processes vertex shaders can be programmed using a huge number of instructions that have a wide range of functionality. This is in contrast to the legacy Fixed-function T&L stage, which needed to be programmed by setting certain pipeline states, making it quite inflexible.

This simplified diagram shows that face culling, user clip planes, frustum clipping, homogenous divide, and viewport mapping operate on pipeline stages after the vertex shader, as seen in Figure 2.1. Therefore, these stages cannot be controlled by a vertex shader; they are controlled by Direct3D API calls and by setting render states.

A vertex shader is incapable of either writing to vertices other than the one it is currently processing or creating new vertices.

New vertices can be created with the help of the tessellator stage that is situated above the vertex shader at the beginning of the graphics pipeline.

The vertex shader generates one output vertex from each vertex it receives as input. This vertex might be culled away right after leaving the vertex shader.

Backface culling removes all triangles that are facing away from the viewer or camera. These are by default the vertices that are grouped counterclockwise with respect to the viewer. On average, half of your game world triangles face away from the camera at any given time, so this culling step helps reduce rendering time.

User clip planes can be set by the developer to clip triangles that are outside of these planes and to therefore reduce the number of calculations.

There are two alternatives to user clip planes:

- Using the pixel shader instruction texkill (this instruction cancels rendering of the current pixel if any of the first three components (UVW) of the texture coordinates is less than zero)
- Using guard band clipping on hardware with a guard band region [Dietrich]

Frustum clipping is performed with the viewing frustum. Traditionally, primitives that lay partially or completely off-screen must be clipped to the screen or viewport boundary, which is represented by a 3D viewing frustum [Watt]. Newer approaches that are used by most hardware avoid those costly clipping tests [Olano].

After the perspective transformation the *homogenous* (or perspective) *divide* happens. This means that the x-, y-, and z-coordinates of each vertex are divided by w.

[Olano] et al. do not need to differentiate anymore between frustum clipping and homogenous divide, because they work entirely in homogenous coordinates.

The clip coordinates or normalized device coordinates (NDC) created by the homogenous divide are then mapped to the screen by transforming them into screen space via *viewport mapping*.

The life of the vertices end and the life of the pixels begin in the *triangle setup*. Traditional approaches compute the parameters required for the rasterization of the triangles one triangle at a time and—among other functions—define the pixel coordinates of the triangle outline. This means it defines the first and last pixel of the triangle, scan-line by scan-line (see Figure 2.2).

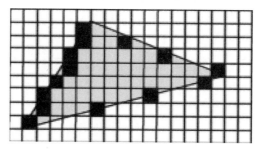

FIGURE 2.2   *Triangle setup.*

Newer approaches like that of [Olano] use an edge function to test if a 2D point is in a triangle [Olano]. This approach achieves better performance on parallel implementations usually found in current graphics hardware.

The *rasterizer* then interpolates the attributes, which are output from the vertex shader across the triangle, and fills in pixels (see Figure 2.3). These attributes include color, depth, and texture coordinates. This interpolation is linear in camera/object/world space but nonlinear in screen space. This is due to the perspective transform. The rasterizer is also responsible for Direct3D *multisampling* (full-scene antialiasing). Because it is done in the rasterizer stage, multisampling only affects triangles and group of triangles; it does not affect lines.

The idea of multisampling is to render multiple samples of a frame, combining them at subpixel level and then filter those subpixels to achieve antialiasing. The application can even specify that only some subsamples be affected by a given rendering pass. Multisampling runs the pixel shader only once per pixel, rather than once per sample, and textures are only fetched once. This way, multisampling increases the resolution of polygon edges and, therefore, the resolution of depth and stencil tests.

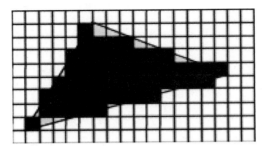

FIGURE 2.3 *Filled triangle.*

Contrary to multisampling, super-sampling renders the actual frame to a resolution that is higher than the required screen resolution. For example, 4x super-sampling the resolution is four times as high as the screen resolution, meaning it has twice the number of pixels in x- as well as in y-direction. This rendering to 4x resolution has the effect that each pixel on the screen is initially represented by four pixels in the back buffer, each being the quarter size of the screen pixel. This way, the subpixel level is reached and the filtering of those four pixels generates the antialiased screen pixel. The result looks good, but the 3D chip has to render four times the screen resolution, which costs a huge amount of fill rate. Super-sampling is used today by all the GeForce and RADEON chips, and its current incarnations have evolved a lot.

There are some problems with multisampling: the instruction texkill or the HLSL intrinsic function clip() or alpha-testing still only work per-pixel, not per-sample. So aliasing effects and jagged edges can be introduced here. Additionally, texture sampling can get tricky. Because there is only one texture fetch per-pixel, not per-sample, you can run into problems at triangle edges. (See in Chapter 3 the section on the CENTROID input pixel shader modifier, which explains how to reduce the texture sampling problems).

GeForce and RADEON graphics cards have another stage in between the triangle setup and the pixel shader stages. They have a visibility subsystem that is responsible for z-occlusion culling (on RADEON cards, Hierarchical-Z). It determines whether a pixel will be hidden behind an earlier rendered pixel. If it is hidden, it will be immediately discarded and it won't enter the pixel shader, thus saving the initial z-buffer read of the pixel-rendering pipeline. During scan-line conversion (see Figure 2.2), the screen is divided into pixel blocks (RADEON 7×00: 8×8; RADEON 8×00, 9000, 9100, and 9200: 4×4), and each block is assigned a bit that determines whether that block is "not cleared," which means visible, or "cleared," which means occluded. A quick z-check is performed on each block to determine whether any pixel in them is visible. If a pixel in a block is visible, the status bit of the whole block is visible. Otherwise, the status bit of the whole block remains set to occluded and the whole block will not be sent to the pixel shader. This saves not only a write into the z-buffer, compared to texkill, but also a read of the z-buffer, although the biggest savings from this technique is avoiding pixel shader operations.

The *pixel shader* is not involved on the subpixel level in any way. It receives the already multisampled pixels along with z, color values, and texture data, that were not occluded by the automatic occlusion culling done by current graphics hardware. To shade the pixel, the pixel shader interface provides instructions that affect the texture addressing (texture instructions or texture operations) and instructions that combine the texture values in different ways with each other (arithmetic instructions, or ALU operations).

> *The hardware unit that modifies vertices or pixels is called a vertex or pixel shader. Similarly, in DirectX terminology, the ASCII file that holds the source code to program the hardware unit is also called a vertex or pixel shader. In OpenGL terminology, the source code is called a vertex program or fragment program.*

Compared to the legacy multitexturing unit, the hardware unit that processes the pixel shader offers much more flexibility by being programmable by a set of instructions that gives the programmer more freedom to implement new algorithms, whereas the multitexturing unit only exposes a very abstract set of pipeline states. How to program the pixel shader with these instructions is shown in this book.

Directly after the pixel shader comes the *occlusion query*. This asynchronous visibility query mechanism counts how many pixels are visible. In other words, an occlusion query returns the number of pixels that pass z-testing. Zero is "fully occluded," which means the pixels are not visible from the current camera position. To use this visibility query mechanism, you must display objects or object groups from front to back when rendering (read more in an article by Dean Sekulic [Sekulic]).

The next stage in the Direct3D graphics pipeline is the *scissor test*. It tests if a pixel is in the specified rectangular area of the window. If the pixel lies in the area, it will be skipped. Otherwise, it will be set. The scissor test is a simplified and therefore more efficient version of the stencil test. However, it is less powerful, because the testing area is rectangular.

The *alpha test* stage outputs pixels with a specific alpha value, and discards the rest. This is one way to map decals that have an alpha mapped texture. The alpha test can be driven by the pixel shader, for example, to reject pixels that are not outlines in the outline rendering pass of cartoon rendering [Card/Mitchell].

The *stencil test* masks the pixel in the render target with the contents of the stencil buffer. This is useful for dissolves, decaling, outlining, or building shadow volumes (see Chapter 24).

The *depth test* determines whether a pixel is visible by comparing its depth value to the stored depth value. The depth test is a pixel-by-pixel logical test that asks "Is this new pixel obscured by the current pixel at this location?" If the answer returned is yes, the pixel gets discarded. If the answer is no, the pixel will travel further through the pipeline and the z-buffer will be updated. The pixel shader can use the depth test with texdepth (ps.1.4 only) or texm3x2depth (ps.1.3 only) instructions. These instructions can calculate the depth value used in the depth buffer comparison test on a per-pixel basis. In pixel shader ps_2_0 upwards, a dedicated depth register is available that is a write-only scalar register that returns a new depth value for a depth test against the depth buffer. Modifying the z value disables the automatic z-occlusion culling mentioned above.

The next stage in the Direct3D pipeline is *fog*. A fog factor is computed and applied to the pixel using a blending operation to combine the fog amount (color) and the already shaded pixel color, depending on how far away an object is. The distance to an object is determined by its z- or w-value or by using a separate attenuation value that measures the distance between the camera and the object in a vertex shader. If fog is computed per-vertex, it is interpolated across the triangles.

> *In pixel shader Version 3, the final fog blending is expected to be performed by the pixel shader. Consequently, the fog blending stage of the pixel pipeline is disabled.*

The *alpha blending* stage blends the pixel's data with the pixel data already in the render target. Because it needs to read back data from the render target to do so (that's why the arrow in Figure 2.1 points in both directions from and to the render target), it is a quite expensive operation. Alpha blending can add, multiply, and even square the colors in several different combinations. This is done with the following blend factors, which control how the source and destination pixels are blended together:

```
FinalColor = SourcePixelColor * SourceBlendFactor + \
DestPixelColor * DestBlendFactor
```

It is useful to blend, for example, two textures in different ways or to simulate different levels of transparency.

Alpha blending is not supported on floating-point buffers on ps_2_0 capable graphics cards such as the ATI RADEON 9500 - X800 (the GeForce 6800 only supports it on 16-bit D3DFMT_A16B16G16R16F floating-point textures). Nevertheless, alpha blending can be simulated with the help of the pixel shader [Caruzzi].

Dithering tries to fool the eye into seeing more colors than are actually present by placing different colored pixels next to one another to create a composite color that the eye will see. For example, a blue pixel next to a yellow pixel would lead to a green appearance. That was a common technique in the days of 8-bit and 4-bit color systems. You switch on the Dithering stage globally with D3DRS_DITHERENABLE, but most recent hardware will not perform any dithering to targets with more than 8-bit color.

The *render target* is usually the backbuffer in which the finished scene is rendered, but it could also be the surface of a texture or one render target of a multiple-render target available on recent hardware (accessed with the oC0-oC3 output registers). This is useful for the creation of procedural textures or for reusing results of previous pixel shader executions. The main render target is read by the stencil test, the depth test, and the alpha blending stage.

To summarize the tasks of the pixel shader in the Direct3D pipeline:

- The pixel shader receives already multisampled pixels along with z, color values, and texture data that were not removed by the automatic z-occlusion culling system.
- The pixel shader is able to support or drive some of the subsequent Direct3D stages and will take over additional responsibilities of subsequent stages in the future. (In pixel shader Version 3, it takes over responsibility of the fog stage.)

Conclusion

Programming vertex and pixel shaders means providing data to the stream-processing data flow and manipulating it mainly in the vertex and pixel shader units. The programmer can directly manipulate the data of one vertex, which makes it more flexible than the legacy fixed-function approach, where it was only possible to manipulate data by setting pipeline states and providing flags.

The pixel shader is also based on the same idea of programmability. Whereas the multitexturing unit exposed a set of pipeline states on a very abstract level, which can be set to achieve a certain effect with an underlying algorithm, the programmable pixel shader is much more flexible with its set of instructions enabling implementations of any algorithm the programmer wants to visualize.

Furthermore, this chapter showed how the vertex shader and the pixel shader play together with the other pipeline stages. This is useful in understanding how data can be fed to them and how data is output by them to subsequent stages. Judging from the developments of recent years, there is also a notion of moving more and more functionality into the programmable parts of the pipeline.

3

HLSL Shader Programming

Now that you understand vertex and pixel shaders, we can start to program them. Throughout most of this book, we achieve this by using a high-level language similar to C, which is a component of the DirectX SDK. This High-Level Shading Language (HLSL) makes learning shader programming faster and makes the shader code easier to read. It also helps the developer to think on the algorithm level while implementing shaders, because it removes the burden of thinking about register read-port limits, instruction co-issuing, and so on. In addition to freeing the developer from hardware details, HLSL offers all the usual advantages of a high-level language, such as easy code reuse, improved readability, and the presence of an optimizing compiler [Peeper/Mitchell].

The upcoming sections will cover the data stream through the vertex and the pixel shader from preparation of data to the output of the pixel shader. This will give you a bird's eye view of how the data streams to the vertex and pixel shaders are set up and will demonstrate the task of the shader programmer.

Vertex Shaders

The vertex shader manipulates data that is part of a structure that describes a vertex. Figure 3.1 shows the data flow in the graphics pipeline; the programmer has to take care of the circled portion when programming vertex shaders.

The vertex shader expects data from the application, and the Direct3D runtime needs to be informed about the structure of this data. Usually the data is provided in

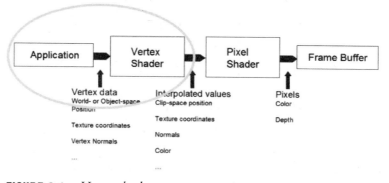

FIGURE 3.1   *Vertex shader stream processing.*

a so-called vertex structure through a vertex buffer. The steps necessary to input this data are as follows:

1. Create a structure that shows the segmentation of the data.
2. Create a vertex declaration that describes this structure.
3. Create a vertex buffer object and an index buffer object (if indexed primitives are needed).
4. Input vertex data into the vertex and index buffers (as shown in the vertex structure and described in the vertex declaration).
5. Create a vertex shader and compile it.
6. Set render states for the nonprogrammable parts of the pipeline.
7. Set the vertex and index buffers as the input stream for the draw primitive functions.
8. Set the vertex and pixel shader constants.
9. Set the vertex shader to modify the vertex data.
10. Execute stream(s) by calling the `DrawIndexedPrimitive()` function.

The following text focuses on the relevant tasks to set up the vertex stream to the programmable vertex shader unit.

Vertex Structure

To feed data to the vertex shader, you must first create a vertex structure that defines the format of that vertex data, as shown below:

```
struct Vertex
{
    D3DXVECTOR3 Position;
    D3DXVECTOR3 Normal;
    D3DXVECTOR2 TexCoord;
    D3DXVECTOR3 Tangent;
};
```

This vertex holds an untransformed position value consisting of x, y, and z, a normal, a pair of texture coordinates, and the tangent vector. All vertices in the vertex buffer should be stored in this format.

Vertex Declaration

A vertex declaration provides the vertex format to the Direct3D runtime. A suitable vertex declaration for the preceding vertex format is as follows:

```
D3DVERTEXELEMENT9 decl[]=
  {
  // stream, offset, type, tessellator processing method, usage, index
  {0, 0, D3DDECLTYPE_FLOAT3, D3DDECLMETHOD_DEFAULT,
      D3DDECLUSAGE_POSITION, 0},
  {0, 12, D3DDECLTYPE_FLOAT3, D3DDECLMETHOD_DEFAULT,
      D3DDECLUSAGE_NORMAL, 0},
  {0, 24, D3DDECLTYPE_FLOAT2, D3DDECLMETHOD_DEFAULT,
      D3DDECLUSAGE_TEXCOORD, 0},
  {0, 32, D3DDECLTYPE_FLOAT3, D3DDECLMETHOD_DEFAULT,
      D3DDECLUSAGE_TANGENT, 0},
   D3DDECL_END()
  };
```

The fourth parameter in each line of the declaration, which describes the *tessellator processing method*, can be used to compute values for higher-order surfaces with the tessellator, for example, for displacement mapping on pre-vs_3_0 hardware. Using D3DDECLMETHOD_DEFAULT as the tessellator processing method means that this vertex element is interpolated; otherwise, the vertex element is copied into the vertex processor's input register. D3DDECLMETHOD_LOOKUP and D3DDECLMETHOD_LOOKUPPRESAMPLED look up a displacement map or a presampled displacement map on pre-vs_3_0 hardware.

The fifth parameter of each line describes the data usage. For example, it marks data as normals, texture coordinates, or tangents. Marking data for use as a normal can be done with the semantic D3DDECLUSAGE_NORMAL. The semantics are generally a binding mechanism between vertex declarations and vertex shaders.

Using semantics enables greater interoperability between various data layouts and vertex shaders.

Please note that the D3DDECLUSAGE_TEXCOORD semantic can be used for all kinds of user-defined fields (that don't have an existing semantic defined by Direct3D).

The last parameter in a declaration line describes the index of the data type. It can be used, for example, to put several texture coordinates into the vertex stream, each with an associated index.

The vertex declaration is created with a call to the CreateVertexDeclaration() function, as follows:

```
m_pd3dDevice->CreateVertexDeclaration(decl, &m_pVertexDeclaration);
```

As we will see in the section on the D3DX effect framework, with effect files, this task can be handled by the effect file framework.

Vertex Streams

Direct3D is able to assemble data for each vertex that is fed into the processing portion of the Direct3D pipeline from one or more data streams. For example, one data stream can hold the positions and normals, while a second holds color values and a third holds texture coordinates. The function that delivers this functionality is `SetStreamSource()`. The declaration of this method is:

```
HRESULT SetStreamSource(
    UINT StreamNumber,
    IDirect3DVertexBuffer9 *pStreamData,
    UINT OffsetInBytes,
    UINT Strides
);
```

The first parameter defines the data stream, and the second parameter holds a pointer to an `IDirect3DVertexBuffer9` interface, representing the vertex buffer to bind to the specified data stream. The next parameter holds the offset from the beginning of the stream to the beginning of the vertex data, in bytes. To find out if the device supports stream offsets, see the `D3DDEVCAPS2_STREAMOFFSET` constant in `D3DDEVCAPS2`. The last parameter holds the stride of the component, in bytes.

Here is an example:

```
m_pd3dDevice->SetStreamSource(0, m_pVertices, 0, sizeof(Vertex));
```

DirectX 7 compatible hardware supports only one stream; newer hardware supports up to 16. An example program that shows a model with fur might use the following pseudocode to use streams.

```
All passes: stream 0: position, normal, diffuse vertex color
if (finpass)
    fin pass stream 1: texture coordinates for fins
if (shellpass)
    shells pass stream 2: texture coordinates for shells
```

In every pass, `SetStreamSource()` sets stream 0 to use the position, normal, and diffuse color values. The user can choose the text coordinate that corresponds to his desired body covering; for example, if he adds a pass in which `SetStreamSource()` is set to 1, the result will be fins. Additionally, he can let `SetStreamSource()` set the stream 2 to use a texture coordinate for the shells in a second pass. Switching on and off the fin and shell passes makes the whole system scalable. For example, if the object with fur is a long distance away, it would not make sense to show its fur, because it is not visible from that distance. Switching off the fur support at long viewing distances can reduce the chance of fill-rate limitation.

Vertex Stream Frequency

Another new feature called vertex stream frequency is available since the release of the DirectX 9.0 Summer Update 2003 SDK and it was updated in the DirectX 9.0 Summer Update 2004. This feature is supported only on hardware that supports the vertex shader Version 3 model, but with this hardware, it runs with every vertex shader version and on the fixed-function pipeline as well.

Vertex stream frequency can manipulate complete streams of vertices by fetching vertex data at different rates so that the same input data can be used for more than a single vertex in the vertex shader. This is done with the `SetStreamSourceFreq()` function:

```
HRESULT SetStreamSourceFreq(UINT StreamIndex, UINT Frequency);
```

`StreamIndex` indicates which stream is to have its frequency set, while `Frequency` is the frequency to which it will be set. One practical use of vertex stream frequency is compressing vertices by separating a 3D model into chunks of vertices, consisting of a base position and an offset. The vertex shader then adds the base position to each offset value to generate the untransformed vertex. The first stream is given a frequency indicating how many offset vertices are to use the same base position data, while the frequency of the second stream remains unchanged (more in [Thibieroz]).

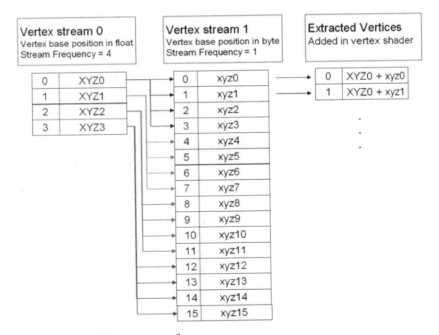

FIGURE 3.2   *Vertex stream frequency.*

Vertex stream frequency can also be used to instance models. The idea here is to draw multiple instances of the same model with one `DrawPrimitive()` or `DrawIndexedPrimitive()`call. This is useful when drawing such things as trees, particle systems, and sprites. For example, drawing a lot of trees can be done by storing one tree model in the vertex stream 0 and the concatenated world-view-projection matrix for all trees in vertex stream 1. Then the pointer for vertex stream 1 is advanced for each rendered instance. The vertex shader would be nearly the same, with the exception that the matrix is stored in the vertex stream instead of the constant registers.

Set Constants for Vertex Shaders

To provide constant data from the application to the vertex shader in case of using assembly shaders we can use the following functions:

```
// four floats (128-bit) in c8
SetVertexShaderConstantF(8, -m_LightDir, 1);
// four integers (128-bit) in i8
SetVertexShaderConstantI(8, iCounter, 1);
// one bool in b8
SetVertexShaderConstantB(8, bSwitch, 1);
```

These functions are supported by the default `IDirect3DDevice9` interface and by the effect file framework with the `ID3DXEffectStateManager` interface.

All floating-point data used in the vertex shader is represented by 128-bit quad floats (4 × 32-bit).

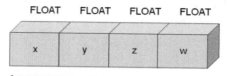

FIGURE 3.3　*128-bit quad float.*

Additionally, the effect file format supports even more handy functions to provide constant—or in HLSL tongue, *uniform*—data to the vertex shader. These include the following:

- `SetFloat()`
- `SetVector()`
- `SetMatrix()`
- `SetString()`

These functions ease the burden of checking if and how data fits into a 128-bit quad float. All these functions are also available for the pixel shader with similar names and functionality.

Once we've set up a vertex buffer and filled it with data, set up the vertex stream processing and provided the constant data from the application to the vertex shader, and written the vertex shader (this is covered extensively in the following parts of this book), we need to compile, create, and set the vertex shader.

Compile, Create, and Set a Vertex Shader

After declaring the vertex layout and setting up the vertex stream processing capabilities requested from hardware, we need to assemble and create the vertex shader. The following code snippet (which assumes the vertex shader is already written) shows how to compile and create a HLSL vertex shader stored in an ASCII file:

```
DWORD dwShaderFlags = 0;
#ifdef DEBUG_VS
    dwShaderFlags = D3DXSHADER_DEBUG | D3DXSHADER_SKIPOPTIMIZATION;
#endif

// Assemble the vertex shader from the file
D3DXCompileShaderFromFile( _T("hlsl.vsh"), NULL, NULL, "TShader",
                    "vs_1_1", dwShaderFlags, &pCode,
                    NULL, &m_pConstantTable );

// Create the vertex shader
m_pd3dDevice->CreateVertexShader( (DWORD*)pCode->GetBuffer-
Pointer(), &m_pVertexShader );

m_pd3dDevice->SetVertexShader( m_pVertexShader );
```

The compilation and resource allocation is done by mainly two functions. D3DXCompileShaderFromFile() compiles the shader and returns in its seventh parameter the compiled shader code in a buffer, as well as any embedded debug and symbol table information. The vertex shader is then created by a call to CreateVertex-Shader(), which stores a handle to the vertex shader in the variable provided in its second parameter. The vertex shader is then set with this handle and SetVertexShader().

The effect file framework provided with the DirectX SDK reduces these three function calls to one that compiles, creates, and sets the vertex shader.

```
DWORD dwShaderFlags = 0;
#ifdef DEBUG_VS
    dwShaderFlags = D3DXSHADER_DEBUG | D3DXSHADER_SKIPOPTIMIZATION;
#endif

if( FAILED( hr = D3DXCreateEffectFromFile( m_pd3dDevice,
                "hlsl.fx", NULL, NULL,
                    dwShaderFlags, NULL, &m_pEffect, NULL ) ) )
                return hr;
```

The function D3DXCreateEffectFromFile() does everything that is necessary to add a complete effect to the effect file framework. But there is even more: whereas there could be only one vertex shader in an ASCII file, there can be as many vertex and pixel shaders as you like in an effect file.

Having a stream of vertices and a vertex shader in place, we can now look at the process of how the vertex shader receives data from this stream by looking into the different data that is received via the vertex shader input semantics.

Vertex Shader Input

HLSL makes a distinction between varying and uniform input data in shaders based on the kind of content the data represents. In the assembly programming model, *varying* input data is delivered to the shader via the input registers, and *uniform* input data is delivered to the shader via constant registers. The easiest way to remember this from an assembly programmer's point of view is to think of input data delivered to the shader via constant registers as uniform and the rest of the input data as varying.

The distinction is important, because varying input data needs to be marked with a semantic, while uniform input data does not. Marking data with a semantic is necessary, because the HLSL compiler needs to know about the nature of the data to put it into the right kind of registers. For example, each pair of texture coordinates needs its own register, the position values in the vertex shader should be stored in the position output register, etc.

Uniform Input

There are two methods for specifying uniform input in HLSL: declaring global variables and marking input parameters as uniform.

```
// Declare a global as uniform
float4 vOrbit;

// Declare a uniform input parameter
float4 VS(uniform float4x4 mWorldViewProj): POSITION
{
    return mul(mWorldViewProj, vOrbit);
}
```

Uniform variables are set by the application via the constant table. This is a symbol table that defines how the uniform variables used by a shader must be loaded into the constant registers prior to shader execution.

Varying Input

Varying data is specified by marking the input parameters of the top-level shader function with an input semantic. The input semantic is a name used to link the given shader input to an output of the previous stage of the graphics pipeline. Vertex and pixel shaders have different sets of input semantics due to the different parts of the graphics pipeline that feed into each shader unit.

The vertex shader input semantics describe the per-vertex information to be loaded from a vertex buffer by the vertex shader (e.g., positions, normals, texture coordinates, colors, tangents, binormals, and so on). Table 3.1 shows the input semantics for vertex shaders.

Table 3.1   Vertex Shader Input Semantics

Semantic	Data
POSITIONn	Position
BLENDWEIGHTn	Blend weights
BLENDINDICESn	Blend indices
NORMALn	Normal vector
PSIZEn	Point size
COLORn	Color
TEXCOORDn	Texture coordinates
TANGENTn	Tangent
BINORMALn	Binormal
TESSFACTORn	Tessellation factor

These input semantics directly map to the combination of the vertex declaration set with the SetVertexDeclaration() function that is used to describe the vertex data elements in a vertex buffer. Input semantics—like all other semantics—are specified by appending a colon (:) and the input semantic name to the input parameter declaration. The following code snippet shows semantics for variables that should hold the position of a vertex, the texture coordinate of a vertex, a vertex normal, and a vertex tangent:

```
VS_OUTPUT VS(float4 Pos : POSITION,
        float2 Tex : TEXCOORD,
        float3 Normal : NORMAL,
        float3 Tangent : TANGENT  )
{
...
}
```

In a nutshell, input semantics help the compiler map data that is fed to the vertex shader from the vertex stream to the suitable hardware registers. To force the mapping of data to a specific register, the register modifier can be used together with the name of the hardware register.

```
float4 scaleFactor : register(c4);
sampler s0 : register(s0);
float3 Normal : NORMAL : register(v3);
```

Forcing the compiler to use a specific register is usually not necessary and requires some shader assembly knowledge.

Having seen so far how the vertex shader is fed by the application with data and how it receives data, we will now focus on how it outputs data. This means we skip the question of how to write a shader here once again, which is covered later in this book, and we follow the data stream through the graphics pipeline/graphics hardware and look at some HLSL language characteristics.

Vertex Shader Outputs

Vertex and pixel shaders provide output to subsequent graphics pipeline stages. The syntax for output semantics is identical to the syntax for specifying input semantics.

The output semantics of the vertex shader, shown in Table 3.2, are used to link the position value to the rasterizer and to link the outputs with the interpolators in the rasterizer (texture coordinate and color values) to the pixel shader post interpolation.

Table 3.2   Vertex Shader Output

Semantic	Data
POSITION	Position
PSIZE	Point size
FOG	Vertex fog
COLOR*n*	Color (example: COLOR0)
TEXCOORD*n*	Texture coordinates (example: TEXCOORD0)

The following example shows different ways to output values from a vertex shader.

```
struct VSOutput
{
    float2 tex2 : TEXCOORD2
};

float4 VS(out float2 tex0 : TEXCOORD0, out VSOutput Out) : POSITION
{
    tex0 = float2(1.0, 0.0);
    Out.tex2 = float2 (0.1, 0.2);
    return float4(0.5, 0.5, 0.5, 1.0);
}
```

The variable tex0 in the first line in the vertex shader is marked as an output value by using the keyword out in the brackets following the shader name. The variable tex2 in the second line is part of an output structure, and this structure is signed as out following the name of the shader. A third 4D vector is returned as an output float4 value by this shader.

The vertex shader needs to output at least a position value to the subsequent stages marked with the semantic POSITION.

Through the stages that follow the vertex shader, the pixel shader will receive the data. Receiving data in the pixel shader follows similar rules as receiving data in the vertex shader.

Data that is coming from the pipeline needs to be marked with a semantic, and data that is provided by the application directly to the pixel shader does not need to be marked.

Pixel Shaders

The pixel shader retrieves interpolated position values, texture coordinates, and—if needed—normals and color values from the previous pipeline stages. Additionally, it will fetch data from textures and receive uniform or constant data from the application. Figure 3.4 shows the data flow in the graphics pipeline. The programmer has to take care of the circled portion when programming pixel shaders.

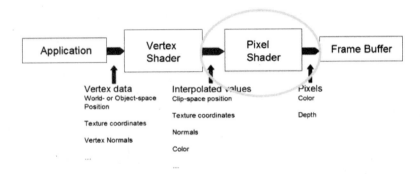

FIGURE 3.4 *Pixel shader stream processing.*

To receive data in the pixel shader, the following steps need to be done.

1. Create a pixel shader and compile it.
2. Set render states for the nonprogrammable parts of the pipeline.
3. Set pixel shader constants.
4. Set pixel shader.
5. Set the textures with SetTexture().
6. Set the sampler states with SetSamplerState() or the sampler_state in the effect file.
7. Execute stream(s) by calling the DrawIndexedPrimitive() function.

Similar to the vertex shader, the pixel shader can be compiled with D3DXCompile-ShaderFromFile(), created with CreatePixelShader(), and set with SetPixelShader().

By using the effect file format, all these steps are done in the effect file framework for the vertex and the pixel shader after a call to D3DXCreateEffectFromFile(). Similar to vertex shaders, uniform input data can be set with the following functions.

```
        // four floats (128-bit) in c8
SetPixelShaderConstantF(8, -m_LightDir, 1);
        // four integers (128-bit) in i8
SetPixelShaderConstantI(8, iCounter, 1);
        // one bool in b8
SetPixelShaderConstantB(8, bSwitch, 1);
```

These functions are supported by the default IDirect3DDevice9 interface and by the effect file framework with the ID3DXEffectStateManager interface. Additionally, the effect file format supports even more handy functions to provide constant data or HLSL tongue uniform data to the pixel shader. These functions include:

- SetFloat()
- SetVector()
- SetMatrix()
- SetString()

These functions are exactly the same as those of the vertex shader. So you cannot see if the data is set for the vertex or pixel shader without looking into the HLSL shader code and looking up the variable.

To provide textures to the pixel shader, the SetTexture()and SetSamplerState() functions are used in the same way they were used for the legacy multitexturing unit. As will be further described in the section on the effect file, the effects framework provides now a keyword to set sampler states directly in the effect file with the name sampler_state.

Input provided from the previous pipeline stages to the pixel shader is marked with a semantic. As you will see in a few seconds the default semantic is TEXCOORDn, whereas n is a number between 0 and 7 in current DirectX versions.

Pixel Shader Input

Pixel shader input semantics describe the information that is interpolated for each vertex of the current primitive and provided by the rasterizer.

Table 3.3 Pixel Shader Input

Semantic	Data
VFACE	Primitive faces front or back
VPOS	Position of pixel in x, y
COLORn	Color
TEXCOORDn_CENTROID	Texture coordinates

The appended character *n* is an optional integer that helps the HLSL compiler choose one of several available registers. Whereas the semantic COLOR*n* is used for data that consists of color values, the semantic TEXCOORD*n* is used for all other data.

Some recent hardware offers a face register that supports pixel shader Version 3, which indicates whether the incoming pixel is part of a front- or back-facing triangle. This face register is exposed by the semantic VFACE. If the value in the variable marked with VFACE is less than zero, the triangle is facing away from the eye (i.e., the primitive is the back face, because the area is negative, or counterclockwise). Therefore, it only makes sense to compare this value against 0 (> 0 or < 0). Using a variable declared with VFACE is only allowed in compare and branch instructions. Here is a simple example:

```
float4 PS(float vFace : VFACE): COLOR0
{
    const float4 FrontColor = {1.0f, 0.0f, 0.0f, 1.0f};
    const float4 BackColor = {0.0f, 1.0f, 0.0f, 1.0f};
    return (vFace > 0) ? FrontColor : BackColor;
}
```

If the triangle is facing front, the pixel shader returns the front color, and if it is facing back, the back color is returned. This is useful for such instances as two-sided lighting.

Additionally, a position register is available on recent hardware. It contains the current pixels (x, y) in screen space in the corresponding channels. The (z, w) channels are undefined. A variable that is marked with the semantic VPOS can only have the following masks: .x, .y, .xy. A typical example for the usage of the VPOS semantic is:

```
float4 PS(float vPos : VPOS, float2 Tex : TEXCOORD0) : COLOR
{
  float fraction = frac(vPos.y * 0.5f);

  if(fraction.y != 0.0f)
  {
    return float4(1.0f, 0.0f, 0.0f, 1.0f);
  }
  else
    return float4(0.0f, 1.0f, 0.0f, 1.0f);
}
```

The intrinsic frac() returns a floating-point value for the y component representing the largest integer that is less than or equal to its source value. In this example, the return value of this instruction can only be 0.0f or 1.0f. The comparison with the if flow control returns the red color if the fraction is greater than 0; otherwise, it returns the green color. The result of this pixel shader is that the application will show red and green stripes for each pixel row.

CENTROID can be added to the TEXCOORD*n* semantic as a pixel shader input semantic modifier to reduce problems with multisampling or when several textures are packed together. Adding this keyword modifies how texture coordinates are interpolated and it helps to ensure that texture coordinates are within the area of the texture specified by the three vertex texture coordinates. Texture sampling can get tricky when multisampling is used. Because there is only one texture fetch per-pixel—not per-sample—you can encounter problems at triangle edges.

When multisample antialiasing, interpolated quantities are generally evaluated at the center of the pixel. However the center of the pixel may lie outside of the primitive, as shown by the pixel in the center of Figure 3.5.

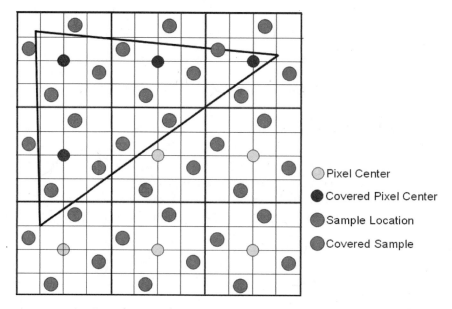

FIGURE 3.5   *Sampling pixels.*

Note that if this is a triangle edge and it's also the texture edge, you are sampling off the edge of the texture. It might wrap around to the other side and be a totally different color. With a projected texture, you might end up dividing by an incorrect w value, which might lead into some completely crazy texels.

With the CENTROID modifier, the interpolation evaluates the interpolated quantity at the centroid of the covered samples. Figure 3.6 shows one centroid in the middle of the figure.

Centroid interpolation evaluates the interpolated quantity at the centroid of the covered samples. Even sampling with the CENTROID semantic may lead to problems: if you have two triangles side by side that sample the same texture, moving the boundary between the triangles changes where the centroids are, therefore changing the

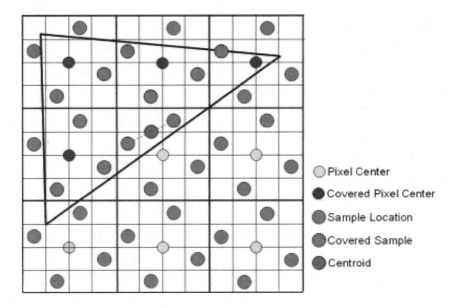

FIGURE 3.6 *Sampling pixels with* CENTROID.

filtering. Clipping triangles produces multiple triangles that look the same, but the caution against this is that the extra seam introduced by the clipping is actually visible now because it changes how the texture is sampled along the seam. There is no universal solution, but on a lot of textures, centroid interpolation helps the first problem and does not help the second one.

After altering the values the pixel shader receives, the shader needs to output at least one value in a variable marked with the semantic COLOR0. This is shown in the following section.

Pixel Shader Output

Pixel shader output semantics, shown in Table 3.4, bind the output colors of a pixel shader with the correct render target, whereas the DEPTH output semantic can be used to change the destination depth value at the current raster location.

Table 3.4   Pixel Shader Output Semantics

Semantic	Data
COLORn	Color for render target n
DEPTH	Depth value

The following examples show different ways to output values from pixel shaders.

```
float4 PS(out float Color1 : COLOR1) : COLOR
{
    // writes color values to render target 1
    Color1 = float4(1.0, 0.0, 0.0, 1.0);

    // writes color values to render target 0
    return float4(0.0, 1.0, 0.0, 1.0);
}
--
// pixel shader output structure
struct PSOutput
{
    float4 Color : COLOR;
    float Depth : DEPTH;
};

PSOutput PS()
{
    PSOutput Out = (PSOutput)0;

    Out.Color = float4(1.0, 0.0, 0.0, 1.0);
    Out.Depth = 1.0;
}
--
// pixel shader output structure
struct PSOutput
{
    float4 Color : COLOR;
    float Depth : DEPTH;
};

// using the out keyword
void PS(out PSOutput Out)
{
    Out.Color = float4(1.0, 0.0, 0.0, 1.0);
    Out.Depth = 1.0;
}
```

The first example just returns one output value in COLOR0. That's why we could use the simplified syntax by adding :COLOR0 as a postfix to the brackets of the pixel shader input values.

The second example shows how to initialize the structure with 0. This is useful if not all variables are used in the shader, which might happen in a case in which branches are used. In that case, the HLSL compiler would show an error message.

The third example uses the keyword out to output values.

Showing how to mark the output of the pixel shader to help the compiler put the right values into the right registers is the final step in following the data stream through the vertex and pixel shader. Before we get deeper into HLSL programming, we need to examine the various vertex and pixel shader versions that are available and how they correspond to specific graphics cards, because this relationship will be mentioned throughout the following text.

Compile Targets

To account for the fact that graphics hardware supports different features, a version system is available in DirectX and also for the HLSL compiler. Usually a game project starts by specifying a minimum hardware configuration in which the game should be able to run. In the case of shader capable graphics cards, this is done regarding their shader capabilities with a very scalable system of different vertex and pixel shader versions. This version system marks different vertex shader versions with the prefix *vs_** and different pixel shader versions with the prefix *ps_**. The following section covers how the HLSL compiler uses different vertex and pixel shader versions and gives an overview of which currently available graphics hardware supports which versions.

Choosing specific target hardware with support for a specific shader version means targeting a specific part of the end-user market (read more in Chapter 28).

As shown in the "Tools of the Trade" section in Chapter 1, the HLSL compiler expects to receive a specific shader version as the compile target. The compiler creates assembly shaders with the specified shader version numbers.

Figure 3.7 shows how the application feeds an HLSL shader to the HLSL compiler and how the compiler provides a compiled binary assembler file back to the application. The HLSL file is provided to the compiler with a call to D3DXCompile-Shader() or, if the effect file framework is used, the function D3DXCompileEffect-File(). Both functions provide the compiled binary version for CreateVertexShader(), which allocates the necessary resources and provides the binary assembly file to the DirectX 9 runtime.

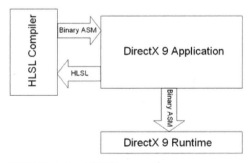

FIGURE 3.7 *HLSL compiler usage.*

Therefore, the output of the HLSL compiler depends on the underlying hardware in the same way that the assembler does. Specifying ps_3_0 on pre-ps_3_0 hardware will lead to a situation in which the application won't run correctly, but the performance will be fine, because the debug runtime will reject any Draw(Indexed)Primitive() calls and the retail runtime might render garbage. Specifying ps_1_1 for a shader that needs many more instruction slots than available will force the compiler to display an error message like the following:

```
error X4532: cannot map expression to pixel shader instruction set
```

One of the main advantages of using the HLSL compiler is the ability to generate different assembly versions from the same HLSL source. As long as the number of used instructions does not exceed the number of available instructions on the target platform, this ability offers an efficient way to optimize for different hardware platforms.

DirectX 9 supports many different shader versions that correspond to existing or upcoming hardware. For DirectX 8 hardware, there is the vertex shader implementation vs_1_1 and the pixel shader implementations ps_1_1-ps_1_4 (vs_1_0 and ps_1_0 are skipped here, because a graphics card that only supports ps_1_0 was never released). Additionally, for the new DirectX 9 hardware, vertex shader implementations vs_2_0, vs_2_a, vs_2_sw, and vs_3_0 and the pixel shader implementations ps_2_0, ps_2_a, ps_2_b, ps_2_sw, ps_3_0, and ps_3_sw are supported. The pixel shader implementations with the appendix _sw are software implementations, which invoke REF if selected, whereas the vertex shader implementations with the appendix _sw invoke a software implementation provided by INTEL or AMD, which runs the vertex shader on the CPU with quite good performance. The capabilities of the different vertex and pixel shader versions are shown in the following table:

Table 3.5 Vertex and Pixel Shader Version Capabilities

Version	Maximum Instruction Slots	Constant Count
vs_1_1	96	cap'd (4)
vs_2_0	256	cap'd (4)
vs_2_a	256	cap'd (4)
vs_2_sw	unlimited	8192
vs_3_0	cap'd (1)	cap'd (4)
vs_3_sw	unlimited	8192
ps_1_1-ps_1_3	8–12	8
ps_1_4	28 in two phases	8
ps_2_0	96	32
ps_2_a	cap'd (2)	32
ps_2_b	cap'd (2)	32
ps_2_sw	unlimited	8192
ps_3_0	cap'd (3)	224
ps_3_sw	unlimited	8192

(1) D3DCAPS9.MaxVertexShader30InstructionSlots
(2) D3DCAPS9.D3DPSHADERCAPS2_0.NumInstructionSlots
(3) D3DCAPS9.MaxPixelShader30InstructionSlots
(4) D3DCAPS9.MaxVertexShaderConst

The column labeled "Instruction Slots" shows the number of instructions that can be used in one vertex shader or pixel shader by the programmer. For example, ps_1_1 supports eight instruction slots, which means that no pixel shader written for this version can use more than eight instructions. The number of available constant registers is presented in the last column, labeled "Constant Count." For example ps_1_1 supports eight constant registers, which can be used to send eight constant vectors to the pixel shader.

All these DirectX shader implementations are supported on the following, currently available, shader-capable graphics cards:

Table 3.6 Shader Support of Available Graphics Cards

Graphics Card	Vertex Shader Version	Pixel Shader Version
GeForce 3	vs_1_1	ps_1_1
RADEON 8500, 9000, 9100, 9200	vs_1_1	ps_1_1-ps_1_4
GeForce 4TI	vs_1_1	ps_1_1-ps_1_3
Parhelia	vs_1_1 + vs_2_0	ps_1_1-ps_1_3
RADEON 9500-9800	vs_1_1 + vs_2_0	ps_1_1-ps_2_0
Wildcat VP 10	vs_1_1	ps_1_1-ps_1_2
GeForce FX	vs_1_1-vs_2_a	ps_1_1-ps_2_a
GeForce 6800	vs_1_1-vs_3_0	ps_1_1-ps_3_0
RADEON X800	vs_1_1-vs_2_0	ps_1_1-ps_2_b (not: ps_2_a))

Checking the availability of a specific shader version can be done with a capability flag delivered by the D3DCAPS9 structure, which is filled by a call to the GetDevice-Caps() function. It is important to note that each newer graphics card needs to support all lower shader versions (exception: ps_2_b offers less functionality than ps_2_a).

Developing for the least common denominator means using vs_1_1 and ps_1_1. The next evolutionary step is vs_2_0 and ps_2_0 and perhaps, in a couple of years, the majority of graphics cards should support vs_3_0 and ps_3_0.

To target a specific platform with the HLSL compiler, the functions D3DXGetVertexShaderProfile() and D3DXGetPixelShaderProfile() are useful. These functions return the name of the highest HLSL profile supported by a given graphics card. At the time of writing, the HLSL compiler supported the profiles listed in Table 3.7

Table 3.7 Profiles Supported by the HLSL Compiler

Shader Profile	Description
vs_1_1	Compile to vs_1_1 assembly
vs_2_0	Compile to vs_2_0 assembly
vs_2_a	Same as the vs_2_0 profile, with the following additional capabilities available for the compiler to target: • Number of Temporary Registers (r#) is greater than or equal to 13 • Dynamic flow control instruction • Predication
vs_2_sw	Compile to vs_2_sw assembly
vs_3_0	Compile to vs_3_0 assembly
ps_1_1	Compile to ps_1_1 assembly
ps_1_2	Compile to ps_1_2 assembly
ps_1_3	Compile to ps_1_3 assembly
ps_1_4	Compile to ps_1_4 assembly
ps_2_0	Compile to ps_2_0 assembly
ps_2_a	Same as the ps_2_0 profile, with the following additional capabilities available for the compiler to target: • 512 instructions (any mix of ALU and texture, `D3DPS20CAPS_NOTEXINSTRUCTIONLIMIT`) • 22 temporary registers • No limit on levels of depency (`D3DPS20CAPS_NODEPENDENTREADLIMIT`) • Arbitrary swizzles (`D3DPS20CAPS_ARBITRARYSWIZZLE`) • Predication (`D3DPS20CAPS_PREDICATION`) • Gradient Instructions (`D3DPS20CAPS_GRADIENETINSTRUCTIONS`)
ps_2_b	Same as the ps_2_0 profile, with the following additional capabilities available for the compiler to target: • 512 instructions (any mix of ALU and texture, `D3DPS20CAPS_NOTEXINSTRUCTIONLIMIT`) • 32 temporary registers
ps_2_sw	Compile to ps_2_sw assembly
ps_3_sw	Compile to ps_3_sw assembly
ps_3_0	Compile to ps_3_0 assembly

Because games have to follow a minimum shader specification to target a certain part of the end-user market, one of the challenges is to adjust your effect to this target segment. The HLSL compiler helps here by giving hints, warnings, and error messages, so that the programmer does not need to know assembly in detail (although it helps to optimize HLSL code).

The following sections will further detail how to program vertex and pixel shaders with HLSL. We will start with a simple example program.

A Simple Example

To illustrate the use of HLSL before presenting an exhaustive description of the language syntax, the vertex and pixel shaders of a diffuse lighting model are shown and explained in the following lines (the underlying lighting algorithm is explained in Chapter 5).

```
// ———————————————————-
// variables that are provided by the application
// ———————————————————-
float4x4 matWorldViewProj;
float4x4 matInvTransposeWorld;
float4 vecLightDir;
// ———————————————————-
// vertex shader output channels
// ———————————————————-
struct VS_OUTPUT
{
    float4 Pos  : POSITION;
    float3 Light : TEXCOORD0;
    float3 Norm : TEXCOORD1;
};
// ———————————————————-
// vertex shader function (input channels)
// ———————————————————-
VS_OUTPUT VS(float4 Pos : POSITION, float3 Normal : NORMAL)
{
    VS_OUTPUT Out = (VS_OUTPUT)0;
    Out.Pos = mul(Pos, matWorldViewProj); // transform Position
    Out.Light = normalize(vecLightDir); // output light vector

    // transform Normal and normalize it
    Out.Norm = normalize(mul(matInvTransposeWorld, Normal));
    return Out;
}
// ———————————————————-
// Pixel Shader (input channels):output channel
// ———————————————————-
float4 PS(float3 Light: TEXCOORD0, float3 Norm : TEXCOORD1) : COLOR
{
    // diffuse albedo
    float4 Dcolor = { 1.0f, 0.0f, 0.0f, 1.0f};

    // ambient albedo * ambient intensity
    float4 Acolor = {0.1,  0.0,  0.0, 1.0};

    return Acolor + Dcolor * saturate(dot(Light, Norm));
}
```

The vertex shader transforms the vertex position with the matWorldViewProj matrix and the normal vector with the matInvTransposeWorld—both provided by the application as global variables (uniform input)—and outputs the position values to the pixel shader. The world view projection matrix, the inverse world matrix, and the light vector are provided by the application to the vertex shader via the variables matWorld-ViewProj, matInvTransposeWorld, and vecLightDir, respectively.

The structure VS_OUTPUT at the beginning of the source describes the output values of the vertex shader. As you can see, the vertex shader looks like a C function with the return value VS_OUTPUT and the input values in the variables Pos and Normal in brackets after its name VS. The input and output values for the vertex shader use the semantic POSITION. Additionally the vertex shader outputs a normal marked with the semantic NORMAL.

The vertex shader VS outputs the normal and light vectors in the variables Light and Norm. Looking at the actual code body of the VS function, you can see that an instrinsic function called mul() is used to multiply the position vector by matWorldViewProj. Whereas the mul() used to calculate the position value uses the matrix as the second argument, the mul() used to calculate the normal uses the inverse world matrix in its first argument.

Both transformations are done with the function mul(a, b), which performs a matrix multiplication between a matrix and a vector. If a is the vector and b is the matrix, the vector is treated as a row vector. If b is the vector and a is the matrix, it is treated as a column vector. In this example, mul() gets the position or normal vector as the first parameter—therefore, it is treated as a row vector—and the transformation matrix, consisting of 16 floating-point values (float4×4), as the second parameter (the mul() intrinsic and other intrinsics are discussed in more detail later in the section "Intrinsics").

Whereas the first mul() uses the position vector as a row vector, the second mul() intrinsic used to calculate the normal uses the normal vector as a column vector. Because the matrix was already inversed in the application, this usage equals to an inverse and transposed world matrix.

The vertex shader outputs a position value, a light vector, and a normal vector to the pixel shader.

The pixel shader receives the light and normal vector as input values and outputs a color value. The output value is shown by the colon followed by the COLOR semantic after the brackets containing the input values.

It returns at least one float4 value, and this value is always treated as a color value by the compiler. It uses a constant diffuse value and a constant ambient value, declared with const.

The names of the vertex and pixel shader are also the entry point for the high-level language compiler and can be provided in its command line. An example command line to compile the pixel shader for Version 1.4 might look like this:

```
fxc.exe /T ps_1_4  /E PS /Fc $(InputName).txt "$(InputName).fx"
```

Illustrating the usage of HLSL before going into language specifications should have given you a first impression of how similar HLSL is to C and some C++ constructs.

The following section covers further similarities and highlights the additions that were made to account for the fact that HLSL is a language for vector graphics.

Language Basics

The language used by the HLSL compiler is a kind of C with graphics-related specifics and should be easy to learn for a C programmer. Compared to C, it has been extended with vector and matrix types to make it more concise for the typical operations carried out in 3D graphics. Additionally, as you will see on the following pages, some mechanisms have also been borrowed from C++.

Once you understand HLSL, you will need to know how to:

- Declare variables
- Declare function prototypes
- Use intrinsic functions
- Define your own data types
- Use semantics to "wire" your shader arguments to other shaders and to the pipeline (that was shown at the beginning of this chapter)

Keywords

Keywords are predefined identifiers that are reserved for the HLSL language and cannot be used as identifiers in your program. Table 3.8 shows all keywords currently used by HLSL. Keywords marked with an asterisk (*) are case insensitive.

Table 3.8   HLSL Keywords

asm *	bool	compile	const
decl*	do	double	else
extern	false	float	for
half	if	in	inline
inout	int	matrix*	out
pass*	pixelshader*	return	sampler
shared	static	string*	struct
technique*	texture*	true	typedef
uniform	vector*	vertexshader*	void
volatile	while		

The in, out, and inout keywords are used to mark parameters that are passed into the shader or passed back by the shader but are not initialized for use when passed in and passed both in and out of the shader. The keyword out is useful for returning several values from a function (an example was given at the beginning of this chapter in the subsection "Pixel Shader Output").

The keywords in Table 3.9 are currently unused but reserved for potential future use.

Table 3.9   Future HLSL Keywords

auto	break	case	catch
char	class	compile	const
const_cast	continue	default	delete
dynamic_cast	enum	explicit	friend
goto	long	mutable	namespace
new	operator	private	protected
public	register	reinterpret_cast	short
signed	sizeof	static_cast	switch
template	this	throw	try
typename	union	unsigned	using
virtual			

As you can see here, HLSL will advance into the syntactical range of C++.

Data Types

HLSL supports a variety of data types, from simple scalars to more complex types, such as vectors and matrices. Table 3.10 shows a list of scalar types.

Table 3.10   HLSL Scalar Types

Data Type	Representable Values
bool	true or false
int	32-bit signed integer
half	16-bit floating-point value
float	32-bit floating-point value
double	64-bit floating-point value

Hardware that does not support the integer data type emulates it. This emulation might lead to unexpected results and a performance decrease will be visible in the assembly source created by the HLSL compiler. A rule of thumb for all recent hardware is to use integer data only for indexing (read more in the upcoming section "Optimizing HLSL Shaders").

Furthermore, double data types will be emulated by float types on hardware platforms that have no native double support.

Vector Data Types

One of the graphics enhancements of HLSL is provided by the vector data types. There are a variety of ways that these vectors can be declared:

```
float3 vecLight;
float vecLight[3];
vector vecPos;
vector <float, 4> vecPos;
bool3 bDecision;
bool bDecision[3];
vector <bool, 3> bDecision;
```

Individual components of a vector can be accessed like this:

```
float4 pos={3.0f, 5.0f, 2.0f, 1.0f};
float value = pos[0];
float value = pos.x;
float value = pos.y;
float2 value = pos.xy;
float3 value = pos.xyz;
```

Please note the first example initializes the variable at declaration time. To access individual components, there are two component namespaces: *.x, *.y, *.z, and *.w and *.r, *.g, *.b, and *.a.

Swizzling

Swizzling refers to the ability to copy any source register component to any temporary register component. Swizzling does not affect the source register data. Before an instruction runs, the data in a source register is copied to a temporary register.

```
float4 vec1 = float4(4.0, -2.0, 5.0, 3.0);
float2 vec2 = vec1.yx;    // vec2 = (-2.0, 4.0)
float scalar = vec1.w;    // scalar = 3.0
float3 vec3 = scalar.xxx; // vec3 = (3.0, 3.0, 3.0)
```

Please note that the first example is also a constructor, which is similar to the C++ version but with some enhancements to deal with complex data types. It helps to initialize values at definition time. The following lines show some different ways to use constructors to initialize variables with a value.

```
float3 vPos = float3(4.0f, 1.0f, 2.0f);
float fDiffuse = dot(vNormal, float3(1.0f, 0.0f, 0.0f));
float4 vPack = float4(vPos, fDiffuse);
```

Constructors are commonly used to temporarily define a quantity with literal values (as in dot(vNormal, float3(1.0f, 0.0f, 0.0f)) in the previous code snippet) or to explicitly pack smaller data types together (as in `float4(vPos, vDiffuse)` in the previous snippet).

Arbitrary swizzling (`D3DPS20CAPS_ARBITRARYSWIZZLE`) works on hardware platforms that support this functionality (vs_1_1-vs_3_0, ps_2_a, and ps_3_0). Swizzling support in pixel shader versions is shown in Table 3.11.

Table 3.11 Swizzling Support in Different Pixel Shader Versions

Pixel Shader Version	ps_ 1_1	ps_ 1_2	ps_ 1_3	ps_ 1_4	ps_ 2_0	ps_ 2_b	ps_ 2_a	ps_ 2_sw	ps_ 3_0	ps_ 3_sw
.x				x	x	x	x	x	x	x
.y	.			x	x	x	x	x	x	x
.z	x*	x*	x*	x	x	x	x	x	x	x
.w	x	x	x	x	x	x	x	x	x	x
.yzxw					x	x	x	x	x	x
.zxyw					x	x	x	x	x	x
.wzyx					x	x	x	x	x	x
arbitrary							x	x	x	x

* Only available if destination write mask is .w (.a).

Write Masks

Masking controls how many components are written.

```
float4 vec3 = float4(4.0, -2.0, 5.0, 3.0);
float4 vec1 = float4(1.0, 2.0, 3.0, 4.0);
vec1.xw = vec3;  // vec1 = (4.0, 2.0, 3.0, 3.0)
vec1.y = vec3;  // vec1 = (4.0, -2.0, 3.0, 3.0)
```

Assignments cannot be written to the same component more than once. So the left side of this statement is invalid:

```
f_4D.xx = pos.xy;   // cannot write to the same destination components
```

Also, the component namespaces cannot be mixed. This is an invalid component write:

```
f_4D.xg = pos.rgrg;   // invalid write: cannot mix component name spaces
```

Write masks work on hardware platforms that support pixel shader Versions ps_1_4 and higher. Figure 3.12 shows the support of write masks in different pixel shader versions.

Table 3.12 Write Mask Support in Different Pixel Shader Versions

Pixel Shader Version	ps_ 1_1	ps_ 1_2	ps_ 1_3	ps_ 1_4	ps_ 2_0	ps_ 2_b	ps_ 2_a	ps_ 2_sw	ps_ 3_0	ps_ 3_sw
.xyz	x	x	x	x	x	x	x	x	x	x
.w	x	x	x	x	x	x	x	x	x	x
arbitrary				x	x	x	x	x	x	x

Matrices

Matrix data types are 2D arrays of data. Like scalars and vectors, matrices may be composed of any of the basic data types: bool, int, half, float, or double. Matrices may be of any size, but you will typically use 4×3 or 4×4 matrices. Like vectors, the individual elements of matrices can be accessed using array or structure/swizzle syntax. For example, the following array indexing syntax can be used to access the top-left element of the matrix matWorldViewProj.

```
float value = matWorldViewProj[0][0];
```

There is also a structure syntax defined for access to and swizzling of matrix elements. For zero-based row-column position, you can use any of the following:

```
_m00, _m01, _m02, _m03
_m10, _m11, _m12, _m13
_m20, _m21, _m22, _m23
_m30, _m31, _m32, _m33
```

For one-based row-column position, you can use any of the following:

```
_11, _12, _13, _14
_21, _22, _23, _24
_31, _32, _33, _34
_41, _42, _43, _44
```

Matrices can also be accessed using array notation. For example:

```
float2x2 fMat = {3.0f, 5.0f,  // row 1
                 2.0f, 1.0f}; // row 2
float value = fMat[0][0];       // value = 3.0f
float value = fMat._m00      // value = 3.0f
float value = fMat._12       // value = 5.0f
float value = fMat[1][1]     // value = 1.0f
float2 value = fMat._21_22   // value = {2.0f, 1.0f}
float2 value = fMat[1]       // value = {2.0f, 1.0f}
```

Matrices can be stored as row_major or column_major:

```
row_major    half1x4 fh1By4;
column_major half4x1 fh4By1;
row_major    half3x2 fh3By2;
column_major half3x2 fh2By3;
```

The type modifier row_major indicates that each row of the matrix will be stored in a single constant register. Likewise, using column_major indicates that each column of the matrix will be stored in a single constant register. Storing matrices in column major order is the default behavior.

Storage Classes

Variables can be stored in different storage classes, which inform the compiler about the intended scope and lifetime of a given variable.

```
extern float variable;
const float variable;
static float variable;
```

The variable with the modifier extern can be set by the Set*ShaderConstant*() API and can be modified by the shader itself (but not read back by Get*ShaderConstant*()). The variable with the modifier const can be set by the Set*ShaderConstant*() API but cannot be modified by the shader itself. The variable with the storage modifier static cannot be set by the Set*ShaderConstant*() API but can be modified within the shader.

Type Casting

HLSL also supports type casting. Type casting often is used to promote or demote a given variable to match a variable to which it is being assigned. For example in the following case, a literal float 0.0f is being cast to a float4{0.0f, 0.0f, 0.0f, 0.0f} to initialize vResult.

```
float4 vResult = 0.0f;
```

The following example shows a situation in which you need to know exactly what type casting is doing.

```
float4 vPos;
float fDisplacement, fResult;
fResult = vPos * fDisplacement;
```

There is a good chance that fResult does not hold the expected result. vPos is cast to a float by using only the first component multiplied with the scalar float fDisplacement. In other words the result in fResult is vPos.x * fDisplacement. Multiplying with vPos.z or declaring fResult as float4 might lead to expected results.

Table 3.13 shows a list of all type casting rules for HLSL.

Table 3.13 HLSL Type Casts

Type of Cast	Casting Behavior

Scalar-to-scalar	**Always valid.** When casting from bool type to an integer or floating-point type, false is considered to be zero, and true is considered to be one. When casting from an integer or floating-point type to bool, a zero value is considered to be false, and a nonzero value is considered to be true. When casting from a floating-point type to an integer type, the value is rounded to zero. This is the same truncation behavior as C.
	
	 Example:
	 ```float4 fValue = float4(4.0, -2.0, 5.0, 3.0);```
	 ```int4 iValue.y = fValue.x;```

Scalar-to-vector	**Always valid.** This cast operates by replicating the scalar to fill the vector.
	
	 Example:
	 ```float4 fValue = float4(4.0, -2.0, 5.0, 3.0);```
	 ```float4 fResult = fValue.x;```

Scalar-to-matrix	This cast operates by replicating the scalar to fill the matrix.
	
	 Example:
	 ```float4 fValue = float4(4.0, -2.0, 5.0, 3.0);```
	 ```float4x4 fMat = fValue.x;```

Scalar-to-structure	This cast operates by replicating the scalar to fill the structure.
	
	 Example:
	 ```struct VS_OUTPUT```
	 ```{```
	 ``` float4 Pos : POSITION;```
	 ``` float3 Normal : TEXCOORD0;```
	 ``` float4 Light : TEXCOORD1;```
	 ``` float3 View : TEXCOORD2;```
	 ``` float3 Half : TEXCOORD3;```
	 ```};```
	 ```VS_OUTPUT Out = (VS_OUTPUT)0;```

Vector-to-scalar	**Always valid.** This selects the first component of the vector.
	
	 Example:
	 ```float4 fValue = float4(4.0, -2.0, 5.0, 3.0);```
	 ```float fResult = fValue;```

Continued on next page

Table 3.13 HLSL Type Casts (continued)

Type of Cast	Casting Behavior
Vector-to-vector	The destination vector must not be larger than the source vector. The cast operates by keeping the left-most values and truncating the rest. For the purpose of this cast, column matrices, row matrices, and numeric structures are treated as vectors.
Vector-to-matrix	The size of the vector must be equal to the size of the matrix. Example: `float4 fValue = float4(4.0, -2.0, 5.0, 3.0);` `float2x2 fMat = fValue;`
Vector-to-structure	Valid if the structure is not larger than the vector and all components of the structure are numeric.
Matrix-to-scalar	**Always valid.** This selects the upper-left component of the matrix. Example: `float2x2 fMat = {3.0f, 5.0f,  // row 1` `                    2.0f, 1.0f}; // row 2` `float fResult = fMat;`
Matrix-to-vector	The size of the matrix must be equal to the size of the vector. Example: `float2x2 fMat = {3.0f, 5.0f,  // row 1` `                    2.0f, 1.0f}; // row 2` `float4 fVector = fMat;`
Matrix-to-matrix	The destination matrix must not be larger than the source matrix, in both dimensions. The cast operates by keeping the upper-left values and truncating the rest.
Matrix-to-structure	The size of the structure must be equal to the size of the matrix, and all components of the structure are numeric.
Structure-to-scalar	The structure must contain at least one member.
Structure-to-vector	The structure must be at least the size of the vector. The first components must be numeric, up to the size of the vector.
Structure-to-matrix	The structure must be at least the size of the matrix. The first components must be numeric, up to the size of the matrix.
Structure-to-object	The structure must contain at least one member. The type of this member must be identical to the type of the object.
Structure-to-structure	The destination structure must not be larger than the source structure. A valid cast must exist between all respective source and destination components.

Structures

Structures are available in HLSL, too. For example, consider the following output structure:

```
struct VS_OUTPUT
{
    float4 Pos  : POSITION;
    float2 Tex : TEXCOORD0;
    float4 Light : TEXCOORD1;
    float3 View : TEXCOORD2;
    float4 Light2 : TEXCOORD4;
    float4 Light3 : TEXCOORD3;
    float4 Light4 : TEXCOORD5;
};
```

Structures are used similarly to how they are used in C. They are declared with the keyword struct and defined and initialized by using HLSL code like this:

```
VS_OUTPUT Out = (VS_OUTPUT)0;
```

Components can be accessed in this example with the structure variable Out followed by a point.

```
Out.Pos = mul(Pos, matWorldViewProj); // transform Position
```

Samplers

There is a sampler keyword in HLSL that corresponds to the assembly sampler registers. To identify samplers in HLSL, each sampler gets a name. Each texture map that should be used in the pixel shader needs to be declared with a sampler. The following example uses a color map and a bump map to calculate a bump-mapped per-pixel diffuse lighting.

```
sampler ColorMapSampler;
sampler BumpMapSampler;

float4 PS(float3 LightDir: COLOR0, float2 Tex: TEXCOORD0, float2
Tex2 : TEXCOORD1) : COLOR
{
    // fetch color map
     float4 color = tex2D(ColorMapSampler, Tex);

    // bump map
     float3 bumpNormal = (2 * tex2D(BumpMapSampler, Tex2) - 1.0f);

    // diffuse comp.
     float4 diff = saturate(dot(bumpNormal, LightDir)); @CODE:

  return color * diff;
}
```

An HLSL sampler has a very direct mapping to the actual silicon in the 3D graphics processor, which is responsible for addressing and filtering textures. A sampler needs to be defined for each texture map but may be used several times in the pixel shader. In the pixel shader Versions vs_3_0, ps_2_a, and ps_3_0 there is no limit for "re-use" (this is shown by the `D3DPS20CAPS_NOTEXINSTRUCTIONLIMIT` and `D3DPS20CAPS_NODEPENDENTREADLIMIT` capability bits in the capability structure).

Re-using samplers is very common in image processing applications, since the input image is often sampled multiple times with different texture coordinates to provide data to a filter kernel expressed in shader code. The following code snippet is part of a bloom filter developed by Masaki Kawase [Kawase]. A bloom filter simulates the occurrence in which film and sensors in cameras can cause oversaturated values to bleed into neighboring cells or regions of the film (read more in Chapter 20). This filter samples the same texture four times each pass.

```
sampler RenderMapSampler;

float4 PSBloom(float2 TopLeft          : TEXCOORD0,
        float2 TopRight                : TEXCOORD1,
        float2 BottomRight             : TEXCOORD2,
        float2 BottomLeft              : TEXCOORD3) : COLOR0
{
  float4 addedBuffer = 0.0f;

  // sample top left
  addedBuffer = tex2D(RenderMapSampler, TopLeft);

  // sample top right
  addedBuffer += tex2D(RenderMapSampler, TopRight);

  // sample bottom right
  addedBuffer += tex2D(RenderMapSampler, BottomRight);

  // sample bottom left
  addedBuffer += tex2D(RenderMapSampler, BottomLeft);

  // average
  return addedBuffer *= 0.25f;
}
```

A modern C-like compiler that is focused on programming graphics does not only provide a way to access textures but also intrinsics (similar to C compilers for CPUs). These are highly optimized functions that are delivered by the compiler vendor to the programmer for his convenience. This way, programmers do not need to reinvent common functions, and they can be sure they're using the most efficient code available.

Intrinsics

Intrinsics are provided by the HLSL compiler to simplify tasks and to allow for optimization (e.g., mathematical instructions). There are intrinsics that cover mathematical operations and intrinsics that cover texture-sampling operations.

Math Intrinsics

The math intrinsics listed in Table 3.14 will be converted to assembly operations by HLSL. In some cases, such as `abs()` and `dot()`, they will map directly to single assembly-level operations, while in other cases, such as refract() and step(), they will map to multiple assembly instructions. Please note that some intrinsics, notably ddx(),ddy(), and fwidth(), are not supported on pixel shader versions other than ps_2_a and ps_3_0. All available math intrinsics are shown in Table 3.14.

Table 3.14 Intrinsic Functions

Intrinsic	Description
abs(x)	Absolute value (per component). Maps to the assembly instruction abs.
acos(x)	Returns the arccosine of each component of *x*. Each component should be in the range [–1, 1].
all(x)	Tests if all components of *x* are nonzero.
any(x)	Tests if any component of *x* is nonzero.
asin(x)	Returns the arcsine of each component of *x*. Each component should be in the range [$-\pi/2$, $\pi/2$].
atan(x)	Returns the arctangent of *x*. The return values are in the range [$-\pi/2$, $\pi\pi/2$].
atan2(y, x)	Returns the arctangent of *y*/*x*. The signs of *y* and *x* are used to determine the quadrant of the return values in the range [$-\pi$, π]. atan2 is well defined for every point other than the origin, even if *x* equals 0 and *y* does not equal 0.
ceil(x)	Returns the smallest integer that is greater than or equal to *x*.
clamp(x, min, max)	Clamps *x* to the range [*min*, *max*].
clip(x)	Discards the current pixel, if any component of *x* is less than zero. This can be used to simulate clip planes, if each component of *x* represents the distance from a plane. This is the intrinsic you use when you want to generate an asm texkill. Please note that this instruction interferes with the automatic occlusion culling mechanism of modern graphics hardware, which leads to a performance decrease. Furthermore, it can cause problems with multisampling.
cos(x)	Returns the cosine of *x*.
cosh(x)	Returns the hyperbolic cosine of *x*.
cross(a, b)	Returns the cross product of two 3D vectors, *a* and *b*.
D3DCOLORtoUBYTE4(x)	Swizzles and scales components of the 4D vector *x* to compensate for the lack of UBYTE4 stream component support in some hardware. Check the flag D3DDTCAPS_UBYTE4 for support.
ddx(x)	Returns the partial derivative of *x* with respect to the screen-space *x*-coordinate. Maps to the assembly instruction ddx.
ddy(x)	Returns the partial derivative of *x* with respect to the screen-space *y*-coordinate. Maps to the assembly instruction ddy.

Continued on next page

Table 3.14 Intrinsic Functions *(continued)*

Intrinsic	Description
degrees(x)	Converts x from radians to degrees.
determinant(m)	Returns the determinant of the square matrix m.
distance(a, b)	Returns the distance between two points, a and b.
dot(a, b)	Returns the dot product of two vectors, a and b. Maps to the assembly instructions dp3 and dp4.
exp(x)	Base-e exponential function. Returns ex.
exp2(x)	Calculates the base 2 exponent of x per component.
faceforward(n, i, ng)	Tests if a face is visible. Returns −n * sign(dot(i, ng))
floor(x)	Returns the greatest integer that is less than or equal to x.
fmod(a, b)	Returns the floating point remainder f of a / b such that a = i * b + f, where i is an integer, f has the same sign as x, and the absolute value of f is less than the absolute value of b.
frac(x)	Returns the fractional part f of x, such that f is a value greater than or equal to 0, and less than 1. Maps to the assembly instruction frc.
frexp(x, out exp)	Breaks a floating-point number into fraction and power of 2. frexp returns the mantissa, and the exponent is stored in the output parameter exp. If x is 0, the function returns 0 for both the mantissa and the exponent.
fwidth(x)	Returns abs(ddx(x))+abs(ddy(x)).
isfinite(x)	Returns true if x is finite, false otherwise.
isinf(x)	Returns true if x is +INF or -INF, false otherwise
isnan(x)	Returns true if x is NAN or QNAN, false otherwise. A NAN, which means "Not-a-Number," indicates that the specified value is not a legal number. The function returns true if the argument is not a number and false if the argument is a number. The classic example of a NAN is zero divided by zero, 0/0.
ldexp(x, exp)	Returns x * 2exp.
len(v)	Vector length.
length(v)	Returns the length of the vector v.
lerp(a, b, s)	Returns a + s(b − a). This linearly interpolates between a and b, such that the return value is a when s is 0, and b when s is 1. Please note that this instruction does not necessarily map to the assembly instruction lrp. If its blending factor is not saturated, it maps to a mul followed by a mad instruction. Otherwise it maps to lrp, which has a value range of [0..1] for its third parameter. If it does not map to lrp, this restriction does not exist.
log(x)	Returns the base-e logarithm of x. If x is negative, the return value is undefined. If x is 0, the function returns +INF. Maps to the assembly instruction log.

Continued on next page

Table 3.14 Intrinsic Functions (continued)

Intrinsic	Description
log10(x)	Returns the base-10 logarithm of x. If x is negative, the return value is undefined. If x is 0, the function returns +INF.
log2(x)	Returns the base-2 logarithm of x. If x is negative, the return value is undefined. If x is 0, the function returns +INF.
max(a, b)	Selects the greater of a and b. Maps to the assembly instruction max.
min(a, b)	Selects the lesser of a and b. Maps to the assembly instruction min.
modf(x, out ip)	Splits the value x into fractional and integer parts, each of which has the same sign as x. The signed fractional portion of x is returned. The integer portion is stored in the output parameter ip.
mul(a, b)	Performs matrix multiplication between a and b. If a is a vector, it is treated as a row vector. If b is a vector, it is treated as a column vector. The inner dimension $a_{columns}$ and b_{rows} must be equal. The result has the dimension $arows \times b_{columns}$.
normalize(v)	Returns the normalized vector v / length(v). If the length of v is 0, the result is indefinite. Maps to the assembly instruction nrm or to a dp3, rsq, mul sequence of instructions.
pow(x, y)	Returns xy. Depending on the compile target and the value of y, it maps to different assembly instructions (e.g., exp).
radians(x)	Converts x from degrees to radians.

reflect(i, n)	Returns the reflection vector v, given the entering ray direction i, and the surface normal n. Such that $v = i - 2 * dot(i, n) * n$.
	```float3 reflect(float3 I, float3 N)```
	```{```
	``` // R = I - 2 * N * (I.N)```
	``` return I - 2 * N * dot(I, N);```
	```}```

refract(i, n, eta)	Returns the refraction vector v, given the entering ray direction i, the surface normal n, and the relative index of refraction *eta*. If the angle between i and n is too great for a given *eta*, refract returns (0,0,0).
	The source code of this intrinsic might look like this.
	```float3 refract(float3 I, float3 N, float ri)```
	```{```
	``` float cosI = dot(-I, N);```
	``` float cosT = 1.0f - ri * ri * (1.0f - cosI * cosI);```
	``` float3 T = ri * I + ((ri * cosI - sqrt(abs(cosT))) * N);```
	``` return T * (float3)(cosT > 0);```
	```}```

Continued on next page

Table 3.14 Intrinsic Functions *(continued)*

Intrinsic	Description
`round(x)`	Rounds x to the nearest integer.
`rsqrt(x)`	Returns 1 / sqrt(x). Maps to the assembly instruction `rsq`.
`saturate(x)`	Clamps x to the range [0, 1]. Maps to the assembly instruction modifier `_sat` (free).
`sign(x)`	Computes the sign of x. Returns -1 if x is less than 0, 0 if x equals 0, and 1 if x is greater than zero.
`sin(x)`	Returns the sine of x.
`sincos(x, out s, out c)`	Returns the sine and cosine of x. sin(x) is stored in the output parameter s. cos(x) is stored in the output parameter c. In ps_2_0 and higher, it maps to the assembly instruction `sincos`.
`sinh(x)`	Returns the hyperbolic sine of x.
`smoothstep(min, max, x)`	Returns 0 if x < *min*. Returns 1 if x > *max*. Returns a smooth Hermite interpolation between 0 and 1, if x is in the range [*min, max*]. The source code of this function might look like the following C code: ```float smoothstep (float edge0, float edge1,
float x)
{
if (x < edge0)
return 0;
if (x >= edge1)
return 1;
// Scale/bias into [0..1] range
x = (x - edge0) / (edge1 - edge0);
return x * x * (3 - 2 * x);
}```
`sqrt(x)`	Square root (per component).
`step(a, x)`	Returns ($x \geq a$) ? 1 : 0.
`tan(x)`	Returns the tangent of x.
`tanh(x)`	Returns the hyperbolic tangent of x.
`transpose(m)`	Returns the transpose of the matrix m. If the source is dimension $m_{rows} \times m_{columns}$, the result is dimension $m_{columns} \times m_{rows}$.

Two of the most used math instrinsics are `normalize()` and `mul(a, b)`, which performs a matrix multiplication between a and b. Please note that for example the `pow()` math instrinsic used in a pixel shader does not necessarily map to the `pow` instruction found in different assembly versions. It might be replaced by the assembly instruction `exp` or by a number of `mul` instructions, depending on the chosen pixel shader version target.

The gradient intrinsics ddx() and ddy()are used to detect the rate of change of a given register across adjacent pixels in horizontal (ddx) and vertical directions (ddy). They help to answer the question "how much does this value change from pixel to pixel, in either the screen-x or screen-y position?" This could be useful in a number of cases in which information about adjacent texels is required (e.g., on-the-fly computation of normals from height data, procedural shaders (see [Rost] for an example on adaptive analytic prefiltering with gradient instructions). Complex filtering depends on knowing just how much of the texture (or shading) we need to filter. The values returned by the graphics hardware for ddx() and ddy() are numerically iterated values. That is, if you evaluate ddx(Var), the graphics card will give you the difference between the value of Var at the current pixel and its value at the pixel next door. It is a straight linear difference, made efficient by the nature of the graphics card architecture (neighboring pixels will be calculated simultaneously).

The texture intrinsics that expect the results of the gradient intrinsics can be used to sample a pixel according to the horizontal and vertical rates of changes (see an article on how to retrieve a similar functionality without ddx() and ddy() support in hardware [Pharr]).

Texture Sampling Intrinsics

There are 20 texture sampling intrinsics used for sampling texture data into a pixel shader. The four types of textures (1D, 2D, 3D, and cubemap) each have five types of texture intrinsic loads (regular, with derivaties, projective, mip-map LOD, and biased). All texture sampling intrinsics are shown in Table 3.15.

Table 3.15 Texture Sampling Functions

tex1D(s, t)	1D texture lookup. s is a sampler. t is a scalar.
tex1D(s, t, ddx, ddy)	1D texture lookup, with derivatives. s is a sampler. t, ddx, and ddy are scalars.
tex1Dproj(s, t)	1D projective texture lookup. s is a sampler. t is a 4D vector. t is divided by its last component before the lookup takes place.
tex1Dlod(s, t)	1D mip-map LOD texture lookup. The particular mip-map level of detail (LOD) being sampled has to be specified as the fourth component of the texture coordinate.
tex1Dbias(s, t)	1D biased texture lookup. s is a sampler. t is a 4D vector. The mip level is biased by t.w before the lookup takes place.
tex2D(s, t)	2D texture lookup. s is a sampler. t is a 2D texture coordinate.
tex2D(s, t, ddx, ddy)	2D texture lookup, with derivatives. s is a sampler. t, ddx, and ddy are 2D vectors.
tex2Dproj(s, t)	2D projective texture lookup. s is a sampler. t is a 4D vector. t is divided by its last component before the lookup takes place.

Continued on next page

Table 3.15 Texture Sampling Functions (continued)

`tex2Dlod(s, t)`	2D mip-map LOD texture lookup. The particular mip-map level of detail (LOD) being sampled has to be specified as the fourth component of the texture coordinate.
`tex2Dbias(s, t)`	2D biased texture lookup. s is a sampler. t is a 4D vector. The mip level is biased by t.w before the lookup takes place.
`tex3D(s, t)`	3D volume texture lookup. s is a sampler. t is a 3D texture coordinate.
`tex3D(s, t, ddx, ddy)`	3D volume texture lookup, with derivatives. s is a sampler. t, ddx, and ddy are 3D vectors.
`tex3Dproj(s, t)`	3D projective volume texture lookup. s is a sampler. t is a 4D vector. t is divided by its last component before the lookup takes place.
`tex3Dlod(s, t)`	3D mip-map LOD texture lookup. The particular mip-map level of detail (LOD) being sampled has to be specified as the fourth component of the texture coordinate.
`tex3Dbias(s, t)`	3D biased texture lookup. s is a sampler. t is a 4D vector. The mip level is biased by t.w before the lookup takes place.
`texCUBE(s, t)`	Cubemap lookup. s is a sampler. t is a 3D texture coordinate.
`texCUBE(s, t, ddx, ddy)`	Cubemap lookup, with derivatives. s is a sampler. t, ddx, and ddy are 3D vectors.
`texCUBEproj(s, t)`	Projective cubemap lookup. s is a sampler. t is a 4D vector. t is divided by its last component before the lookup takes place.
`texCUBElod(s, t)`	Mip-map LOD cubemap texture lookup. The particular mip-map level of detail (LOD) being sampled has to be specified as the fourth component of t.
`texCUBEbias(s, t)`	Biased cubemap lookup. s is a sampler. t is a 4D vector. The mip level is biased by t.w before the lookup takes place.

The texture loading intrinsics that take `ddx` and `ddy` parameters compute texture LOD using these explicit derivatives, `ddx()` and `ddy()` math intrinsics.

The `tex*proj()` intrinsics are used to do projective texture reads, where the texture coordinates used to sample the texture are divided by the last component prior to accessing the texture. `tex2Dproj()` is used for projective shadow maps and similar effects. The `tex*bias()` perform biased texture sampling, where the bias can be computed per pixel. It was used to over-blur the textures in ATI's Animusic Pipe example [Peeper/Mitchell]:

```
...
// Blur reflectioni by extension amount
float3 vCubeLookup = vReflection + i.Pos/fEnvMapRadius;
float4 cReflection = texCUBEbias(tCubeEnv, float4(vCubeLookup,
fBlur * fTextureBlur)) * vReflectionColor;
...
```

The product of `fBlur` and `fTextureBlur` is provided to the fourth component of the 4D vector used in `texCUBEbias()` to fetch the cubemap. It determines the bias to be used when accessing the cubemap.

If the underlying hardware supports vs_3_0, a HLSL vertex shader can fetch a texture with the following texture intrinsic (covered more thoroughly in Chapters 25 and 26).

```
tex2Dlod(s, t)
```

`tex2Dlod()` allows you to fetch a texture in the vertex shader by specifying the mip-map in the fourth component of *t.w*, which is to be sampled using up to three channels of the texture coordinates. This value can be negative, in which case the LOD selected is the zeroeth one (biggest map) with the magnification filter `MAGFILTER`. Because *t.w* is a floating-point value, the fractional value is used to interpolate (if the mip-map filter used during minification (`MIPFILTER`) is set to `LINEAR`) between two mip levels.

s identifies the source sampler (*s#*), where # specifies which texture sampler number to sample. The sampler has an associated texture and a control state defined by the `D3DSAMPLERSTATETYPE` enumeration (for example, `D3DSAMP_MINFILTER`). A vertex texture is set in the application with the constants `D3DVERTEXTURESAMPLER0`-`D3DVERTEXTURESAMPLER3` provided to the first parameter of `SetTexture()`.

```
// texture look up in the vertex shader
m_pEffect->SetTexture(D3DVERTEXTURESAMPLER0, m_pDispMap);
```

Similar to the pixel shader texture intrinsics, there is no texture dependent read limit in the vertex shader. A dependent read is a read from a texture map using a texture coordinate that was calculated earlier in the shader.

Vertex texturing has an impact on performance, because all texture accesses come with high latencies, meaning that the period between fetching a value from a texture and being able to use the result can be quite long. There will be a lot of clock cycles spent moving the data from external memory into the chip (on a cache miss), through the cache, through a texture filtering calculation, and eventually into the vertex shader. For this reason, throughput when using vertex texturing can potentially be quite low, but it also means that if the shader has instructions that do not rely on the result of the texture fetch, the texture fetch can be free since non-dependent instructions can be executed while waiting for the texture data to arrive (read more in Beets [Beets]). Vertex textures are not filtered by current hardware, so only point sampling is supported.

Flow Control

Flow-control statements determine which statement block to execute next. HLSL offers `if`, `do`, `for`, and `while` flow controls that are used in the same way as in C/C++.

An `if`/`else` statement is shown in the following code snippet (read more on this example in Chapter 9).

```
if (Shadow > 0.0f)
{ // R
  float3 Reflect = normalize(2 * Diffuse * Normal - LightDir);

  // gloss map in color.w restricts spec reflection
  float Specular = min(pow(saturate(dot(Reflect, ViewDir)), 3),
Color.w);

  return 0.2 * Color + (Color * Diffuse + Specular);
}
else
  return 0.2 * Color + Color * Diffuse;
```

Curly braces ({}) start and end a statement block. When a statement block uses a single statement, the curly braces are optional. A `for` statement is for example useful to average a 4×4 block of pixels.

```
for(int iSample = 0; iSample < 16; iSample++)
{
  // Compute the sum of colors throughout the sample points
  fResampleSum += tex2D(s0, vScreenPosition +
                  g_avSampleOffsets[iSample]);
}
```

The `do`/`while` and `while` statements break out of a loop, if the conditional expression fails.

```
while ( color.a > 0.33f )
{
 color /= 2;
}

do
{
 color /= 2;
}while ( color.a > 0.33f )
```

The main difference between the two statements comes down to the comparison: ask before you shoot (`while`) or shoot before you ask (`do`/`while`). In other words, the `while` statement checks the condition before it executes the statements in its brackets and the `do`/`while` statement checks the condition after the execution of its statement.

Depending on the chosen shader profile, flow control statements can be compiled by the HLSL compiler into very different assembly sequences. If they are not supported in the target shader profile, the compiler will try to enroll the statement and base the flow on a comparison, as long as it fits into the available number of instruction slots.

If flow controls are supported, these statements are compiled to assembly static branching and looping, predicated instructions, static looping, and dynamic looping. The most important difference for HLSL programmers is between dynamic and static flow controls. Flow controls are static if they depend on a variable that is changed on a per-shader runtime basis. In other words, the value of the condition that "drives" the flow control does not change during the execution of a vertex or pixel shader. Flow controls are dynamic, if the variable that holds the condition can change in the shader. For example, a value that is altered in the vertex shader and then used as a condition for a flow control is used in a dynamic branch.

A typical static branch is an if statement that depends on a BOOL variable that is set in the application. If this variable is changed by the shader during shader runtime, it is a dynamic branch. A typical static loop is a for loop, which cannot be changed in the shader, and a typical dynamic loop is a while or do/while statement with a condition based on a decision to be made in the shader.

Table 3.16 should give you an idea of which flow controls are supported and how. To get a more thorough understanding on the support of flow controls, the support of the assembly instructions needs to be examined. (This is shown in Appendix A.)

Table 3.16 Flow Control Support in Vertex and Pixel Shaders

Shader Version	vs_ 2_0	vs_ 2_a	vs_ 2_sw	vs_ 3_0	vs_ 3_sw	ps_ 2_0	ps_ 2_b	ps_ 2_a	ps_ 2_sw	ps_ 3_0	ps_ 3_sw
Static Flow Control	x*	x*	x	x	x	-	-	x*	x	x	x
Dynamic Flow Control	-	x*	x	x	x	-	-	x*	x	x	x

*Check in VS20Caps or PS20Caps. DynamicFlowControlDepth > 0, D3DVS20CAPS_PREDICATION == YES and StaticFlowControlDepth > 0 for static and dynamic flow control support.

The shader versions vs_1_x, ps_2_0, and ps_2_b do not support flow control assembly instructions at all. The HLSL compiler will try to mimic flow controls here. In some cases, it might be better to avoid HLSL flow control statements or to use only statements in which the compiler can "unroll" or simply mimic the flow control behavior. The shader versions that support flow controls might do this on different support levels. Regarding Version 2 shaders, the level of support needs to be checked via three capability bits (DynamicFlowControlDepth, D3DVS20CAPS_PREDICATION, and StaticFlowControlDepth) in the PS20Caps structure.

One of the gotchas regarding the support of flow controls in ps_2_a and ps_3_0 is that the result of a gradient calculation on a computed value inside dynamic flow control is ambiguous when adjacent pixels may go down separate paths. Hence, nothing that requires a derivative of a computed value may exist inside of dynamic flow controls. This includes most texture sampling intrinsics with the exception of `tex*lod()` and `tex*()` with derivatives, since you have to compute the LOD or derivatives outside of the dynamic flow control. Only with these texture intrinsics will the HLSL compiler create an assembly output that uses assembly flow control instructions. Using any other texture intrinsic in the flow control will lead to a situation in which the HLSL compiler will mimic the behavior of this flow control, which might lead to non-optimal code.

With the quite inconsistent support of flow controls throughout available shader profiles, writing HLSL flow control code that compiles well on as many shader profiles as possible is difficult. The way of least resistance is to avoid using flow controls on lower target platforms and to utilize flow controls if the application has a minimum specification that targets shader profiles 2 and 3 only. It helps to have a deeper knowledge of the flow control assembly instructions to optimize the HLSL code according to the capabilities of the hardware and to understand the subtleties here (for example, the different nesting depth of different assembly instructions that might lead to error messages in the HLSL compiler output; see Appendix A).

A similar situation exists regarding the support of the ps_1_x shader profiles by the HLSL compiler.

Using the ps_1_x Compile Targets

Writing pixel shaders in HLSL with compile targets of ps_2_0 and higher is common nowadays, whereas writing pixel shaders in HLSL to target ps_1_1 – ps_1_4 requires some knowledge of assembly programming, to force the compiler to support certain assembly features. Quite often it is easier to use HLSL to write the vertex shader that targets vs_1_1 and use assembly for the ps_1_1 – ps_1_4 pixel shaders, because it takes less time to write 8–28 assembly instructions than slightly changing the HLSL source code several times by checking the assembly output to see if the result fits into the restrictions of the compile target.

If you want to target ps_1_x compile targets with HLSL, the following hints should help to do so.

Instruction Count Limitation

ps_1_x target platforms can use a very limited number of assembly instructions. In other words, the HLSL compiler can compile only to a few assembly instructions. Table 3.5 shows the available number of instructions. Pixel shader Version 1 compile targets are used together with the vertex shader 1 model vs_1_1. This vertex shader model supports at least 96 instructions slots, whereas the ps_1_1-ps_1_3 compile targets only support 8–12 assembly instruction slots, and ps_1_4 supports 28 slots in two phases. The compiler needs some additional guidance to efficiently compile the HLSL source code to such a small number of instructions.

Restricted Arbitrary Swizzle and Write Mask

Tables 3.11 and 3.12 show the support swizzles and write masks in ps_1_x. ps_1_ 1-ps_1_3 compile targets that do not support arbitrary write masks or replicate swizzles (i.e., .r, .g, .b, or .a). ps_1_4 supports replicate swizzles and arbitrary write masks. If the HLSL code uses swizzles or write masks that are not supported by the target platform, it will use extra instructions to emulate the swizzle or write mask. This can quickly cause programs to overrun the available number of assembly instructions slots. To assure the efficient assembly generation of the HLSL compiler, you need to examine the assembly code.

ps_1_x Assembly Modifiers

An advantage of the ps_1_x compile targets is the availability of free instruction or register modifiers. The compiler automatically matches all modifiers that it can, but it is helpful if the programmer thinks in terms of using these modifiers to accomplish certain operations. The easiest and best known case to get a free modifier is the saturate() intrinsic, which adds in all shader versions a free _sat modifier to the assembly instruction.

The _bx2 assembly register modifier (available in ps_1_1-ps_1_4), which biases the value in the register and multiplies it by 2, will be generated by the HLSL compiler by using code fragments like the following:

```
float2 TexCoord = Tex * 2.0f - 1.0f;
...
float2 TexCoord = Tex * 2.0f;
TexCoord -= 1.0f;
...
float2 TexCoord = (Tex - 1.0f) * 2.0f;
```

The HLSL compiler will generate from these code snippets the following assembly code.

```
mov r0, t0_bx2
```

To cause the compiler to generate an assembly _bias modifier (available in ps_1_1-ps_1_4 but with a restricted range in ps_1_1-ps_1_3: [0..1]), one might use for example the following code snippet.

```
float2 TexCoord = Tex - 0.5f;
// assembly: mov r0, t0_bias
// works in ps_1_1 - ps_1_3 only on values with range [0..1]
```

To cause the HLSL compiler to generate an _x2 source modifier (ps_1_4 only), the following code snippet can be used.

```
float2 TexCoord = Tex * 2.0f;
// assembly: mov r0, t0_x2
```

To attach instruction modifiers _x2, _x4, _x8, _d2, _d4, and _d8 to an assembly instruction, the HLSL compiler might be fed by the following source code.

```
float2 TexCoord = (Tex1 + Tex2) * 2.0f;
// assembly: add_x2 r0, t0, t1
```

Please note that ps_1_1-ps_1_3 only supports _x2, _x4, and _d2, whereas ps_1_4 supports all modifiers.

Additionally, all assembly pixel shader versions support a negate and a complement modifier. To force the HLSL compiler to create these, the following source code can be used.

```
// complement modifier: works only on values in the range [0..1]
float2 TexCoord = 1.0f - Tex;
// assembly: mov r0, 1-t0;

// negate modifier
float2 TexCoord = -Tex;
// assembly: mov r0, -t0;
```

Please note that constants in ps_1_x cannot be negated. The HLSL compiler might emulate this by moving the value first into a temporary register.

Strategy for Targeting ps_1_x with HLSL Shaders

The best strategy to create HLSL shaders for the ps_1_x compile target is to create a working shader with the ps_2_0 compile target and then downsize the shader so that it fits into the restricted number of instructions of the ps_1_x models. This is done by disabling the validation of the HLSL compiler with the -Vd switch and then examining the assembly code created by the HLSL compiler. By altering the HLSL code and examining the assembly output, you can optimize the code step by step so that it fits.

This is similar to the way a HLSL shader is optimized. How this can be done is shown in the next section.

Optimizing HLSL Shaders

HLSL source code is optimized by inspecting the assembly code created by the HLSL compiler. This requires some knowledge of writing and optimizing assembly shaders, which is discussed in Appendix A. The following HLSL writing rules should help the compiler to create optimal assembly source code and should therefore help to reduce the time necessary to optimize your code.

The most important optimization rule is: optimize on an algorithmic level first. If you feel that the algorithm can't be optimized anymore without losing the necessary flexibility, the following code optimization rules can be used to optimize HLSL code.

Rule #1: Use Intrinsics

Intrinsic functions should be used whenever feasible, because you don't need to reinvent the wheel by writing your own function, and there is a good chance that they are optimized for specific shader profiles. It won't make sense to use an instrinsic, if the intrinsic would recalculate a value that is already calculated in previous shader instructions and can be re-used here or if the precision or functionality provided by the intrinsic is not necessary and a reduced version would require less instruction slots.

Rule #2: Use the Appropriate Data Type

By using the appropriate data type, you help the compiler and the optimizer in the driver to optimize code and pair shader instructions. For example, using a `float4` data type instead of a `float` data type prevents the compiler from arranging the output assembly instructions in a way that they can be co-issued on hardware that supports this.

Rule #3: Reduce Type Casting

Eliminate type casts whenever possible. It is more efficient to initialize the alpha channel by choosing a `float4` data type than it is to choose a `float3` data type and rely on the type casting of the compiler.

```
sampler texSampler;
float3 diff, amb;

float4 PS(float2 tex : TEXCOORD0) : COLOR
{
   float3 color = tex2D(texSampler, tex);
   color *= diff + amb;

 return float4(color, 1.0);
}
```

Leads to the following assembly code:

```
ps_2_0
def c2, 1, 0, 0, 0
dcl t0.xy
dcl_2d s0

texld r0, t0, s0
mov r1.xyz, c0
add r1.xyz, r1, c1
mul r0.xyz, r0, r1
mov r0.w, c2.x
mov oC0, r0
```

Using the following HLSL pixel shader reduces the number of assembly instructions by one (although if the hardware can pair instructions, this should not lead to a difference in performance).

```
sampler texSampler;
float4 diff, amb;
float4 PS(float2 tex : TEXCOORD0) : COLOR
{
   float4 color = tex2D(texSampler, tex);
   return color *= diff + amb;
}
...
ps_2_0
dcl t0.xy
dcl_2d s0

texld r0, t0, s0
mov r1, c0
add r1, r1, c1
mul r0, r0, r1
mov oC0, r0
```

Rule #4: Use Integer Data Types Carefully

All ps_2_x and ps_3_0 hardware lacks support for native integer data types, with the exception of the indexing registers. Therefore, the compiler emulates integer data types by using a `frc`, `mad`, `cmp`, `cmp`, `mad` instruction sequence, or similar. The following piece shows this.

```
float4 PS(int k : TEXCOORD0) : COLOR
{
   int n = k / 3;
   return n;
}
...
ps_2_0
def c0, 0.333333, 0, 1, 0
dcl t0.x

mul r0.w, t0.x, c0.x
frc r0.w, r0.w
mad r2.w, t0.x, c0.x, -r0.w
cmp_pp r1.w, -r0.w, c0.y, c0.z
cmp_pp r0.w, t0.x, c0.y, c0.z
mad r0, r0.w, r1.w, r2.w
mov oC0, r0
```

Integers are more efficient than floats, if they are used to index into an array of constant registers.

```
float4x4 m[10];
float4 VS(
   float4 Pos : POSITION,
   float2 index : BLENDINDICES,
   float blend : BLENDWEIGHT) : POSITION
{
 float4 p1 = mul(Pos, m[index.x]);
 float4 p2 = mul(Pos, m[index.y]);
return lerp(p1, p2, blend);
}
...
vs_2_0
def c40, 4, 0, 0, 0
dcl_position v0
dcl_blendindices v1
dcl_blendweight v2

frc r0.xy, v1
add r0.xy, -r0, v1
mul r0.xy, r0, c40.x
mova a0.xy, r0
dp4 r0.x, v0, c0[a0.y]
dp4 r0.y, v0, c1[a0.y]
dp4 r0.z, v0, c2[a0.y]
dp4 r0.w, v0, c3[a0.y]
dp4 r1.x, v0, c0[a0.x]
dp4 r1.y, v0, c1[a0.x]
dp4 r1.z, v0, c2[a0.x]
dp4 r1.w, v0, c3[a0.x]
add r0, r0, -r1
mad oPos, v2.x, r0, r1
```

This is another example in which the HLSL compiler creates code that emulates integer data types, in this case because an integer data type is required in the index register. This is not necessary if we declare the indices as int2.

```
float4 VS(
   float4 Pos : POSITION,
   int2 index : BLENDINDICES,
   float blend : BLENDWEIGHT) : POSITION
{
float4 p1 = mul(Pos, m[index.x]);
float4 p2 = mul(Pos, m[index.y]);

return lerp(p1, p2, blend);
}
...
vs_2_0
def c40, 4, 0, 0, 0
dcl_position v0
dcl_blendindices v1
dcl_blendweight v2
```

```
mul r0.xy, v1, c40.x
mova a0.xy, r0
dp4 r0.x, v0, c0[a0.y]
dp4 r0.y, v0, c1[a0.y]
dp4 r0.z, v0, c2[a0.y]
dp4 r0.w, v0, c3[a0.y]
dp4 r1.x, v0, c0[a0.x]
dp4 r1.y, v0, c1[a0.x]
dp4 r1.z, v0, c2[a0.x]
dp4 r1.w, v0, c3[a0.x]
add r0, r0, -r1
mad oPos, v2.x, r0, r1
```

Declaring the indices as int2 saves three instruction slots here.

Rule #5: Pack Scalar Constants

To reduce the number of constants used and to allow the HLSL compiler to work around hardware limitations (can read only from one constant register), it is good HLSL programming practice to pack scalar constants into one constant.

```
float scale, bias;

float4 VS(float4 Pos: POSITION) : POSITION
{
    return(Pos * scale + bias);
}
...
vs_2_0
dcl_position v0
mov r0.w, c0.x
mad oPos, v0, r0.w, c1.x
```

Packing the scale and bias variable into one constant gives the compiler the opportunity to optimize this code to one mad instruction.

```
float2 scale_bias;

float4 VS(float4 Pos: POSITION) : POSITION
{
    return(Pos * scale_bias.x + scale_bias.y);
}
...
vs_2_0
dcl_position v0
mad oPos, v0, c0.x, c0.y
```

Rule #6: Read the Assembly Output of the HLSL Compiler to Optimize HLSL Code

Watch out for assembly optimization rules as shown in Appendix A and in [ATI] and [Rege] and force the HLSL compiler to output optimized assembly code. This is done by examining the assembly code produced by the compiler and then altering the HLSL code so that the compiler creates the expected assembly code.

D3DX Effect Files Framework

The DirectX SDK comes with an effect file framework that helps to organize shaders together with rendering states. This framework helps you to manage shaders by simplifying and organizing shader management in a very natural way.

Here are some features of effects:

- Effects contain global variables. These variables can be set by either the effect itself or by the application.
- Effects manage pipeline states. This includes states for setting transformations, lighting, materials, and rendering options.
- Effects manage texture state and sampler state. This includes specifying texture files, initializing texture stages, creating sampler objects, and setting sampler state.
- Effects manage shader state. This includes creating and deleting shaders, setting shader constants, setting shader state, and rendering with shaders.
- Effects contain multiple rendering options called techniques. Each technique encapsulates global variables, pipeline state, texture and sampler state, and shader state. A single style is implemented in a rendering pass. One or more passes can be encapsulated in a technique. All the passes and techniques can be validated to see if the effect code will run on the hardware device.
- Effects can save and restore state, leaving the device in the same state as before the effect was run.
- Effects can use preshaders: shader code that is constant at runtime and has therefore been extracted by the HLSL compiler from the pixel or vertex shader to be used as uniform data.
- The new DirectX Standard Annotation and Semantics (DXSAS) even offers semantics for parameters and a scripting interface that brings effects a new level of self-described operation and versatility.

The following text features some of the frequently used features of the D3DX Effect File framework by showing typical real-world examples.

 Effect files are natively used by the examples in the SDK, especially the SDK example EffectEdit and by NVIDIA's FX Composer.

Techniques and Passes

An effect in an effect file uses effect parameters, one or more techniques, and one or more passes. A logical structure of an effect looks like this.

```
Effect file parameters
    Technique
        pass0
        ...
        pass1
    Technique2
    ...
```

Here is a typical example of an effect file:

```
float4x4 matWorldViewProj;
float4x4 matWorld;
float4 vecLightDir;
...
// vertex and pixel shader goes here ...

technique TShader
{
    pass P0
    {
        // compiler directives
        VertexShader = compile vs_1_1 VS();
        PixelShader  = compile ps_1_1 PS();
    }
}
```

The first three lines of this code snippet are occupied by global variables, representing the effect file parameters. These parameters might be used in every vertex or pixel shader in this effect file. The line that starts with the keyword technique shows one technique named TShader in this effect file. This technique uses only one pass. The two lines in the pass statement are telling the compiler that the name of the vertex shader is VS() and the name of the pixel shader is PS(). To differentiate between the vertex and the pixel shader, the keywords VertexShader and PixelShader are used. To provide the compiler with its target platform, the keywords vs_1_1 and ps_1_1 are used.

One Technique Several Passes

A technique encapsulates the effect state that determines a rendering style. A technique is made up of one or more passes. An effect file that uses one technique with multiple passes is shown in the following lines:

```
technique TShader
{
    pass P0
    {
```

```
          VertexShader = compile vs_1_1 VS();
          PixelShader  = compile ps_2_0 PS();
     }
     pass P1
     {
          Sampler[0] = (RenderMapSampler);
          Sampler[1] = (ProjTexMapSampler);

          VertexShader = compile vs_1_1 VSProjTexture();
          PixelShader  = compile ps_2_0 PSProjTexture();
     }
}
```

The syntax for calling a technique is as follows:

```
technique [ id ]  [< annotation(s) >]
     { pass(es) }
```

Where parameter id is an optional unique identifier. This is the word TShader in the previous example. An annotation is not used in any way by the effect framework, but it can be used by the application to identify certain techniques by providing specific descriptions (see the section "DirectX Standard Annotation and Semantics").

Each pass is marked by the keyword pass. The syntax for calling a pass is as follows:

```
pass  [ id ]  [< annotation(s) >]
     { state assignment(s) }
```

Parameter id is an optional unique identifier. We use P0 or P1 here to identify passes. To execute a pass from within the application, you can call the number of the pass by counting from top to bottom.

The example uses two passes, where the second pass depends on the result of the first pass. Therefore pass P0 will be called first and then pass P1. The pixel shader in PSProjTexture() blends a projected texture in ProjTexMapSampler with the result from a render target in RenderMapSampler that was filled in the first rendering pass.

Several Techniques
Using several techniques in an effect file is useful in providing fallback paths for older graphics cards. So part of the id of the technique might be the name of the supported shader version.

Here is an effect file with several techniques:

```
technique HLSLShader
{
     pass
     {
          Sampler[0] = (ColorMapSampler);
          Sampler[1] = (BumpMapSampler);
```

```
        VertexShader = compile vs_1_1 VS();
        PixelShader  = compile ps_2_a PS();
    }
}

technique ASM30Shader
{
    pass
    {
        Sampler[0] = (ColorMapSampler);
        Sampler[1] = (BumpMapSampler);
        VertexShaderConstant4[0] = (matWorldViewProj);
        VertexShaderConstant4[4] = (matWorld);
        VertexShaderConstant1[8] = (vecLightDir);
        VertexShaderConstant1[9] = (vecLightDir2);
        VertexShaderConstant1[10] = (vecLightDir3);
        VertexShaderConstant1[11] = (vecLightDir4);
        VertexShaderConstant1[12] = (vecEye);
        VertexShaderConstant1[13] = {0.2, 0.0, 0.0, 1.0};

        VertexShader = <VS30>;
        PixelShader  = <PS30>;
    }
}
```

Both techniques are functionally identical; the main difference is that the first technique uses an HLSL shader with the HLSL compiler, and the second technique is written in *s_3_0 assembly.

Depending on the availability of *s_3_0 hardware, the application might choose the appropriate technique. Please note in the second technique the use of the VertexShaderConstant*[] keywords. This is necessary if an assembly shader is used in an effect file, to tell the compiler the constant register in which it should store the uniform data.

Shaders in Effect Files

Effect files can store HLSL as well as assembly shader code. The following example shows this.

```
float4x4 matWorldViewProj;

VERTEXSHADER VS11 =
asm
{
    vs_1_1
    dcl_position v0
    m4x4 oPos, v0, c0
};
PIXELSHADER PS11 =
asm
{
    ps_1_1
```

```
            def c0, 1.0,0.0,0.0,0.0
            mov r0, c0
    };

    struct VS_OUTPUT
    {
        float4 Pos  : POSITION;
    };

    VS_OUTPUT VS(float4 Pos  : POSITION)
    {
        VS_OUTPUT Out = (VS_OUTPUT)0;
        Out.Pos = mul(Pos, matWorldViewProj);
        return Out;
    }

    float4 PS() : COLOR
    {
        return float4(1.0, 0.0, 0.0, 0.0);
    }


    technique HLSLShader
    {
        pass
        {

            VertexShader = compile vs_1_1 VS();
            PixelShader  = compile ps_1_1 PS();
        }
    }

    technique ASM11Shader
    {
        pass s_1_1
        {
            VertexShaderConstant4[0] = (matWorldViewProj);

            VertexShader  = <VS11>;
            PixelShader   = <PS11>;
        }
    }
```

There are two techniques, each with one pass, that are functionally identical. The technique HLSLShader uses an HLSL vertex shader named VS() and an HLSL pixel shader named PS(). The technique ASMShader uses a vs_1_1 vertex shader named VS11 and a ps_1_1 pixel shader named PS11. Please note that the names of assembly shaders are provided to the compiler by using angular brackets.

Textures in Effect Files

Textures can be set and sampled with the help of an effect file. The effect file can also store the SetSamplerState() functionality. The following example shows how to integrate texture sampler states in an effect file:

```
...
texture ColorMap;
sampler2D ColorMapSampler = sampler_state
{
   Texture = <ColorMap>;
   MinFilter = Linear;
   MagFilter = Linear;
   MipFilter = Linear;
   AddressU  = Clamp;
   AddressV  = Clamp;
};

texture BumpMap;
sampler2D BumpMapSampler = sampler_state
{
   Texture = <BumpMap>;
   MinFilter = Linear;
   MagFilter = Linear;
   MipFilter = Linear;
   AddressU  = Clamp;
   AddressV  = Clamp;
};
...
float4 PS(float2 Tex: TEXCOORD0,
          float4 Light : TEXCOORD1,
          float3 View : TEXCOORD2,
          float4 Light2 : TEXCOORD4,
          float4 Light3 : TEXCOORD3,
          float4 Light4 : TEXCOORD5) : COLOR
{
...
   // fetch color map
   float4 color = tex2D(ColorMapSampler, Tex);

   // fetch bump map
   float4 bumpNormal = (2 * tex2D(BumpMapSampler, Tex)) - 1.0;
...
}
```

The texture is declared with the texture keyword, which represents an IDirect3D Texture9 object. By using texture objects we can associate the texture for a particular sampler stage directly in the effect file. This is done by applying the sampler description to the sampler as shown in the following code snippet:

```
technique TShader
{
   pass P0
   {
      Sampler[0] = (ColorMapSampler);
      Sampler[1] = (BumpMapSampler);
```

```
                         // compile shaders
                         VertexShader = compile vs_1_1 VS();
                         PixelShader  = compile ps_2_0 PS();
             }
     }
```

A sampler for a 2D texture is defined with the `sampler2D` keyword. The sample stages of the texture are set with the `sampler_state`keyword followed by the state values in brackets. Both textures in this example are trilinearly filtered and clamped. The keywords for the sampler states follow the functionality provided by the `SetSampler-State()` functions and should therefore look very familiar to you.

DirectX Standard Annotation and Semantics

When Microsoft created Direct3DX Effects, it was designed to be as open and versatile as possible. To drive a more general operating logic and data input mechanism, Microsoft later added a DirectX Standard Annotation and Semantics (DXSAS) specification. DXSAS offers three major components: semantics that characterize the content of a variable more than the already available shader input and output semantics, annotation, and scripts.

New Semantics

Semantics can now also applied to data send from the application to the shader (parameter). For example, to label a matrix as a world view-projection transform matrix and to label a float4 a diffuse color:

```
             float4x4 myTransform : WORLDVIEWPROJECTION;
             float4 myColor : DIFFUSE;
```

DXSAS contains most usable combinations of joint, world, view, projection, inverse, and transpose matrices along with standard lighting, coloring, and bounding definitions.

Annotations

Annotations are not used by the DirectX Effect file framework, but can be used by the application. An example of an annotation might be a hint to associate a file with a texture type, which is defined as a string.

```
             string filename = "Colormap.dds";
```

Using right and left angle brackets and a semicolon around a string makes it an annotation.

```
             <string filename = "Colormap.dds";>
```

Annotations serve to attach a note to a variable.

```
texture Colormap <string filename = "Colormap.dds";>;
```

You might store even more data like this.

```
texture EnvironmentMap
<
    string type = "CUBE";
    string name = "lobbycube.dds";
>;
```

The most important annotations are:

```
// the object the paramter is bound to
String Object;
// the frustum the view dependent parameter is bound to
String Frustum;
// define the space which the data should be represented
String Space;
// define operating logic scoped by annotation placement
String Script;
```

Although annotations cannot be used by the effect API, they can be accessed by the application through the `ID3DXEffect::GetAnnotationByName()` function.

This way, references to data files, such as texture filenames and *.x files, can be encapsulated in the effect file. For example, texture names can be provided in the effect file to load them by the application. This is done for example by EffectEdit, delivered by the DirectX SDK and NVIDIA's FX Composer.

Scripts

The new scripting interface in the Direct3DX Effect framework brings effects a new level of self-described operation and versatility. They are capable of exposing standard materials, but can also expose magnificent post-processing effects such as a high-dynamic range, per-light shadow-buffers, and other complex connected shader networks without being tied directly to one application. The annotation script strings break down into a stream of statements in which each statement is a command-value pair.

```
String Script="command=value;";
```

Values are either strings or parameter names that provide the necessary data for that command. Commands exposed by DXSAS are loops assigning render targets, changing frustum, setting techniques and passes, drawing, and deferring operations to other effects in a shader network. As an example, the following script fragment is applied to a technique in an .fx file to implement a bloom effect in which a scene is down-sampled into a render target, and an alpha channel is used to apply a brightness bloom to the whole scene. The complete .fx file ships with FX Composer 1.5 and can be found at MEDIA\HLSL\scene_bloom.fx.

```
            //The DXSAS startup parameter
            float std : StandardsGlobal <
               //is it applied to the object or scene?
               string ScriptClass = "scene";
               //in what order?
               string ScriptOrder = "postprocess";
               //What will be in the set render targets?
               string ScriptOutput = "color";
               //This is the main script!
               string Script =
               //It sets the technique to glow and runs it's script
                          "Technique=Glow;";
            > = 0.80; //version number

            Technique Glow<
            //This is the glow technique's script!
               String Script=
                    //It is hiding the default render target
                    "RenderColorTarget0=SceneMap;"
                    //It is hiding the default depth-stencil
                    "RenderDepthStencilTarget=DepthBuffer;"
                    //Prepare the default clear color
                    "ClearSetColor=@farColor;"
                    //Prepare the default clear depth
                    "ClearSetDepth=@farDepth;"
                    //Clear the color
                    "Clear=Color0"
                    //Clear the depth
                    "Clear=Depth"
                    //What do we expect in our render targets?
                    "ScriptSignature0=color;"
                    //Allow another shader to render
                    "ScriptExternal=GlowDefaultRender;"
                    //Set pass and jump to it's script
                    "Pass=BlurGlowBuffer_Horz;"
                    //Set pass and jump to it's script
                    "Pass=BlurGlowBuffer_Vert;"
                    //Set pass and jump to it's script
                    "Pass=BlurGlow_Composite;";
               //this is a value being fetched from the script
               float3 farColor= (0,0,0);
               //this is a value being fetched from the script
               float farDepth= 1.0;>
            {
            Pass BlurGlowBuffer_Horz<
                //This is the pass's script!
                String Script=
                    //It will blur onto this target
                    "RenderColorTarget0=HBlurMap;"
                    //Use D3D Draw call with a full screen quad
                    "Draw=Buffer;";>
            {/*put device state here*/}
```

```
Pass BlurGlowBuffer_Vert<
   //This is the pass's script!
   String Script=
      //It will blur onto this target
      "RenderColorTarget0=VBlurMap;"
      //Use D3D Draw call with a full screen quad
      "Draw=Buffer;";>
{/*put device state here*/}

Pass BlurGlow_Composite<
   //This is the pass's script!
   String Script=
      //It will blur onto the default target
      "RenderColorTarget0=;"
      //It will blur onto the default depth-stencil
      "RenderDepthStencilTarget=;"
      //Use D3D Draw call with a full screen quad
      "Draw=Buffer;";>
{/*put device state here*/}
}
```

Scripts help to abstract the shader and its environment even more from the application. They are useful in making shaders more tweakable for artists and programmers, because both do not need to write C or C++ code to set up, for example, an additional render target (read more in [Maughan]).

Device States in Effect Files

An effect file can also store device states. That means you might write all the render states into the effect files, extending the capabilities of an effect file to store all data that is needed for one or more objects. For example, alpha blending might look like this.

```
technique TShader
{
   pass alphablend
   {
...
      // enable alpha blending
      AlphaBlendEnable = TRUE;
      SrcBlend        = ONE;
      DestBlend       = ONE;
...
   }
}
```

Preshaders

A preshader is code that is constant at runtime that has been extracted from a pixel or vertex shader by the HLSL compiler. This is indicated by the assembly output of the compiler like this:

```
vertexshader =
asm {
//
// Generated by Microsoft (R) D3DX9 Shader Compiler 4.09.00.0904
//
// Parameters:
//
//   float fIteration;
//   float4 pixelSize;
//
//
// Registers:
//
//   Name            Reg   Size
//   ------          ---   ---
//   fIteration      c0      1
//   pixelSize       c1      1
//

preshader
mul r2.xy, (0.5, 0.5), c1.xy
mul r1.xy, c0.x, c1.xy
add r0.xy, r2.xy, r1.xy
neg c0.x, r0.x
neg c3.x, r0.y
mov c1.x, r0.y
mov c2.x, r0.x

// approximately 7 instructions used
//
// Generated by Microsoft (R) D3DX9 Shader Compiler 4.09.00.0904
vs_1_1
def c4, 1, 0, 0.5, 0
dcl_position v0
dcl_texcoord v1
mad oPos, v0.xyxx, c4.xxyy, c4.yyzx
add r0.y, v1.x, c0.x
add r0.z, v1.y, c1.x
mov oT0.xy, r0.yzzw
add r0.x, v1.x, c2.x
mov oT1.xy, r0.xzzw
add r0.w, v1.y, c3.x
mov oT2.xy, r0.xwzw
mov oT3.xy, r0.ywzw

// approximately 9 instruction slots used
};
```

By using the preshader code in a constant table similar to constants, the preshader functionality is an optimization technique of the compiler. Nevertheless, it might be interesting to think about code that was identified by the compiler as preshader code when approaching other optimization strategies.

The Effect File API

Effects can be stored in ASCII files usually with the postfix *.fx or *.fxl (you might choose any other postfix). They are opened, read-in, and compiled by the function D3DXCreateEffectFromFile(). Assuming this function call succeeds, we can use the effect API to set the appropriate variables needed by our effect.

For example, setting the matrices in the application source with the SetMatrix() function is done like this:

```
D3DXMATRIX mWorldViewProj = m_matWorld * m_matView * m_matProj;
m_pEffect->SetMatrix( "matWorldViewProj", &mWorldViewProj );
m_pEffect->SetMatrix( "matWorld", &m_matWorld);
```

A vector can be set with the SetVector() function:

```
m_pEffect->SetVector("vecEye",
&D3DXVECTOR4(vEyePt.x,vEyePt.y,vEyePt.z,0));
```

A specific technique can be set with SetTechnique(), a pass can be specified with BeginPass()/EndPass(), and a texture can be set with the SetTexture() function.

The following steps summarize what needs to be done in the application to use an effect:

- Set the constants with SetFloat(),SetVector(), SetMatrix(),SetString(),SetTexture()
- Obtain a handle to the technique in the effect with GetTechniqueByName()
- Activate the technique with SetTechnique()
- Get the number of passes that the technique uses with BeginPass()
- Call CommitChanges() to update device states
- Render the number of passes
- End the pass with EndPass()
- End the technique with End()

The following source code snippet shows all these steps with the exception of step 1.

```
if( m_pEffect != NULL )
{
    D3DXHANDLE hTechnique = m_pEffect->GetTechniqueByName(
                          "ASM3OShader" );
    m_pEffect->SetTechnique( hTechnique );

    m_pEffect->SetTexture("ColorMap", m_pColorMap);
    m_pEffect->SetTexture("BumpMap", m_pBumpMap);

    m_pEffect->Begin( &nPasses, 0 );

    for(iPass = 0; iPass < nPasses; iPass++)
    {
     m_pEffect->BeginPass(iPass);
```

```
                    // set the instance data for the current draw call
                    m_pEffect->CommitChanges()

                    // Render Geometry

                    m_pEffect->EndPass();
                    }
                    m_pEffect->End();
        }
```

The function `Begin()` saves all the states the user selected for saving. If no state is stored, very little work is done. The function `BeginPass()` is a heavyweight function. It applies all states explicitly listed in a pass in an effect file. Additionally, it uses the constant tables of vertex and pixel shaders to determine what constant registers are updated. Then, it updates all samplers referenced by pixel shaders and applies the states specified by these samplers.

All `Set*` calls are cached if the `Set*` call is called between the `BeginPass()` and `EndPass()` functions. These calls are put on a list to be updated at the next call to `CommitChanges()`. Only when `CommitChanges()` is called will the device state get updated. This is the only method other than `BeginPass()` that applies device states. It only updates the device state that has been affected by `Set*` calls since the last `CommitChanges()/BeginPass()`.

`EndPass()` is a lightweight function. It just indicates that the current pass is done, whereas `End()` indicates the end of the effect and is used as such as the last effect file API function.

Having seen the whole effect file API, we see that using effect files is a straightforward process that hides several unnecessary burdens from the application. For example, the application never needs to know into what hardware constant register to load data or to which sampler a texture is bound. These details are all managed by the D3DX Effects framework.

Summary

This chapter helped you set up your working environment and provided a fundamental understanding of the overall capabilities of the vertex and pixel shader units. HLSL programming allows you to program longer shaders on an algorithmic level without the intricacies of thinking about register usage rules and all other hardware restrictions. HLSL optimization is something that is definitely worth investing time into.

Another level of abstraction from the underlying shader source code can be added to an application by using the effect file framework. It assures that shaders, render states, textures, and texture states are handled in a simplified way and optimizes for performance by offering meaningful caching capabilities for all of these.

With the necessary knowledge on how to program shaders, we can start now to practice this in the rest of the book.

Lighting Algorithms

This second part of the book covers the implementation of some common reflection algorithms. A reflection model is the model that describes how the incoming light reacts when it hits a certain type of surface (material).

We examine two global reflection models (simple ambient and hemispheric lighting), a diffuse reflection model that follows Lambert's law, and two specular reflection models (Phong and Blinn-Phong) together with point light and spot light sources. These are the most common lighting algorithms used today in games with dynamic lighting.

When we combine specular and diffuse reflections with their contributions to intensity with an ambient component, we get the standard lighting equations used by the Direct3D and OpenGL fixed-function pipelines.

$$I = I_{amb} + I_{diff} + I_{spec}$$

This equation demonstrates how intensities (I stands for light intensity) from different kinds of reflections can be calculated separately. It can be implemented in the vertex shader (per-vertex lighting) or in the pixel shader (per-pixel lighting). Because there are more pixels than vertices, calculating lighting per-pixel has a certain impact on the performance of the application, but leads also to much better visual quality, as shown in Figure 1.

The first row in this figure shows the geometry involved, the second row shows how per-vertex lighting looks on this geometry, and the third row shows how per-pixel lighting looks on the same geometry. Using per-pixel lighting makes the visual appearance of the lighting effect nearly independent from the underlying geometry. This must be weighed against the higher demands of per-pixel calculations.

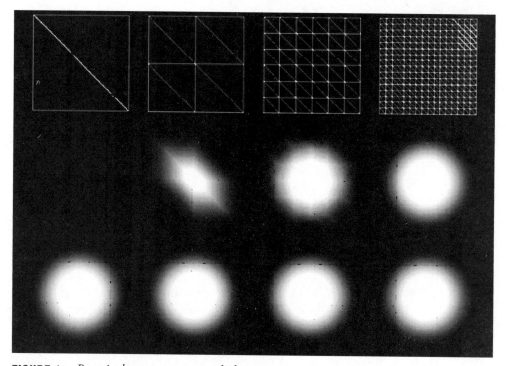

FIGURE 1   *Per-pixel versus per-vertex lighting.*

Graphics engines use and will use a combination of lighting models calculated per-vertex or per-pixel. Balancing this combination is a way to scale the graphics engine on different hardware platforms.

4   Ambient Lighting

There is light in the real world that just "exists" in the environment; it has no direction but it has intensity and color. This light has been scattered and reflected in the world for so long it has lost these properties. In computer graphics, we call this kind of lighting ambient.

The following chapter will cover how the simplest form of ambient lighting can be implemented.

Background

In an ambient lighting model, all light beams fall uniformly from all directions onto an object. This is an example of a "global lighting model," although its visual quality is poor. No real calculation is made for this light; it is used to set the "miminum" amount of light that falls onto all surfaces.

The ambient lighting component is usually described with the formula

$$I = A_{\text{intensity}} \times A_{\text{color}}$$

The intensity value describes the lighting intensity, and the color value describes the color of the light.

Implementation

Implementing a simple ambient lighting model as shown here is quite straightforward. The following source code snippet shows the implementation of the ambient lighting formula in HLSL.

```
// ———————————————————————————-
// variables that are provided by the application
// ———————————————————————————-
float4x4 matWorldViewProj;
// ———————————————————————————-
// vertex shader output channels
// ———————————————————————————-
struct VS_OUTPUT
{
   float4 Pos: POSITION;
};
// ———————————————————————————-
// vertex shader function (input channels)
// ———————————————————————————-
VS_OUTPUT VS( float4 Pos: POSITION )
{
   VS_OUTPUT Out = (VS_OUTPUT) 0;
   Out.Pos = mul(Pos, matWorldViewProj); // transform Position
   return Out;
}
// ———————————————————————————-
// Pixel Shader (input channels):output channel
// ———————————————————————————-
float4 PS() : COLOR
{
  float Aintensity = 0.8f;
  float4 Acolor =  float4(1.0,  0.075,  0.075, 1.0);

  return Aintensity * Acolor;
}
// ———————————————————————————-
// Name technique | pass | how to compile
// ———————————————————————————-
technique HLSLShader
{
   pass P0
   {
      // compiler directives
      VertexShader = compile vs_1_1 VS();
      PixelShader  = compile ps_1_1 PS();
   }
}
```

The structure VS_OUTPUT at the beginning of the source describes the output values of
the vertex shader. The vertex shader looks like a C function with the return value
VS_OUTPUT and the input value in the variable Pos in brackets after its name VS.

The input and output values for the vertex shader use the semantic POSITION,
which is identified by a colon (:) that precedes it. Semantics help the HLSL compiler
to bind the right shader registers for the data. The semantic in the vertex shader input

structure identifies the input data to the function as position data. The semantic in the vertex shader output structure identifies the vertex shader return value as position data that will be an input value to the pixel shader (this is the only obligatory output value of the vertex shader). Inside the brackets, the vertex shader transforms the vertex position with the matWorldViewProj matrix provided by the application as a uniform variable and outputs the position values.

The pixel shader follows the same C-function–like approach as the vertex shader. Its return value is float4, which is treated as a color value by the compiler because it is marked with the semantic COLOR. Unlike the vertex shader, the pixel shader takes no explicit input value (except the not visible position value of the pixel). This is documented by the empty bracket after its name PS.

Please remember that the names of the vertex and pixel shaders are also the entry point for the high-level language compiler and must be provided in its command line.

This example uses an effect file, therefore a technique must be named together with the name of the pass and the compiler directives.

```
technique HLSLShader
{
    pass
    {
        // compiler directives
        VertexShader = compile vs_1_1 VS();
        PixelShader  = compile ps_1_1 PS();
    }
}
```

The name of the technique is HLSLShader, and the pass does not use an id. The two lines in the pass statement are telling the compiler that the name of the vertex shader is VS() and the name of the pixel shader is PS(). They use the keywords VertexShader and PixelShader to differentiate between vertex and pixel shaders.

Results

Figure 4.1 shows a screenshot from the ambient lighting example program, which can be found in the directory Chapter 4 - Ambient.

Notice the knob of the top of the teapot is not visible when it is turned toward the viewer. This is because all light beams are coming from all directions uniformly onto the object. Therefore, the whole teapot is painted with exactly the same color.

FIGURE 4.1   *Ambient lighting.*

Conclusion

If a scene needs a simple global lighting model, which is very efficient and quite handy in situations where a remaining light only needs to show a color but does not need to show contour information, ambient lighting does the job.

Beyond this, a visually more pleasant global lighting model is shown with the hemispheric lighting model in Chapter 11.

5 Diffuse Lighting

Whereas the ambient lighting model shown in the previous chapter just exists in the environment without source or direction, in real-world situations, the lighting has some direction to it. The simplest lighting model that supports this is the diffuse lighting model. This chapter covers a diffuse lighting model that follows a law developed by Lambert [Lambert] in 1760.

Background

In a diffuse lighting model, reflections are independent of the observer's position. Therefore, the surface of an object in a diffuse lighting model reflects equally well in all directions (meaning it does not change as the observer moves). This is why diffuse lighting is commonly used to simulate matte surfaces.

The Lambertian diffuse lighting model utilizes two vectors. The light vector L describes the direction of the light, and the normal vector N describes the surface orientation, as illustrated in Figure 5.1.

The diffuse reflection has its peak $\cos(\alpha) = 1$ when L and N are aligned; in other words, when the surface is perpendicular to the light beam. The diffuse reflection diminishes for smaller angles. Therefore, the light intensity is proportional to $\cos(\alpha)$ (read more in [RTR] and [Savchenko]).

To implement the diffuse reflection in an efficient way, the following property of the dot product is used

$$N \cdot L = \|N\| \times \|L\| \times \cos(\alpha)$$

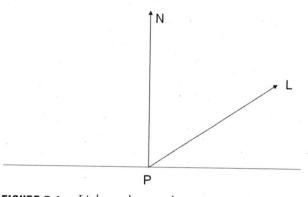

FIGURE 5.1   *Light and normal vectors.*

If the light and normal vectors are of unit length (normalized), this leads to the following simplification

$$\mathbf{N} \cdot \mathbf{L} = \cos(\alpha)$$

The dot product equals $\cos(\alpha)$, if $\mathbf{N}$ and $\mathbf{L}$ are unit vectors. Together with the ambient component, the example of this chapter uses the equation

$$I = A_{intensity} \times A_{color} + D_{intensity} \times D_{color} \times \mathbf{N} \cdot \mathbf{L}$$

Implementation

Implementing a Lambertian diffuse lighting model is shown in the following HLSL vertex and pixel shaders.

```
// ————————————————————————-
// variables that are provided by the application
// ————————————————————————-
float4x4 matWorldViewProj;
float4x4 matInvTransposeWorld;
float4 vecLightDir;
float4 vDic;
// ————————————————————————-
// vertex shader output channels
// ————————————————————————-
struct VS_OUTPUT
{
    float4 Pos   : POSITION;
    float3 Light : TEXCOORD0;
    float3 Norm  : TEXCOORD1;
};
```

```
// ——————————————————————-
// vertex shader function (input channels)
// ——————————————————————-
VS_OUTPUT VS(float4 Pos : POSITION, float3 Normal : NORMAL)
{
    VS_OUTPUT Out = (VS_OUTPUT)0;

    // transform Position
    Out.Pos = mul(Pos, matWorldViewProj);

    // output light vector
    Out.Light = normalize(vecLightDir);

    // transform Normal and normalize it
    Out.Norm = normalize(mul(matInvTransposeWorld, Normal));
    return Out;
}
// ——————————————————————-
// Pixel Shader (input channels):output channel
// ——————————————————————-
float4 PS(float3 Light: TEXCOORD0, float3 Norm : TEXCOORD1) : COLOR
{
    // ambient albedo * ambient intensity
    float4 A = {0.5, 0.0,  0.0, 1.0};

    // vDic = Dintensity * Dcolor
    return A + vDic * saturate(dot(Light, Norm));
}
```

Compared to the ambient lighting example of the previous chapter, this vertex shader has an additional parameter for the vertex normal. The semantic NORMAL shows the HLSL compiler how to bind the data to the vertex shader registers. The world-view-projection matrix, the inverse and transposed world matrix, and the light vector are provided to the vertex shader via the constants matWorldViewProj, matInvTranspose-World, and vecLightDir. All these uniform input variables are provided by the application to the vertex shader.

The normal vector is transformed by being multiplied with the inverse and transposed world matrix. You can think of a normal transform in the following way: normal vectors (unlike position vectors) are simply directions in space, and as such they should not get squished in magnitude, and translation doesn't change their direction. They should simply be rotated in some fashion to reflect the change in orientation of the surface. This change in orientation is a result of rotating and squishing the object but not moving it. The information for rotating a normal can be extracted from the 4x4 transformation matrix by performing transpose and inversion. A more math-related explanation is given in [RTR2][Turkowski].

So the bullet-proof way to transform normals is to use the transpose of the inverse of the matrix that is used to transform the object. If the matrix used to transform the object is called M, then we must use the matrix N to transform the normals of this object.

$$N = \text{transpose}\left(\text{inverse}\left(M\right)\right)$$

Nevertheless, the normal can be transformed with the transformation matrix (usually the world matrix) that is used to transform the object in the following cases:

- *Matrix formed from rotations (orthogonal matrix), because the inverse of an orthogonal matrix is its transpose.*
- *Matrix formed from rotations and translation (rigid-body transforms), because translations do not affect vector direction.*
- *Matrix formed from rotations and translation and uniform scalings, because such scalings affect only the length of the transformed normal, not its direction. A uniform scaling is simply a matrix that uniformly increases or decreases the object's size, as opposed to a non-uniform scaling, which can stretch or squeeze an object. If uniform scalings are used, the normals do have to be renormalized.*

Using the transformation matrix to transform the normal instead of the inverse and transposed transformation matrix is useful in reducing the number of matrices send to the vertex shader. For example, if the world space position value is needed to subtract it from the light vector, it is more efficient to use the world matrix to transform the normal and the position value rather than using a separate matrix to transform the normal. This is shown in Chapter 7.

The transformation of the normal is done with the function `mul(a, b)`, which performs a matrix multiplication between a and b. If a is a vector, it is treated as a row vector. If b is a vector, it is treated as a column vector. In this example, `mul()` gets the position vector as the second parameter—therefore, it is treated as a column vector—and the transformation matrix, consisting of 16 floating-point values (float4×4), as the first parameter. Using the column vector with the inverse matrix is equivalent to using a row vector with a transposed inverse matrix.

The dot product of the light and normal vector is than clamped to 0 with the `saturate()` intrinsic, since lights that are backfacing to the surface should have no effect. The diffuse color and the diffuse intensity constants are multiplied in the application, because they do not change on a per-vertex or per-pixel basis and their result is sent via the constant vDic to the pixel shader.

Results

Figure 5.2 shows a screenshot from the diffuse lighting example program, which can be found in the directory Chapter 5 - Diffuse. Use the E and D keys to change the intensity of the diffuse lighting contribution and the R and F keys to change the green component of the diffuse color.

FIGURE 5.2 *Diffuse lighting.*

By looking at this screenshot, the viewer can tell where the light is coming from, and compared to the ambient lighting model shown in the previous chapter, it is also possible to see the contour of the knob.

Conclusion

Diffuse reflection gives contour to objects. Despite the fact that the Lambertian diffuse reflection model is quite capable of handling a lot of lighting necessities in modern games, it can only cover matte surfaces with one level of surface roughness.

This motivates researchers to develop new diffuse reflection models that can account for differing roughness of the surface, such as the one developed by Oren-Nayar [Oren][Fosner][Valient]. (Read more in Chapter 13.)

Although most reflections are diffuse, most research efforts have focused on surfaces that are smooth enough to create a view-dependent highlight, as shown in the next chapter.

6 | Specular Lighting

Specular reflectance takes into account the location of the viewer, in contrast to both ambient and diffuse reflectance. It is used to simulate smooth, shiny, and/or polished surfaces. The location of the viewer is accounted for by adding an additional input vector. This is done differently for the two common specular reflectance models used in most current and upcoming games and featured in this chapter.

These are the original Phong specular reflectance models developed by Bui Tong Phong [Phong][Foley] in 1975 and Jim Blinn's modification of this reflectance model in 1977, which is now called Blinn-Phong specular reflectance model [Blinn].

Background of Phong Reflectance

To account for the position of the viewer for the specular highlight, Bui Tong Phong uses two vectors to calculate the specular component: the viewer vector **V** that describes the direction of the viewer (in other words the camera), and the reflection vector **R** that describes the direction of the reflection from the light vector. This is shown in Figure 6.1.

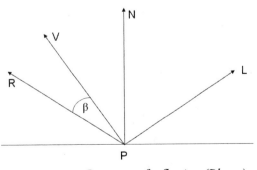

FIGURE 6.1 *Geometry of reflection (Phong).*

The angle between **V** and **R** is β. The more **V** is aligned with **R**, the brighter the specular light should be. Therefore $\cos \beta$ can be used to describe the specular reflection. To simulate surface roughness, an exponent n is applied to the cosine function. It simulates the "sharpness" or "glossiness" of the reflection.

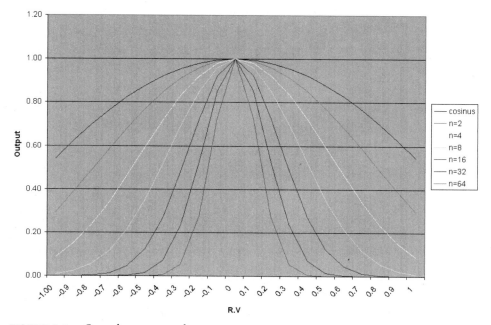

FIGURE 6.2 *Specular power value.*

Therefore, the specular reflection can be described with the following equation:

$$\cos(\beta)^n$$

To compute specular reflectance, the following property of the dot product can be used:

$$\mathbf{R} \cdot \mathbf{V} = \|\mathbf{R}\| \cdot \|\mathbf{V}\| \cdot \cos \beta$$

If both vectors are of unit length, $\mathbf{R} \cdot \mathbf{V}$ is equal to $\cos \beta$. Therefore, the specular reflection can be written as follows:

$$(\mathbf{R} \cdot \mathbf{V})^n$$

The reflection vector is calculated with the following formula (read more in [Foley2]):

$$\mathbf{R} = 2 \times (\mathbf{N} \cdot \mathbf{L}) \times \mathbf{N} - \mathbf{L}$$

The entire reflectance formula, with ambient, diffuse, and specular reflectance, is therefore as follows:

$$I = A_{\text{intensity}} \times A_{\text{color}} + D_{\text{intensity}} \times D_{\text{color}} \times \mathbf{N} \cdot \mathbf{L} + S_{\text{intensity}} \times S_{\text{color}} \times (\mathbf{R} \cdot \mathbf{V})^n$$

Implementation Phong

To evaluate the Phong reflectance per-pixel, the whole formula needs to be implemented in the pixel shader. The following HLSL shader shows how the reflection vector is calculated in the pixel shader and how it is used to achieve the reflection.

```
// ─────────────────────────────-
// variables that are provided by the application
// ─────────────────────────────-
float4x4 matWorldViewProj;
float4x4 matWorld;
float4 vecLightDir;
float4 vecEye;
float4 vDIC;
float4 vSpecIC;
// ─────────────────────────────-
// vertex shader output channels
// ─────────────────────────────-
struct VS_OUTPUT
{
    float4 Pos   : POSITION;
    float3 Light : TEXCOORD0;
    float3 Norm  : TEXCOORD1;
    float3 View  : TEXCOORD2;
};
// ─────────────────────────────-
// vertex shader function (input channels)
// ─────────────────────────────-
VS_OUTPUT VS(float4 Pos : POSITION, float3 Normal : NORMAL)
{
    VS_OUTPUT Out = (VS_OUTPUT)0;

    // transform Position
    Out.Pos = mul(Pos, matWorldViewProj);

    // transform Normal
    Out.Norm = mul(Normal, matWorld);

    float4 PosWorld = mul(Pos, matWorld);
```

```
        Out.Light = vecLightDir;      // L
        Out.View = vecEye - PosWorld; // V
        return Out;
    }
    // ——————————————————————————-
    // Pixel Shader (input channels):output channel
    // ——————————————————————————-
    float4 PS(float3 Light: TEXCOORD0, float3 Norm : TEXCOORD1,
              float3 View : TEXCOORD2) : COLOR
    {
        float4 A = { 0.1f, 0.0f, 0.0f, 1.0f};

        float3 Normal = normalize(Norm);
        float3 LightDir = normalize(Light);
        float3 ViewDir = normalize(View);

        // diffuse component
        float Diff = saturate(dot(Normal, LightDir));

        // R = 2 * (N.L) * N - L
        float3 Reflect = normalize(2 * Diff * Normal - LightDir);

        // R.V^n
        float Specular = pow(saturate(dot(Reflect, ViewDir)), 8);

        // I = A + Dcolor * Dintensity * N.L + Scolor * Sintensity *
    (R.V)^n
        return A + vDIC * Diff + vSpecIC * Specular;
    }
```

Like the previous example, the vertex shader input values are the position values and a normal vector. Additionally, the vertex shader gets as a global variable the matWorld-ViewProj matrix, the matWorld matrix, the eye position in vecEye, and the light vector in vecLightDir as global variables, which are set from the application. Please note that we transform the normal here with the world matrix, because we can reuse this matrix then to calculate the viewer vector. This is more efficient than sending down a separate inverse and transposed world matrix to transform the normal.

You might also provide vecLightDir directly to the pixel shader, because we treat the light vector as a light source with parallel light beams, and therefore the direction of L is always the same for all vertices. This is shown in the Blinn-Phong example in the next section.

The vertex shader outputs the position, the light, and the normal and viewer vector. These vectors are also the input values of the pixel shader.

All three vectors are normalized with normalize() in the pixel shader, which returns:

$$vector\ v = v\ /\ length(v)$$

If the length of v is 0, the result is undefined.

Normalization of vectors is necessary, because the interpolators between the vertex and the pixel shader do not necessarily output vectors that are of unit length. Figure 6.3 shows how an interpolated vector might look.

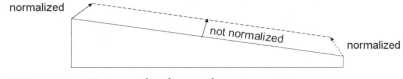

FIGURE 6.3   *Un-normalized normal.*

The two vectors at the left and right are the vertex normals. The vector in the middle represents a vector of non-unit length. The line that connects the vertex normals represents the length of the vectors that are lying between the vertex normals.

Normalizing vectors in the pixel shader is quite expensive on most recent hardware (exception: a half-precision `normalize()` is free on a GeForce 6800). On the other hand, using vectors with a slightly reduced magnitude can cause the interiors of triangles to appear darker than they should. This performance/quality trade-off led to the decision to skip the normalization in the pixel shader in the previous example (diffuse lighting example).

An alternative approach to normalize vectors is using a cube normalization map as covered in Chapter 16. This approach trades the cost of the `normalize()` *intrinsic against the latency of a cubemap fetch.*

In the pixel shader, the function `saturate()` is used to clamp all values to the range [0..1]. The reflection vector is retrieved by re-using the result from the diffuse reflection calculation. To get the specular power value, the function `pow()` is used. It is declared as `pow(x, y)` and returns x^y. This function is only available in pixel shaders above and including ps_2_0. Getting a smooth specular power value in pixel shader versions lower than ps_2_0 is quite a challenge (read more in [Beaudoin/Guardado], [Halpin]).

In the last line of the pixel shader, the return statement corresponds to the implementation of the reflectance formula shown previously, whereas the diffuse intensity, diffuse color, specular intensity, and specular color are prepared in the application and provided to the pixel shader via the `vDIC` and `vSpecIC` uniform variables.

Results Phong

The following figure shows a screenshot from the Phong specular reflectance example program, that can be found in the directory CD-ROM\Chapter 6 - Specular\Phong Specular. You might zoom in and out with the W and S keys and move the light with the arrow keys. To move the light on the *z*-axis, use Home and End. Use the E and D keys to change the intensity of the diffuse lighting contribution, the R and F keys to change the green component of the diffuse color and the T and G and Q and A keys to change the intensity and color of the specular light component.

FIGURE 6.4   *Phong reflectance.*

Running a Phong reflection model in the pixel shader results in an evenly distributed reflection as can be seen in Figure 6.4. Changing the specular power value alters the size of the highlight and its intensity.

The major drawback of this reflectance model is the high cost of calculating the reflection vector in the pixel shader. Getting rid of this calculation was the target of Jim Blinn's modification of the Phong specular reflectance model.

Background Blinn-Phong Specular Reflectance

At the time of the invention of the Blinn-Phong reflectance model in 1977, people did not have the luxury of running lighting models in real-time on the hardware available at that time. Therefore, it was a huge step forward when Jim Blinn [Blinn] replaced the dot product between **R** and **V** with the dot product of a new vector and **N** and established the most popular specular reflection model until today. He used an (until then) new vector that lies in the middle between **V** and **L**, as shown in Figure 6.5, and named it halfway vector, or **H**. You might think of **H** as the "surface normal" that leads to the maximum highlight in the direction of **V**. Because **H** depends on **V** it is still view-dependent, whereas the position of the surface is represented by the normal vector **N**.

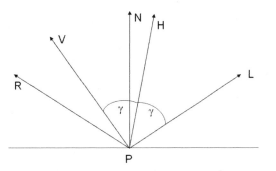

FIGURE 6.5   *Geometry of reflection (Blinn-Phong).*

H is defined as:

$$H = \frac{L+V}{len(L+V)}$$

Because only the direction is important, we can skip the division and write:

$$H = L + V$$

 Using $(L+V)/2$ is not correct, because in case of a view vector nearly parallel to the surface and a light vector perpendicular, the sum of L and V will be ~1.414, not 2.

The cosine of the angle between **H** and **N** is used as a measure of the distance a particular surface is away from the maximum specular direction. The degree of sharpness of the highlights is adjusted by taking the cosine to some power. Blinn uses here

50 to 60. The example program can be found in Chapter 25. The resulting Blinn-Phong formula looks like this

$$I = A_{\text{intensity}} \times A_{\text{color}} + D_{\text{intensity}} \times D_{\text{color}} \times \mathbf{N} \cdot \mathbf{L} + S_{\text{intensity}} \times S_{\text{color}} \times \left(\mathbf{N} \cdot \mathbf{H} \right)^{n}$$

Implementation Blinn-Phong

The Blinn-Phong model uses the dot product of **N** and **H** to calculate the specular reflection. **N** is transformed in the vertex shader and sent through the interpolators to the pixel shader. To calculate **H**, **V** is retrieved in the vertex shader and sent to the pixel shaders.

```
// ─────────────────────────────-
// variables that are provided by the application
// ─────────────────────────-
float4x4 matWorldViewProj;
float4x4 matWorld;
float4 vecLightDir;
float4 vecEye;
float4 vDIC;
float4 vSpecIC;
// ──────────────────────────────-
// vertex shader output channels
// ──────────────────────────────-
struct VS_OUTPUT
{
    float4 Pos  : POSITION;
    float3 Light : TEXCOORD0;
    float3 Norm : TEXCOORD1;
    float3 View : TEXCOORD2;
};
// ────────────────────────────────-
// vertex shader function (input channels)
// ──────────────────────────────-
VS_OUTPUT VS(float4 Pos : POSITION, float3 Normal : NORMAL)
{
    VS_OUTPUT Out = (VS_OUTPUT)0;

    // transform Position
    Out.Pos = mul(Pos, matWorldViewProj);

    // transform Normal
    Out.Norm = mul(Normal, matWorld);

    float4 PosWorld = mul(Pos, matWorld);
```

```
        Out.Light = vecLightDir;      // L
        Out.View = vecEye - PosWorld; // V

    return Out;
}
// ————————————————————————————-
// Pixel Shader (input channels):output channel
// ————————————————————————————-
float4 PS(float3 Light: TEXCOORD0, float3 Norm : TEXCOORD1,
          float3 View : TEXCOORD2) : COLOR
{
    float4 Acolor = { 0.1f, 0.0f, 0.0f, 1.0f};

    float3 Normal = normalize(Norm);
    float3 LightDir = normalize(Light);
    float3 Half = normalize(LightDir + normalize(View));

    // diffuse component
    float Diff = saturate(dot(Normal, LightDir));

    // N.H^n
    float Specular = pow(saturate(dot(Normal, Half)), 25);

    // I = Acolor + Dintensity * Dcolor * N.L + Sintensity *
Scolor(N.H)n
    return Acolor + vDIC * Diff + vSpecIC * Specular;
}
```

Compared to the Phong model shown in the previous example, the light vector is used directly in the pixel shader here. Because we treat the light vector as a light source with parallel light beams, the direction of **L** is always the same for all vertices.

The most important line is that in which the half vector is calculated. Please note that **H** is calculated in the pixel shader because it varies nonlinearly across the surface. Alternatively, on less capable hardware it is sufficient to do this in the vertex shader and send **H** through the interpolators to the pixel shader.

To achieve a similar specular highlight as seen in the Phong implementation, we chose a higher power value.

Results Blinn-Phong

Looking at the screenshot in Figure 6.6 shows that the Blinn-Phong model creates an evenly distributed highlight, which looks comparable to the Phong model. The Blinn-Phong example program offers the same amount of functionality as the Phong example program.

ON THE CD The source code of this example program can be found in Chapter 6 - Specular\ Blinn-Phong Specular.

FIGURE 6.6   *Blinn-Phong example program.*

Comparison

Figure 6.7 shows a visual comparison of the two models. The Phong model is shown on the left and the Blinn-Phong model is shown on the right. At first glance, there does not appear to be much difference between the Phong and the Blinn-Phong models.

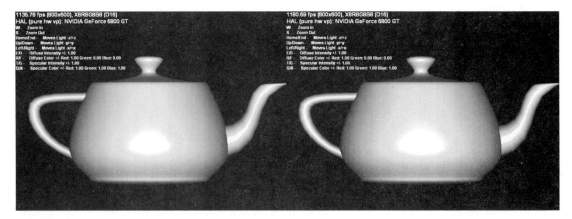

FIGURE 6.7   *The Blinn-Phong lighting model (left) and the Phong lighting model (right).*

A closer look reveals a different shape of the highlight. The Blinn-Phong model spreads a little bit more and therefore leads to different reflections, especially with models that consist of thin parts. Nevertheless, this is not a disadvantage, because you can adjust this by choosing another specular power value.

The Phong model looks better but eats up more instruction slots, whereas the Blinn-Phong model looks good enough and is faster. This is a classic performance/quality trade-off, in which most developers nowadays opt for the Blinn-Phong model.

Both specular reflectance models can be optimized by moving some vector normalizations into the vertex shader and using a lookup table to calculate or approximate the power value (see [Beaudoin/Guardado], [Halpin]).

Conclusion

The Phong and Blinn-Phong models each provide a very efficient way to simulate shiny, smooth surfaces. As long as these surface properties are suitable for a specific type of game, these reflectance models are quite useful. If there is a need to differentiate more between different kind of reflectance properties, more complex reflectance models need to be involved. This is shown in Part III, "Advanced Lighting."

A handy property of per-pixel lighting models is the capability to mimic surface roughness by using a texture map consisting of perturbed normals. This technique is called bump mapping and will be discussed in the next chapter.

7 Bump Mapping

Bump mapping, a technique developed by Jim Blinn [Blinn2], is an elegant device that enables a surface to appear as if were wrinkled or dimpled without the need to model these depressions geometrically. Instead, the surface normal is angularly perturbed according to information given in a two-dimensional normal map and this "tricks" a local reflection model. One problem with bump mapping is that because the pits or depressions do not exist in the model, a silhouette edge will not follow the line of the model, because it is faked.

There are two common frames of references used to store normals in normal maps. For object bump mapping, the normals are stored in object or world space and are tied this way very closely to the geometry. For the most commonly used tangent space bump mapping, the normals are stored in tangent or texture space, which requires all vectors that should be compared to the normal to be in tangent or texture space as well. The following text will focus on tangent space bump mapping.

Background

Bump mapping simply uses perturbed angles to fake the existence of geometry (for example, in creating grooves and bulges). Whereas a color map stores color values, a normal map is a graphics file (e.g., *.dds, *.tga, etc.) that stores normals, which are used instead of the vertex normals to calculate the lighting. Bump maps can be created with a Photoshop plug-in available from the developer Web site of NVIDIA (*http://developer.nvidia.com*).

In the most common bump mapping method, these normals are stored in what is called *texture space* or *tangent space*. The light vector is usually handled in object or world space, so to obtain proper lighting results the light vector has to be transformed into the same space as the normals in the normal map. This is done with the help of a *texture* or *tangent space coordinate system*.

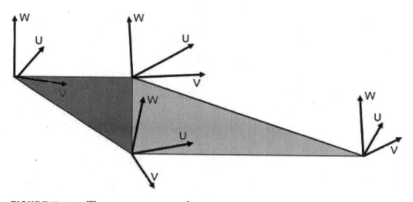

FIGURE 7.1   *Texture space coordinate system.*

The easiest way to obtain such a texture space coordinate system is to use the D3DXComputeNormal() and D3DXComputeTangent() functions provided with the Direct3D utility library Direct3DX. Source code implementations of the functionality covered by these functions can be found in the NVMeshMender library, which can be downloaded from the NVIDIA Web site (*http://developer.nvidia.com*). Calculating the tangent vectors for a texture space coordinate system is shown in [Lengyel2].

The bump mapping example creates a **W** vector for the texture space coordinate system by using the normal and calculates the **U** vector with the help of the D3DXComputeTangent() function. The **V** vector is retrieved by calculating the cross product of the **W** and the **U** vector.

AN ASIDE ON OBJECT SPACE BUMP MAPPING

In contrast to tangent space bump mapping discussed previously, object space bump mapping works in the following way. A normal map holds the normals in object space (e.g., very colorful). The light vector is provided in object space as a pixel shader constant. There is no need to build up a texture space coordinate system the traditional way and therefore no need for a transform of the light vector in the vertex shader. In the pixel shader, a simple dot product operation can be done between the normal from the normal map and the light vector to get a diffuse reflection (both in object space).

You can even perform object space bump mapping with the fixed-function pipeline by providing the light color in tfactor. This way, only a single dp3 operation has to be done.

Some advantages and disadvantages of object space bump mapping include:

Cons:

- Cannot tile or reuse the normal map. Geometry and normal map are tied explicitly.
- Normal maps with normals in object space:
  - Do not palettize.
  - Behave badly with mip-mapping.
  - Change overall brightness as the object moves into the distance.
  - Cannot be compressed with DXT or the 3Dc compression format.
  - Sharp edges cannot share normal map edges. (One texel will map on both sides of a sharp edge.)

Pros:

- Faster.
- No need to store per-vertex frame, a.k.a. the texture space coordinate system, so less memory is used.
- You can use more per-pixel calculated lights with ps.1.1.
- Such a unique normal map can be used to store bullet holes or to update clothing, etc.

Implementation

Tangent space bump mapping is implemented by creating a 3×3 transformation matrix in the vertex shader, which transforms all vectors from object or world space to tangent space. All transformed vectors are then sent to the pixel shader and treated there in the same way as if they were in their original frame of reference.

The following example source shows the creation of the tangent space system and the transformation of the light and view vector to tangent space in an HLSL vertex shader.

```
float4x4 matWorldViewProj;
float4x4 matWorld;
float4 vecLightDir;
float4 vecEye;

struct VS_OUTPUT
{
    float4 Pos  : POSITION;
    float2 Tex : TEXCOORD0;
    float3 Light : TEXCOORD1;
    float3 View : TEXCOORD2;
};
```

```
VS_OUTPUT VS(float4 Pos : POSITION,
  float2 Tex : TEXCOORD,
  float3 Normal : NORMAL,
  float3 Tangent : TANGENT  )
{
    VS_OUTPUT Out = (VS_OUTPUT)0;
    Out.Pos = mul(Pos, matWorldViewProj); // transform Position

    // compute the 3x3 tranform matrix
    // to transform from world space to tangent space
    float3x3 worldToTangentSpace;
    worldToTangentSpace[0] = mul(Tangent, matWorld);
    worldToTangentSpace[1] = mul(cross(Tangent, Normal), mat-
World);
    worldToTangentSpace[2] = mul(Normal, matWorld);

    Out.Tex = Tex;

    float4 PosWorld = mul(Pos, matWorld);

    // L
    Out.Light = mul(worldToTangentSpace, vecLightDir);

    // V
    Out.View = mul(worldToTangentSpace, vecEye - PosWorld);

    return Out;
}
```

The 3×3 matrix is created with the tangent and the normal provided by the application via the vertex buffer to the vertex shader. The binormal is the result of the cross product of these two vectors.

The light and view vectors are then transformed with the tangent space matrix and the result is sent to the pixel shader via the output structure VS_OUTPUT.

The following pixel shader fetches a color map and the normal map. The sampler states of these textures are set with the D3DX effect file framework in an effect file. Both textures are trilinear filtered and clamped (read more on the problems with trilinear filtered normal maps in [Wloka3]).

```
texture ColorMap;
sampler ColorMapSampler = sampler_state
{
   Texture = <ColorMap####;
   MinFilter = Linear;
   MagFilter = Linear;
   MipFilter = Linear;
   AddressU  = Clamp;
   AddressV  = Clamp;
};
texture BumpMap;
sampler BumpMapSampler = sampler_state
```

```
    {
        Texture = <BumpMap>;
        MinFilter = Linear;
        MagFilter = Linear;
        MipFilter = Linear;
        AddressU  = Clamp;
        AddressV  = Clamp;
    };
    ....
    float4 PS(float2 Tex: TEXCOORD0, float3 Light : TEXCOORD1, float3
View : TEXCOORD2) : COLOR
    {
        // fetch color map
        float4 Color = tex2D(ColorMapSampler, Tex);

        // normal map
        float3 Normal =(2 * (tex2D(BumpMapSampler, Tex)))- 1.0;

        float3 LightDir = normalize(Light); // L
        float3 ViewDir = normalize(View); // V

        // diffuse component
        float Diffuse = saturate(dot(Normal, LightDir));

        // reflection vector
        float3 Reflect = normalize(2 * Diffuse * Normal - LightDir);

        // gloss map in Color.w restricts spec reflection
        float Specular = min(pow(saturate(dot(Reflect, ViewDir)), 3),
                        Color.w);

        return 0.2 * Color + Color * Diffuse + Specular;
    }
```

Both textures are fetched with a tex2D() function. The function tex2D() is declared as tex2D(s, t), where s is a sampler object and t is a 2D texture coordinate.

The normal from the normal map is used instead of the normal from the vertex throughout the entire pixel shader. The value in the normal map is scaled by 2.0 and biased by -1.0 to recover the tangent space normal. These steps are necessary, because the normal map is stored in an unsigned texture format with a value range of [0..1] to allow older hardware to operate correctly. Therefore, the normals have to be mapped back to the signed range [-1..1].

Compared to previous examples, this pixel shader restricts the region in which a specular reflection might happen to the water regions of the earth model. This is done with the help of the min() function and a gloss map that is stored in the alpha values of the color map. min() is defined as min(a, b) and it selects the lesser of a and b. This way some pixels show a specular reflection and others do not. Gloss maps are useful in mimicking material with a reflection behavior that changes on a per-pixel basis (e.g., rusty metal).

In the return statement, the ambient term is replaced by an intensity-decreased color value from the color map. The constant values used in the previous examples to describe the intensity and the color of the diffuse and specular component are skipped here. So we can assume that these values are 1.0f each.

Results

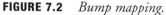 The example program gives the viewer the illusion that mountainous regions of the **ON THE CD** Earth are higher than watery regions. The screenshot in Figure 7.2 is taken from the example program for this chapter, which can be found in the directory Chapter 7 - Bump Mapping.

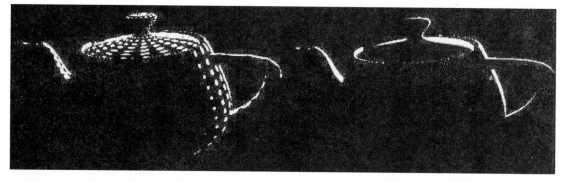

FIGURE 7.2 *Bump mapping.*

Please note how the desert zone of Africa is highlighted. This follows the idea that sand reflects the sun better than plants do.

Conclusion

Bump mapping fakes surface details by perturbing the normals in such a way that the resulting lighting effect tricks the eye into perceiving bulges and depressions without altering the geometry.

Using tangent space bump mapping is straightforward due to the availability of the D3DXComputeNormal() and D3DXComputeTangent() functions. To create a normal map, you can use a Photoshop plug-in or one of the several standalone programs that are available free of charge.

Faking the existence of surface details by perturbing normals does not offer convincing results in a situation in which a surface needs to relatively move to another under different viewing directions (e.g., a stone wall), because a bump mapped surface is still flat. This parallax effect can be faked by using parallax mapping as shown in the next chapter.

8

Parallax Mapping with Offset Limiting

At the beginning of 2004, a thread in the OpenGL discussion forum [Parallax-Thread] attracted the game programming community. A few days after he started the thread, Terry Welsh posted a paper on a technique he called "Parallax Mapping with Offset Limiting" [Welsh]. The underlying idea of this paper can also be found in the paper "Detailed Shape Representation with Parallax Mapping" written by Tomomichi Kaneko, et al. [Kaneko].

Parallax is exhibited when areas of a surface appear to move relative to one another as the view position changes. This can be observed on any surface that is not flat, such as tree bark, wavy beach sand, or rock walls.

With the method presented in this chapter, motion parallax is realized by mapping a texture that is distorted dynamically to correspond to the destination shape. The distortion is realized by shifting the texture coordinates of each drawn pixel as the texture is mapped to the polygon.

This chapter will cover the implementation of Welsh's paper and the ongoing discussions regarding this technique.

Background

Any parallax effect depends on the point of view. Compare a real surface and a bump-mapped polygon that simulates that surface, as shown in Figure 8.1. If the real surface has variations in height, it will exhibit parallax effects. Point A on the real surface corresponds to texel T_{actual} on the polygon, and point B corresponds to texel TB.

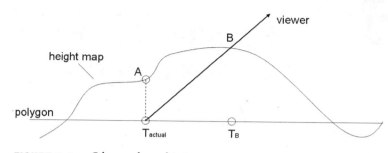

FIGURE 8.1 *Observed texel is incorrect.*

Imagine viewing a point on the surface from a position indicated by the view vector. In the real world, the viewer vector would intersect point *B*, and this point would be seen by the observer.

With bump mapping, the eye would perceive point *A*, because the viewer vector intersects *Tactual*. This is because the different height is simulated on a flat polygon.

In an ideal world, to see point *B*, an offset can be added to *Tactual* to produce *TB*. Adding such an offset shifts high areas of the surface away from the eye, while low areas of the surface are shifted toward the eye. Thus, parallax is achieved for the simulated surface. Because calculating such an offset is quite expensive, an approximation is used here.

The offset is found by tracing a ray from point A at the height of the real surface parallel to the polygon until it intersects the viewer vector as shown in Figure 8.2.

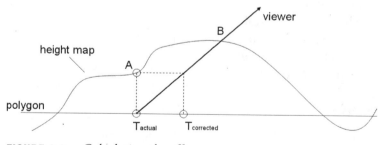

FIGURE 8.2 *Calculating the offset.*

The point where the ray intersects the viewer vector does not necessarily lie on the real surface. This is why this technique is only an approximation and not an exact simulation of parallax.

Tcorrected is obtained by modulating the view vector by the surface height. The tangent space viewer vector has components x and y, which lie in the plane of the surface, and a z component, which is perpendicular to the surface. These can be represented by V(x,y) and V(z).

The height value *h* is retrieved from a height map and must be scaled and biased to account for the surface being simulated. For example, a brick wall texture might cover a 2×2 meter area. Also imagine the surface of the bricks and the recessed grout give the surface a thickness of 0.02m. The correct scale factor *s* for this material would be 0.02/2 = 0.01. A bias *b* of 0.0 would give the appearance that the grout lies in the plane of the polygon, while a bias of −0.01 would give the appearance that the surface of the bricks lies in the plane of the polygon and the grout sinks below it. Scaling and biasing leads to the following equation for *hsb*.

$$h_{sb} = (h \times s) + b$$

Finally, the modified texture coordinate *Tcorrected* from Figure 8.2 can be calculated as in the following equation.

$$T_{corrected} = T_A + \frac{V_{(x,y)} \times h_{sb}}{V_{(z)}}$$

Although this equation is correct, it leads to visual problems as the angle between the viewer vector and the polygon approaches zero, *V(z)* also approaches zero. This creates a very large texture offset and the parallax mapping approach is no longer convincing.

To avoid this problem, the denominator in this equation can be dropped. This modification limits the texture coordinate offset to values lower than *hsb* (this is where the part of the name "offset limiting" is coming from), while causing little difference in the result when the viewer vector makes a steep angle and preserving the texture when this angle is shallow. So we end up with the following equation:

$$T_{corrected} = T_A + V_{(x,y)} \times h_{sb}$$

This is an approximation that works well enough, and it reduces the code in the pixel shader. The new texture coordinate in *Tcorrected* is then used to index the color map and the bump map and could be used to index any other map.

Implementation

The implementation of parallax mapping is based on the bump mapping example of the previous chapter. This example uses three texture maps: a color map, a normal map, and a height map. The latter provides the height value that is used to calculate the new texture coordinate.

```
float4 PS(float2 Tex: TEXCOORD0, float3 Light : TEXCOORD1, float3
          View : TEXCOORD2): COLOR
{
  const float scale = {0.04f};
  const float bias = {0.02};
  float3 LightDir = normalize(Light); // L
  float3 ViewDir = normalize(View); // V

  // fetch height map
  float Height = scale * tex2D(HeightMapSampler, Tex) - bias;

  // compute new texture coordinates
  float2 TexCorrected  = Height * ViewDir + Tex;
  float4 Color;
  float3 Normal;

  if (fSwitchParallax)
  {
     // fetch color map
     Color = tex2D(ColorMapSampler, TexCorrected);

     // bump map
     Normal =(2 * (tex2D(BumpMapSampler, TexCorrected )))- 1.0;
  }
  else
  {
     Color = tex2D(ColorMapSampler, Tex);
     Normal =(2 * (tex2D(BumpMapSampler, Tex)))- 1.0;
  }
  // diffuse comp.
  float Diff = saturate(dot(Normal, LightDir));

  return 0.2 * Color + Color * Diff;
}
```

The *hsb* value is stored in height and *Tcorrected* is stored in TexCorrected. This pixel shader only uses diffuse lighting but should work as well with every lighting algorithm.

Results

ON THE CD   The example program shown in Figure 8.3 is based on the example of the previous chapter and can be found in Chapter 8 - Parallax Mapping. Pressing P switches on parallax mapping with offset limiting.

The screenshot on the right shows regular bump mapping. Although you look at it from the side, you can still see the bottom of the grooves. If there is a groove between rocks, you should not be able to see its bottom when looking from this direction onto it. The left screenshot shows parallax mapping, which achieves more believable results. You can see that there are grooves, but you can not see the bottom of the groove.

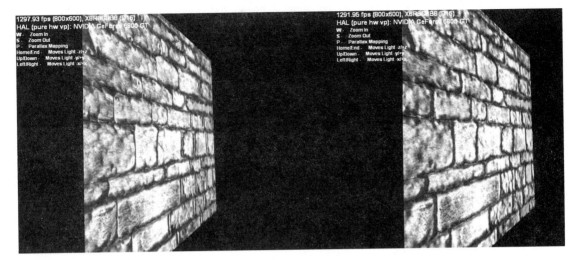

FIGURE 8.3 *Parallax mapping.*

Conclusion

Overall, parallax mapping is an easy to implement, inexpensive, and nice looking approximation that adds some level of plausibility to the bump mapping effect-through the addition of a parallax effect.

The obvious disadvantage of parallax mapping is the false assumption that points A and B in Figure 8.1 are the same distance from the polygon. This assumption results in artifacts that are apparent near steep height changes on the surface, which occur for example in a height map with a high frequency. Therefore, this technique is applicable only to low frequency height maps, leaving the creation of finer details to detail maps or bump maps.

9

Self-Shadowing

With all the lighting models covered so far, the calculation of the specular component still happens when the light vector and the normal vector point in opposite directions. The target of the term developed during this chapter is to prevent this. Additionally, it allows a linear scaling of the light intensity and helps reduce pixel popping when the light gets extremely close to the polygon and bump mapping is performed, because we get a linear scaling of light brightness when the light is in front of the polygon.

Because this term prevents the light beams from shining under certain conditions on the surface of the object, it is called a self-shadowing term (more complex self-shadowing terms are covered in Part III of this book).

Background

The screenshot in Figure 9.1 shows an example using a self-shadowing term on the right and an example that does not use a self-shadowing term on the left.

FIGURE 9.1 *Without (left) or with (right) a self-shadowing term.*

What happened here was that the light vector was moved into or behind the red teapot lit by a Phong light. This way from the point of view of the camera it was occluded by geometry. Whereas the screenshot on the right shows the expected result, the screenshot on the left shows a completely white teapot. This effect should be prevented by the self-shadowing term.

There are several ways to achieve a self-shadowing term. The main idea here is to restrict the diffuse and specular lighting component, so that the ambient lighting component is left. This can be done by multiplying these components with a factor that approaches zero if the light vector is hidden by geometry.

$$I = A_{intensity} \times A_{color} + S \times \left(D_{intensity} \times D_{color} \times \mathbf{N} \cdot \mathbf{L} + S_{intensity} \times S_{color} \times \left(\mathbf{R} \cdot \mathbf{V} \right)^n \right)$$

If S approaches zero, the whole term in brackets will be zero (read more in [Frazier]). A different way to restrict the contribution of the diffuse and specular lighting models in case the light vector is occluded is to switch them off.

$$I = A_{intensity} \times A_{color} + if \left(S > 0.0 f \right) \left(D_{intensity} \times D_{color} \times \mathbf{N} \cdot \mathbf{L} + S_{intensity} \times S_{color} \times \left(\mathbf{R} \cdot \mathbf{V} \right)^n \right)$$

Implementation

To implement a self-shadowing term, we need to find a way to track whether the light vector is occluded by geometry. Frazier uses the dot product of the normal and the light vector to track this.

```
...
S = saturate(4.0f * N.L)
...
```

Using the N.L has the advantage of re-using a part of the diffuse component. So the computational overhead is quite small. Multiplying $\mathbf{N} \cdot \mathbf{L}$ here by four raises the threshold from which the shadowing effect is visible.

This approach works well on non-bumped surfaces, but if perturbed normals stored in tangent space are retrieved from a bump map, we need to follow a different approach. This is because the perturbed normal can point in the direction of the light vector, although it is hidden by geometry as shown in Figure 9.2.

The screenshot on the left side shows a bump-mapped teapot. The tangent space bump map simulates dents in the teapot. Therefore, the normals are bent toward the surface of the teapot. Although the light source is hidden partly behind the teapot, dents are lit, because their normals are pointing toward the light vector.

The screenshot on the right side shows the proper reflectance behavior. This is because the light vector is in texture space. This allows us to use the z value of the light vector similar to the $\mathbf{N} \cdot \mathbf{L}$ result on a non-bump mapped surface, because $\mathbf{L}.z$ equals $\mathbf{N} \cdot \mathbf{L}$ if the light vector is in tangent space.

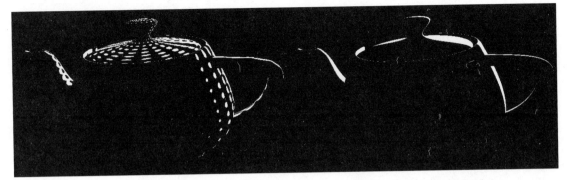

FIGURE 9.2 *Bump mapping with* **N·L** *(left) or with* **L**.z *as self-shadowing term (right).*

Therefore in the case of tangent-space bump mapping, the self-shadowing term in HLSL can be expressed as follows:

```
S = saturate(4* LightDir.z);
```

A third way to calculate the self-shadowing term is to use an if statement as follows:

```
...
float shadow = 4.0f * LightDir.z;

if (shadow > 0.0f)
{
...
}
...
```

The advantage of this approach is that on graphics hardware that supports dynamic branches, all the computations in the if statement do not need to be executed, if the pixels are shadowed.

The implementation of the first two approaches is shown in the following pixel shader.

```
float4 PS(float3 Light: TEXCOORD0, float3 Norm : TEXCOORD1,
float3 View : TEXCOORD2) : COLOR
    {
        float4 DiffColor = { 1.0f, 0.0f, 0.0f, 1.0f};
        float4 Ambient = {0.3,  0.0,  0.0, 1.0};

        float3 Normal = normalize(Norm);
        float3 LightDir = normalize(Light);
        float3 ViewDir = normalize(View);
```

```
    // diffuse component
    float Diffuse = saturate(dot(Normal, LightDir));

    // compute self-shadowing term
    float Shadow = saturate(4* Diffuse);
//    float Shadow = saturate(4 * LightDir.z);

    // reflection vector
    float3 Reflect = normalize(2 * Diffuse * Normal - LightDir);

    // specular component
    float Specular = pow(saturate(dot(Reflect, ViewDir)), 8);

    return Ambient + Shadow * (DiffColor * Diffuse + Specular);
}
```

The self-shadowing term reduces the diffuse and specular component of the lighting model to zero, in case the diffuse component or the *z* channel of the light vector is zero. In other words, the diffuse component or the *z* component of the light vector is used to diminish the intensity of the specular component.

The third approach modifies the previous pixel shader slightly by adding if and else statements. On ps_3_0 hardware, this might be more efficient than the previous approaches (rule of thumb: if the branch can skip about 12–15 assembly instruction slots).

```
...
    // diffuse comp.
    float Diffuse = saturate(dot(Normal, LightDir));

    // self-shadowing term
    float Shadow = 4.0f * LightDir.z;

    if (Shadow > 0.0f)
    {// R
     float3 Reflect = normalize(2 * Diffuse * Normal - LightDir);

     // gloss map in color.w restricts spec reflection
     float Specular = min(pow(saturate(dot(Reflect, ViewDir)), 3),
                     Color.w);

     return 0.2 * Color + (Color * Diffuse + Specular);
    }
    else
        return 0.2 * Color + Color * Diffuse;
...
```

If LightDir.z is greater than 0, the if branch will be executed and the Phong lighting will be calculated. Otherwise, the ambient and diffuse term is returned.

Conclusion

ON THE CD This chapter is accompanied by three example programs that can be found on the CD-ROM in the directories Chapter 9 - Self-Shadowing Term\HLSL Self-Shadowing Term; Chapter 9 - Self-Shadowing Term\HLSL Bump Mapping Self-Shadow L.z, and Chapter 9 - Self-Shadowing Term\HLSL Bump Mapping Self-Shadow if.

The first example program is a modified version of the Phong example from Chapter 6. By moving the light vector into the teapot or behind the teapot by pressing End on your keyboard, you can see the effect visualized in Figure 9.1. The second and third examples are modified versions of the bump mapping example from Chapter 7.

Whereas all examples so far have used a directional light, in which all light beams are treated as parallel to simulate light beams coming from the sun, the following chapter presents light sources that mimic point and spot lights.

10 Light Sources

Light sources are commonly categorized according to the distribution of their light beams as directional, point, and spot light sources. In this chapter, we will learn about each and discover how to implement them.

Point Lights

All the previous chapters examine the visual quality of the reflectance of light on surfaces. All examples so far used the same vector to describe the direction from which light is falling onto the surface. This way, all light beams are treated as parallel beams. This mimics the kind of light beams coming from the sun, and is called a *directional* light source.

This section examines light beams of a *point* light, which are spread out from one position uniformly in all directions, as shown in Figure 10.1.

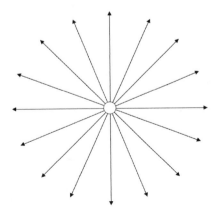

FIGURE 10.1 *Point light.*

Background

Point lights are usually characterized by having a position in space and an attenuation factor that falls off with increasing distance. You give a light source a position by subtracting the position of the vertex of the mesh that should be illuminated from the light vector.

To attenuate a light source, a so-called attenuation factor is used.

The following attenuation factor offers a good ratio between quality and efficiency for current graphics hardware. (Read more in [Dietrich2], [Ginsburg] and [Dempski].)

$$attenuation = 1 - d \times d \, / / \, d = distance$$

This equation can be expanded as follows:

$$attenuation = 1 - \left(x \times x + y \times y + z \times z \right)$$

To be able to adjust the range of distance, each distance component can be divided through a range constant.

$$attenuation = 1 - \left(\left(x/r \right)^2 + \left(y/r \right)^2 + \left(z/r \right)^2 \right)$$

Vectorizing this formula leads to:

$$attenuation = 1 - dot\left(L/r, L/r \right)$$

The lighting formula used so far and extended to support point lights is then:

$$I = A_{intensity} \times A_{color} + \left(Shadow \times \left(D_{intensity} \times D_{color} \times \mathbf{N} \cdot \mathbf{L} + S_{intensity} \times S_{color} \times \left(\mathbf{R} \cdot \mathbf{V} \right)^n \right) \right) \times \left(1 - dot\left(L/r, L/r \right) \right)$$

If the attenuation value is zero, the only lighting contribution still visible is ambient lighting.

Implementation

Implementing a point light source means adding an attenuation factor and making the light beams spread out from one position uniformly in all directions. The following vertex shader calculates the attenuation factor per-vertex and sends the result in the fourth component of the light vector via the interpolators to the pixel shader.

```
VS_OUTPUT VS(float4 Pos : POSITION,
  float2 Tex : TEXCOORD,
  float3 Normal : NORMAL,
  float3 Tangent : TANGENT  )
{
    VS_OUTPUT Out = (VS_OUTPUT)0;
    Out.Pos = mul(Pos, matWorldViewProj); // transform Position
```

```
                // compute the 3x3 tranform matrix
                // to transform from world space to tangent space
                float3x3 worldToTangentSpace;
                worldToTangentSpace[0] = mul(Tangent, matWorld);
                worldToTangentSpace[1] = mul(cross(Tangent, Normal), mat-
        World);
                worldToTangentSpace[2] = mul(Normal, matWorld);

                Out.Tex = Tex.xy;

                float3 PosWorld = normalize(mul(Pos, matWorld));

                float LightRange = 0.5;

                float3 Light = LightPos - PosWorld;
                Out.Light.xyz = normalize(mul(worldToTangentSpace, Light)); //
        L

                // 1 - Attenuation
                Out.Light.w = saturate(1 - dot(Light * LightRange, Light *
                            LightRange));

                float3 Viewer = vecEye - PosWorld;
                Out.View = mul(worldToTangentSpace, Viewer); // V

            return Out;
        }
```

To achieve the spread out of the light beams, the light vector is calculated by subtracting the light vector from the vertex position. Instead of dividing the light vector
through the range value, we use a "smaller than 1.0f" value that can be multiplied,
which is more efficient than division.

The corresponding pixel shader shows bump mapping with a self-shadowing
term. The main addition is the multiplication with the attenuation term.

```
        float4 PS(float2 Tex: TEXCOORD0, float4 Light : TEXCOORD1, float3
    View : TEXCOORD2) : COLOR
        {
            // fetch color map
            float4 Color = tex2D(ColorMapSampler, Tex);

            // fetch bump map
            float3 Normal = 2 * (tex2D(BumpMapSampler, Tex) - 0.5);

            float3 LightDir = normalize(Light.xyz);
            float3 ViewDir = normalize(View);

            // diffuse component
            float Diffuse = saturate(dot(Normal, LightDir));

            // compute self-shadowing term
            float Shadow = saturate(4 * LightDir.z);
```

```
            float3 Reflect = normalize(2 * Diffuse * Normal - LightDir);
    // R

            // gloss map in color.w used to restrict spec reflection
            float Specular = min(pow(saturate(dot(Reflect, ViewDir)), 3),
    Color.w);

            // I = A + (Shadow * (D * N.L + (R.V)n)) * (1 - dot(L/r, L/r))
            return  0.2 * Color + (Shadow * (Color * Diffuse + Specular) *
    (Light.w)));
        }
```

By multiplying the diffuse and specular terms with the fourth component of the light vector, which holds the attenuation value computed in the vertex shader, these terms can be diminished to zero. Calculating the attenuation factor with a look-up texture or natively in the pixel shader would further improve its visual quality.

Results

The point light example program can be found in the directory Chapter 10 - Light Sources\Point Light.

To see the visual effect of light beams distributed from one point in space uniformly in all directions with attenuation based on distance, you need to press the Home and End keys. The screenshot in Figure 10.2 shows a point light that is far away from the sphere. Moving closer to the sphere with the earth texture would lead to a wider spread of light.

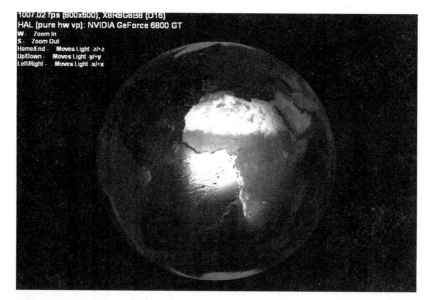

FIGURE 10.2 *Point light.*

The screenshot in Figure 10.2 shows that using one-point light is usually not enough to light a scene. Therefore point lights are commonly used as an additional light source to accentuate parts of a scene.

This point light model creates a performance/quality trade-off that gives remarkable results especially if used with other nondynamic or dynamic light sources that distribute light evenly or that mimic or attend scattered light much more. It works well even on ps_1_1 capable hardware.

Four Point Lights

Having four dynamic point lights in a scene at once can be achieved by running the same shader multiple times. This multipass approach has the disadvantage that geometry needs to be processed four times. Creating the same effect in one pass would reduce the vertex throughput. The following section shows how to create a single pixel shader that creates four point lights of the same quality as shown in the previous section.

Background

To account for more light sources, we need to enhance the lighting formula in the following way:

$$I = A + \sum_{\ell} \left(S_{\ell} \times \left(\left(D \times \mathbf{N} \cdot \mathbf{L}_{\ell} + \left(\mathbf{R}_{\ell} \cdot \mathbf{V} \right)^{n} \right) \times Att_{\ell} \right) \right)$$

The variable Att symbolizes here the attenuation value, which reduces the intensity of the point light. For each light source, we need an individual shadow term, light vector, reflection vector, and attenuation factor. In other words, whereas the ambient and diffuse term, normal vector, and viewer vector are the same for all point lights, the light and reflection vector, self-shadowing term, and attenuation factor are unique to each point light.

Implementation

To implement four point lights, all unique terms need to be computed individually in the pixel shader, which leads to a higher amount of instructions compared to the example program used in the previous section.

The following HLSL code focuses on the necessary modifications to the example program shown in the previous section.

```
...
float3 PosWorld = normalize(mul(Pos, matWorld));
float LightRange = 0.2;

float3 Light = LightPos- PosWorld;
Out.Light.xyz = normalize(mul(worldToTangentSpace, Light)); // L
```

```
// 1 - Attenuation
Out.Light.w = saturate(1 - dot(Light * LightRange, Light *
                       LightRange));

float3 Light2 = LightPos2- PosWorld;
Out.Light2.xyz = normalize(mul(worldToTangentSpace, Light2));
Out.Light2.w = saturate(1 - dot(Light2 * LightRange, Light2 *
                        LightRange));

float3 Light3 = LightPos3 - PosWorld;
...
```

The position of each light vector is sent from the application to the vertex shader in LightPos - LightPos4. The vertex shader is used to retrieve an individual vector L for each light source and store it in the xyz channel of the output register. The attenuation factor is stored in the fourth channel w of the same output register. The constant value LightRange holds the value that adjusts the point light for different ranges. You might use an individual value for each point light here.

The pixel shader retrieves these four light vectors together with their attenuation values and calculates the reflection vector for each light individually.

```
float4 PS( float2 Tex: TEXCOORD0,
           float4 Light : TEXCOORD1,
           float3 View : TEXCOORD2,
           float4 Light2 : TEXCOORD4,
           float4 Light3 : TEXCOORD3,
           float4 Light4 : TEXCOORD5) : COLOR
{
    // fetch color map
    float4 Color = tex2D(ColorMapSampler, Tex);

    // fetch bump map
    float3 Normal = (2 * tex2D(BumpMapSampler, Tex)) - 1.0;

    float3 LightDir = normalize(Light.xyz);
    float3 LightDir2 = normalize(Light2.xyz);
    float3 LightDir3 = normalize(Light3.xyz);
    float3 LightDir4 = normalize(Light4.xyz);

    float3 ViewDir = normalize(View);
    float Diff = saturate(dot(Normal,  LightDir));
    float Diff2 = saturate(dot(Normal, LightDir2));
    float Diff3 = saturate(dot(Normal, LightDir3));
    float Diff4 = saturate(dot(Normal, LightDir4));

    float3 Reflect = normalize(2.0f * Normal * Diff - LightDir);
    float Spec = pow(saturate(dot(Reflect, ViewDir)), 15);

    float3 Reflect2 = normalize(2.0f * Normal * Diff2 - LightDir2);
    float Spec2 = pow(saturate(dot(Reflect2, ViewDir)), 15);
```

```
float3 Reflect3 = normalize(2.0f * Normal * Diff3 - LightDir3);
float Spec3 = pow(saturate(dot(Reflect3, ViewDir)), 15);

float3 Reflect4 = normalize(2.0f * Normal * Diff4 - LightDir4);
float Spec4 = pow(saturate(dot(Reflect4, ViewDir)), 15);

return Color * 0.6 + (((Color * Diff + Spec) * (Light.w)) +
                      ((Color * Diff2 + Spec2) * (Light2.w)) +
                      ((Color * Diff3 + Spec3) * (Light3.w)) +
                      ((Color * Diff4 + Spec4) * (Light4.w)));
}
```

The results of the lighting calculations for each light are added in the return statement. A possible oversaturation might be prevented by reducing the range of the attenuation factor in the vertex shader.

Results

The four lights of the example program are moved simultaneously by pressing the arrow keys. This simplification can easily be removed by dedicating each light source its own keys on the keyboard. Moving the four lights to the left side, for example, shows how the lights are attenuated. Additionally, one can see that the attenuation, together with the property of point lights to spread out from one position uniformly in all directions, leads to a distribution that follows a sphere (see Figure 10.3).

ON THE CD The example can be found in the directory Chapter 10 - Light Sources\Four Phong Lights.

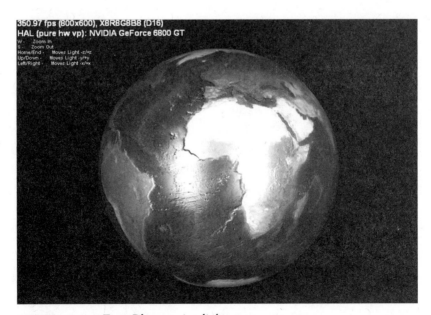

FIGURE 10.3 *Four Phong point lights.*

Conclusion

The two previous sections covered a point light model that is simple enough to be implemented in ps_1_1 capable hardware while still being visually good enough to produce believable results.

Balancing the quality/performance ratio of this point light model can be done by

- Using a Blinn-Phong reflection model
- Using a more or less complex attenuation formula and/or storing the formula in a texture
- Calculating the attenuation per-vertex or per-pixel
- Reducing precision where it does not count by not re-normalizing vectors
- Using a simpler lighting formula by combining the light contributions in simpler ways

Spot Lights

A spot light offers a location, an orientation, and an angle of dispersion to create a cone of light. This chapter covers a spotlight implementation that is ported from the spotlight implementation shown in "The RenderMan Companion" [Upstill].

Background

A spotlight's light ray emanates from a point, resulting in rays that are not parallel. Furthermore, spotlights have an inner cone that is brighter and an outer cone that has a very soft edge. Figure 10.4 shows these cones.

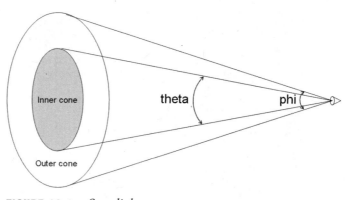

FIGURE 10.4   *Spot light.*

The angle phi is the penumbra angle, or the outer cone angle, and the angle theta is the umbra angle, or the inner cone angle. In the Direct3D fixed-function pipeline, light has the same intensity up to the border of the inner cone's area, falling off to darkness at the edge of the outer cone. The way the light falls off from the inner to the outer cone is typically linear.

Spot lights are more expensive than point lights, because they require a way to determine whether pixels are inside the inner cone and to compute the exponential or linear fall-off from the center of the light cone.

Implementation

To implement a spot light in a pixel shader, we need to account for the angles describing the inner and outer cone, and we need to simulate a fall-off from the center of the light cone. In the following pixel shader, the cone direction vector is SpotDir, and the angle between the cone center and the direction to the surface point is described by LightDir. The dot-product of these vectors represents the angle phi.

```
float lerpstep( float lower, float upper, float s )
{
    return saturate( ( s - lower )  / ( upper - lower ) );
}

float4 PS(float2 Tex: TEXCOORD0, float4 Light : TEXCOORD1, float3
View : TEXCOORD2) : COLOR
{
    // fetch color map
    float4 color = tex2D(ColorMapSampler, Tex);

    // fetch bump map
    float3 bumpNormal = 2 * (tex2D(BumpMapSampler, Tex) - 0.5);

    float3 LightDir = normalize(Light.xyz);
    float3 ViewDir = normalize(View);

    // diffuse component
    float diff = saturate(dot(bumpNormal, LightDir));

    float cosAngle = dot( SpotDir, LightDir );
    float spotFactor = smoothstep( cosOuter, cosInner, cosAngle );
//    float spotFactor = lerpstep( cosOuter, cosInner, cosAngle );

    return  0.2 * color + (spotFactor * lightColor * (color *
            diff)) * Light.w;
}
```

The variable cosInner represents the inner cone shown in Figure 10.4 with values in the range [0.5..1.0], whereas the variable cosOuter represents the outer cone with values of [0.0..0.5]. smoothstep() or lerpstep() interpolates between these values based on the result cosAngle (in Figure 10.4, phi) of the dot-product between the vector that describes the cone center SpotDir and the vector that describes the direction to a surface point LightDir. Whereas smoothstep() uses a hermite interpolation to interpolate between the minimum and maximum values, the lerpstep() function interpolates linearly. This more efficient approach leads to a slightly lower visual quality.

Light attenuation is realized in the same way as in the point light example from the previous chapter: by multiplying the main lighting term with the attenuation value in `Light.w` that was computed in the vertex shader.

Results

ON THE CD The example program accompanying the "Spot Light" section can be found in the directory Chapter 10 - Light Sources\Spot Light.

The following keys influence the appearance of the spot light:

- E, D changes the inner cone value and therefore the max value of the interpolation function
- R, F changes the outer cone value and therefore the max value of the interpolation function
- Home, End attenuates the light
- T, G changes the red channel of the light's color
- Up, Down, Right, Left changes the light's direction

The screenshot in Figure 10.5 shows the spot light contribution modulated with diffuse lighting. To make the spot light effect more visible, the color map is not applied to the object here.

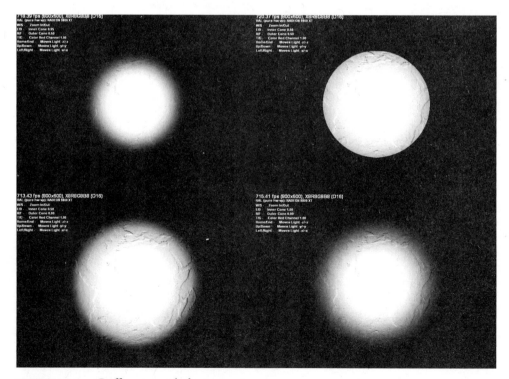

FIGURE 10.5 *Different spot light properties.*

In the top left screenshot, the inner cone value is 0.95 and the outer cone value is 0.50. In the top right screenshot, the inner cone value is 0.50 and the outer cone value is 0.50. Because both values are of the same size, interpolation does not happen. You can see here the spotlight cone with a sharp edge. In the bottom left screenshot, the inner cone value is 0.50 and the outer cone value is 0.0 and in the bottom right screenshot, the inner cone value is raised to 1.0f, so that the interpolation happens in the range [0.0..1.0].

Conclusion

This chapter covered the two most common light sources—point lights and spot lights—in an efficient implementation. There are obviously several other ways to implement these light sources, and you should feel encouraged to discover the way that works best for your particular project.

11 Hemispheric Lighting

None of the lighting models shown thus far are capable of mimicking reflected light from the ground or from other surrounding objects. Just think of a car moving around in the sunlight. The problem with conventional lighting models is that in the real world, the majority of light does not come from a single source. In an outdoor setting, some of it does indeed come straight from the sun, but more comes equally from all parts of the sky, and still more is reflected back from the ground and other surrounding objects. These indirect light sources are extremely important, because they will often provide a much larger percentage of the total illumination than the sun itself. Hemispheric lighting can imitate the contributions of indirect light sources.

Background

Hemispheric lighting simulates the effect of the sunlight coming from above and reflected from all directions. It differentiates between an upper and a lower hemisphere as shown in Figure 11.1.

The upper hemisphere is blue and represents the sky color, and the lower hemisphere is green and represents the ground. Think of the light beams coming from all directions to the microfacet.

As a "global lighting model" it can be used in a lighting formula as a replacement for the ambient term covered in Chapter 5. There are slightly different ways to implement the hemispheric lighting model.

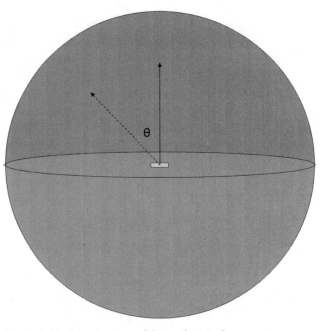

FIGURE 11.1   *Upper and lower hemisphere.*

Implementation: N.y as the Blend Factor

The first example feeds the y value of the normal as the blend factor to the `lerp()` function, as shown in the following source code snippets. Therefore, the y value of the vertex normal determines how much color is blended together.

Areas with normals with high y values are "sky" colored.
Areas with normals with low y values are "ground" colored.

This is shown in the following source code snippet.

```
VS_OUTPUT VS(float4 Pos : POSITION, float2 Tex : TEXCOORD, float3
        Normal : NORMAL)
{
    VS_OUTPUT Out = (VS_OUTPUT)0;

    Out.Pos = mul(Pos, matWorldViewProj); // transform Position
    Out.Norm = mul(Normal, matWorld);
    Out.Norm.w = (Out.Norm.y * 0.5f) + 0.5f;        // offset

...
    return Out;
}
```

```
float4 PS(float3 Incident : TEXCOORD0, float4 Norm : TEXCOORD1,
          float3 PosAdj : TEXCOORD2) : COLOR
{
...
   //         GroundColor  SkyColor
   return lerp(GroundColor, SkyColor, Norm.w);
}
```

They linearly interpolate between x and y, such that the return value is x when s is 0, and y when s is 1. The y value of the normal can have values in the range [−1..1]. This value range is biased and shifted so that we end up with a [0..1.0].

Using the y value of the normal is a simple way of emulating the indirect light contributions found in a typical outdoor scene. Adding an offset value to the y value of the normal would enhance the amount of scattered light reflection and therefore light that does come directly from the sky.

ON THE CD A screenshot of the example program, which can be found in the directory Chapter 11 - Hemisphere Lighting\Hemisphere Lighting N.y is shown in Figure 11.2. Please note how hemispheric lighting provides self-shadowing.

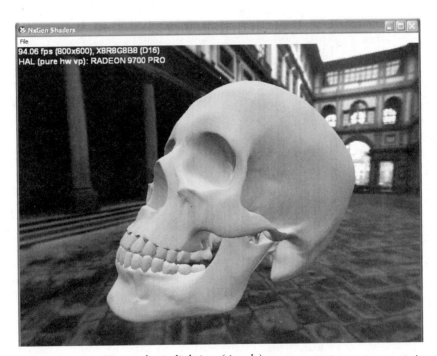

FIGURE 11.2 *Hemispheric lighting (simple).* Background lighting environment is the Uffizi Light Probe Image © 1999 Paul Debevec, www.debevec.org/Probes/. Used with permission.

This approach does not account for the direction of the sun, which is not a problem when representing certain lighting situations, such as a cloudy day, an area with many skyscrapers, or a situation in which you do not want to account for different times of day.

The following examples offer the capability to account for the direction of the sun.

Implementation: N.S as the Blend Factor

ON THE CD The next examples in the directory Chapter 11 - Hemisphere Lighting\Hemisphere Lighting dot(N, Sky) can account for the direction of light by using a sky vector as shown in Figure 11.1. To achieve this, they use the dot product between the normal and the sky vector as the blending factor for the lerp instruction. Therefore, the vertex normal determines how much color is blended together.

- Areas with normals pointing toward the sky are "sky" colored.
- Areas with normals pointing toward the ground are "ground" colored.

This is shown by the following source code additions.

```
...
// direction of light from sky
const float3 DirFromSky = {0.0f, 1.0f, 0.0f};
const float4 ModelColor = { 1.0f, 1.0f, 1.0f, 1.0f};
const float4 GroundColor = { 0.2f, 0.2f, 0.2f, 1.0f};
const float HemiIntensity = {0.9f};
...
    float4 temp = HemiIntensity * lerp(GroundColor, ModelColor,
(dot(N, DirFromSky) * 0.5f) + 0.5f);
```

Calculating the dot product between the sky direction and the normal vector in the pixel shader gives the example program the ability to account for the position of the sun. Compared to the previous example, there is no visible difference as long as the sky direction is (0.0, 1.0, 0.0).

Implementation: Adding an Occlusion Term

Adding an occlusion term to the previous examples to improve the visual quality of self-shadowing is shown by Chas. Boyd [Boyd]. Figure 11.3 shows a comparison between the previous example program and the example program that uses the occlusion term.

The screenshot on the right in Figure 11.3 shows that using an occlusion term leads to a more evenly distributed self-shadowing term. This term is calculated by sending out rays from each facet of the model to see how many intersect the object. Some rays will hit the object and others will miss it. The ratio of hits/misses is then stored as a texture coordinate in the vertex data of the file that holds the geometry as the occlusion term.

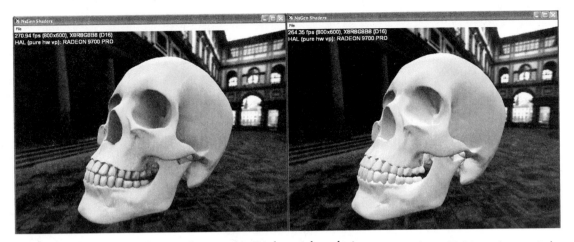

FIGURE 11.3 *Left: without occlusion term/Right: with occlusion term. Background lighting environment is the Uffizi Light Probe Image © 1999 Paul Debevec, www.debevec.org/Probes/. Used with permission.*

This term is then used to weight the blending factor consisting of the dot product between N and the sky vector.

This example program can be found in the directory Chapter 11 - Hemisphere Lighting\Hemisphere Lighting dot(N, Sky) + Occ.

ON THE CD

Conclusion

Hemispheric lighting accounts for the indirect light sources common in outdoor scenes by blending between a color from a top hemisphere and a color from a bottom hemisphere. In the case of a car or a motorbike, to achieve a very natural effect the color of the car or motorbike is retrieved from the texture map that is used for the vehicle.

If the vehicle drives in a wide outdoor scene—e.g., in a rally or in a race—the ground color can be retrieved from the color of the ground map and the sky color can be retrieved from a sky texture or just by using a blue color, depending on the main color that comes from the sky. Using an environmental map as shown in the previous examples would be not efficient enough here. In MotoGP and MotoGP 2 instead of using an environment map for the ground color, Shawn Hargreaves [Hargreaves] uses a scaled down version of a top shot of the terrain, blurs it, and adds some noise and blends it with the color of the vehicle.

To create the color of the sky, he uses a static environment map with a "typical" scene of the environment and re-uses this all the time.

In scenes where the ground is always similar—e.g., driving a car through a town—it might be even easier to use a color for the bottom hemisphere (as shown in the examples here) and to use a more sophisticated environment mapping approach for the upper hemisphere. For example, a blurred 32x32x32 cube environment map that is dynamically updated every five frames. (Read more on cube environment maps in Part IV.)

Having seen the implementation of the most common lighting models of current games, you should now have some idea how to create your own lighting model. Implementing lighting models is always a performance/quality trade-off, closely matched to the requirements of the game genre. A factor that must be considered is the mood and the environment of a scene. Lighting an outdoor scene requires different approaches than an indoor scene. Some lights in indoor and outdoor scenes can be pre-calculated in light maps and some lights can be dynamic, similar to the approaches shown earlier in this chapter. In outdoor scenes, very rough approximations can lead to believable environment effects.

Being creative is very important in all cases. This part of the book laid out the foundation for you to start to develop your own ideas.

Advanced Reflectance Algorithms

The following part of the book should show you how to implement some of the lighting algorithms that were discussed in the last two decades at universities.

We can expect some of these reflectance algorithms to be adopted in the next couple of years and to be further simplified, making them suitable for the demands of real-time environments. We examine two isotropic lighting models and two anisotropic lighting models here that might be good candidates for use in game environments.

In 1981, Robert L. Cook and Kenneth E. Torrance [Cook] presented a reflectance model that was based on physics by using measured data from real materials and using physically measurable factors, such as energy and wavelength. Between 1992 and 1994, Michael Oren and Shree K. Nayar [Oren] published several papers on a diffuse lighting model that is based on both physics and observation. The starting point was a physics model, and after dropping terms that did not substantially contribute to the overall result, the lighting model was refined by observation without relying any more on the concepts of physics. Both models are isotropic lighting models, meaning that both are invariant under a rotation about the normal vector N, as long as the angle between V and L, the angle between these vectors and N, and the distribution of microfacets all remain constant. Many surfaces, however, possess different degrees of roughness in different directions. These surfaces are called anisotropic reflectors and include materials such as brushed metal, hair, and certain fabrics.

The first anisotropic lighting model that will be presented here was developed by Gregory J. Ward and presented on SIGGRAPH 1992 in his paper "Measuring and Modeling Anisotropic Reflection." Ward's goal was to find the "... simplest empirical formula that will do the job ..." [Ward].

In 2000, Michael Ashikhmin and Peter Shirley [Ashikhmin] developed a Fresnel-weighted Phong-style model that is anisotropic. One of the most interesting properties of this model for game developers is that there is an efficient way to factorize the whole model. That was shown by Mauro Steigleder and Michael McCool [Steigleder] at the University of Waterloo.

Let's start with the Cook-Torrance model.

12 | Cook-Torrance Reflection

The previously discussed lighting models are largely the result of a common-sense, practical approach to graphics. Although the equations used approximate some of the ways light interacts with objects, they do not have a physical basis.

The Cook-Torrance reflection model [Cook] presented by Robert L. Cook and Kenneth E. Torrance on SIGGRAPH 1981 is a reflectance model for rough surfaces that is based on a physical method. It surpasses Phong's model because it was developed using measured data from real materials and uses physically measurable factors, such as energy and wavelength [Foley3].

Background

Similar to most of the lighting models shown in the previous part of this book, the Cook-Torrance model consists of an ambient, a diffuse, and a specular term and a few other terms that will be explained in the following text. Most of the material in this chapter will deal with the specular component, because it was the main research interest of Cook and Torrance. This specular component is based on three main concepts:

- A microfacet model for surface roughness, based on the Torrance-Sparrow model from 1967 [Torrance]. The distribution of the microfacet slope is represented by Beckmann's microfacet distribution function.
- A geometric attenuation factor for self-shadowing and masking of the microfacets.
- Fresnel's equation to compute the amount of light refracted when it strikes a material boundary.

The following text will cover each of these areas in detail. They are nowadays the cornerstones of several newer reflection models.

Microfacet Model

The starting point for the Cook-Torrance reflection model is the geometric description of a surface, developed by K.E. Torrance and E.M. Sparrow. Torrance-Sparrow assumed that a surface is composed of many small V-shaped grooves, which are lined with flat mirrors called microfacets. They assumed that the surface consists of specularly reflecting V-cavities of infinite length.

Figure 12.1 shows a V-cavity with two faces, where both faces are fully illuminated by a distant light source on the right side.

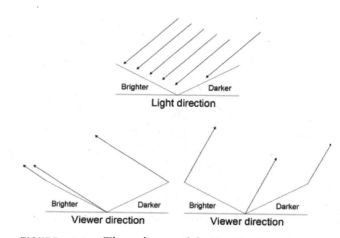

FIGURE 12.1   *The radiance of the V-cavity increases as the viewer moves toward the illumination direction.*

If the faces are viewed from the left side by a distant observer, a larger fraction of the foreshortened cavity area is dark and a smaller fraction is bright. As this observer moves to the right, toward the light source direction, the fraction of brighter area increases while that of the darker area decreases. The radiance of the cavity increases as the observer approaches the light source direction. This effect is in contrast to Lambertian surfaces whose brightness does not vary with the viewing direction.

Due to complexity of computation, actual rendering does not use real facets. Instead, reflectance models use some probability distribution function that predicts an approximate number of facets with a specific normal. Such a function is called a microfacet distribution function.

The Microfacet Distribution Function

A microfacet distribution function characterizes the distribution of the slopes of the microfacets. As light arrives at different angles, different distributions of the slope of the microfacets will cause different patterns of reflection. We use the term D to describe a mircofacet distribution function and the constant m to describe the root mean square slope of the microfacets. The distribution of the microfacets is retrieved in the Cook-Torrance reflectance model by the Beckmann [Beckmann] distribution function for rough surfaces. Given the halfway vector **H**, **D** returns the fraction of microfacets whose normal vectors point along the direction of **H**, which is shown in Figure 12.2.

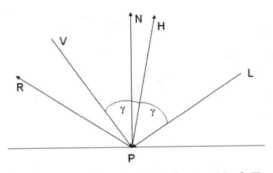

FIGURE 12.2   *Geometry of reflection (Cook-Torrance).*

The halfway vector **H** is defined as halfway between **L** and **V**. As already shown in Chapter 6 for the Blinn-Phong lighting model, the halfway vector is

$$H = L + V$$

The angle γ can be found between **V** and **H** and between **H** and **L**, so that

$$\cos(\gamma) = V \cdot H = L \cdot H$$

Figure 12.3 shows how these vectors are oriented in a microfacet.

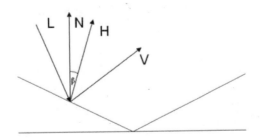

FIGURE 12.3   *Geometry of reflection (Cook-Torrance).*

β is the angle between **N** and **H**. Cook-Torrance uses Beckmann's microfacet distribution function.

$$D = \frac{1}{m^2 \cos^4 \beta} e^{-\left[\left(\tan^2 \beta\right)/m^2\right]}$$

To implement the function in vector form, we compute the squared tangent with the ratio of dot products:

$$\tan^2 \beta = \frac{\sin^2 \beta}{\cos^2 \beta} = \frac{1 - \cos^2 \beta}{\cos^2 \beta} = \frac{1 - (\mathbf{N} \cdot \mathbf{H})^2}{(\mathbf{N} \cdot \mathbf{H})^2}$$

Substituting, we get:

$$D = \frac{1}{m^2 \mathbf{N} \cdot \mathbf{H}^4} e^{\frac{-(1 - \mathbf{N} \cdot \mathbf{H}^2)}{m^2 (\mathbf{N} \cdot \mathbf{H})^2}}$$

The original Beckmann function has a 4 in the denominator in front of m^2. It has a "normalization" effect for high roughness. The results of this function are in the range [0..1]. Leaving out the 4—as Cook-Torrance did—leads to a nice "ring" effect.

m is the root-mean-square slope of the microfacets. Small values of m indicate that the surface is smooth and the grooves are shallow, and it produces a sharp highlight. Large values of m indicate a rough surface with deep grooves and produce more spread-out highlights.

Figure 12.4 shows four screenshots of the example program with different values for m.

The upper-left screenshot in Figure 12.4 was taken with an m value of 0.1, the upper right screenshot was taken with an m value of 0.2, the lower left with 0.4, and the lower right screenshot with 0.8.

You can use m per-pixel in a texture and you can even model multiple scales of roughness by calculating a weighted average of microfacet distribution functions, such as in:

$$D = \sum_{i=1}^{n} w_i D_{mi}$$

where mi is the root-mean-square slope of the ith distribution and wmi is the weight of the ith distribution.

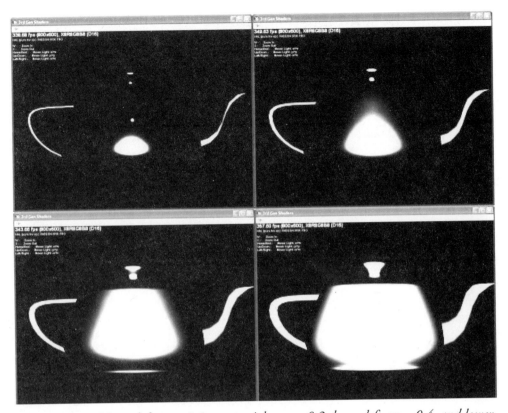

FIGURE 12.4 *Upper left: m = 0.1, upper right: m = 0.2, lower left: m = 0.4, and lower right: m = 0.8.*

$$D = w1 \times D1 + w2 \times D2 + wn \times Dn... // \quad where \quad w1 + w2 + wn = 1$$

Implementing Beckmann's microfacet distribution function can be done with the following pseudo code, which accounts for only one scale of roughness.

```
float D = pow(e, -((1 - N.H2) / (m2 * N.H2))) / (m2 * N.H2 *
N.H2);
```

As you can see, this pseudocode follows the previous equation thoroughly. Although D distributes microfacets, it does not handle the situation in which light is blocked by adjacent microfacets before it reaches the surface or after it has been reflected. This is done with a geometrical attenuation factor.

The Geometrical Attenuation Factor

The geometrical attenuation factor (GAF), which is labeled G in the Cook-Torrance reflection model, represents the masking and shadowing effects of the microfacets.

G accounts for three cases. The geometry of grooves means that the walls of grooves can block some of the light that would otherwise fall on a facet (called shadowing), as in Figure 12.5 (c), and that some of the light reflected from a facet can be blocked on its way out (called masking), as in Figure 12.5 (b).

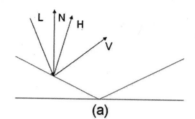

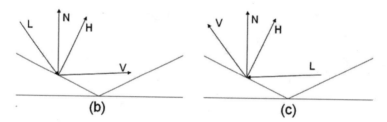

FIGURE 12.5   *Light rays reflecting from the surface microfacet in the Torrance-Sparrow model. (a) No interference. (b) Partial interception of reflected light. (c) Partial interception of incident light.*

Calculation of G assumes that the microfacets exist in the form of V-shaped groves with the sides at equal but opposite angles to the average surface normal, as shown in Figure 12.5.

For the simplest case, in Figure 12.5 (a) G is 1.0. To compute G for case (b), James F. Blinn [Blinn] and Eric Lengyel [Lengyel] give a trigonometric derivation of the proportion of the reflected light. Figure 12.6 shows x in relation to w.

When light is blocked after being reflected by a microfacet, we can use the following fraction.

$$G_1 = \frac{x}{w}$$

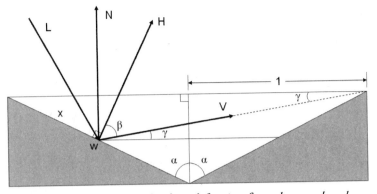

FIGURE 12.6 *Fraction of L from left microfacet that reaches the viewer equals x/w.*

Let's start by retrieving w.

For α, the trigonometric function is as follows:

$$\sin\alpha = \frac{y}{w}$$

We know that y is 1, therefore we can say:

$$\sin\alpha = \frac{1}{w}$$

Solving for w leads to:

$$w = \frac{1}{\sin\alpha}$$

Please take a look at the triangle made from V, x, and the base of the whole triangle ($2 \times y$). There are two angles of interest here: γ, which is given, and β and the angle between x and H, which is 90 degrees or $\pi/2$. Therefore, the angle between x and V is $\pi/2 + \beta$.

According to the law of sines:

$$\frac{x}{\sin\alpha} = \frac{y}{\sin\beta}$$

we end up with:

$$\frac{x}{\sin\gamma} = \frac{2}{\sin(\beta + \pi/2)}$$

which leads to the following equation:

$$x = \frac{2\sin\gamma}{\sin(\beta + \pi/2)}$$

All the sine functions in the previous equations can be expressed as cosine functions by shifting them by $\pi/2$.

$$\sin(\beta + \pi/2) = \cos\beta = \mathbf{V}\cdot\mathbf{H}$$

$$\sin\gamma = \cos(\pi/2 - \gamma) = \mathbf{N}\cdot\mathbf{V}$$

$$\sin\alpha = \cos(\pi/2 - \alpha) = \mathbf{N}\cdot\mathbf{H}$$

Plugging these into the fraction G_1 shown earlier leads to:

$$G_1 = \frac{x}{y} = \frac{2(\mathbf{N}\cdot\mathbf{H})(\mathbf{N}\cdot\mathbf{V})}{\mathbf{V}\cdot\mathbf{H}}$$

This function handles the case in which light is blocked after being reflected by the microfacet. When light is blocked before reaching a microfacet, we can calculate the fraction G_2 by replacing $\mathbf{V}$ with $\mathbf{L}$.

$$G_2 = \frac{x}{w} = \frac{2(\mathbf{N}\cdot\mathbf{H})(\mathbf{N}\cdot\mathbf{L})}{\mathbf{L}\cdot\mathbf{H}}$$

Now we account for all three cases. If light is not blocked (Figure 12.4 (a)), G will be 1. The case that light is blocked after being reflected by a microfacet (Figure 12.4 (b)) is handled by G_1 and the case in which light is blocked by geometry (Figure 12.4 (c)) before reaching a microfacet is handled by G_2.

$$G = \min(1, G_1, G_2)$$

The whole geometric attenuation factor can be written like this:

$$G = \min\left(1, \frac{2(\mathbf{N}\cdot\mathbf{H})(\mathbf{N}\cdot\mathbf{V})}{\mathbf{L}\cdot\mathbf{H}}, \frac{2(\mathbf{N}\cdot\mathbf{H})(\mathbf{N}\cdot\mathbf{L})}{\mathbf{V}\cdot\mathbf{H}}\right)$$

Because the angle between **L** and **H** and between **V** and **H** is the same, you might replace **L·H** with **V·H**, which leads to:

$$G = \min\left(1, \frac{2(N \cdot H)(N \cdot V)}{V \cdot H}, \frac{2(N \cdot H)(N \cdot L)}{V \cdot H}\right)$$

Figure 12.7 is a screenshot that shows the effect of the geometrical attenuation factor.

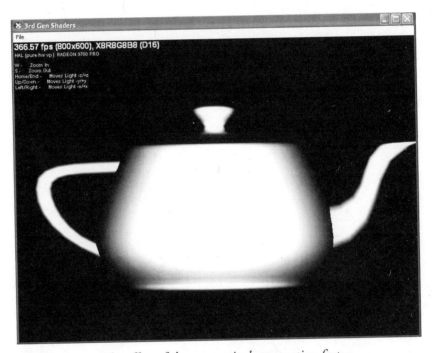

FIGURE 12.7   *The effect of the geometrical attenuation factor.*

Comparing Figure 12.7 to Figure 12.4 highlights the effect of attenuation. The following pseudocode calculates the geometric attenuation factor with the equation shown earlier:

```
float G = min(1.0f, min((2 * N.H * N.L) / V.H, (2 * N.H * N.V) /
V.H));
```

So far we have learned that the microfacet distribution function together with the geometrical attenuation factor simulate interaction of light with a rough surface. One additional feature of the Cook-Torrance reflection model is the Fresnel reflection formula, which simulates the light reflection at the interface between two media having different refractive indices.

The Fresnel Term

The amount of reflectance you see on a surface depends on the viewing angle. If you look straight down from above at a pool of water, you will not see very much reflected light on the surface of the pool, and can see down through the surface to the bottom of the pool. At a glancing angle (looking with your eye level with the water), you will see much more specularity and many reflections on the water surface, and you might not be able to see what's under the water.

This is called the Fresnel reflectance (pronounced "fre-nel," the "s" is silent). It can be thought of as a top-layer interface. Some light is reflected and the remainder is transmitted through. How much light is reflected depends on the surface material and the incident angle. Figure 12.8 shows three different Fresnel effects depending on the angle of incoming light.

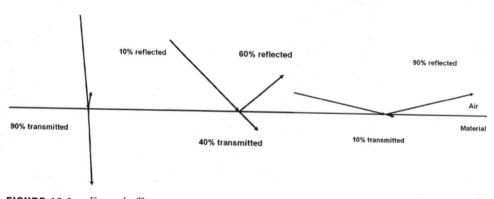

FIGURE 12.8   *Fresnel effect.*

The Fresnel term is particularly important for semitransparent materials such as plastic, glass, water, skin, and car paint. It quantifies the reflection of a portion of the incident light at a discrete interface between two media having different refractive indices. (It also occurs when viewing opaque materials such as metal or paper.)

All materials become fully reflective at the shallowest grazing angle. (Read more in [Wloka2], [Fosner].)

An efficient but approximated formula is given by Schlick [Schlick]. It is accurate to within 1%:

$$F = f_\lambda + \left(1 - f_\lambda\right)\left(1 - \mathbf{N} \cdot \mathbf{V}\right)^5$$

The f_γ is the Fresnel reflectance index (spectral distribution) of the material at normal incidence, **V** points to the eye, and **N** is the normal. Please note that using these vectors excludes the light direction from the calculation of the Fresnel term. This is an acceptable approximation for outdoor games, but it would fail in indoor games, in which light sources that have a position and attenuation are most often used.

 Using the angle between the view and the normal for the Fresnel factor is correct for environment mapping, but when used in the context of a microfacet model, the angle between the view and the half-angle vector should be used. Because this would make it more difficult to factorize the whole Cook-Torrance model and store it in a texture, we use **N·V** *here.*

Figure 12.9 shows several different quantities for the specular reflectance at normal incidence.

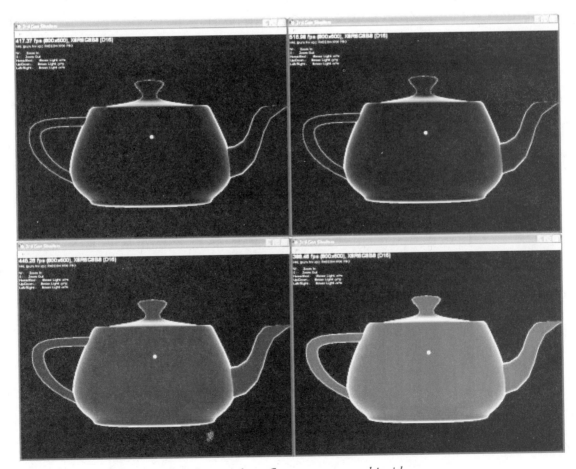

FIGURE 12.9 *Different values for specular reflectance at normal incidence.*

The upper-left screenshot shows a specular reflectance at normal incidence of 0.0001, the upper-right screenshot of 0.01, the lower-left screenshot of 0.1, and the lower-right index of 0.2.

The Fresnel term can be implemented with the following pseudocode.

```
float F = RI  +  (1 - RI) * pow((1 - N.V), 5.0f);
```

Let's summarize what we have learned so far. The Cook-Torrance reflectance model treats a surface as being composed of planar microscopic facets called microfacets. Each microfacet is treated as a perfect reflector that obeys the reflective laws of electromagnetic theory. The roughness of a surface is characterized by the slopes of the microfacets.

So far, we have discussed all necessary main components of the specular term of the Cook-Torrance reflection model. We now need to examine how Cook-Torrance set up the specular reflection model.

Putting It All Together: Cook-Torrance Reflection Formula

The following equation symbolizes the specular term of the Cook-Torrance reflection model.

$$R_s = \frac{F\lambda}{\pi} \frac{DG}{(\mathbf{N}\cdot\mathbf{V})(\mathbf{N}\cdot\mathbf{L})}$$

D is the microfacet distribution function, which returns the fraction of microfacets oriented in a given direction. G is the geometrical attenuation factor, which accounts for self-shadowing of the microfacets. f_γ is the Fresnel term, which describes the amount of light reflected as a function of the angle of incidence.

The π appearing in the denominator of the previous equation is a normalization factor (read more in [Lengyel]). $\mathbf{N}\cdot\mathbf{V}$ makes the equation proportional to the surface area (and hence the number of microfacets) that the viewer sees in a unit piece of foreshortened surface area, whereas $\mathbf{N}\cdot\mathbf{L}$ makes the equation proportional to the surface area that the light sees in a unit piece of foreshortened surface area.

The specular component shown earlier is embedded in the following formula that describes the Cook-Torrance reflectance model.

$$L_I = R_a L_{ia} + \sum \ell L_{i\ell} \left(\mathbf{N}\cdot\mathbf{L}_\ell\right) d\omega_{i\ell} \left(sR_s + dR_d\right)$$

The first part of the formula represents the ambient component, the second part accounts for light sources with different intensities and different projected areas, and the final part represents the specular (sR_s) and diffuse (sR_d) reflectance.

In the second part of the equation, $d\omega$ is the unit solid angle. As shown in Figure 12.10, it is measured in terms of the area on a sphere intercepted by a cone whose apex is the sphere's center.

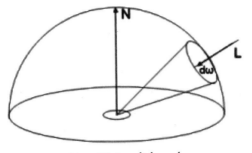

FIGURE 12.10   *Unit solid angle.*

Solid angles are measured in steradians (sr). The solid angle is the concept of a two-dimensional angle extended to three dimensions. In two dimensions, an angle of 2π radians covers the whole unit circle. Extending this to three dimensions, a solid angle of 4π steradians would cover the whole area of a unit sphere.

In this case, $\mathbf{N}\cdot\mathbf{L}$ represents the angle of illumination of the light beam, whereas it represented the diffuse reflection in the Lambertian lighting models shown in the previous part of the book. For example, an illuminating beam with the same intensity L_i (in Part II we used the I for intensity) and angle of illumination ($\mathbf{N}\cdot\mathbf{L}$) as another beam, but with twice the solid angle ($d\omega_i$) of that beam, will make a surface appear twice as bright. An illuminating beam with twice the intensity of another beam, but with the same angle of illumination and solid angle, will also make a surface appear twice as bright.

The implementation of the Cook-Torrance reflectance model with one light can be prototyped with the following pseudo-code.

$$L_I = A_{\text{intensity}} \times A_{\text{color}} + L_i\left(\mathbf{N}\cdot\mathbf{L}\right)dw \times \left(D_{\text{intensity}} \times D_{\text{color}} \times \mathbf{N}\cdot\mathbf{L} + S_{\text{intensity}} \times S_{\text{color}} \times R_s\right)$$

The specular term Rs consists of the result of the previous section and is multiplied with a specular intensity constant and a specular color constant.

Please note that implementing a more sophisticated ambient lighting model and/or a more sophisticated diffuse lighting model might improve the overall visual experience even more.

Implementation

The following implementation of the Cook-Torrance reflectance model in a pixel shader is done in the same order as described in the previous text. The implementation starts with the distribution function, calculates the geometric attenuation factor, and then calculates the Fresnel term.

```
float4 PS(  float3 Normal : TEXCOORD0,
            float4 Light : TEXCOORD1,
            float3 View : TEXCOORD2,
            float3 Half : TEXCOORD3) : COLOR
{
  const float PI = 3.1415926535;
  const float m = 0.2f;              // roughness
  const float RI = 0.01f;            // Fresnel reflection index

  const float Si = 0.3f;             // specular intensity
  const float Di = 0.7f;             // diffuse intenstiy
  const float Ai = 0.1f;             // ambient intensity
  const float dw = 1.5f;             // unit solid angle

  // copper-like color RGB(184, 115, 51)
  const float4 C = {1/256.0f * 184.0f, 1/256.0f * 115.0f, \
                    1/256 * 51.0f, 1.0f};

  float3 N = normalize(Normal);
  float3 L = normalize(Light.xyz);
  float3 V = normalize(View);
  float3 H = normalize(Half);

  float NH = saturate(dot(N, H));
  float VH = saturate(dot(V, H));
  float NV = saturate(dot(N, V));
  float NL = saturate(dot(L, N));

  // Compute Beckmann's distribution function
  //                    -[(1 - N.H^2) / m^2 * (N.H)^2]
  // D =      1        e^
  //      m^2 N.H^4
  // ß is the angle between N and H
  // m is the root-mean-square slope of the microfacets
  float NH2 = NH * NH;
  float m2 = m * m;
  float D = (1 / m2 * NH2 * NH2) *
          (exp(-((1 - NH2) / (m2 * NH2))));

  // Compute self shadowing term
  // G = min(1, 2 * N.H * N.L, 2 * N.H * N.V)
  //               V.H           V.H
  float G = min(1.0f, min((2 * NH * NL) / VH, (2 * NH * NV) / VH));

  // Compute Fresnel term (Schlick's approximation)
  // F = IR + (1-IR)*(1 - (N.V))^5
  // IR + (1 - N.V)^5 * (1 - IR)
  float F = RI  +  (1 - RI) * pow((1 - NV), 5.0f);
```

```
// Compute final Cook-Torrance specular term
// Rs = (F * D * G) * 1 / PI * N.V * N.L
float S = (F * D * G) / (PI * NL * NV);

// Original: Ir = Ai * Ac + Ii(N.L)dw * (Si * Sc + Di * Dc * N.L)
// My formula: Ir = Ia * C + N.L * sat(dw * (Di * C * N.L +
//                  Si * Rs))
return Ai * C + (NL * saturate(dw * ((Di * NL * C) + (Si * S))))\
       * Light.w;
}
```

The formula in the return statement is modified slightly by adding a saturate modifier. The intensity of the light beam is covered by the attenuation value in Light.w.

Factorizing the Cook-Torrance Model

It turns out that most lighting models in computer graphics can be factored into independent components that only depend on one or two angles [Heidrich]. Factorizating the Cook-Torrance model and storing the components in one or more textures is shown in the following section. To enable viewing the textures resulting from the following functions, the textures are stored in files with the D3DXSaveTextureToFile() function.

Beckmann Distribution Function

The microfacet distribution function, which defines the percentage of facets oriented in the direction *H*, depends on the angle between *H* and *N* and a roughness parameter. This is true for a wide variety of distribution functions. Providing these two parameters to a function that creates a lookup texture for the microfacet distribution function is shown here.

```
VOID WINAPI Beckmann (D3DXVECTOR4* pOut, const D3DXVECTOR2*
pTexCoord,
                      const D3DXVECTOR2* pTexelSize, LPVOID pData)
{
    /*
    *                              -[(1 - N.H^2) / (m^2 * (N.H)^2)]
    * D =      1               e^
    *       m^2 * N.H^2 * N.H^2
    */
    #define PI 3.141592653f

    float NH2 = pTexCoord->x *pTexCoord->x;
    float m2 = pTexCoord->y * pTexCoord->y;
    float D = (1.0f / m2 * NH2 * NH2) * (exp(-((1.0f - NH2) / (m2 *
NH2)))));
    pOut->x = D;
}
```

Although floating-point textures are available, it is still challenging to store values in textures, because floating-point textures are only filtered on the latest hardware (at the time of this writing the floating-point format `D3DFMT_A16B16G16R16F` on a GeForce 6800). To get bilinear filtering on a wide range of graphics cards, this example uses an L16 texture of size 512×512.

After fetching the textures in the HLSL shader, the resulting value is multiplied by 5.0f to account for the reduced precision of the texture format.

 To prevent precision, the values could be stored in the texture as the `log2` value and recreated in the shader with an `exp2` function.

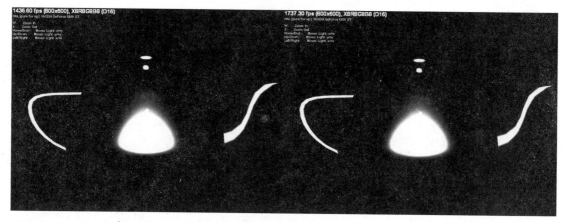

FIGURE 12.11   *Left: Beckmann/right: Beckmann factorized.*

On the left of Figure 12.11, you can see a screenshot of the example program with the distribution function calculated in the pixel shader, and on the right you see the screenshot of the example program using the result of a texture that holds the distribution function.

Using a roughness term that is constant for a given surface, we end up with a univariate function $D(\mathbf{N} \cdot \mathbf{H})$.

The Geometrical Attenuation Factor

The geometrical attenuation factor, which represents the masking and shadowing effects of the microfacets, uses four different parameters in the formula used in this chapter so far. By trading off visual quality, we can simplify this to the following equation.

```
float G = min(1.0f, 2.0f * N.H);
```

The screenshots in Figure 12.12 show how the simplified GAF looks.

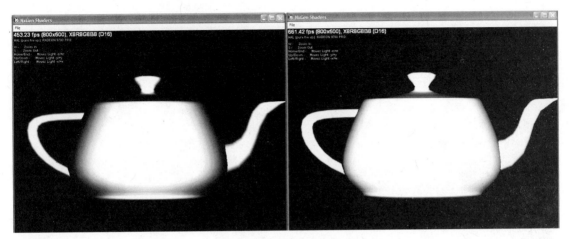

FIGURE 12.12 *Left: Cook-Torrance GAF/right: simplified GAF.*

The screenshot on the right shows that the simplified GAF is not distributed as evenly as the original version, but this version only takes two assembly instructions, so it does not make sense to store it in its own texture.

The Fresnel Term

The Fresnel term, which is the reflection of a portion of incident light at a discrete interface between two media having different refractive indices, is a bivariate function, by depending on the angle between **N** and **V** and the refraction index as parameters. These two parameters can be provided to a function that creates a lookup texture for the Fresnel term, as shown here.

```
VOID WINAPI Fresnel (D3DXVECTOR4* pOut, const D3DXVECTOR2*
pTexCoord,
                     const D3DXVECTOR2* pTexelSize, LPVOID pData)
    {
    //─────────────────
    // Compute Fresnel term (Schlick's approximation)
    // float F = RI + (1 - RI) * pow((1 - NV), 5.0f);
    //─────────────────
    float NV = pTexCoord->x;
    float RI = pTexCoord->y;
    pOut->x = RI + (1 - RI) * (FLOAT)pow((1 - NV), 5.0f) / 10.0f;
    }
```

Storing this Fresnel term in an L16 texture leads to precision losses. Multiplying the result from the texture map in the shader by 5.0f accounts for these losses, as shown in Figure 12.13.

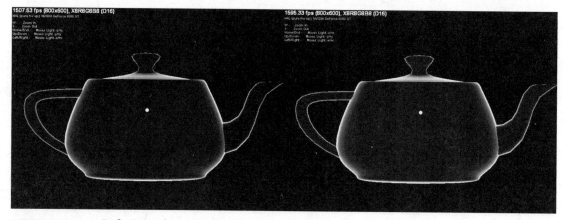

FIGURE 12.13   *Left: Fresnel term/right: Fresnel term factorized.*

The screenshot on the right shows the approach that stores the Fresnel term in an 8×8 texture. Please note that by using a reflection index that is constant for a given surface, we can end up with a univariate function $F(\mathbf{N} \cdot \mathbf{V})$.

Putting all this together leads to a nice lighting effect that needs substantially fewer instruction slots. We can go a step further and put everything in one texture.

One Texture for Everything

The whole specular term as shown in the previous section can be stored in one texture. This assumes that the same refraction index and the same roughness value m are used all the time. In this case, the distribution function and the Fresnel term only expect one parameter each.

```
VOID WINAPI CookTorrance (D3DXVECTOR4* pOut, const D3DXVECTOR2*
pTexCoord,
    const D3DXVECTOR2* pTexelSize, LPVOID pData)
{
    #define PI 3.1415926535897

    float NH = pTexCoord->x;
    float NH2 = NH * NH;
    const float m2 = 0.2f * 0.2f;
    float D = (1.0f / m2 * NH2 * NH2) * ((FLOAT)exp(-((1.0f - NH2) /
(m2 * NH2))));
```

```
        // float F = RI  +  (1 - RI) * pow((1 - NV), 5.0f);
        float NV = pTexCoord->y;
        const float RI = 0.01f;
        float F = RI  +  (1 - RI) * (FLOAT)pow((1 - NV), 5.0f);

        float G = min(1.0f, 2.0f * NH);

        // specular term without NL
        float S = (D * F * G) / (PI * NV);
        pOut->x = S;
    }
```

The texture creation function follows exactly the approach we have taken in the last section, where we separated the distribution function and the Fresnel term into different textures. It also incorporates the geometric attenuation function into the texture and stores nearly all the other calculations. The HLSL code for this function is shown here.

```
    float4 PS( float3 Normal : TEXCOORD0,
               float4 Light : TEXCOORD1,
               float3 View : TEXCOORD2,
               float3 Half : TEXCOORD3) : COLOR
{
   // specular intensity
   const float Si = 0.3f;
   const float Di = 0.7f; // diffuse intenstiy
   const float Ai = 0.1f; // ambient intensity
   const float dw = 3.0f; // unit solid angle

   // copper-like color RGB(184, 115, 51)
   const float4 C = {1/256.0f * 184.0f, 1/256.0f * 115.0f, 1/256 *
51.0f, 1.0f};

   float3 N = normalize(Normal);
   float3 L = normalize(Light.xyz);
   float3 V = normalize(View);
   float3 H = normalize(Half);

   float NH = saturate(dot(N, H));
   float NV = saturate(dot(N, V));
   float NL = saturate(dot(L, N));

   //...
   float2 Tex = float2(NH, NV);
   float DFGThroughPINV = tex2D(CookTorranceMapSampler, Tex) *
5.0f;

   //...
   float S = DFGThroughPINV / NL;

   //...
   return Ai * C + (NL * saturate(dw * ((Di * NL * C) + (Si * S)))) *
Light.w;
   }
```

Because this example uses the simplified geometric attenuation factor, $\mathbf{V} \cdot \mathbf{H}$ is not used here. Therefore we can save one dot product.

To further reduce the number of instructions, $\mathbf{N} \cdot \mathbf{L}$ can also be integrated into the texture by using an L16 32×32×32 volume texture. Together with hardware bilinear filtering support, this improves the visual appearance on graphics hardware that supports volume textures. Only slight changes are necessary to add $\mathbf{N} \cdot \mathbf{L}$ to the function that creates the look-up texture. In the HLSL code the texture is sampled with `tex3d()` and $\mathbf{N} \cdot \mathbf{L}$ is passed as an additional texture coordinate.

Further simplifying this source code might lead to an approach that runs on ps_1_1 or ps_1_4 hardware.

Storing D and F in non-floating point textures with 8-bit precision on pre-ps_2_0 hardware can be realized by storing the range [0..1] in the red channel, subtracting by one and storing the remainder in the range [1..2] in the green channel, subtracting by one and storing the range [2..3] in the blue channel and the remainder [3..4] in the alpha channel. The original value can be restored in the pixel shader with three add instructions.

add r2.r, r2.r, r2.g   // R + G
add r2.r, r2.r, r2.b   // R + G + B
add r2.r, r2.r, r2.a   // R + G + B + A

A value range of [0..6] can be used on pre-ps_2_0 hardware by storing the range [0..1] in the red channel, subtracting one and storing the remainder in the range [1..2] in the green channel, subtracting by two and storing the remainder in the range [2..4] in the blue channel and after another subtraction of two, storing the remainder in the alpha channel [4..6]. The original value can be restored in the pixel shader with three add instructions.

add r2.r, r2.r, r2.g   // R + G
add r2.r, r2.r, r2.b_x2   // R + G + B_x2
add r2.r, r2.r, r2.a_x2   // R + G + B_x2 + A_x2

Results

This chapter is accompanied by seven example programs, which can be found in the directory Chapter 12 - Cook-Torrance. The names of the examples in the directory are as follows:

- Cook-Torrance shows a pure implementation in the pixel shader. This implementation does not use any lookup textures and strives for the highest quality.
- Cook-Torrance Lookup Table shows an implementation with two textures that store Beckmann's distribution function and the Fresnel term in a 2D texture. This implementation uses the same geometric attenuation factor as the first example.

- Cook-Torrance Lookup Table One Texture uses one texture to store Beckmann's distribution function, the Fresnel term, and a simplified geometric attenuation factor.
- Cook-Torrance Lookup Table One Volume Texture stores everything in a volume texture and expects $N \cdot H$, $N \cdot V$, and $N \cdot L$ as parameters.

Overall, we end up with four different approaches.

1. Everything is implemented in the pixel shader.
2. Beckmann distribution function is in one 2D texture and Fresnel term is in one 2D texture.
3. Beckmann distribution function, the Fresnel term, and a simplified GAF together with a simplified specular term are in one 2D texture.
4. Beckmann distribution function, the Fresnel term, a simplified GAF, and the complete specular term are in one 3D texture.

The following figure shows screenshots of each approach.

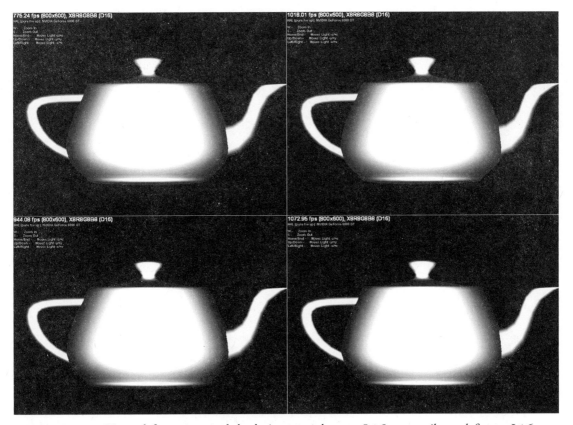

FIGURE 12.14 *Upper left: native pixel shader/upper right: two L16 textures/lower left: one L16 texture/lower right: one volume texture*

Upper left shows approach 1, upper right shows approach 2, lower left shows approach 3, and lower right shows approach 4. The native pixel shader implementation has a nice ring of orange/yellow tones around the highlight. The factorized implementations do look quite good even if the light source is moved, the results are comparable. Performance is getting better from 1–4, although volume textures might invalidate the texture cache system of the graphics card, giving performance different from what is expected in a larger application.

Conclusion

This chapter showed some of the cornerstones of modern lighting algorithms developed since the early 80s. These fundamental features are:

- Microfacet surface simulated by a distribution function
- Geometric attenuation factor used to simulate shadowing and masking of light beams
- Fresnel term to simulate materials with two media with different refraction indices

13 | Oren-Nayar Reflection

Michael Oren and Shree K. Nayar [Oren] published a reflectance model in 1992 that enhances the standard Lambertian model, which only considers surfaces as smooth diffuse surfaces, by accounting for surface roughness.

Rough surfaces—such as sandpaper, plaster, clay, sand, and clothes—exhibit much more of a backscattering effect, particularly when the light source direction is near to the view direction.

If the full moon followed the Lambertian distribution, the edges of the moon would be in near darkness. In fact, the edges look as bright as the center of the moon. This is because the moon's surface is made of a jumble of dust and rock with diffuse reflecting surfaces at all angles. Thus, the number of the reflecting surfaces is uniform for any orientation of the surface; hence, no matter the orientation of the surface to the viewer, the amount of light reflecting off the surface is nearly the same.

Background

The Oren-Nayar reflection model is based on the following techniques.

- To describe direction, Oren-Nayar use spherical coordinates.
- A microfacet model for surface roughness, based on the Torrance-Sparrow Model from 1967 [Torrance]. The distribution of the microfacet slope is done in an early implementation of the model by the Gaussian distribution function.
- A geometric attenuation factor for complex geometrical effects such as self-shadowing, masking, and compared to the Cook-Torrance model, additional interreflections of the microfacets.

Let's start by examining spherical coordinates.

Spherical Coordinates

Since lighting equations are more about directions than positions, it is often better to describe a vector not in Cartesian coordinates like $V = (V_x, V_y, V_z)$ but with a pair of angles θ (polar or elevation; small greek theta), Φ (azimuth, big greek phi), and the length of the vector. Figure 13.1 shows a sphercial coordinate system.

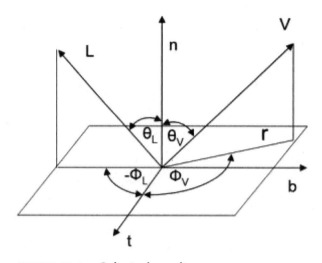

FIGURE 13.1   *Spherical coordinates.*

To locate a point with spherical coordinates, you need two angles and the distance from the origin of the system. The polar angle is taken relative to the normal vector *n* and the azimuth angle is taken relative to the tangent vector *t*. Spherical coordinates are described by (*r*, θ, Φ), but because we use unit vectors, we can ignore the distance parameter *r*. The polar angle θ lies in the range $0 \leq \theta \leq \pi$, and Φ takes values in the range $0 \leq \phi \leq 2\pi$ 0.

This way the direction of **V** can be described as $V(\theta_V, \phi_V)$.

To convert the spherical coordinates to 3D Cartesian coordinates (*x*, *y*, *z*), we will project **V** onto the t-b plane. That leads to the vector *r*. As shown in Figure 13.2, *r* can be described in the plane *t-b* with its length and Φ.

To solve for *r*, we use the following trigonometric function:

$$\sin\theta = \frac{r}{V}$$

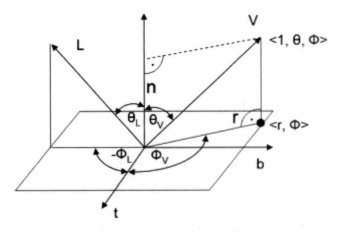

FIGURE 13.2   *Projecting V on the t-b plane.*

Because **V** is a unit vector, we can simplify to

$$r = \sin\theta$$

To solve for *n*, we use the following trigonometric function:

$$\cos\theta = \frac{n}{V}$$
$$n = V \times \cos\theta$$
$$n = \cos\theta$$

In the *t-b* plane, we know that:

$$t = r \times \cos\phi$$
$$b = r \times \sin\phi$$

Plugging *r* into these equations leads to

$$t = \sin\theta \times \cos\phi$$
$$b = \sin\theta \times \sin\phi$$
$$n = \cos\theta$$

This equation converts from spherical to Cartesian coordinates.

Microfacet Model

Similar to the Cook-Torrance reflection model shown in the previous chapter, the starting point for the development of the Oren-Nayar model was the geometric description of a surface developed by K.E. Torrance and E.M. Sparrow. Torrance-Sparrow assumed that a surface is composed of many small V-shaped grooves, which are lined with flat mirrors called microfacets. They assumed that the surface consists of specularly reflecting V-cavities of infinite length and that the upper edges of each V-cavity lie in the same plane. Additionally, in the Cook-Torrance model we assumed that all facets have the same slope and that they are uniformly distributed in orientation on the surface plane (in other words, they are oriented perpendicular to the surface plane), whereas Oren-Nayar extended this model to arbitrarily shaped V-cavities. They assume that each facet area *da* is small compared to the area *dA* of the surface patch that is imaged by a single pixel, as shown in Figure 13.3. Hence, each pixel includes a very large number of facets.

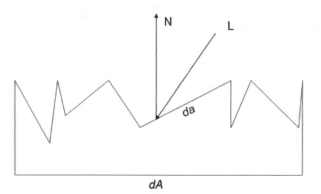

FIGURE 13.3   *V-cavities in the Oren-Nayar reflection model.*

The Microfacet Distribution Function/Geometric Attenuation Factor

To be able to model Lambertian rough surfaces with interreflection, the Oren-Nayar model includes a variety of different facet slopes. In the first incarnation of the Oren-Nayar model, the distribution of the slope areas was done by the Gaussian distribution function with zero mean and standard deviation σ to describe the roughness of the surface. If σ is zero, all facet normals are aligned with a surface normal. The greater σ is, the deeper the cavities are.

$$D = C \times e^{-\theta^2/\sigma^2}$$

C is the normalization constant and θ is the polar angle of the facet normal with respect to the surface patch normal. The overall brightness of a surface patch is the sum of the intensities of all its facets. This includes masked facets, shadowed facets, and some facets that are lit by the reflection from others.

Because this approach was not usable on the hardware of its time and even on today's hardware, Oren and Nayar simplified their model by comparing it to actual data and reducing it to the terms that had the most significant impact. They ended up with the following formula:

$$I = P \times E_o \times \cos(\theta_L) \times \left(A + B \times \max\left(0, \cos(\phi_V - \phi_L)\right) \times \sin(\alpha) \times \tan(\beta)\right)$$

P/π is a surface reflectivity property, which we can replace with our surface diffuse color (in the following example, the color of the texture) and E_0 is a light input energy term, which we can replace with our light diffuse color (in the following example, white). $\cos(\theta_L)$ equals $\mathbf{N} \cdot \mathbf{L}$ and will be replaced by this term.

A, B, σ, and β are described with the following equations.

$$A = 1 - 0.5 \times \sigma^2 / \sigma^2 + 0.33$$
$$B = 0.45 \times \sigma^2 / \sigma^2 + 0.09$$
$$\alpha = \min(\theta_L, \theta_V)$$
$$\beta = \max(\theta_L, \theta_V)$$

σ is the surface roughness parameter. It's the standard deviation in radians of the angle of distribution (root-mean-square slope) of the microfacets in the surface roughness model. The larger the value, the rougher the surface.

θ_V is the angle between the vertex normal and the view direction.

θ_L is the angle between the vertex normal and the light direction.

$\Phi_V - \Phi_L$ is the circular angle (about the vertex normal) between the light vector and the view vector.

Note that if the roughness value is zero, the model is the same as the Lambertian diffuse model. Oren and Nayar also note that you can replace the value 0.33 in coefficient A with 0.57 to better account for surface reflection.

Implementation

The part of the formula between B and sin is named C in the following HLSL code, and the part that includes the sin and tan, named *sintan*, is fetched from a lookup texture map named SinTanSamp.

```
float4 PS(float2 Tex: TEXCOORD0, float3 Light : TEXCOORD1, float3
View : TEXCOORD2) : COLOR
    {
```

```
float4 Color = tex2D(ColorMapSampler, Tex); // fetch color map
float4 N = tex2D(BumpMapSampler, Tex);      // bump map
float3 N_bx2 = 2 * N.xyz - 1.0f;

float3 L = normalize(Light);
float3 V = normalize(View);
float NL = dot(L, N_bx2);
float VN = dot(V, N_bx2);

// fetch texture with sin(alpha) * tan(alpha)
float sintan = tex2D( SinTanSamp, float2(saturate(NL), satu-
rate(VN))).x;

float3 LProjected = normalize(L - NL * N_bx2);
float3 VProjected = normalize(V - VN * N_bx2);
float C = saturate(dot(LProjected, VProjected));

// A in Color.w and B in N.w
return Color * saturate((NL * (Color.w + N.w * C * sintan)));
}
```

The variable sintan holds the $\sin(\alpha) \times \tan(\beta)$ of the previous equation. It is stored in a lookup texture that is created with the following callback function.

```
VOID WINAPI SinTan (D3DXVECTOR4* pOut, CONST D3DXVECTOR2*
pTexCoord,
   CONST D3DXVECTOR2* pTexelSize, LPVOID pData)
   {
     UNREFERENCED_PARAMETER( pTexelSize );
     UNREFERENCED_PARAMETER( pData );

     FLOAT NL = pTexCoord->x;
     FLOAT VN = pTexCoord->y;
     FLOAT min = ((NL < VN) ? NL : VN);
     FLOAT max = ((NL < VN) ? VN : NL);

     pOut->x = sinf(acosf(min)) * tanf(acosf(max));
   }
```

Depending on which value is smaller, the sinf() function receives the return value of the acosf() function from $N \cdot L$ or $N \cdot V$ and the tanf() function receives the return value of the arccosine of the bigger value. To store the values with minimum loss, a 512×512 R16F texture is used.

To solve for

$$C = \max\left(0, \cos\left(\phi_V - \phi_L\right)\right)$$

we project L and V into the $t\text{-}b$ plane in the previous HLSL code.

$$L' = L - NL \times N$$
$$V' = V - VN \times N$$

The resulting vectors $\mathbf{L'}$ and $\mathbf{V'}$ are normalized and can therefore be described with Φ_V and Φ_L. Subtracting these azimuth angles from each other and taking the cosine is equal to a dot product between the projected light and the projected view vector.

The same $\mathbf{A}$ and $\mathbf{B}$ values can be used for the whole model and therefore stored as constants. One of the example programs allows you to change this value with the Q and W keys. Alternatively, these values can be stored per-pixel in the alpha channels of two textures. This is shown in the example programs that implement the Oren-Nayar reflection model together with bump mapping.

The example program that creates these maps gets input from a color map with the roughness value in the alpha component and from a bump map with an empty alpha value. It uses the roughness value to compute $\mathbf{A}$ and $\mathbf{B}$ and stores these values in the alpha channel of the color map and the alpha channel of the bump map. This pro-gram can be found in Chapter 13 - Oren-Nayar\Oren-Nayar Create A and B value in

ON THE CD color and bump map.

Results

ON THE CD This chapter is accompanied by three example programs, which can be found in the directory Chapter 13 - Oren-Nayar. The names of the examples in the directory are as follows:

- The example in the directory Oren-Nayar Compare is shown in Figure 13.4. It allows the roughness value for the whole model to be changed interactively.
- A screenshot of the example in the directory Oren-Nayar Bump Mapping is shown in Figure 13.5. This covers an Oren-Nayar reflection model together with bump mapping, where the $\mathbf{A}$ value is stored in the color map and the $\mathbf{B}$ value is stored in the normal map.
- A utility example program is provided in directory Oren-Nayar Create A and B value in color and bump map. It can be used to store the $\mathbf{A}$ and $\mathbf{B}$ values in the alpha channels of the color and normal map. This is done with a color map that holds the sigma values provided by an artist. These sigma values are used to create the $\mathbf{A}$ and $\mathbf{B}$ values for each pixel.

Screenshots

The screenshot in Figure 13.4 shows the Oren-Nayar reflection model with a sigma value of 1.0 on the left side and with a sigma value of 0 on the right side. The latter is therefore reduced to a diffuse reflection model following Lambert's law.

The following screenshot (Figure 13.5) shows the Oren-Nayar reflection model together with bump mapping. The A and B values are stored in the alpha channel of the color and the normal map.

Comparing this screenshot to the screenshots of the bump mapping example pro-grams highlights the visual effect of being able to set different roughness values per pixel.

FIGURE 13.4 *Left Oren-Nayar/right: diffuse based on Lambert's law.*

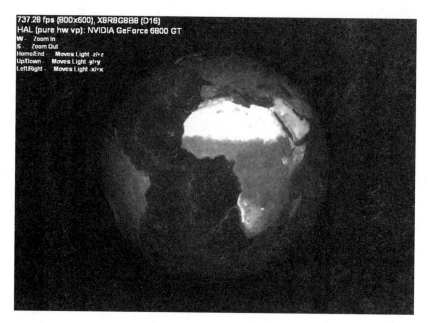

FIGURE 13.5 *Oren-Nayar and bump mapping.*

Roughness Map

By painting values into the alpha channel of the color map, the artist can influence the appearance of the reflection effect directly.

The top half of Figure 13.6 shows the RGB values of the color map, and the bottom half shows the alpha map, which holds the roughness value.

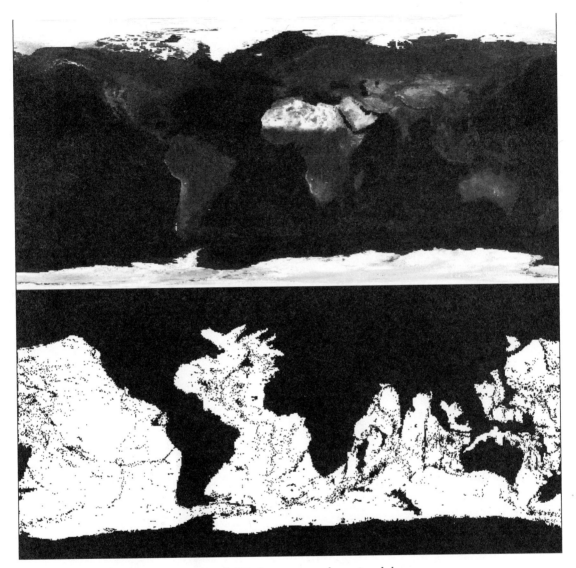

FIGURE 13.6 *Roughness map—top: RGB, bottom: roughness in alpha.*

Conclusion

This chapter showed a reflection model, in which lights have a position in space but do not account for the position of the viewer. Therefore, this model can be used to replace the diffuse lighting model based on Lambert's law. Compared to this model, it is much better at representing rough surfaces. Implementing the roughness value on a per-pixel basis, steered by a sigma value that is painted by the artist into the color map, gives good results. This might be used, for example, to simulate the fair wear and tear of objects.

14 Ward Reflection Model

All the reflection models discussed so far mimic an isotropic surface. For any given point on an isotropic surface, the light reflected does not change when the surface is rotated about the normal. In other words, the function that describes the reflection model is invariant under a rotation about the normal vector N. As long as the angle between the direction of the viewer V and the direction to light L remains constant, and the angle between each of these vectors and the normal vector remains constant, the distribution of microfacets also remains constant.

However, many surfaces such as brushed metal, hair, and certain fabrics possess different degrees of roughness in different directions. These surfaces are called anisotropic reflectors. This chapter will cover a simple anisotropic model, developed by Gregory J. Ward and presented at SIGGRAPH 1992 in his paper "Measuring and Modeling Anisotropic Reflection." It is an accurate, easy to use anisotropic reflection model. It was his goal to find the "simplest empirical formula that will do the job . . ." [Ward].

Background

Ward developed a model with physically meaningful parameters without adding undue complexity. Therefore, he did not use a geometric attenuation factor nor the Fresnel term. He asserts that these terms are difficult to integrate and tend to cancel each other out, and they may be reasonably replaced with a single term that will normalize the function. He started with an isotropic reflection model (equation 4 in [Ward]). His general BRDF lighting equation is:

$$L = \rho_{bd} \times L_i \times \cos(\theta_i) \times dw_i$$

in which:

L_r: Reflected light intensity
ρ_{bd}: The BRDF
L_i: Incident light intensity
$\cos(\theta_i)$: Angle between the light and the surface patch normal
w_i: Incident light direction

Ward's BRDF is

$$\rho_{bd} = \frac{\rho_d}{\pi} + \rho_s \frac{1}{\sqrt{N \cdot L N \cdot V}} \frac{1}{4\pi m^2} e^{\frac{-[(1 - N \cdot H^2)]}{m^2 (N \cdot H)^2}}$$

in which:

- ps: The specular reflectance term
- m: The standard deviation (root-mean-square) of the surface slope

The normalization factor $1/4\pi \, m^2$, which replaces the geometric attenuation factor and the Fresnel term, is accurate as long as m is not much greater than 0.2, at which point the surface becomes mostly diffuse.

 Balancing the incoming and outgoing energy in a reflectance model is called normalization.

Ward extended this isotropic reflectance model to surfaces with two perpendicular (uncorrelated) slope distributions, *mx* and *my* (see equation 5a in [Ward] and also equation 6.72 in [Lengyel]).

$$\rho_{bd} = \frac{\rho_d}{\pi} + \rho_s \frac{1}{\sqrt{N \cdot L N \cdot V}} \frac{1}{4\pi_{mx} y_{my}{}^2} e^{\frac{(T \cdot \rho)^2}{m_x{}^2} + \frac{1 - (T \cdot \rho)^2}{m_y{}^2} \times \frac{(N \cdot H)^2 - 1}{(N \cdot H)^2}}$$

in which:

- ρ_d: The diffuse reflectance term
- ρ_s: The specular reflectance term
- m_x: The standard deviation of the surface slope in the x direction
- m_y: The standard deviation of the surface slope in the y direction

$\mathbf{T}$ is the tangent to the surface aligned to the direction in which the roughness is m_x, and $\mathbf{P}$ is the normalized projection vector $\mathbf{H}$ onto the tangent plane.

$$\mathbf{P} = \mathbf{H} - (\mathbf{N} \cdot \mathbf{H}) \times \mathbf{N} / \left\| \mathbf{H} - (\mathbf{N} \cdot \mathbf{H}) \times \mathbf{N} \right\|$$

The tangent vectors $\mathbf{T}$ and $\mathbf{P}$ in this case are whatever you want to supply. For instance, if you have a disk that has concentric grooves in its surface, align the tangents so they're perpendicular to the radial direction. These tangents may or may not be the same as the texture-aligned tangents.

Ward also developed a computationally convenient approximation (see equation 5b in [Ward]).

$$\rho_{bd} = \frac{\rho_d}{\pi} + \rho_s \frac{1}{\sqrt{\mathbf{N} \cdot \mathbf{L} \mathbf{N} \cdot \mathbf{V}}} \frac{1}{4\pi_{mx} y_{my}^2} exp \frac{\left(-2 \times \dfrac{\mathbf{H} \cdot \mathbf{t}^2}{m_x} + \dfrac{(\mathbf{H} \cdot \mathbf{L})^2}{m_y} \right)}{(1 + \mathbf{H} \cdot \mathbf{n})}$$

n, t, b is the local coordinate frame. t and b are two perpendicular tangent directions on the surface plane. They represent the grooves in the surface. The mx and my terms are the standard derivation of the slope (root-mean-square) in the t and b direction. They control the sharpness of the highlight (the smaller the sharper), and the ratio mx: my controls anisotropy.

As long as $p_d + p_s < 1$ and m_x, $m_y < 0.2$, this model has been shown to match measured data rather well.

The model considers scratches on the surface leading to different roughness (defined by m_x and m_y) when considering directions parallel or perpendicular to the scratches: the more m_x and m_y are different, the more anisotropy is created.

Implementation

The native approach and the approximated approach were implemented in a reference implementation in the pixel shader and in an optimized implementation with a lookup texture.

Reference Implementation

Here is the non-approximated implementation.

```
float4 PS(float4 Color : COLOR0,
          float3 Normal : TEXCOORD0,
          float3 Light : TEXCOORD1,
          float3 View    : TEXCOORD2,
          float3 Tangent : TEXCOORD4) : COLOR
{
  const float PI = 3.141592653f;
  const float mx = 0.5f; // standard derivation of the slope in the
T1 direction
  const float my = 0.1f; // standard derivation of the slope in the
T2 direction
  const float mx2 = mx * mx;
  const float my2 = my * my;

  const float Si = 0.7f;
  const float Di = 0.3f;

  float3 N = normalize(Normal);
  float3 L = normalize(Light);
  float3 T = normalize(Tangent);
  float3 V = normalize(View);
  float3 H = normalize(L + V);

  float NL = saturate(dot(L, N));
  float NV = saturate(dot(V, N));
  float NH = saturate(dot(H, N));
  float NH2 = NH * NH;

  float3 P = normalize(H - NH * N);
  float TP = dot(T,P);
  float TP2 = TP * TP;

  float E = exp (((TP2 / mx2) + ((1 - TP2) / my2)) * (NH2 - 1) /
                 NH2);

  return ((Di * Color * NL) / PI  + (Si * (((1 /  sqrt(NL * NV)) *
(1/(4 * PI * mx * my)))) * E)) * NL;
}
```

Please note that the **T** and **P** vectors are not saturated, because their value range is [-1.0...1.0]. To reduce the number of instructions necessary, you might do the following:

- Remove the `normalize()` intrinsics and therefore remove some visual quality.
- Use a cube normalization map as shown in the upcoming Chapter 16.
- Remove the term $\left(1/sqrt\left(\mathbf{NL}\times\mathbf{NV}\right)\right)$. This does not seem to lead to a visually remarkable loss.

The approximated implementation can be handled in a similar way.

```
float4 PS(float4 Color : COLOR0,
          float3 Normal : TEXCOORD0,
          float3 Light : TEXCOORD1,
          float3 View : TEXCOORD2,
          float3 Binormal : TEXCOORD3,
          float3 Tangent : TEXCOORD4) : COLOR
{
  const float PI =
3.14159265358979323846264338327950288419716939937510582097494459592f;
  const float mx = 0.3f; // standard derivation of the slope in the
T1 direction
  const float my = 0.05f; // standard derivation of the slope in
the T2 direction

  const float Si = 0.9f;
  const float Di = 0.1f;

  float3 N = normalize(Normal);
  float3 L = normalize(Light);
  float3 V = normalize(View);
  float3 H = normalize(L + V);
  float3 T = normalize(Tangent);
  float3 B = normalize(Binormal);

  float NL = saturate(dot(L, N));
  float NV = saturate(dot(V, N));
  float HN = saturate(dot(H, N));

  float HT1 = dot(H, T);
  float HT2 = dot(H, B);

  float E = exp (-2 * (((HT1 / mx) * (HT1 / mx) + (HT2 / my) * (HT2
/ my))/ (1 + HN)));

  return ((Di * Color * NL)/ PI + (Si * ((1 /  sqrt(NL * NV) * (1/
(4 * PI * mx * my))) * E))) * NL;
}
```

To optimize this shader, the same ideas covered in the non-approximated version of the Ward model can be used.

Both implementations can be improved by storing the exponent in a lookup texture.

One Texture for Everything

The exponent of both Ward models can be stored in a L16 2D texture. The following function shows how to create the lookup texture for the non-approximated version.

```
    VOID WINAPI Ward (D3DXVECTOR4* pOut, const D3DXVECTOR2*
pTexCoord,
                    const D3DXVECTOR2* pTexelSize, LPVOID pData)
    {
      UNREFERENCED_PARAMETER( pTexelSize );
      UNREFERENCED_PARAMETER( pData );

      const float PI = 3.141592653f;
      const float mx = 0.4f; // standard derivation of the slope in the
T1 direction
      const float my = 0.1f; // standard derivation of the slope in the
T2 direction
      const float mx2 = mx * mx;
      const float my2 = my * my;

      float NH = pTexCoord->x;
      float NH2 = NH * NH;
      float TP = 2.0f * pTexCoord->y - 1.0f;
      float TP2 = TP * TP;
      float S = exp (((TP2 / mx2) + ((1 - TP2) / my2)) * (NH2 - 1) /
NH2) * (1/(4 * PI * mx * my));
      pOut->x = S;
    }
```

This texture creation function creates a texture that stores nearly the whole specular term of the Ward reflection model, whereas the term (1 / sqrt(NL * NV)) was left out.

The advantage of the non-approximated equation over the approximated equation is that it only needs two parameters $\mathbf{T} \cdot \mathbf{P}$ and $\mathbf{N} \cdot \mathbf{H}$, whereas the approximated Ward formula needs to be stored in a volume texture because it needs three parameters.

```
    VOID WINAPI Ward (D3DXVECTOR4* pOut, const D3DXVECTOR3*
pTexCoord,

  const D3DXVECTOR3* pTexelSize, LPVOID pData)
    {
      UNREFERENCED_PARAMETER( pTexelSize );
      UNREFERENCED_PARAMETER( pData );
```

```
// standard derivation of the slope in the T1 direction
const float mx = 0.8f;
// standard derivation of the slope in the T2 direction
const float my = 0.1f;

float HT1 = 2.0f * pTexCoord->x - 1.0f;
float HT2 = 2.0f * pTexCoord->y - 1.0f;
float HN = pTexCoord->z;

// exp (-2 * ((H.T1 / mx)2 + (H.T2 / my)2) / (1 + H.N)))
float E = (float) exp (-2.0f * ((HT1 / mx) * (HT1 / mx) + (HT2 /
my) * (HT2 / my))/ (1 + HN));

pOut->x = E;
}
```

To further improve the performance of these implementations, I removed the vector renormalization code from the pixel shader wherever visually acceptable. As a result, the pixel shader now uses a similar number of instructions in each case.

Volume textures can have a negative effect on the texture cache system of modern graphics cards. This penalty can lead to a performance decrease in bigger applications. What seems to count at the end, while comparing the approximated with the non-approximated approach, is the use of a volume texture in the approximated approach. This gives the non-approximated approach an advantage.

Results

ON THE CD This chapter is accompanied by four example programs, which can be found in the directory Chapter 14 - Ward.

- In the directory Ward is the reference implementation of the non-approximated Ward reflectance model.
- In the directory Ward Lookup 2D Texture is the implementation that stores the exponent of the non-approximated Ward model in a 2D lookup texture.
- The reference implementation of the approximated Ward reflection model can be found in the directory Ward Approximated.
- The implementation that uses a 3D volume texture to store the exponent of the approximated Ward model can be found in the directory Ward Approximated Lookup Volume Texture.

The screenshots in Figure 14.1 show the non-approximated Ward reflection model with different values for *mx* and *my*.

Please note that if both values are bigger than 0.2, the reflectance gets weaker.

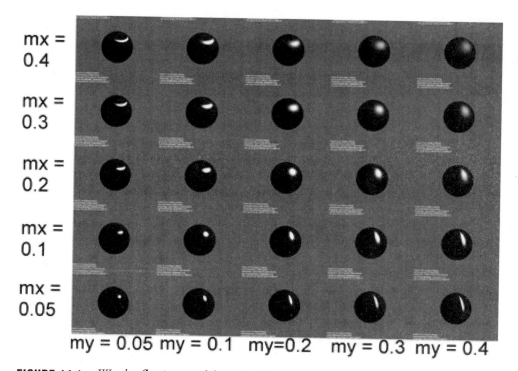

FIGURE 14.1 *Ward reflection model with different values for mx and my.*

Figure 14.2 shows the non-approximated reference implementation on the left and the optimized version with a texture lookup on the right. The distribution of the highlight is similar, although because we removed the term $(1\ /\ \text{sqrt}(NL\ *\ NV))$, distortions in the middle of the half moon-like reflection are visible with lower values. This should be acceptable when used in games.

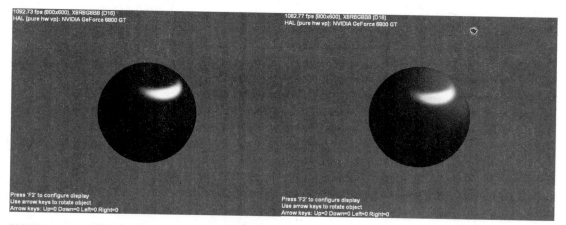

FIGURE 14.2 *Ward reflection model optimized.*

Conclusion

Although most available implementations of the Ward reflection model use the approximated Ward reflection model, the non-approximated version seems to be the better choice for real-time applications, because the exponent can be stored in a 2D lookup texture rather than in a 3D look-up texture, which is likely to give reduced performance.

15 Ashikhmin-Shirley Reflection Model

The goal of Michael Ashikhmin and Peter Shirley [Ashikhmin] was to make a Fresnel-weighted Phong-style model that is anisotropic, physically plausible, and has intuitive parameters. This chapter presents an analytical factorization developed by Mauro Steigleder and Michael McCool [Steigleder] of this model that is suitable for real-time implementations even on ps_1_1 capable graphics cards.

Background

Even though the Ashikhmin-Shirley model is based on the Blinn-Phong model shown in Chapter 6, it includes enhancements to take into account the Fresnel effect and the energy tradeoff between diffuse and specular reflections. The model is defined as a weighted sum of a diffuse term and a specular term.

$$\mathbf{L} = \mathbf{N} \cdot \mathbf{L}\left(k_d \times (1 - k_s) \times D_c + k_s \times S_c\right)$$

where D_c is the diffuse component, S_c is the specular component, k_d specifies the diffuse reflectance, and k_s specifies the specular reflectance at normal incidence. $\mathbf{N} \cdot \mathbf{L}$ is added here for self-shadowing. In other words, the intensity of the overall effect depends on the intensity of the diffuse light.

Diffuse Term

The diffuse term of the Ashikhmin-Shirley model is based on Schlick's approximation of the Fresnel factor. It is based on the assumption that directional diffuse reflectance is due to subsurface scattering, so that diffusely scattered light is subject to the Fresnel effect both going into the surface and coming out from it.

This term leads to a lower diffuse reflectivity at glancing angles, where the specular reflectivity dominates.

The diffuse term of the Ashikhmin-Shirley model is defined as

$$R_d = \frac{28k_d}{23\pi}\left(1-k_s\right)\left(1-\left(1-\frac{N \cdot V}{2}\right)^5\right)\times\left(1-\left(1-\frac{N \cdot L}{2}\right)^5\right)$$

Specular Term

The specular term is given by

$$R_s = \sqrt{\frac{\left(\left(m_x+1\right)\left(m_y+1\right)\right)}{8\pi}}\frac{N \cdot H^{\left(m_x \times t \cdot H^2 + m_y \times b \cdot H^2\right)/\left(1-H \cdot n^2\right)}}{H \cdot L \times \max\left(N \cdot V, N \cdot L\right)}\times F\left(H \cdot L\right)\times N \cdot L$$

Similar to the Ward reflection model shown in the previous chapter, the Ashikhmin-Shirley reflection model uses two perpendicular (uncorrelated) slope distributions, m_x and m_y. These slopes are the standard derivation of the slope in the direction of two perpendicular tangent directions on the surface plane named t and b. Ashikhmin and Shirley use the approximated Fresnel formula developed by Schlick [Schlick], which we have already used to implement the Cook-Torrance reflection model.

$$F = f_\lambda + \left(1-f_\lambda\right)\left(1-N \cdot V\right)^5$$

The f_λ is the Fresnel reflectance index (spectral distribution) of the material at normal incidence.

Implementation

To have a benchmark for a factorization of the model, we implement first a reference model that runs completely in the pixel shader without any accommodation to precision.

Reference Implementation

The reference implementation of the Ashikhmin-Shirley model tries to implement as precisely as possible the original formula by not sacrificing precision. To reduce the complexity of the specular component, we will divide it into three parts like this.

$$\mathbf{R}_s = \sqrt{\frac{\left((m_x+1)(m_y+1)\right)}{8\pi}}$$

$$\mathbf{N}\cdot\mathbf{H}^{\left(m_x\times T1\cdot H^2 + m_y\times T2\cdot H^2\right)/\left(1-N\cdot H^2\right)}$$

$$f_\lambda + (1-f\lambda)(1-\mathbf{H}\cdot\mathbf{L})^5$$

$$\max(\mathbf{N}\cdot\mathbf{V}, \mathbf{N}\cdot\mathbf{L})$$

The following pixel shader implements all these parts in ps_2_0 shader.

```
float4 PS(float4 Color    : COLOR0,
          float3 Normal   : TEXCOORD0,
          float3 Binormal : TEXCOORD1,
          float3 Tangent  : TEXCOORD2,
          float3 View     : TEXCOORD3,
          float3 Light    : TEXCOORD4) : COLOR0
{
   const float PI =
3.1415926535897932384626433832795028841971693993751105820974944592f;
   const float RI = 0.7f;

   float ks = 1.0f - kd;

   float3 N = normalize(Normal);
   float3 Bi = normalize(Binormal);
   float3 T = normalize(Tangent);
   float3 V = normalize(View);
   float3 L = normalize(Light);
   float3 H = normalize(L + V);

   float NV = saturate(dot(N, V));
   float NL = saturate(dot(N, L));
   float NH = saturate(dot(N, H));
   float HL = saturate(dot(H, L));
   float T1H = dot(Bi, H);
   float T2H = dot(T, H);

   // Calculate diffuse
   // Rd = 28 * kd (1 - ks) (1 - (1 - N.V)5) * (1 - (1 - N.L)5)
   //      23p                          2                    2
   float Rd = (28 /(23 * PI)) * (1 - pow(1 - (NV / 2), 5.0f)) * (1 -
           pow(1 - (NL / 2), 5.0f));

   // Calculate specular
   //                       B
   //   (mx * T1.H^2 + my * T2.H^2) / (1 - (H.N)^2)
   // N.H
   float B = (pow(NH,(mx * T1H * T1H + my * T2H * T2H) / (1 - NH *
           NH)));
```

```
//            F
//RI + (1 - RI)(1 - H.L)^5
//HL * max(NV, NL)
float F = (RI + (1 - RI) * pow(1 - HL, 5.0f)) / HL * max(NV, NL);

// A is a uniform value provided by the application
float Rs = A * B * F;

// Lr = N.L (kd * (1 - ks) * Dc + ks * Sc)
return NL * (kd * (1 - ks) * Rd + ks * Rs);
}
```

Part A of the specular component is sent as a uniform variable from the application to the pixel shader. Part B covers the power value of $\mathbf{N}\cdot\mathbf{H}$, and F follows Schlick's approximated Fresnel equation.

Factorized Implementation

The Ashikhmin-Shirley model is a weighted sum of a diffuse and a specular component. While factorizing this reflection model, it is helpful to differentiate between the diffuse and the specular components.

The diffuse term depends only on the two parameters $N.V$ and $N.L$ and can therefore be stored in a 2D texture directly. To prevent the reduction of the value range in the texture, the constant $28/23\pi$ is not included in the texture. The values stored in the texture are as follows.

$$\left(1-\left(\frac{1-\mathbf{N}\cdot\mathbf{V}}{2}\right)^{5}\right)\times\left(1-\left(\frac{1-\mathbf{N}\cdot\mathbf{L}}{2}\right)^{5}\right)$$

The following function stores the proper values in a 2D texture.

```
    VOID WINAPI Diffuse (D3DXVECTOR4* pOut, CONST D3DXVECTOR2*
pTexCoord,
                    CONST D3DXVECTOR2* pTexelSize, LPVOID pData)
  {
    FLOAT NV = pTexCoord->x;
    FLOAT NL = pTexCoord->y;

    FLOAT temp = 1 - powf(1 - NV/2, 5);
    FLOAT temp2 = 1 - powf(1 - NL/2, 5);

    pOut->x = (temp * temp2);
  }
```

The specular term can be decomposed into a product of three functions with two parameters. This allows us to store these factors in 2D texture maps and then combine the results during rendering.

$$R_s = \sqrt{\frac{\left((m_x+1)(m_y+1)\right)}{8\pi}}$$

$$N \cdot H^{\left(m_x \times T1 \cdot H^2 + m_y \times T2 \cdot H^2\right)/\left(1-N \cdot H^2\right)}$$

$$f_\lambda + \left(1-f\lambda\right)\left(1-H \cdot L\right)^5$$

$$\max\left(N \cdot V, N \cdot L\right)$$

Part A of the equation is a constant and occupies only one constant register. For the rest of the specular term, a factorization has been developed by Michael McCool and Mauro Steigleder [Steigleder] at the University of Waterloo. Taking advantage of the separability of the exponential in Part B of the equation, they divided this part into three factors:

$$N \cdot H^{\left(m_x \times T1 \cdot H^2\right)/\left(1-N \cdot H^2\right)} \times N \cdot H^{\left(m_y \times T2 \cdot H^2\right)/\left(1-N \cdot H^2\right)}$$

$$\frac{1}{\max\left(N \cdot V, N \cdot L\right)}$$

Adding F leads to the following equation.

$$N \cdot H^{\left(m_x \times T1 \cdot H^2\right)/\left(1-N \cdot H^2\right)} \times N \cdot H^{\left(m_y \times T2 \cdot H^2\right)/\left(1-N \cdot H^2\right)}$$

$$\frac{f_\lambda + \left(1-f_\lambda\right)\left(1-H \cdot L\right)^5}{\max\left(N \cdot V, N \cdot L\right)}$$

It is possible to store the first two factors in one texture named *Gs*, and the last factor in another texture, named *Gp*. McCool and Steigleder use the following formula to store part B of the equation above in *Gs*.

$$g_s(u,v) = u^{\frac{v^2}{1-u^2}}$$

where u is $N \cdot H$ and v is $m_x \times T1 \cdot H^2$ or $m_y \times T2 \cdot H^2$. In other words, this equation is used to store the exponents for both factorized parts of B in the 2D texture.

This implementation needs to account for some numerical limitations. Using $1 - u^2$ in the denominator can lead to a numerical singularity at $u == 1$. Another singular situation is as u -> 0, when the function tends toward a Dirac impulse.

Solving the first singularity can be done by finding an appropriate limit and replacing the evaluation of

$$g_s(u,v) = u^{\frac{v^2}{1-u^2}}$$

with

$$g_s(u,v) = e^{\frac{-v^2}{2}}$$

This is done by tracking the $\mathbf{N \cdot H}$ value and replacing the first equation by the second equation that does not use $\mathbf{N \cdot H}$ anymore, if $\mathbf{N \cdot H}$ approaches 1.0.

To remove the singularity as u -> 0, a small bias α to u can be added to avoid aliasing here. Additionally, it is useful to add in a scale factor so we need to represent only the "important" (where it varies rapidly) part of the function. Assuming a scale factor β, we can use $\beta(v - 0.5)$ instead of v in the definition of the function and make the corresponding change in the parameterization. With these changes, the modified function becomes

$$e^{\frac{-(\beta(v-0.5))^2}{2}} \; if \; u + \alpha \geq 1 \; otherwise \; gs(u,v) = (u+\alpha)^{\frac{(\beta(v-0.5))^2}{1-(u+\alpha)^2}}$$

Choosing 10-6 for α and 5 for β leads to good results. The function that stores this equation in a texture named *Gs* is as follows.

```
VOID WINAPI Gs (D3DXVECTOR4* pOut, CONST D3DXVECTOR2* pTexCoord,
                CONST D3DXVECTOR2* pTexelSize, LPVOID pData)
{
  // u = N.H
  // v = sqrt(mx) * T2H / 5.0f + 0.5f
  //     or
  // v = sqrt(my) * T1H / 5.0f + 0.5f
  FLOAT u = pTexCoord->x;
  FLOAT v = pTexCoord->y;
  FLOAT g;

  // limit:
  // (-5.0f * 5.0f * (v - 0.5f) * (v - 0.5f) / 2.0f)
  // e
  //
```

```
// Replacing v with the input value leads to
// (-5.0f * 5.0f * ((sqrt(mx) * T2H / 5.0f + 0.5f) - 0.5f) * \
//    ((sqrt(mx) * T2H / 5.0f + 0.5f) - 0.5f) / 2.0f)
// e
// To use this limit only in case the H.N raises to 1, a 1/256.0f
// is used as a soft clamp value.
// if u is bigger than 0.99609375
if(1.0f - 1.0f/256.0f > u)
{
  g = expf(-5.0f * 5.0f * ((v - 0.5f) * (v - 0.5f)) / 2.0f);
}
// else if u is smaller than 0.99609375
else
{
  g = powf(u, 5.0f * 5.0f * (v - 0.5f) * (v - 0.5f)/(1.0f - u *
      u));
}
pOut->x = g;
}
```

After these modifications, the parameterization of *gs* becomes

$$gs\left(\mathbf{N\cdot H}, \frac{sqrt(mx)\times \mathbf{T1\cdot H}}{\beta} + 0.5 \right)$$

and similarly for $\mathbf{T2\cdot H}$ and m_y. The texture with the name *Gs* is therefore accessed with the following parameters.

```
float fu = tex2D( GsSamp, float2(NH, (sqrt(mx) * T2H) \
           / 5.0f + 0.5f)).x;
float fv = tex2D( GsSamp, float2(NH, (sqrt(my) * T1H) \
           / 5.0f + 0.5f)).x;
```

The third part of part B of the Ashikhmin-Shirley reflection model is

$$gp = \frac{f_\lambda + \left(1 - f_\lambda\right)\left(1 - \mathbf{H\cdot L}\right)^5}{\max\left(\mathbf{N\cdot V}, \mathbf{N\cdot L}\right)}$$

gp also has singularities at $u = 0$ and $v = 0$, where the denominator goes to zero. These singularities are removed by approximating this function by adding a small value ε to the denominator. Replacing the maximum function with a simple product also produces smoother results and doesn't affect the plausibility of the model. After these modifications, the factor *gp* becomes

$$gp = \frac{f_\lambda + \left(1 - f_\lambda\right)\left(1 - \mathbf{H\cdot L}\right)^5}{\varepsilon + \max\left(\mathbf{N\cdot V}, \mathbf{N\cdot L}\right)}$$

This factor is now parameterized as

$$gp\Big(\mathbf{H}\cdot\mathbf{L}, \max\big(\mathbf{N}\cdot\mathbf{V}, \mathbf{N}\cdot\mathbf{L}\big)\Big)$$

The functions that store the factor in a 2D texture are as follows.

```
FLOAT Fresnel(FLOAT n)
{
  FLOAT RI = 0.5f; // hard coded RI

  return RI + (1 - RI) * (1 - powf(n, 5));
}

VOID WINAPI Gp (D3DXVECTOR4* pOut, CONST D3DXVECTOR2* pTexCoord,
               CONST D3DXVECTOR2* pTexelSize, LPVOID pData)
{
  /*
  *  u = H.L
  *  v = max(VN, LN)
  */
  FLOAT u = pTexCoord->x;
  FLOAT v = pTexCoord->y;
  FLOAT g;
  g = Fresnel(u)/(1.0f/256.0f + u * v);

  pOut->x = g;
}
```

A good value for ε is 1/256.0f when using an 8-bit texture representation, and 1.0f/65536.0f when using a 16-bit texture representation. The singularity situation only occurs at near-grazing angles, so the introduction of ε still results in very close visual approximation to the original model.

Results

This chapter is accompanied by two example programs in the directory Chapter 15 - Ashikhmin.

ON THE CD

- Ashikhmin contains the reference implementation
- Ashikhmin Lookup Table contains the implementation that stores the factorized terms in three lookup textures.

The screenshot in Figure 15.1 show various m_x and m_y values in the reference implementation.

Figure 15.2 compares the reference implementation with the factorized implementation. On the y axis the m_x values raise from 10, 100, 1000, and 10000 and on the x axis the m_x values raise from 10, 100, 1000, and 10000.

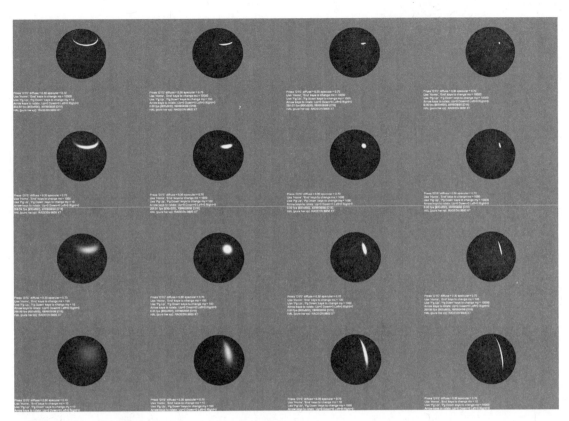

FIGURE 15.1 *Ashikhmin with various exponents.*

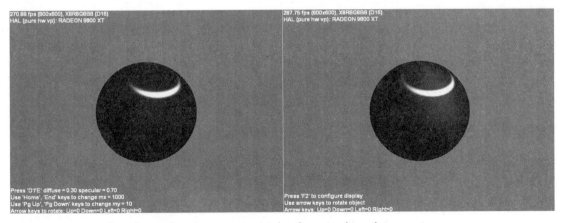

FIGURE 15.2 *Left: reference implementation/right: factorized implementation.*

As you can see, it is difficult to find a difference between the two screenshots. The screenshot on the left shows the reference implementation, and the screenshot on the right shows the factorized implementation. Due to the reduced precision, the factorized version works only with combinations of the values 1.000 and 10 for m_x and m_y.

Summary

The factorization of the Ashikhmin-Shirley reflection model leads to an anisotropic reflection model that is cheap to produce and very flexible. It is physically plausible and fulfills most requirements of a modern reflection model.

Conclusion

Having seen reference implementations of the most common advanced lighting models from the last 20 years, you can now try out the factorization ideas shown in this part of the book and develop your own factorization schemes on these. Further ideas can be found in [Latta] and in [McCool].

The goal of all factorization activities should be to receive one or more textures that cover the whole model. Recent hardware provides floating-point textures with or without filtering. This should simplify the factorization process and make it much easier to create your advanced lighting procedural texture collection.

 All lighting models covered in this and the previous part of the book can also be implemented per-vertex (in the vertex shader), as it is done in the DirectX and OpenGL fixed-function pipeline. As long as the objects in the scene are tessellated enough, this should lead to good results. If the tessellation level of the objects is not high enough or bump/parallax mapping effects should be achieved, calculating the lighting formulas per-pixel will be necessary.

IV
Environment Cube Mapping

This part of the book features a technique called cube environment mapping, which reflects the environment of an object in its surface. Understanding the idea behind this technique will open many doors to more advanced gaming techniques that might be implemented in the next couple of years.

The surfaces of real-life objects are characterized by the degree to which light is absorbed, reflected, or transmitted. To replicate the visual richness of natural objects, the eye must perceive that light is accurately reflected off objects in real-time, without objectionable artifacts. The complexity involved in modeling the physical behavior of light by explicitly tracing secondary light rays throughout a scene, however, has led to alternative techniques to simulate realistic reflections. By far, the most popular environment reflection method implemented in modern hardware, due to its speed and flexibility, was introduced by Ned Green [Green] in 1986.

Green stored a picture of the environment on the inner six sides of a cube by placing the camera in the center of the environment and then projecting the environment onto the sides of a cube positioned with its center at the camera's location. The images of the cube are then used as the environment map. This is called cubic environment mapping, or simply cube maps.

Cube environment maps can be created dynamically in the application or offline. Most of the material in the following part of the book will deal with cubic environment mapping, but cube maps can do many other things. A better way to think about cube maps is to think of them as functions that are based on directions instead of the *u*, *v* coordinates typically used in texture addressing.

Cube maps can be used to achieve the following techniques.

Lighting algorithms: Cube maps can store factorized lighting equations.
[Wynn][Hurley][Latta].

Phong Shading: Since cube maps can be used to interpolate vectors
spherically, you can achieve Phong shading.

Shadow Maps: See the article from Emil Perrson in ShaderX2 [Perrson] for a
shadow map implementation that uses cube maps to store shadow data.

Refraction: Cube maps can be used to approximate refraction, as shown in
this chapter.

Renormalization: By treating the cube map as a vector lookup, you can
perform vector renormalization. This is shown in the following section.

16

Generate and Access Cube Maps

The following two sections show how to construct cube maps for environment mapping and for normalizing vectors. Vector normalization is useful in situations where the underlying pixel shader version does not support the HLSL intrinsic `normalize()` or its assembly incarnations consisting of a `dp3`, `rsq`, `mul` instruction sequence (`rsq` is only available in versions ps_2_0 and up) or where the number of available pixel shader instruction slots does not allow normalization with these instructions.

Constructing Cube Environment Maps

Conceptually, cube environment maps represent the environment as six sides of a cube that surround one or more of the objects in your scene. To generate a cube environment map, replace the object on which you want to put reflections with a camera at the object's position and take snapshots in six directions (positive *x*, negative *x*, positive *y*, negative *y*, positive *z*, and negative *z*). Each snapshot should have a 90-degree field-of-view and a square aspect ratio, so that the six cube faces fit tightly to create an omnidirectional panorama.

Figure 16.1 shows how to use these images as the six faces of your cube map.

Due to how it's created, a cube environment map cannot reflect the object itself and cannot simulate multiple reflections, such as when two shiny objects reflect each other. A cube map can be created in a pre-processing step or generated dynamically.

This section showed how to fill a cube map, so that it holds images of an object's environment. The next section will cover how to fill a cube map with normalized vectors, so that it can be used to normalize vectors in the pixel shader.

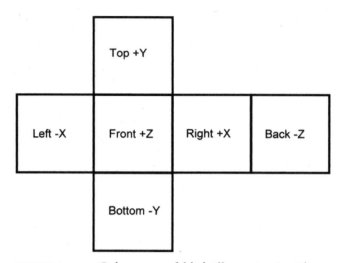

FIGURE 16.1   *Cube map unfolded, illustrating its sides.*

Constructing a Cube Normalization Map

A cube normalization map is generated by storing an array of vectors in the cube map instead of storing color images. To illustrate a cube normalization map, Figure 16.2 shows how a vector is provided to the cube map as a 3D texture coordinate and how the normalized vector is fetched from the cube map.

Each texel on the cube represents a unit light vector, oriented to this origin. In other words the faces of the normalization cube map are constructed such that the texel pierced by any given direction vector contains the normalized version of that vector.

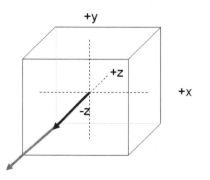

FIGURE 16.2   *Cube normalization map.*

The orange vector in Figure 16.2 represents the vector provided to the cube map, and the blue vector is the normalized vector returned by the cube normalization map.

A cube normalization map like this can be constructed for older hardware using a signed texture format. If signed texture components are unavailable, the normalized version of the vector may be stored range-compressed and then expanded prior to use as a normalized vector. A normalized vector is created as follows.

```
vector v = v/length(v);
```

When using an usigned texture format, the components of this vector are encoded as unsigned RGB colors:

$$red = \frac{x+1}{2}$$

$$green = \frac{y+1}{2}$$

$$blue = \frac{z+1}{2}$$

The range is reduced from [-1..1] to [0..1] by adding 1 and dividing by 2.

Recent hardware can also store unsigned floating-point cube maps in the range [0..1]. A resolution of 32×32 texels is typically sufficient for a normalization cube map even with 8-bit color components. A resolution of 16×16—or even 8×8—can also generate acceptable results. Figure 16.3 shows four screenshots of an example program that can be found in Chapter 16 - Generate and Access Cube Maps\Cook-Torrance Lookup Table accompanying this chapter, which uses cube normalization maps of different formats.

ON THE CD

Top left is a D3DFMT_A8R8G8B8 cube map , top right uses D3DFMT_Q8W8V8U8, bottom left uses D3DFMT_A2B10G10R10, and bottom right uses D3DFMT_A16B16G16R16F. All four vectors (**N**, **L**, **V**, and **H**) of the underlying Cook-Torrance reflection model are normalized in the pixel shader with this cube map. All cube maps are 256×256×256. The Cook-Torrance model is factorized into a volume texture as shown in Chapter 12 and uses the pixel shader profile ps_1_4.

The function CreateNormalCubeMap() in the example source code fills, depending on the availability of signed or unsigned textures, the cube map with vectors in the value range [-1..1] or [0..1]. Using a D3DFMT_A16B16G16R16F or D3DFMT_A2B10G10R10 cube map leads to remarkably better results than with Q8W8V8U8, especially if all four vectors are normalized.

If the graphics hardware does not support a four-channel floating-point texture format, two channel textures with the format D3DFMT_R16G16F might be a good alternative to an integer 8-bit format (also called Hi-Lo format). (Read more in [Harris] on using cube normalization maps and performance considerations.)

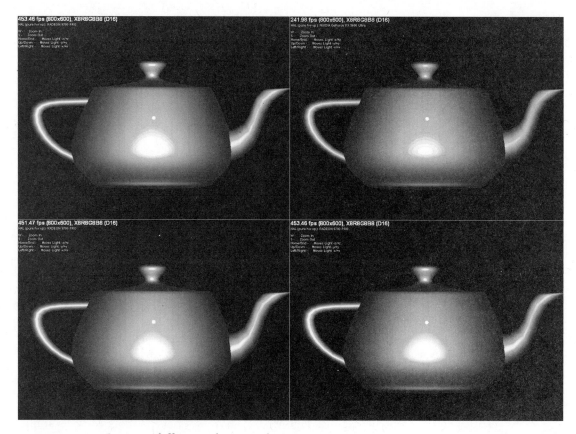

FIGURE 16.3   *Compare different cube normalization maps.*

*If a rsq instruction is not supported by the target hardware (previous to ps_2_0), there is another technique for normalizing vectors that is based on the fact that vectors to be interpolated are usually close to unit length. For a nearly unit-length vector **V**, we can approximate $1/\|\mathbf{V}\|$ by the first terms of the Taylor expansion of*

$$1/ sqrt\left(x\right) \text{ at } x = 1:$$

$$1/ sqrt\left(x\right) \approx 1 + \left(1 - x\right)/2$$

*The approximation for **V** is therefore*

$$\mathbf{V}/\|\mathbf{V}\| = \mathbf{V}/ sqrt\left(\|\mathbf{V}\|2\right) \approx \mathbf{V} + \mathbf{V} \times \left(1 - \|\mathbf{V}\|2\right)/2$$

This computation can be implemented using the following two assembly instructions.

dp3_sat r1, r0, r0

mad_d2 r1, r0, 1-r1, r0

Accessing Cube Maps

You access a cube map much like you create a cube map. Think of the texture coordinates as a 3D vector pointing from the center of the cube out toward the sides. The point where the vector **R** intersects a cube wall is the matching texel for that texture coordinate. In case of an environment cube map, you create **R**, which is used to access the cube map, with the help of the incident ray vector **I**, which is the negated eye vector. Please note that the reflection vector in Figure 16.2 is not the same reflection vector used in the Phong lighting equation in Chapter 7. It is calculated with the following formula, where **I** is the vector from eye to vertex.

$$R = I - 2 \times N \times (I \cdot N)$$

The geometry of accessing cube maps using these vectors is shown in Figure 16.4.

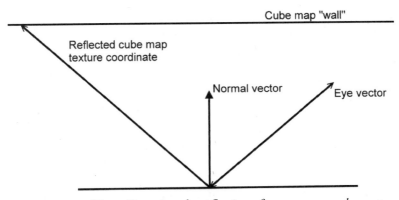

FIGURE 16.4   *Vector **R** tracing the reflection of a ray onto a cube map.*

You can find a mathematical proof for **R** on many Web sites and in numerous textbooks. A geometrical proof by inspection might look like Figure 16.5.

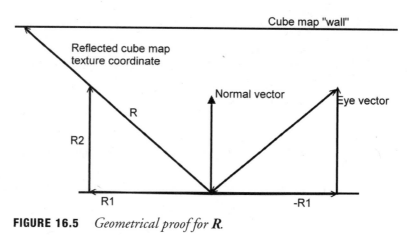

FIGURE 16.5   *Geometrical proof for **R**.*

The following equations demonstrate the geometric proof.

$$R = R1 + R2$$
$$R1 = I - R2$$

This leads to

$$R = I - 2 \times R2$$
$$R = N \times (I \cdot N)$$

which leads to

$$R = I - 2 \times N \times (I \cdot N)$$

A cube environment map is accessed by providing **R** as a 3D texture coordinate. The largest magnitude of this texture coordinate selects the corresponding face of the cube to use, e.g., the vector (–3.2, 5.1, –8.4) selects the **–Z** face. The remaining two coordinates are divided by the absolute of the largest magnitude coordinate, i.e., 8.4. They now range from –1 to 1 and are simply remapped to [0..1] to compute the texture coordinates. For example, the coordinates (–3.2, 5.1) are mapped to (–3.2 / 8.4 + 1), (5.1 / 8.4 +1), which leads to about (0.31, 0.80).

Conclusion

This chapter covered the basics of using cube maps and showed how to construct cube normalization maps. Cube normalization maps have very different performance characteristics on different hardware and by using different texture formats. To receive a performance increase from the usage of cube normalization maps requires a thorough knowledge of these characteristics, and they need to be measured and tested in the game scenario in which they are used.

17

Cube Environment Mapping

To achieve static reflective environment mapping, a cube map with the image that should be reflected by the object is loaded and used as the material of the object. This is done by indexing the cube map with a vector that points from each vertex or point of the surface into the cube map. This so-called reflection vector is calculated in the vertex shader and sent through the interpolators to the pixel shader. In the pixel shader, the reflection vector is used directly to fetch the cube map.

```
VS_OUTPUT VS(float4 Pos : POSITION, float2 Tex : TEXCOORD, float3
           Normal : NORMAL)
{
    VS_OUTPUT Out = (VS_OUTPUT)0;
    Out.Pos = mul(Pos, matWorldViewProj); // transform Position
    float3 Norm = normalize(mul(Normal, matWorld));

    // get a vector toward the camera/eye -> V
    float3 PosWorld  = normalize(mul(Pos, matWorld));
    float3 Incident = normalize(PosWorld  - vecEye);

    // Reflection Vector for cube map: R = I - 2*N * (I.N)
    Out.Reflect = reflect(Incident, Norm);
    // Out.Reflect = Incident - 2 * Norm * dot(Incident, Norm);

    return Out;
}
...
float4 PS(float3 Ref : TEXCOORD4) : COLOR
{
    return texCUBE(CubeMapSampler, Ref);
}
```

Please note that the reflection vector does not need to be normalized, because all that matters is its direction and not its magnitude when sampling a cube map.

The incident ray **I** is calculated by subtracting the eye position from the position of the vertex in world space. The reflection vector is calculated with the help of the intrinsic `reflect()`. You can see what this intrinsic does in the source line below the line where `reflect()` is used. This line is commented out but offers the same functionality as the line above, which is calculating **R**. An implementation of this function might look like this:

```
float3 reflect(float3 I, float3 N)
{
    return I - 2 * N * dot(I, N);    // R = I - 2 * N * (I.N)
}
```

This follows the formula for calculating the reflection vector, postulated in the previous section. To sample the cube map in the pixel shader, the texture instrinsic `texCUBE()` is used. This instrinsic maps down to the assembly instruction `texld`.

ON THE CD

Figure 17.1 shows a screenshot from the example program available in Chapter 17 - Cube Environment Mapping\Static Cube Environment Map.

FIGURE 17.1   *Static reflective environment mapping* Background lighting environment is the Uffizi Light Probe Image © 1999 Paul Debevec, www.debevec.org/Probes/. Used with permission.

As you can see, cube environment mapping creates a chrome-like reflective surface, because it is the only "material" used for the surface of the object here.

To improve this program, you might use an additional color map and a reflectivity parameter, which might be delivered into the pixel shader via a constant value or the alpha channel of the texture map. The alpha channel of the texture map can be used to set the amount of reflectivity on a per-pixel basis.

Static Refractive and Reflective Environment Mapping

Adding a refraction effect to the previous example allows simulation of transparent materials.

In the real world, light rays that pass through one medium into another are bent at the interface between the two media. This is called refraction. The most common example of this is when you stand at the edge of the water and look at a fish below the surface. The light rays reflected off the fish bend as they leave the water. The light also bends differently as the shape of the water's surface changes. The change in direction that leads to the visual effect of refraction happens because light travels more slowly in denser material. For example, light travels quickly in the air, but much slower in water (although the difference is quite small).

Willebrord van Roijen Snell (1580–1626), a Dutch mathematician, discovered a simple formula that is used to calculate the refraction of light when traveling between two media of differing refractive index (although the most common form was actually published first by Descartes). Snell's Law states that the ratio of the sines of the incoming and outgoing angles (relative to the surface normal) is equal to the ratio of the indices of refraction of the two materials.

This is expressed by the following equation with four variables (Read more at [Weisstein]):

$$\eta_1 \sin\theta_I = \eta_2 \sin\theta_T$$

The refracted vector is represented by **T**, which stands for *transmitted* and the incident vector is represented by **I**. The Greek letter η (eta) is used for a single material's index of refraction as shown in Figure 17.2.

A medium's index of refraction measures how the medium affects the speed of light. The higher the index of refraction for a medium, the slower light travels in it.

Using the ratio of indices of refraction is more efficient in practice, because it saves the vertex shader from having to calculate the ratio for each vertex. This formula is implemented in the intrinsic function refract(), delivered with the HLSL compiler. The source code of this intrinsic might look like this.

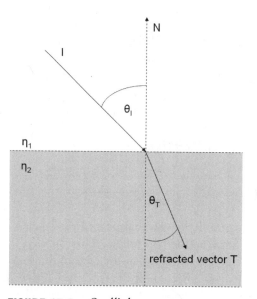

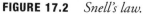

FIGURE 17.2 *Snell's law.*

```
float3 refract(float3 I, float3 N, float ri)
{
  float cosI = dot(-I, N);
  float cosT = 1.0f - ri * ri * (1.0f - cosI * cosI);

  float3 T = ri * I + ((ri * cosI - sqrt(abs(cosT))) * N);

  return T * (float3)(cosT > 0);
}
```

Notice that we only simulate the first refracted ray. Any incident ray should really be refracted twice: once as it enters the object and again as it leaves. While leaving the object, another refraction should happen between medium with $\eta2$ and then a medium with $\eta3$. The problem with this second refraction is that you don't have any sense of the volume of the object. This means you cannot follow the complete path of the light as it passes through the object.

Nevertheless, using the first refracted vector **T** gives good enough results, so that the trade-off between accuracy and performance is appropriate.

Another approach—let's call it Short-Normal-Approach—is to approximate the refraction even more. This can be done by using the reflection equation and a scaled (but not renormalized) normal vector [Dempski2]. This refraction factor has nothing to do with the index of refraction (Snell's law). Indeed, the refraction factor is a made up term. What the refraction factor does is weight the normal's contribution to the final expression.

Shortening the normal leads to a bend vector that might look like an extension of the eye vector as shown in Figure 17.3.

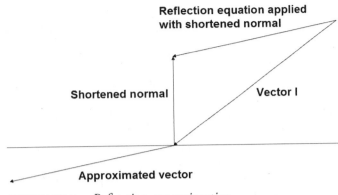

FIGURE 17.3 *Refraction approximation.*

It is easy to see that if the normal were shortened to a zero length, the refraction vector would be the same as the eye vector, whereas with a longer normal, the refraction vector is bent more to the surface.

Both approaches are implemented in the following HLSL shader. The cube map is fetched twice in the pixel shader—first with the reflection vector and then with an approximated refracted vector.

```
VS_OUTPUT VS(float4 Pos : POSITION, float2 Tex : TEXCOORD, float3
        Normal : NORMAL)
{
    VS_OUTPUT Out = (VS_OUTPUT)0;
    Out.Pos = mul(Pos, matWorldViewProj); // transform Position
    float3 Norm = normalize(mul(Normal, matWorld));

    // get a vector toward the camera/eye -> V
    float3 PosWorld  = normalize(mul(Pos, matWorld));
    float3 Incident = normalize(PosWorld  - vecEye);

    // Reflection Vector for cube map: R = I - 2*N * (I.N)
    Out.Reflect = reflect(Incident, Norm);

    float3 ShortNorm = mul(Norm, 0.4);

    // approximated refracted vector
    Out.Refract = reflect(Incident, ShortNorm);

    // Snell's law in refract()
    // Out.Refract = refract(Incident, Norm, 0.99);

    return Out;
}

float4 PS(float3 Ref : TEXCOORD4, float3 Refract : TEXCOORD5) :
        COLOR
{
```

```
float4 tex1 = texCUBE(CubeMapSampler, Ref);
float4 tex2 = texCUBE(CubeMapSampler, Refract);

return tex2 * 0.9 + tex1;
}
```

The normal is shortened for the Short-Normal-Approach in the vertex shader and stored in the variable ShortNorm. This shortened normal is used to calculate the approximated refraction vector. Using a higher value to shorten the normal (near 1.0) results in something that looks very much like reflection, whereas lower values (near zero) lead to a normal that is closer to vector **I** and might cause a zooming effect.

Snell's law implementation uses the refract() instrinsic to calculate the refraction vector. This part of the code is commented out in the vertex shader in the previous example.

The reflection and the refraction vectors are sent via the interpolators to the pixel shader, where they are used to sample the same cube map twice. The example program reduces the intensity of the color fetched from the cube map with the refraction vector by multiplying it by 0.5. It is then added to the value fetched with the reflection vector.

Figure 17.4 shows a screenshot of the example program, which features a refraction effect. It shows a partly reflective, partly refractive teapot and can be found at Chapter 17 - Cube Environment Mapping\Static Refractive and Reflective Environment Map.

FIGURE 17.4 *Static refractive and reflective environment mapping Background lighting environment is the Uffizi Light Probe Image © 1999 Paul Debevec, www.debevec.org/Probes/. Used with permission.*

Although the reflections of the environment dominate what is visible on the teapot, the big archway still shines through.

Chromatic Dispersion

Refraction not only depends on the surface normal, incident angle, and ratio of indices, but also on wavelength of the incident light. For example, the color red gets refracted more than blue light. To account for this fact, the beam of light is separated into its wavelength components, each of which travels at a slightly different speed. This is called chromatic dispersion (read more in [Fernando/Kilgard]).

Figure 17.5 shows how the three color channels are refracted differently in $\eta 2$.

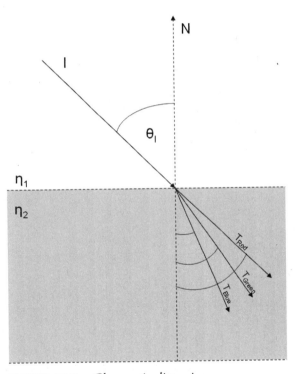

FIGURE 17.5 *Chromatic dispersion.*

Keep in mind that real light is a band of wavelengths rather than three particular and discrete wavelengths. Still, this approximation is effective enough to be useful. Figure 17.6 shows a screenshot from the example program available from Chapter 17 - Cube Environment Mapping\Chromatic Dispersion.

FIGURE 17.6 *Chromatic dispersion in action. Background lighting environment is the Uffizi Light Probe Image © 1999 Paul Debevec, www.debevec.org/Probes/. Used with permission.*

The surface of the teapot looks like the surface of a bubble. To get a visual effect that looks more like a crystal, Fernando and Kilgard combine chromatic dispersion with a reflection factor based on the Fresnel effect.

Use your imagination to find new and interesting effects. There is a lot of unexplored territory.

Dynamic Reflective and Refractive Environment Mapping

Whereas all cube maps used so far were created in an offline process, the following examples will use a dynamically created cube map. To do this, you need to render the scene to the faces of the cube map. The underlying idea is exactly the same as rendering to a 2D render target. The only difference is that a cube map has six different faces.

ON THE CD The example program that presents dynamic reflective and refractive environment mapping can be found at Chapter 17 - Cube Environment Mapping\Dynamic Cube Environment Map. To highlight the dynamic update, an airplane is flying around the teapot. Because the cube map is created for each frame, the reflection of the airplane is visible on the teapot, as shown in Figure 17.7.

323.37 fps (800x600), X8R8G8B8 (D16)
HAL (pure hw vp): RADEON 9700 PRO

FIGURE 17.7 *Dynamically updated cube map Background lighting environment is the Uffizi Light Probe Image © 1999 Paul Debevec, www.debevec.org/Probes/. Used with permission.*

In the framework function RestoreDeviceObjects(), a RenderToEnvMap object and a cube map render target are created by calling the D3DXCreateRenderToEnvMap() and D3DXCreateCubeTexture() functions. Similar to the D3DXFillTexture() functions, the RenderToEnvMap object provides a convenient way to render into the cube map, and it can also handle the depth and stencil buffer.

The D3DXCreateCubeTexture() function together with the D3DUSAGE_RENDERTARGET flag creates six different surfaces for the cube map, and all of which are valid render targets.

The RenderToEnvMap object retrieves each six surface, sets it as a render target, sets the depth/stencil buffer, and restores both buffers after rendering. The view matrix is used to position the camera in the same position as the reflective object and to change the orientation of the camera to point in the direction that matches the current face. Here is the main part of the source code that does this:

```
...
D3DXMATRIXA16 matProj;
D3DXMatrixPerspectiveFovLH( &matProj, D3DX_PI * 0.5f, 1.0f, 0.5f,
1000.0f );
```

```
    // Get the current view matrix, to concat it with the cubemap view
vectors
    D3DXMATRIXA16 matViewDir( m_matView );
    matViewDir._41 = 0.0f; matViewDir._42 = 0.0f; matViewDir._43 =
0.0f;

    // store old render target and old depth/stencil buffer
    // set stencil buffer
    if(FAILED(hr = m_pRenderToEnvMap->BeginCube( m_pCubeMap )))
        return hr;

    for( UINT i = 0; i < 6; i++ )
    {
        // gets cube map render target surface and set it as render
target
        m_pRenderToEnvMap->Face( (D3DCUBEMAP_FACES) i, 0 );

        // Set the view transform for this cubemap surface
        D3DXMATRIXA16 matView;
        matView = D3DUtil_GetCubeMapViewMatrix( (D3DCUBEMAP_FACES) i
);

        // Render the scene (except for the teapot)
        RenderScene( &matView, &matProj, FALSE );
    }
    // Restore depth-stencil buffer and render target
    m_pRenderToEnvMap->End( 0 );
    ...
```

The function `RenderScene()` renders the scene into the selected cube map face.

The HLSL shader code is identical to the shader code of the second example in this chapter.

ON THE CD   The following example program, shown in Figure 17.8, combines the bump mapping example from Chapter 9 with the previous example. It can be found at Chapter 17 - Cube Environment Mapping\Bumped Dynamic Cube Environment Map.

The directional light source can be moved with the arrow keys. The cube mapping contribution (`tex2 * 0.5 + tex1`) is combined here with the ambient component that consists of the `color` value fetched from the color map and multiplied by 0.2.

```
        return (0.2 * color  + (tex2 * 0.5 + tex1)) + shadow * (color
               * diff + spec);
```

On the backside of the earth, only the original texture together with the combined reflected and refracted effect is visible, whereas on the side where the light shines, the diffuse and specular component is added.

FIGURE 17.8   *Bumped dynamic updated cube map. Background lighting environment is the Uffizi Light Probe Image © 1999 Paul Debevec, www.debevec.org/Probes/. Used with permission.*

Accurate Cube Environment Mapped Reflection and Refraction by Adjusting for Object Distance

One of the common problems encountered in environment mapping is that flat surfaces do not render well. There is very little variation in the reflection vector direction itself, and because environment maps are indexed from the exact center, it does not take into account that a reflection vector can be originated off-center and therefore end up reflecting a different object. This deficiency would make a flat mirror appear to reflect all the same point, by magnifying only a few texels.

Environment mapping based solely on the reflection vector direction acts as if the objects in the environment map are infinitely far away. Chris Brennan [Brennan] describes a way to alleviate this by adjusting the use of the environment map such that it has a finite radius that is close to the real proximity of the objects. The most precise way to do this is by intersecting the reflection or refraction ray with the environment map sphere and then using the vector from the center of the map to the intersection point to index the map. Calculating the intersection of a sphere and a vector is expensive in a shader, therefore we need to find an approximation.

The reflection vector is adjusted by multiplying the vertex position in world space by 10.0f in the vertex shader. This equals the scaling factor of the surrounding sky box with the environment and gives good results. The scaled vertex position vector is then sent through the interpolators to the pixel shader, and there it is added to the reflection vector. For the cube used in this example, Figure 17.9 represents these adjustments to the reflection vector graphically.

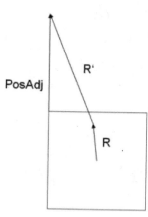

FIGURE 17.9   *Graphical representation of how the reflection vector is adjusted.*

The formula that represents this adjustment is

$$R' = R + \left(VertexPosition \times 10.0f \right)$$

The vertex and the pixel shader that use the adjusted reflection vector are as follows.

```
VS_OUTPUT VS(float4 Pos : POSITION, float2 Tex : TEXCOORD, float3
          Normal : NORMAL)
{
    VS_OUTPUT Out = (VS_OUTPUT)0;

    Out.Pos = mul(Pos, matWorldViewProj); // transform Position
    Out.Norm = mul(Normal, matWorld);

    float OneOverRadius= 10.0f;

    // get a vector toward the camera/eye -> V
    float3 PosWorld  = normalize(mul(Pos, matWorld));
    Out.Incident = normalize(PosWorld  - vecEye);
    Out.PosAdj = PosWorld * OneOverRadius;
```

```
       return Out;
   }
   ...
   float4 PS(float3 Incident : TEXCOORD0, float3 Norm : TEXCOORD1,
            float3 PosAdj : TEXCOORD2) : COLOR
   {
      float3 N = normalize(Norm);
      float3 I = normalize(Incident);

      float3 ref = reflect(I, N);
      float3 refr = reflect(I, N * 0.4f);
      float3 coord = PosAdj + ref;

      float4 tex1 = texCUBE(CubeMapSampler, coord);
      float4 tex2 = texCUBE(CubeMapSampler, refr);

      return tex2 * 0.5 + tex1;
   }
```

The vertex shader calculates the adjusted position value and sends it through a texture interpolator to the pixel shader. This value is then added to the reflection vector that is used to sample the cube map.

ON THE CD The screenshot on the left side of Figure 17.10 uses the reflection vector as calculated in the previous example programs, and the screenshot on the right shows the example program with an adjusted reflection vector. The example program can be found at Chapter 17 - Cube Environment Mapping\Accurate Refractive and Reflective Static Environment Map.

FIGURE 17.10   *Left: unadjusted reflection vector/right: adjusted reflection vector.*

Conclusion

This chapter covered the most common ways cube maps are used by using them as an environment reflection and refraction map. There are several other methods to use cube maps to achieve certain effects (e.g., cube shadow maps), but the main idea is always very similar to the ones shown in this chapter.

18

High Dynamic Range Cube Maps

Up until now, games have not been able to use a dramatic contrast. Artists have had to stay in between 0.2 and 0.8 of the [0.0 .. 1.0] 8-bit color range. If backgrounds are dark enough to provide good contrast, they look bad when lit later because of banding quantization artifacts. If objects are lit too brightly, they saturate and no one can ever see them again. Both cases can be solved with a higher color range.

The first step in implementing a high-dynamic range rendering system is using a texture format that can store values with such a high range. The following text shows three ways to store a high-value range in currently supported texture formats.

Therefore, this chapter will present techniques that allow the use of higher dynamic range in cube maps. It will cover the following techniques:

- How to use floating point cube textures
- How to extend the traditional 4×8-bit integer texture format to achieve a higher value range
- How to use a 16-bit per-component integer texture format to achieve a higher value range
- How to bilinear filter floating-point textures
- How to filter floating-point cube map textures efficiently

Let's start by looking into the most obvious way to achieve a higher value range in textures.

fp16 Format

The most obvious way to achieve a higher value range is by using a floating-point environment texture map and processing all calculations in floating-point format.

Figure 18.1 shows a screenshot of an example program that uses floating-point textures. This example program can be found in the directory Chapter 18 - High Dynamic Range Cube Maps\FP16 Dynamic Cube Environment Map.

FIGURE 18.1   *16-bit floating-point cube map (Background lighting environment is the Uffizi Light Probe Image © 1999 Paul Debevec, www.debevec.org/Probes/. Used with permission.*

You might notice some "stair" effects at the roofs of the buildings. This is because floating-point textures cannot be bilinear filtered, at the time of this writing, on ATI RADEON 9500+ and newer ATI hardware. The later section, "Filtering of High Dynamic Range Cube Maps," will present a solution to this.

Another drawback of a floating-point texture format is that it is still not widely supported in hardware. So some tricks are needed when targeting older graphics hardware. Furthermore, the memory footprint of the 16-bit per channel floating-point data format textures is substantially higher than that of the 8-bit per-channel integer texture formats.

Both problems can be addressed by using a compressed texture format. The two most promising methods for compressing data are shown in the following two sections.

RGBE8 **Format**

It is possible to pack three floating-point values into a single 32-bit texture (D3DFMT_ A8R8G8B8), where RGB channels keep mantissas of the original floating-point values and the alpha channel keeps the common exponent. This format is known as Radiance RGBE format. It was first described by Greg Ward [WardG] and it was applied to cube maps by Arkadiusz Waliszweski [Waliszewski].

The main idea behind this format is to encode floating-point values to RGBE8 values by dividing the floating-point value through the exponent of the largest value and then multiplying the result that has a value range of [0.5 ..1.0] with 255 to get it into a value range of [0..255]. The common exponent is then stored in the alpha channel (this is where the E in RGBE is coming from). This technique leads to a loss of precision in channels, which keep values significantly smaller than a channel with the greatest exponent, but this loss of data is acceptable, because significantly small components would not be visible after conversion from high-dynamic range values to the visible range (8-bit back buffer). Following is the pseudo-code that shows the encoding formula.

```
Original floating point values:
R = 537.0, G = 0.01, and B = 125.0

Encoded in three 8-bit values:
10 = exp;
8bitAlpha = 128 + exp;
133 = 8bitMantissaRed =   (R                 ) * 255
            2^(8bitAlpha - 128)
  0 = 8bitMantissaGreen = (G                 ) * 255
            2^(8bitAlpha - 128)
 31 = 8bitMantissaBlue =  (B                 ) * 255
             2^(8bitAlpha - 128)
```

The `RGBE8` values are decoded to floating point values with the following formula:

```
534.08 = Red = 8bitMantissaRed   / 255 * 2^(8bitAlpha - 128);
     0 = Green = 8bitMantissaGreen / 255 * 2^(8bitAlpha - 128);
124.48 = Blue = 8bitMantissaBlue  / 255 * 2^(8bitAlpha - 128);
```

Here is another example:

```
Original floating point values:
R = 0.1, G = 0.01, and B = 0.05

Encoded in three 8-bit values:
2 = exp;
8bitAlpha = 128 + exp;
6 = 8bitMantissaRed =   (R                 ) * 255
            2^(8bitAlpha - 128)
0 = 8bitMantissaGreen = (G                 ) * 255
            2^(8bitAlpha - 128)
3 = 8bitMantissaBlue =  (B                 ) * 255
            2^(8bitAlpha - 128)

Decoding leads to:
0.094 = Red = 8bitMantissaRed   / 255 * 2^(8bitAlpha - 128);
0.0 = Green = 8bitMantissaGreen / 255 * 2^(8bitAlpha - 128);
0.047 = Blue = 8bitMantissaBlue  / 255 * 2^(8bitAlpha - 128);
```

The tricky part here is to find the right exponent, because the result of $2^{exponent}$ needs to be higher than or equal to the floating-point value that should be encoded. Otherwise, we would not be able to reduce the floating-point value to the range [0.5..1]. Therefore the following equation must be true:

$$maxComponent \leq 2^{exponent}$$

To achieve a very fast convergence, the following code snippet is used to detect the suitable exponent.

```
int iExpMax = 256;
int iExpMin = 0;

while( iExpMax - iExpMin > 1 )
{
    int iMiddle = (iExpMax + iExpMin) / 2;

    if( maxComponent > pow(2, iMiddle))
        iExpMin = iMiddle;
    else
        iExpMax = iMiddle;
}
```

There are a maximum and a minimum value, which are changed depending on whether the value lies in the upper half of 128 or in the lower half. If the desired exponent lies in the lower half in the first iteration of this code snippet, the next search will use 64 as the exponent. If we use a 16-bit floating-point texture that can store values in the range $[0..2^{16}]$, there is a good chance that the second and third iteration will reduce the value in iExpMax to 16.

Here is the C version of the encoding algorithm:

```
inline VOID EncodeRGBE8( D3DXFLOAT16* pSrc, BYTE** ppDest )
{
    FLOAT r, g, b;

    // pointers to the color channels
    r = (FLOAT) *(pSrc+0);
    g = (FLOAT) *(pSrc+1);
    b = (FLOAT) *(pSrc+2);

    // Determine the largest color component
    float maxComponent = max( max(r, g), b );

    // the following lines are looking for an exponent
    // that results as 2^x to a higher value that the value
    // of the floating point number that should be
    // encoded
    int iExpMax = 256;
    int iExpMin = 0;
    while( iExpMax - iExpMin > 1 )
    {
        int iMiddle = (iExpMax + iExpMin) / 2;
```

```
        if( maxComponent > pow(2, iMiddle))
            iExpMin = iMiddle;
        else
            iExpMax = iMiddle;
    }

    // Divide the components by the shared exponent
    FLOAT fDivisor = (FLOAT) pow(2, iExpMax);
    r /= fDivisor;
    g /= fDivisor;
    b /= fDivisor;

    // Constrain the color components
    // min() selects the lesser of x and y -> no color value bigger
       than 1
    // max() selects the greater of x and y -> no color value
            smaller than 0
    // value range [0..1]
    r = max( 0, min(1, r) );
    g = max( 0, min(1, g) );
    b = max( 0, min(1, b) );

    // pDestColor: pointer to access the three color channels
    // ppDest: pointer-pointer to move the pointer
    D3DCOLOR* pDestColor = (D3DCOLOR*) *ppDest;

    // multiplying the color values with 255 expands the value
range from [0..1]
        // to a value range of [0..255] == unsigned 8-bit value range
        *pDestColor = D3DCOLOR_RGBA( (BYTE)(r*255), (BYTE)(g*255),
(BYTE)(b*255), iExpMax + 128 );

    // move pointer to the next RGBA value.
    *ppDest += sizeof(D3DCOLOR);@CODE2:    }
```

To improve the performance of the encoding process, a power-of-two lookup table might be used.

The following HLSL code handles encoding and decoding RGBE8 to fp values in the shader. Please note that we don't need to reduce the value range in the vertex or pixel shader to [0.5..1.0] and then multiply it again with 255, because in the vertex or pixel shader only floating-point formats are used for storage, and the result does not need to fit into a unsigned 8-bit value. If we write into a render target with unsigned 8-bit channels, the conversion will be done by the graphics hardware.

```
float4 EncodeRGBE8( in float3 rgb )
{
float4 vEncoded;

// Determine the largest color component
float maxComponent = max( max(rgb.r, rgb.g), rgb.b );
```

```
// Round to the nearest integer exponent
float fExp = ceil( log2(maxComponent) );

// Divide the components by the shared exponent
vEncoded.rgb = rgb / exp2(fExp);

// Store the shared exponent in the alpha channel
vEncoded.a = (fExp + 128) / 255;

return vEncoded;
}
```

More accurate but slower encoding can be achieved by using the following function:

```
// More accurate encoding
#define EXP_BASE    (1.04)
#define EXP_OFFSET  (64.0)

// a^n = b
#define LOG(a, b)   ( log((b)) / log((a)) )

float4 EncodeRGBE8(in float3 rgb)
{
 float4 rgbe;

 // determine the largest color component
 float fMax = max(max(rgb.r, rgb.g), rgb.b);

 float fExp = floor( LOG(EXP_BASE, fMax) );
 rgbe.a = clamp( (fExp + EXP_OFFSET) / 255, 0.0, 1.0 );
 rgbe.rgb = rgb / pow(EXP_BASE, rgbe.a * 255 - EXP_OFFSET);
 return rgbe;
}
```

The following pseudo-code snippet decodes RGBE values back to floating point.

```
float3 DecodeRGBE8( in float4 rgbe )
{
 float3 vDecoded;

 // Retrieve the shared exponent
 float fExp = rgbe.a * 255 - 128;

 // Multiply through the color components
 vDecoded = rgbe.rgb * exp2(fExp);

 return vDecoded;
}
```

The following function decodes slower but with more precision:

```
float3 DecodeRGBE8(in float4 rgbe)
{
```

```
// retrieved the shared exponent
float fExp = rgbe.a * 255 - EXP_OFFSET;
float fScaler = pow(EXP_BASE, fExp);
return (rgbe.rgb * fScaler);
}
```

Having two pairs of encode and decode functions offers the choice for a performance/quality trade-off. Because of the different underlying algorithm, these pairs cannot be intermixed.

An example program that uses the RGBE8 format can be found in the following directory Chapter 18 - High Dynamic Range Cube Maps\RGBE8 Dynamic Cube Environment Map.

The biggest advantage of the RGBE8 format is that it is supported on all hardware that supports 32-bit integer formats, which should be all available consumer graphics hardware on the market. Its disadvantage is the computational overhead created by the ongoing encoding and decoding process that excludes pre-DX9 hardware from the minimum specification for this technique. The following texture format might have a higher value loss, but is computationally significantly faster.

RGB16 Format

The RGB16 format scales a 16-bit (0 to 65535) value linearly between 0.0f and RGB16_MAX (an arbitrary maximum value above which data is clipped). The following pseudo-code encodes and decodes floating-point data to and from RGB16 data.

```
// encode
OutputColor = RGB / ConstantValue;

// decode
OutputColor = RGB * ConstantValue;
```

This kind of encoding is pretty straightforward and efficient. You might experiment with values other than 100 as the maximum value.

The advantage of the 16-bit integer format is that it is filtered by all hardware that supports it. This is shown in a screenshot of the example program, which can be found in the following directory Chapter 18 - High Dynamic Range Cube Maps\ RGB16 Dynamic Cube Environment Map, in Figure 18.2 on the left side.

Filtering of High Dynamic Range Cube Maps

Although recent hardware supports floating-point cube maps, not all hardware can bilinear filter these textures.

The cube map examples first apply the cube map texture onto the faces of the skybox, and then onto the teapot by fetching texels with the reflection vector.

In the first case, we sample a 2D texture, and in the second case, we sample a cube map with a 3D vector. Filtering can be involved in both processes, but a different filtering method needs to be used for each process. We therefore need to differentiate between filtering a 2D floating-point texture and filtering a cube map floating-point texture.

Filtering a 2D Floating-Point Texture

Mapping a 16-bit per-channel floating-point cube map to the skybox leads to significant stair effects, as seen in the example program at the roofs of the buildings, whereas the RGBE8 version on the right side of Figure 18.2 is bilinear filtered by hardware and therefore looks much better.

FIGURE 18.2   *Left: 16-bit floating-point cube map/ Right: RGBE8 cube map* Background lighting environment is the Uffizi Light Probe Image © 1999 Paul Debevec, www.debevec.org/Probes/. Used with permission.

Bilinear filtering solves blockiness by taking 4 neighboring pixels of the texture map and averaging between them. This gives a more gradual change in color instead of the normally abrupt change.

> *However, since bilinear filtering samples neighboring pixels from a square area, it can only produce convincing results for surfaces at a right angle to the viewer. For angled or uneven surfaces, anisotropic filtering is required.*

To linearly filter a one-dimensional texture, the texture coordinate needs to be converted from the floating-point value range [0..1] to the "texel space" with the range [0.. width of 1D texture]. Then the two texels that lie closest to the converted coordinate need to be fetched, and the contribution or weight of each texel based on the distance from the coordinate value in texel space needs to be calculated.

For example, if the texel space texture coordinate is 1.35 in the 1D texture shown in Figure 18.3, the weight of texel 1 is calculated with its fractional part 0.35 as $(1 - 0.35)$ and the weight of texel 2 is 0.35.

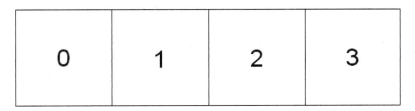

0	1	2	3

FIGURE 18.3   *Filtering 1D texture.*

By using a 2D texture, we will end up with two fractional parts for each texture coordinate, and we need to fetch four texels. You might consider the origin of the texel to be the upper-left corner of the texture. If the texture coordinates point to this origin (0, 0), the origin gets the full intensity of the current texel and none of the remaining three of the nearest four texels. As the point you are sampling the texture from moves right, along the top edge of that texel, you start to incorporate the next texel over, and the two values get blended. If the sampling point moves down, the texel beneath this texel and the one below and to the right of the texel where the sampling happens need to be observed. Figure 18.4 shows a 2D texture with texel space coordinates.

0, 0	1, 0	2, 0	3, 0
0, 1	1, 1	2, 1	3, 1
0, 2	1, 2	2, 2	3, 2
0, 3	1, 3	2, 3	3, 3

FIGURE 18.4   *Filtering 2D texture.*

Let's say the sampled point should be (1.35, 1.1). The current texel is (1,1). The upper-right texel is (2,1), the lower texel is (1,2), and the lower-right texel is (2,2). Then the steps necessary to bilinear filter a texture are:

1. Convert the texture coordinates into texel space and compute their fractional part.
2. Fetch four texels, one on the right of the current texel, one below the current texel, and one below the texel to the right of the current texel.
3. Compute the weights necessary to leap between the texels by retrieving the fractional part.

The following code snippet of the HLSL vertex shader source code uses a constant variable named `dimension` to store the texture coordinates in texel space.

```
...
const float2 oneZero  = float2(1.0f, 0.0f);
const float2 dimension = float2(1/512.0f, 1/512.0f);

Out.TopLeft = Tex + oneZero.yy * dimension; // Top Left
Out.TopRight = Tex + oneZero.xy * dimension; // Top Right
Out.BottomLeft = Tex + oneZero.yx * dimension; // Bottom Left
Out.BottomRight = Tex + oneZero.xx * dimension; // Bottom Right
...
```

Depending on which texel should be fetched, the constant variable `oneZero` reduces the value that should be added to the texture coordinate to null or multiplies the value stored in one of the channels of dimension with 1.0f.

In this code snippet, the top-left texel of the square that gets filtered is equal to the texture coordinates that are sent to the vertex shader. For the top-right texel we add 1/(the x dimension of the texture) to the x value of the top-left texel and to access the bottom-left texel we add 1/(the y dimension of the texture) to the y value of the top-left texel. To access the bottom-right texel, we need to add to the x value of the top-left pixel 1/(through the x dimension of the texture) and 1/(through the y dimension of the texture) to the y value.

The four 2D vectors `TopLeft`, `TopRight`, `BottomLeft`, and `BottomRight` are sent through the texture coordinate registers to the pixel shader, and they are used there to fetch the four texels.

```
float4 PSSkybox(float2 TopLeft : TEXCOORD0,
                float2 TopRight : TEXCOORD1,
                float2 BottomLeft : TEXCOORD2,
                float2 BottomRight : TEXCOORD3) : COLOR

{
    float4 topleftC     = tex2D(CubeFaceSampler, TopLeft);
    float4 toprightC    = tex2D(CubeFaceSampler, TopRight);
    float4 bottomleftC  = tex2D(CubeFaceSampler, BottomLeft);
    float4 bottomrightC = tex2D(CubeFaceSampler, BottomRight);
```

```
        const float2 dimension = float2(512.0f, 512.0f);
        float2 Weight = frac(TopLeft * dimension);

        float4 top    = lerp(topleftC,    toprightC,    Weight.xxxx);
        float4 bottom = lerp(bottomleftC, bottomrightC, Weight.xxxx);
        return lerp(top, bottom, Weight.yyyy);
    }
```

Two weight factors are stored in the variable Weight. They are retrieved by using the fraction of the product of the texture coordinates of the top left texel and the texture coordinates in texel space.

Then the result of the texture fetch with the top-left texture coordinates is lerped with the result of the texture fetch of the top-right texture coordinates. The same happens for the bottom texels and to retrieve the end result, the result of both rows is lerped.

ON THE CD Figure 18.5 shows a screenshot of the example program on the right and the unfiltered version on the left side. The example program can be found in the directory Chapter 18 - High Dynamic Range Cube Maps\Bilinear Filtered FP16 Dynamic Cube Environment Map.

FIGURE 18.5 *Left: unfiltered 2D texture/right: filtered 2D texture* Background lighting environment is the Uffizi Light Probe Image © 1999 Paul Debevec, www.debevec.org/Probes/. Used with permission.

Bilinear filtering of 2D textures as described in this section does not have a high computational cost. Counting instructions leads to about four texture and nine arithmetic assembly instructions.

Using bilinear filtering on floating-point textures on hardware that does not support filtering of floating-point textures seems like a great quality improvement but increases the cost of using floating-point textures instead of integer textures even more.

Filtering a Cube Map Floating-Point Texture

The effect of a filtered cube map is visible on the object to which the cube map is applied.

Arkadiusz Waliszewski [Waliszewski] fetches eight texels from the cube map by using 3D texture coordinates and lerps them to produce the final pixel. By not needing to select a cube map face before filtering, he avoids possible problems due to the fact that the edges of the cube map are not filtered. The steps necessary to filter the cube map this way are the following.

- Multiply each component of the texture coordinate by the size of the texture (in pixels) to the coordinate in texel space.
- For each texture coordinate component, compute the two closest integer values (e.g., 123.4 values gives 123 and 124).
- Compute the contribution of each integer part by using the fractional part of the texture component. For example, the fraction of the contribution of 123 with a value of 123.4 is 1 − 0.4 (= 0.6), whereas the fraction of the contribution of 124 is 1 − 0.6 (=0.4).
- Construct eight texture coordinates and divide these by the texture size to get the coordinates in the range [0..1]. Then fetch eight texels.
- Compute the final pixel value using contributions and fetched texels by lerping everything.

This filtering method fetches the texels as shown in Figure 18.6.

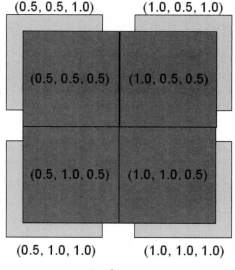

FIGURE 18.6   *Fetch pattern.*

The gray left-upper texel is fetched first, then the texel with the same x and y values but with a 0.5 higher z-value is fetched. The third fetch is done with the pixel that is below the first pixel, and the fourth fetch just changes the z-value by +0.5 to fetch the fourth pixel and so on.

Lerping happens first between the gray texel (0.5, 0.5, 0.5) and the second texel (1.0, 0.5, 0.5), then between the second row of texels.

After that, the first row of pixels that are behind the gray pixels is lerped, followed by the second row.

The results of the lerps of the first row are then lerped with the results of the second row for the gray and the texels behind, and the two results are lerped to the color value that is the output value of the pixel shader. Here is the HLSL pixel shader code:

```
float4 PS(float3 Ref : TEXCOORD4) : COLOR
{
    float3 textureSize = float3(64, 64, 64);
    float3 textureSizeDiv = float3(0.03125, 0.03125, 0.03125);
    float3 halfPixel   = float3(0.5, 0.5, 0.5);
    float3 oneConst    = float3(1.0, 1.0, 1.0);

    // multiply coordinates by the texture size
    float3 texPos = Ref * textureSize;

    // compute first integer coordinates
    float3 texPos0 = floor(texPos + halfPixel);

    // compute second integer coordinates
    float3 texPos1 = texPos0 + oneConst;

    // perform division on integer coordinates
    texPos0 = texPos0 * textureSizeDiv;
    texPos1 = texPos1 * textureSizeDiv;

    // compute contributions
    float3 blend = frac(texPos + halfPixel);

    // construct 8 new coordinates
    float3 texPos000 = texPos0;
    float3 texPos001 = float3(texPos0.x, texPos0.y, texPos1.z);
    float3 texPos010 = float3(texPos0.x, texPos1.y, texPos0.z);
    float3 texPos011 = float3(texPos0.x, texPos1.y, texPos1.z);
    float3 texPos100 = float3(texPos1.x, texPos0.y, texPos0.z);
    float3 texPos101 = float3(texPos1.x, texPos0.y, texPos1.z);
    float3 texPos110 = float3(texPos1.x, texPos1.y, texPos0.z);
    float3 texPos111 = texPos1;

    // sample cube map
    float3 C000 = texCUBE(CubeMapSampler, texPos000);
    float3 C001 = texCUBE(CubeMapSampler, texPos001);
    float3 C010 = texCUBE(CubeMapSampler, texPos010);
    float3 C011 = texCUBE(CubeMapSampler, texPos011);
    float3 C100 = texCUBE(CubeMapSampler, texPos100);
```

```
float3 C101 = texCUBE(CubeMapSampler, texPos101);
float3 C110 = texCUBE(CubeMapSampler, texPos110);
float3 C111 = texCUBE(CubeMapSampler, texPos111);

// compute final pixel value by lerping everything
float3 C = lerp(
            lerp(lerp(C000, C010, blend.y),
                lerp(C100, C110, blend.y),
                blend.x),
            lerp(lerp(C001, C011, blend.y),
                lerp(C101, C111, blend.y),
                blend.x),
            blend.z);

return float4(C.r, C.g, C.b, 1.0f);
}
```

ON THE CD

Figure 18.7 shows a comparison of the filtered cube map created by the example program in the directory Chapter 18 - High Dynamic Range Cube Maps\Filtered Cube Map FP16 Dynamic Cube Environment Map and an unfiltered floating-point cube map.

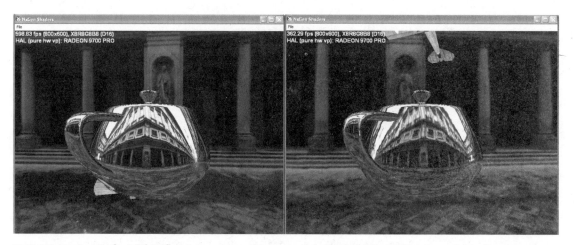

FIGURE 18.7   *Left: 16-bit floating-point cube map with 256×256×256/right: 16-bit floating-point cube map with 64×64×64 filtered.*

The left screenshot uses a 16-bit floating-point cube map texture in the size 256x256x256, whereas the example on the right screenshot uses a filtered 16-bit floating-point cube map texture in the size 64x64x64 with a small quality loss. Even using 32x32x32 leads to acceptable results here. This should get even more important if the graphics card is running out of memory bandwidth.

Conclusion

This part of the book has given you all the tools to use cube maps in different environments. To normalize vectors in the pixel shader, cube normalization maps can be used if the number of instruction slots are low, the `normalize()` intrinsic is not supported, or the `rsq` assembly instruction is not supported. Don't forget that the cost of a cube normalization map fetch varies substantially between different graphics hardware.

Another area of application is the reflection of the environment on an object in the scene. Some games use a static cube map here that shows a typical scene of the game and move this cube map over the object. Using a dynamic cube environment map can be computationally quite expensive. Here are a few tips to help you create an effective implementation of cubic environment mapping.

- Use one environment map for all objects.
- Use static cube maps instead of dynamic ones when possible.
- If you need a dynamic cube map, write only every fifth frame.
- Switch off cube mapping based on distance to the viewer.

Using cube maps to get a higher dynamic range for storing values is still an expensive task. Using an RGBE8 texture format requires an encoding and decoding process each time the texture is fetched or stored, but it is supported widely on graphics cards. An RGB16 texture format seems to offer a good quality/performance ratio but is not supported widely. Floating-point formats offer the highest dynamic range but are quite expensive, because most recent hardware executes them slower and because filtering is not supported in most current hardware, it needs to be done in the pixel shader, eating up a quite moderate number of instruction slots. .

Overall, the RGBE8 format looks like the clear winner based on quality and—especially—availability.

V

High Dynamic Range Lighting

In the real world, the difference between the brightest point in a scene and the darkest point can be much higher than in a scene shown on a computer display or on a photo. The ratio between highest and lowest luminance is called *dynamic range*.

The range of light we experience in the real world is vast. It might be up to 1012:1 for viewable light in everyday life, from starlight scenes to sunlit snow, and up to a dynamic range of 104:1, from shadows to highlights in a single scene. However, the range of light we can reproduce on our print and screen display devices spans at best a dynamic range of about 102:1. The human visual system is capable of a dynamic range of around 103:1 at a particular exposure. To see light spread across a high dynamic range, the human visual system automatically adjusts its exposure to light, selecting a narrow range of luminances based on the intensity of incoming light. This light adaptation process is delayed, as you'll notice when entering or exiting a dark building on a sunny day, and is known as *exposure adjustment*.

The idea behind all *high-dynamic range lighting* techniques is to prevent losing color data during the calculation process and to move the dynamic range of an image to the range that counts for the eye of the user and the mood of the image. In other words because the computer cannot display a higher value range, we just use its available range of values better.

This part of the book will cover rendering techniques that are used to imitate the behavior of the human visual system under changing light intensities and that are useful for preserving the value range of colors during the rendering process. The characteristics of high-dynamic range lighting are the following:

- Higher dynamic range of the human visual system compared to the computer display
- Light adaptation behavior similar to the human visual system: human eye adapts to compensate for color light sources
- Blooming under intense lighting to imitate very bright areas that overload the optic nerve of the eye

The most sophisticated approach would be to analyze the result of the rendering process, decide which areas of the image have a value range that is more or less important for the viewer, and amplify or attenuate the luminance in these areas.

Although we are not able to implement such an approach with current consumer hardware, there are a bunch of post-processing techniques that help to balance the luminance in an image with good results. We will start with the simplest approach as covered by Hugo Elias [Elias].

19 Simple Exposure

Hugo Elias's approach is based on the chemical process that happens during the exposure of film in a photo camera. This can be visualized with a graph that shows how the amount of chemical remaining on the film falls as more light hits it.

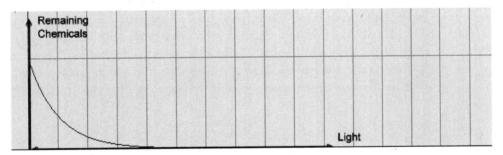

FIGURE 19.1   *Chemical remaining on the film.*

The Y-axis of Figure 19.1 shows the chemical remaining in a film and the *x*-axis shows the amount of light hitting the film. This is an exponential decay graph ($f(x) = \exp(-x)$), which shows that the chemical breaks down quickly initially, but as less and less chemical is left, it breaks down more slowly until there is none remaining.

To reverse this process, Elias suggests turning this function upside down to find out how transparent the film becomes after a certain amount of light has hit it, and thus, how bright the resulting photograph should be. This leads to the following equation:

$$brightness = 1 - \exp^{-light}$$

The graph for this equation is shown in Figure 19.2.

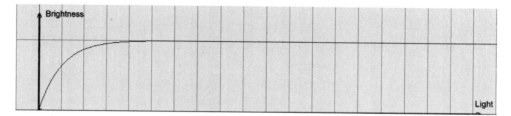

FIGURE 19.2   *Brightness of photograph.*

Figure 19.2 shows clearly that the graph is the negation of the graph in Figure 19.1. In other words, it reverses the effects of the chemical process going on in the camera and helps to reconstitute the brightness of the original scene.

To make the previous equation even more flexible in imitating the functionality of a camera, Elias adds a variable named "exposure control" to it. This variable mimics the fact that the amount of light that hits the film is simply the product of the light entering the camera, the aperture, and the length of time the shutter is open.

$$brightness = 1 - \exp^{-light \times exposure}$$

An exposure value higher than 1.0 makes the picture darker, and a lower exposure value makes the picture brighter.

Implementation

The implementation of this formula is quite straightforward. The HLSL code snippet is:

```
    ...
        return 1 - exp(-tex2D(ColorMapSampler, Tex) * exposure) *
    1.75f; // fetch color map
    ...
```

Results and Conclusion

ON THE CD   The example program is available in the directory Chapter 19 - Simple Exposure.
To review this technique, a photo with the wrong brightness and an oversaturated area is used.

FIGURE 19.3   *Left: original photo/right: corrected photo.*

The original photo was taken with a Sony DSC-P1 Digital Camera on the Maldives. The Maldives are a group of more than 1,000 islands situated southeast of India in the Indian Ocean and therefore south of the equator. They are famous for their bright light (which is why fashion photos are often shot there). Cameras without manual exposure time setting have trouble capturing images here because they expect lighting conditions similar to Europe, Asia, or the U.S., so the images look as though they were taken on a cloudy day.

This is easily seen by looking into the faces of the people in the left picture. The camera reduced the ratio of the highest and lowest luminance value on the photo and most areas darkened. Additionally, there are reflections on the lower-right side of the picture that look like a few oversaturated areas.

The picture on the right was corrected with the Hugo Elias technique, and it shows the correct distribution of luminance over the whole photo. The faces are lit correctly and the reflections of the water and especially the color of the water are correct. It even conveys the fact that the light is unusually bright there.

Although this approach shows a good result with the photo used in Figure 19.3, it does not handle the blurring of very bright areas in an image. This is possible with the approach in the next chapter.

20

Faked High Dynamic Range Lighting

One of the graphically most impressive games of the last couple of years is *WRECKLESS: The Yakuza Missions* (Japanese Version Title: *DOUBLE-S.T.E.A.L*). When it was released for the XBOX™ in 2002 it was one of the first games that used techniques that provided the user with the impression of a better distributed luminance.

An interesting interview regarding the techniques used in the game was given by Masumi Nagaya (producer, lead programmer) and Masaki Kawase (shader programmer) [Kawase2], and Masaki Kawase talked in 2003 and 2004 at the Game Developer Conference [Kawase].

Background

The approach developed by Masaki Kawase fakes the existence of a higher dynamic range of luminance in a scene by using some clever tricks. A simplified overview on what the example program accompanying this chapter is doing is shown in Figure 20.1.

Figure 20.1 shows that the scene is first rendered into a 32-bit integer render target, with 8-bit components for each color channel and the alpha channel. The image in this render target is then down sampled by rendering into another render target of 1/16 the size and at the same time luminance values are calculated, stored in the alpha channel, and then multiplied with the color channels. This operation is called bright-pass filtering, because the result of the operation is an image that shows only the bright areas of the original image.

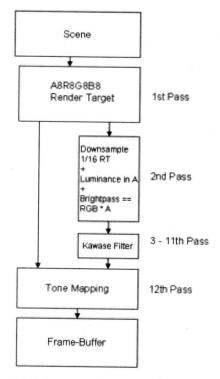

FIGURE 20.1   *Overview of Kawase's approach.*

Luminance Plus Bright Pass

The Luminance value is created by using the dot product of the color with a constant value that is known to create the luminance data.

```
Luminance = dot(color, float3(0.299f, 0.587f, 0.114f));
```

The result of the bright-pass filter is then retrieved with the following equation.

$$Color = RGB \times Luminance$$

The resulting render target holds the scaled luminance values of the original image.

Blooming

To imitate the overloading of the optic nerve if extremely bright areas are watched by the viewer—called blooming—a filter developed by Masaki Kawase is used. It works with the low number of texture stages available on XBOX and DX8 hardware by using several smaller blur filter kernels in several passes.

In each pass, this filter fetches four texels by moving the sampling points away from the pixel being rendered.

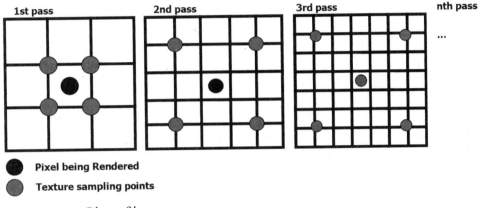

FIGURE 20.2   *Bloom filter.*

The result of one pass is used as the input of the next pass by switching between two render targets in a ping-pong manner.

Using eight iterations leads to very good results. Each iteration takes the previous results as input and applies a new kernel to increase bluriness.

Figure 20.3 shows the first, fourth, and eighth iterations of this filter. The end result after eight iterations has a nice shape.

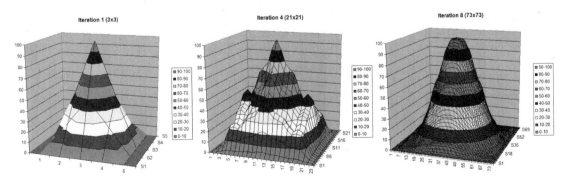

FIGURE 20.3   *Different iterations of Kawase's bloom filter.* Figure adapted from work of Christopher Oat, ATI Research.

Tone Mapping

Tone mapping describes the process of mapping a high dynamic range image into a low dynamic range space. There are numerous ways to achieve different effects with tone mapping. This example does not rely on a sophisticated tone mapping process, because it does not use data that has a higher value range than the output channels. It just lerps between the original image and the blurred image.

Implementation

Implementing Kawase's dynamic range image approach is possible on ps_1_1 hardware. Nevertheless, there are some gotchas while doing this, especially using his bloom filter.

Luminance Plus Bright Pass

The luminance and bright pass are done in one pixel shader pass. It is just a dot product between the original color values and the luminance values and a multiplication of the color values with the result of the luminance calculation.

```
float4 PSScaleBuffer(float2 Tex : TEXCOORD0) : COLOR
{
  float4 RGBA = tex2D(RenderMapSampler, Tex);
  float Luminance = dot(RGBA, float3(0.299f, 0.587f, 0.114f));

  return RGBA * Luminance;
}
```

The bright-pass filter pass scales the image down to 1/16 of its size by copying from a render target with the same size as the scene shown on the display to a render target with 1/16 of this size. Because we use integer textures, the texture is bilinear filtered.

Blooming

Each iteration of the Kawase filter ping-pongs between two renderable textures used for storing intermediate results. These render targets are switched like this.

```
// Provide even numbers, because of the ping-pong buffer
int iteration = 8;

// eight passes for bloom filter
for (int pass = 0; pass < iteration; pass++)
{
  // ping-pong between render targets
  if(bOne)
  {
    m_pEffect->SetTexture(m_hMap, m_pRenderTarget2);
    m_pd3dDevice->SetRenderTarget(0, m_pSurface3);
    bOne = FALSE;
```

```
    }
    else
    {
      m_pEffect->SetTexture(m_hMap, m_pRenderTarget3);
      m_pd3dDevice->SetRenderTarget(0, m_pSurface2);
      bOne = TRUE;
    }

    m_pEffect->SetFloat(m_hIteration, (float)pass);
    m_pEffect->Begin( NULL, 0 );
    m_pEffect->Pass( 0 );
    m_pd3dDevice->DrawPrimitive (D3DPT_TRIANGLESTRIP, 0, 2);
    m_pEffect->End();
}
```

Every pass renders a quad consisting of two stripped triangles into a render target. Each pass the filter reads from the previous render target and fetches the texels in this render target as shown in Figure 20.2. The vertex shader sets up the texture coordinates depending on the current iteration like this.

```
VS_OUTPUTBloom VSBloom(float4 Pos   : POSITION,
                       float2 Tex   : TEXCOORD0)
{
    VS_OUTPUTBloom Out = (VS_OUTPUTBloom)0;
    Out.Pos.xy = Pos.xy;
    Out.Pos.z = 0.5f;
    Out.Pos.w = 1.0f;

    float2 halfPixelSize = pixelSize.xy / 2.0f;
    float2 dUV = (pixelSize.xy * fIteration) + halfPixelSize.xy;

    // compute top left sample
    Out.TopLeft = float2(Tex.x - dUV.x, Tex.y + dUV.y);

    // compute top right sample
    Out.TopRight = float2(Tex.x + dUV.x, Tex.y + dUV.y);

    // compute bottom right sample
    Out.BottomRight = float2(Tex.x + dUV.x, Tex.y - dUV.y);

    // compute bottom left sample
    Out.BottomLeft = float2(Tex.x - dUV.x, Tex.y - dUV.y);

    return Out;
}
```

The texture coordinates are set up by using the size of the texture in texel space. The region where the four texels are fetched moves away with each iteration of the filter from the pixel being rendered into the render target, as shown in Figure 20.2. The pixel shader just adds the results of the four texture fetches and divides them by 4 and stores the result in the destination render target.

```
float4 PSBloom(float2 TopLeft     : TEXCOORD0,
               float2 TopRight    : TEXCOORD1,
               float2 BottomRight : TEXCOORD2,
               float2 BottomLeft  : TEXCOORD3) : COLOR0
{
  float4 addedBuffer = 0.0f;

  // sample top left
  addedBuffer = tex2D(RenderMapSampler, TopLeft);

  // sample top right
  addedBuffer += tex2D(RenderMapSampler, TopRight);

  // sample bottom right
  addedBuffer += tex2D(RenderMapSampler, BottomRight);

  // sample bottom left
  addedBuffer += tex2D(RenderMapSampler, BottomLeft);

  // average
  return addedBuffer *= 0.25f;
}
```

This pixel shader can run on ps_1_1 hardware, and because of the small size of the render target, it is highly efficient on any hardware. Although this opens up a wide target group of end users, the glare algorithm can only create a predictable result with a specific number of iterations in a specific resolution of the render target. In other words, you must always render the scene of the game into a 1024×768 render target that is scaled down to a 256×192 render target to get predictable results. That makes this algorithm suitable for consoles but more complicated for PC games.

> *This filter might be extended by adjusting the scaling of the texture coordinates in the vertex shader, depending on the render target size.*

Tone Mapping

The tone mapping function used in this example is quite simple. The value of the original image and the value from the blurred image are lerped based on a fixed value. Because the blurred image brings in a lot of dark color values, the result is then multiplied by 6.0f to make it brighter.

```
float4 PSScreen(float2 Tex : TEXCOORD0) : COLOR0
{
  float4 FullScreenImage = tex2D(FullResMapSampler, Tex);
  float4 BlurredImage = tex2D(RenderMapSampler, Tex);

  float4 color = lerp(FullScreenImage, BlurredImage, 0.75f);
```

```
    return color * 6.0f;

//    return (1 - exp(-color) * 1.0f) * 8.0f;
}
```

Depending on the mood you want to create in the game, these parameters might be tweaked. You might even use an exponential function, as shown in the previous chapter, or take the power 0.55f of the color values (read more in the next chapter).

DirectX Rasterization Rules

All examples that render to several render targets need to account for a problem that comes from the way DirectX rasterizes. DirectX has always rasterized to render target pixel centers, and has always looked up textures from texel edges. If you render from one render target into another render target without adjusting the texture coordinates for this fact, the picture will move to the bottom right.

Ideally, when you wish to use graphics hardware to process one texture to another, you should not have to care about how many texels your source and destination image have; you should be able to deal with the whole thing in viewport and texture coordinates. The following vertex shader lets Direct3D rasterize into the pixel edges and accounts the texel coordinates for this.

```
VS_OUTPUTScaleBuffer VSScaleBuffer(float4 Pos : POSITION)
{
    VS_OUTPUTScaleBuffer Out = (VS_OUTPUTScaleBuffer)0;
    Out.Pos.xy = Pos.xy + pixelSize.xy;

    Out.Pos.z = 0.5f;
    Out.Pos.w = 1.0f;
    Out.Tex = float2(0.5f, -0.5f) * Pos.xy + 0.5f.xx;
    return Out;
}
```

The only data sent from the application to the vertex shader is the *x* and *y* values of the position. The texture coordinates are derived from the position value. With the high number of render–to–render-target passes, sending only the *x* and *y* values reduces the amount of vertex data sent to the vertex shader substantially. (Although the overall workload of the vertex shader is very low, this might count if there is more work to do.)

Result

The results are achieved by using the reference implementation of the Ashikhmin-Shirley reflection model. Having only one well-defined and movable bright area in the example makes it easier to predict the end result.

ON THE CD The following example programs are available in the directory Chapter 20 - Faked High Dynamic Range.

- High Dynamic Range Kawase RGBA8 uses 32-bit values consisting of four 8-bit components.
- High Dynamic Range Kawase RGBE8 uses compressed RGBE8 values, with the exponent stored in the fourth channel (see Chapter 18 for more information on this format).

Both examples let you choose the

- Exposure level with the R and F keys
- Diffuse and specular contribution with the D and E keys
- *mx* and *my* values of the Ashikhmin-Shirley reflection model with the Home, End and Pg Up, Pg Down keys

Luminance Plus Bright Pass

Figure 20.4 shows the original scene in the screenshot on the left and the result of the luminance and bright-pass filter in the screenshot on the right.

FIGURE 20.4 *Bright-pass filter.*

Please note that the screenshot on the right is a little bit darker than in reality. This is due to reproduction issues.

Blooming

Figure 20.5 shows the result of the bloom filter used by Kawase on the bright-pass filtered image.

FIGURE 20.5   *Kawase's bloom filter.*

Using a different number of iterations leads to different results. For example, using only four iterations, as shown in Figure 20.3, leads to several clouds. More than eight iterations do not lead to better results but will blur out the bright zone so that everything gets dark. Please note that these screenshots are taken from a render target with the size 256×192. Using another resolution might lead to different looking results.

Tone Mapping

The goal for the tone mapping process here was to achieve a look similar to the original image with the addition of the blooming effect. In both example programs, tone mapping just lerps between the blurred and bloomed image and the original image. Increasing the exposure value might compensate for the darkened values in the blurred image.

Using a different technique to modify the color data here is a good way to give your game a certain look and feel.

Figure 20.6 shows that the filter creates a nicely blurred highlight at the point with the highest brightness. This is different from a Gaussian blur, which would follow more closely the reflection first, which will be shown in the next chapter.

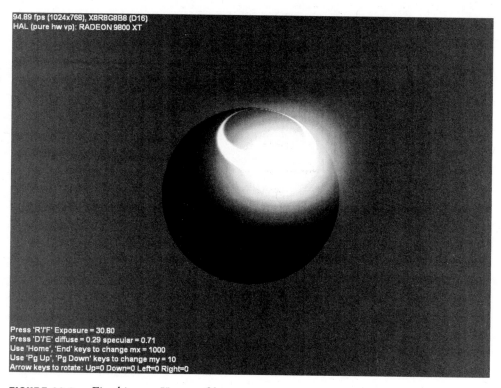

FIGURE 20.6 *Final image Kawase filter.*

Conclusion

Masaki Kawase's approach fakes the existence of high dynamic range in a scene by blurring bright areas in a scene. The original approach utilizing RGBA values is even capable of running on DX8 hardware but is restricted to a fixed-size render target for predictable results, which makes it better suited to console platforms than to PC games. The enhanced RGBE8 version shown in Figure 20.6 requires a more powerful graphics card, due to the higher amount of pixel shader instructions, but leads to even better visual results.

21

High Dynamic Range Lighting

A higher dynamic range of luminance values can be stored in floating-point render targets. Using floating-point render targets allows you to use a higher value range and reduces the loss of precision during all computations. This allows the preservation of a higher range of luminance values throughout the rendering pipeline.

ATI showcased an example program called *Rendering with Natural Light* on SIGGRAPH 2002 (*http://www.ati.com/developer*), which covered a real-time implementation of a non-real-time example presented by Paul Debevec on SIGGRAPH 1998 (*http://www.debevec.org*). ATI's approach follows Paul Debevec's ideas of high dynamic range lighting very closely, and the following pages will cover some techniques found in this demo.

Background

The simplified diagram in Figure 21.1 shows the high-level approach to rendering that is used in the real-time and non-real-time renderings of the *Rendering with Natural Light* example program. The bulk of these operations need to be performed with a high dynamic range of values to truly represent the wide range of radiances present in a real-world scene. The scene is first rendered into a 16-bit floating-point render target, then the render target is scaled down and a bloom filter is applied to the image to simulate light scattering in the eye.

In this example, the bloom filter consists of a two-pass Gaussian filter. This filter is very flexible and its parameters can be tweaked to fit the needs of an application very closely.

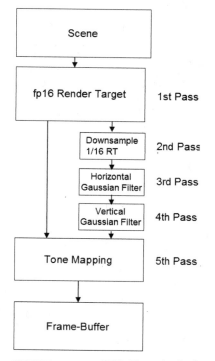

FIGURE 21.1   *ATI's Time high-dynamic range approach.*

Gaussian Filter

The Gaussian filter can be used to blur 2D images by sampling a circular neighborhood of pixels from the input image and computing their weighted average, according to the following equation.

$$g_{2d}(x,y) = \frac{1}{\sqrt{2\pi}\sigma} e^{\frac{-x^2+y^2}{2\sigma^2}}$$

where σ is the standard deviation of the Gaussian and x and y are the coordinates of image samples relative to the center of the filter. The Gaussian can be rearranged and made separable in the following manner.

$$g_{2d}(x,y) = \frac{1}{\sqrt{2\pi}\sigma} e^{\frac{-x^2}{2\sigma^2}} \times \frac{1}{\sqrt{2\pi}\sigma} e^{\frac{y^2}{2\sigma^2}}$$

Factorizing the equation this way lets us compute the Gaussian filter with a series of 1D filtering operations: in the first pass a weighted sum of a column of 13 pixels centered on the current pixel and in its second pass a weighted sum of a row of 13 pixels centered on the current pixel.

To target ps_2_0 capable graphics cards, the samples need to be divided into three types: inner taps, outer taps, and the center tap. The center tap and inner taps shown in Figure 21.2 are calculated by using interpolated texture coordinates.

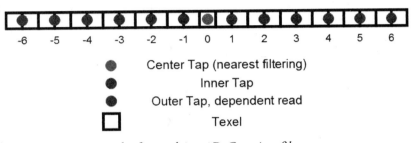

FIGURE 21.2 *Samples for applying 1D Gaussian filter.*

Because we have only eight texture coordinate interpolators in a ps_2_0-capable graphics card, the texture coordinates of the outer taps need to be derived in the pixel shader as deltas from the center tap location.

All samples are weighted based on the predefined weight thresholds and blurriness values and added together. This results in a weighted sum of 25 texels from the source image.

Tone Mapping

The tone mapping pass maps a high dynamic range image into a low dynamic range space to make it suitable for output by the frame buffer. One of the simplest techniques creating a high dynamic range is to multiply the color values with a high exposure value and then reduce this to a low dynamic range by using a power function.

```
color *= ExposureLevel;
return pow(color, 0.55f);
```

By raising or lowering the color values with an exposure value, the difference of the darkest and the brightest point in a scene gets higher or lower. Using a power function to adjust this value range to [0..1] offers the opportunity to adjust the gamma value of the image by choosing a specific power value. Gamma measures the brightness of midtone values produced by a device (often a monitor). A higher gamma value yields an overall darker image. Windows systems use a higher gamma value than Mac OS systems, with the result that the same image is noticeably darker on a Windows system than on a Mac OS system.

Implementation

The main techniques in the example program are the Gaussian filter and the tone mapping technique used here.

Gaussian Filter

The separable filter is implemented in two passes. For each pass, the texture coordinates and texel weights are calculated by the application in the render function and then sent via SetValue() to the pixel shader. The vertex shader calculates the texture coordinate values for the center tap and the six inner taps.

```
VS_OUTPUT_GaussX VSGaussX(float4 Pos      : POSITION)
{
    VS_OUTPUT_GaussX Out = (VS_OUTPUT_GaussX)0;
    Out.Pos.xy = Pos.xy + pixelSize.xy;
    Out.Pos.z = 0.5f;
    Out.Pos.w = 1.0f;

    float2 Tex = float2(0.5f, -0.5f) * Pos.xy + 0.5f.xx;

    Out.Tap0 = Tex;
    Out.Tap1 = Tex + horzTapOffs[1];
    Out.Tap2 = Tex + horzTapOffs[2];
    Out.Tap3 = Tex + horzTapOffs[3];
    Out.Tap1Neg = Tex - horzTapOffs[1];
    Out.Tap2Neg = Tex - horzTapOffs[2];
    Out.Tap3Neg = Tex - horzTapOffs[3];
    return Out;
}
```

The seven texture coordinates are sent to the pixel shader and used to calculate the texture coordinates for the six outer taps.

```
float4 PSGaussX( float2 Tap0 : TEXCOORD0,
                float2 Tap1 : TEXCOORD1,
                float2 Tap2 : TEXCOORD2,
                float2 Tap3 : TEXCOORD3,
                float2 Tap1Neg : TEXCOORD4,
                float2 Tap2Neg : TEXCOORD5,
                float2 Tap3Neg : TEXCOORD6) : COLOR0
{
  float4 Color[7];
  float4 ColorSum = 0.0f;
```

```
// sample inner taps
Color[0] = tex2D(RenderMapSampler, Tap0);
Color[1] = tex2D(RenderMapSampler, Tap1);
Color[2] = tex2D(RenderMapSampler, Tap1Neg);
Color[3] = tex2D(RenderMapSampler, Tap2);
Color[4] = tex2D(RenderMapSampler, Tap2Neg);
Color[5] = tex2D(RenderMapSampler, Tap3);
Color[6] = tex2D(RenderMapSampler, Tap3Neg);

ColorSum = Color[0] * TexelWeight[0];
ColorSum += Color[1] * TexelWeight[1];
ColorSum += Color[2] * TexelWeight[1];
ColorSum += Color[3] * TexelWeight[2];
ColorSum += Color[4] * TexelWeight[2];
ColorSum += Color[5] * TexelWeight[3];
ColorSum += Color[6] * TexelWeight[3];

// compute texture coordinates for other taps
float2 Tap4 = Tap0 + horzTapOffs[4];
float2 Tap5 = Tap0 + horzTapOffs[5];
float2 Tap6 = Tap0 + horzTapOffs[6];
float2 Tap4Neg = Tap0 - horzTapOffs[4];
float2 Tap5Neg = Tap0 - horzTapOffs[5];
float2 Tap6Neg = Tap0 - horzTapOffs[6];

// sample outer taps
Color[0] = tex2D(RenderMapSampler, Tap4);
Color[1] = tex2D(RenderMapSampler, Tap4Neg);
Color[2] = tex2D(RenderMapSampler, Tap5);
Color[3] = tex2D(RenderMapSampler, Tap5Neg);
Color[4] = tex2D(RenderMapSampler, Tap6);
Color[5] = tex2D(RenderMapSampler, Tap6Neg);

ColorSum += Color[0] * TexelWeight[4];
ColorSum += Color[1] * TexelWeight[4];
ColorSum += Color[2] * TexelWeight[5];
ColorSum += Color[3] * TexelWeight[5];
ColorSum += Color[4] * TexelWeight[6];
ColorSum += Color[5] * TexelWeight[6];

return ColorSum;
}
```

Please note that the same weight is used for texels that are lying on opposite sides of the center texel. The vertical Gaussian filter creates the texture coordinates in a different direction, but other than this, it is equal to the one shown in the previous example.

Tone Mapping

The tone mapping pass in this example lerps between the blurred and the original image. Then a vignette is added to the color value. A vignette is an effect that surrounds an image with a round border. Therefore, the vignette is based on the distance to the center of the image. A vignette gives the appearance of a shining object by producing a kind of halo around the object.

```
float4 PSScreen(float2 Tex : TEXCOORD0) : COLOR0
{
  static float fExposureLevel = 32.0f;

  float4 FullScreenImage = tex2D(FullResMapSampler, Tex);
  float4 BlurredImage = tex2D(RenderMapSampler, Tex);

  float4 color = lerp(FullScreenImage, BlurredImage, 0.4f);

  Tex -= 0.5f; // range -0.5..0.5
  float vignette = 1 - dot(Tex, Tex);

  // multiply color with vignette^4
  color = color * vignette * vignette * vignette * vignette;

  color *= fExposureLevel; // apply simple exposure
 return pow(color, 0.55f);
}
```

The final image is multiplied by an exposure value to get a high dynamic range, and then the value range is scaled down to [0..1.0] by applying a power of 0.55f to the color value. This value controls the brightness of midtone values (gamma) in a suitable way in this scene, but you might try out other values as well. Higher values will darken the image and lower values will brighten it.

Results and Conclusion

All results are achieved by using the Ashikhmin-Shirley reflectance model developed in Chapter 15. This reflectance model offers one well-defined and movable bright area in the example that helps to predict the end-result.

ON THE CD The following example program is available in the directory Chapter 21 - High Dynamic Range: High-Dynamic Range Gaussian FP16.
This example let you choose the:

- Exposure level with the R and F keys
- Diffuse and specular contribution with the D and E keys
- *mx* and *my* values of the Ashikhmin-Shirley reflection model with the Home, End and Pg Up, Pg Down keys

The output of the example program is shown in Figure 21.3.

The top-left screenshot in Figure 21.3 shows an exposure value of 1.0. Please note how the vignette is visible on this screenshot. The top-right screenshot uses an exposure value of 4.0 and the bottom-left screenshot an exposure level of 8.0. To raise the amount of light energy in the screenshot, the portion of the diffuse component was raised to 40%.

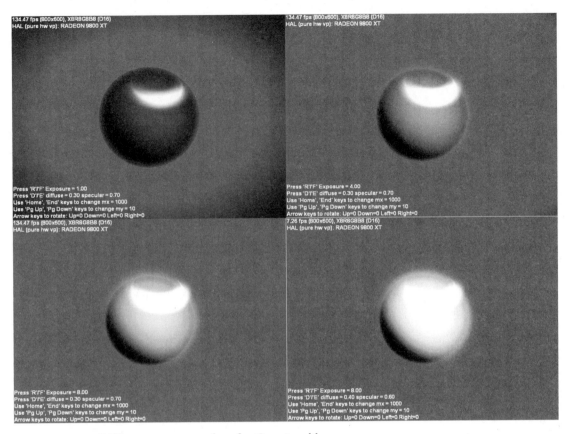

FIGURE 21.3 *Different exposure values for Gaussian blur.*

Using a high dynamic range of luminance values is possible with graphics hardware that supports floating-point render targets and ps_2_0 as the minimum pixel shader model. Floating-point render targets are required to store a higher value range to preserve precision in intermediate calculations, and the ps_2_0 shader specification is necessary because it supports eight texture coordinates as a minimum for the implementation of the Gaussian blur.

Overall, the Gaussian blur is much more flexible than the blooming filter used in the previous chapter. It is less dependent on the size of the render target and leads to more predictable results.

22

Advanced Tone Mapping

An advanced tone mapping system is capable of mimicking the light adaptation behavior of the human visual system. The most important effect is the capability of imitating the light adaptation process that happens when a human comes from a dark room to the sunny outside or vice versa.

Background

To be able to mimic the light adaptation process of a human, the approach in this chapter covers the following steps:

- Measure luminance
- Adapt luminance
- Scale intensity of scene
- Tone mapping

Figure 22.1 outlines these steps.

As shown in Figure 22.1, the example program needs 12 passes to render the scene. Compared to the previous example program, the Gaussian blur filters receive an image in which only the bright areas are left. This image was generated by a bright-pass filter with a similar functionality as the bright-pass filter used in Chapter 20. It is also dependent on the result of the light adaptation process and will be described later in this chapter more thoroughly.

The main improvement is the way the luminance value of the image is measured. This example follows the approach taken by Erik Reinhard, et al. [Reinhard]. To account for the three different images that go into the tone mapping process, this process is more complex than the one used in the previous chapters.

Let's start on how to measure luminance.

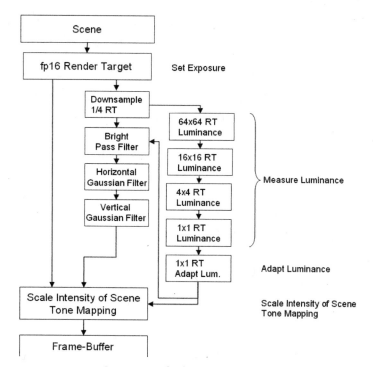

FIGURE 22.1   *Overview of advanced tone mapping.*

Measure Luminance

Before a program can scale the intensity of a scene, it needs to determine how bright the scene is to begin with. The goal is to calculate a good estimate for the average scene luminance.

To measure luminance, two steps are involved. First, the luminance of the whole scene is calculated for each pixel of the scene, and then the luminance values of all pixels are averaged and the result is stored in a 1×1 texture.

The intuitive approach to calculating the luminance value would be the same approach as used in Chapter 20.

```
Lum(x, y) = dot(color, float3(0.2125f, 0.7154f, 0.0721f));
```

Erik Reinhard et al. [Reinhard] have developed a more sophisticated way to average scene luminance. They use the antilogarithm of the average log values for all sampled pixels.

$$Lum_{avg} = \exp\left(\frac{1}{N^{x,y}} \sum \log\big(\delta + Lum(x,y)\big) \right)$$

where $L(x, y)$ is the luminance for a pixel at the location (x, y), N is the total number of pixels in the image and δ is a small value to avoid the singularity that occurs if black pixels are present in the image.

The retrieved average luminance value is then fed to the light adaptation function.

Adapt Luminance

The human visual system does not adjust instantly for changing light conditions. To simulate this behavior, the adaptation to a new luminance value under changing lighting conditions needs to be decelerated. This deceleration process uses the luminance data from the current frame and interpolates it with the luminance data stored in the previous frame. The latter was the result of the interpolation between the luminance value of the previous frame and the frame before that.

This algorithm will output a luminance value that is between these values until it reaches the level of the current luminance.

$$Lum_{\text{Adapted}}(x, y) = Lum_{\text{Previous}} \times \left(Lum_{\text{Current}} - Lum_{\text{Previous}} \right) \times \left(1.0f - pow\left(0.98f, 30 \times ElapsedTime \right) \right)$$

The previous luminance value is multiplied with the difference between the current and the previous luminance value. To apply a time passed scaling, the power of 0.98 with a time-based power value is subtracted from 1.0. Each luminance value output by the luminance adaptation stage is used to scale the intensity of the scene.

Scale Intensity of Scene

With an adapted luminance value in a 1×1 texture, we can scale the scene according to this value. This is done by defining a middle-gray value on the scale from zero to one. This suggests the following equation.

$$FullScreenImage_{\text{Scaled}}(x, y) = \frac{\alpha}{Lum_{\text{Adapted}}(x, y)} \times FullScreenImage(x, y)$$

where $FullScreenImage_{\text{Scaled}}$ is the scaled luminance, Lum_{Adapted} is the adapted luminance value resulting from the previous stage, and α is the middle-gray value. Good choices for the middle gray value are are 0.18f, 0.36f, and 0.54f.

Tone Mapping the Scene

To map the scaled scene from its high dynamic range of values to the low dynamic range of values that can be displayed, Reinhard covers two different tone mapping operators: a simple one and a more advanced one. The simple tone mapping operator compresses mainly the high luminance values.

$$Color(x,y) = \frac{FullScreenImage_{Scaled}(x,y)}{1.0f + FullScreenImage_{Scaled}(x,y)}$$

Note that high luminances are scaled by approximately 1.0/*Lum*, while low luminances are scaled by 1.0. This operator is guaranteed to bring all luminances with displayable reach. To allow higher luminance values to burn out in a controllable fashion, the following tone mapping operator uses *LumWhite* as the smallest luminance that will be mapped to pure white.

$$Color(x,y) = \frac{FullScreenImage_{Scaled}(x,y) \times 1 + \left(\left(FullScreenImage_{Scaled}(x,y)\right)/LumWhite^2\right)}{1.0f + FullScreenImage_{Scaled}(x,y)}$$

If *LumWhite* is set to the maximum luminance in the scene or higher, no burnout will occur, if it is set to infinity, the function reverts to the previous function. Setting *LumWhite* to the maximum luminance in the scene achieves a subtle contrast enhancement in scenes with a low dynamic range.

Bright-Pass Filter

Similar to the bright-pass filter used in Chapter 20, the bright-pass filter in this chapter determines first what areas of the final scene image will be bright, and then excludes the remaining data. The main difference is that the incoming value range in Chapter 22 is [0..1], whereas in this chapter, we have to deal with an incoming high dynamic range of values.

Because the result of the bright-pass filter will be an image mainly consisting of black, gray, and white values, it is not necessary to prevent a high dynamic range in the following render stages of the rendering pipeline of the example. Therefore, the bright-pass filter scales and tone-maps the results to the range [0..1.0] in this example.

The bright-pass filter uses the scaling formula shown in the section "Scale Intensity of Scene" and the simple tone mapping operator of the section "Tone Mapping the Scene." In other words, the bright-pass filter scales and tone-maps the image with the same or similar techniques as the final rendering path scales the original image.

Because of the low dynamic range of values used throughout the following stages, we can feed the blurred result of the Gaussian blur filter stages directly to the final pass, without the need to adjust the value range. So the blurred image can be added directly to the scene output; this offers the advantage of using integer render target formats that are bilinear filtered on most current hardware.

Implementation

All the algorithms covered earlier map very well to HLSL pixel shader instructions. The most challenging is the algorithm used to measure luminance here.

Measure Luminance

To measure the average luminance as in the following equation, three different pixel shaders are used in four passes.

$$Lum_{avg} = \exp\left(\frac{1}{N^{x,y}} \sum \log\left(\delta + Lum(x,y)\right) \right)$$

The first pass takes care of $\log(\delta + Lum(x, y))$, by providing the luminance value retrieved by

```
Lum(x, y) = dot(color, float3(0.2125f, 0.7154f, 0.0721f));
```

with the addition of 0.001f (δ) to the `log()` instrinsic. The pixel shader `PSSample-AverageLuminance()` fetches 3×3 pixels per pass and averages the results.

```
    ...
    fLogLumSum += log(dot(tex2D(RenderMapSampler, TexCoord[7]),
                LUMINANCE_VECTOR)+ Delta);
    fLogLumSum += log(dot(tex2D(RenderMapSampler, TexCoord[8]),
                LUMINANCE_VECTOR)+ Delta);

    // Divide the sum to complete the average
    fLogLumSum /= 9;
    ...
```

The resulting 64×64 texture that holds the luminance values is then downscaled in the pixel shader `PSReSampleAverageLuminance()` to a 16×16 surface, and this surface is downscaled in a third pass by the same pixel shader to a 4×4 texture. Downscaling is done in both passes by fetching 4×4 pixels and averaging the results.

In the fourth and final pass that is necessary to measure luminance, the 4×4 texture is downscaled by fetching 4×4 pixels, and the averaged result is provided to the `exp()` intrinsic as shown in the following source code snippet taken from `PSReSampleAverageLuminanceExp()`.

```
    ...
    fSum += tex2D(ToneMapSampler, TexCoord[14]);
    fSum += tex2D(ToneMapSampler, TexCoord[15]);

    // Divide the sum to complete the average
    fSum = exp(fSum/16);
    ...
```

Downsampling the surface that holds the luminance values this way assures that all pixels are covered. By scaling directly from the original size surface or a scaled down version of the original image to a 4×4 or 1×1 surface, you can still get some averaging, and it might be acceptable for games (read more in [Sousa]), but it might be only the

16 pixels you happen to hit that are averaged. So if there is high-frequency information in there (such as in a black texture with some bright white stripes), you could completely miss the white pixels and your result would be completely black.

 One idea for making this downscaling process more efficient might be to use automatic mip-map generation. If supported in hardware, this might take (compared to the previous approach), some shortcuts in down sampling the surfaces to create the mip-maps. Additionally, this way the overhead involved by the Direct3D can be avoided.

Adapt Luminance

To adapt luminance for imitating the light adjustment behavior of the human visual system, the light adaptation formula is used in a HLSL pixel shader.

```
float4 PSCalculateAdaptedLuminance( float2 Tex :TEXCOORD0): COLOR
{
    float AdaptedLum = tex2D(AdaptedLuminanceMapSampler,
float2(0.5f, 0.5f));
    float CurrentLum = tex2D(ToneMapSampler, float2(0.5f, 0.5f));

    return AdaptedLum + (CurrentLum - AdaptedLum) * ( 1 - pow(
0.98f, FPS * ElapsedTime) );
}
```

This pixel shader decelerates the adaptation to new luminance values under changing lighting conditions. It uses the luminance data from the current frame in `CurrentLum` and interpolates them with the luminance data from the previous frame in `AdaptedLum`. The values stored in `AdaptedLum` were the result of the interpolation between the luminance value of the previous frame and the frame before that. The output of this pixel shader is a luminance value that is between the values in `CurrentLum` and `AdaptedLum` until it reaches the level of the current luminance.

Scale Intensity of Scene

The formula to scale the intensity of the scene uses the result of the 1×1 texture from the previous pass to scale the full screen image according to its intensity.

$$FullScreenImage_{Scaled}(x, y) = \frac{\alpha}{Lum_{Adapted}(x, y)} \times FullScreenImage(x, y)$$

Scaling the intensity of the scene is done in the final rendering pass. The HLSL implementation is straightforward.

```
FullScreenImage.rgb *= MiddleGray / (AdaptedLum + 0.001f);
```

Tone Mapping the Scene

To map the scene from a high dynamic range of values to a low dynamic range of values, the following operator is used.

$$Color(x,y) = \frac{FullScreenImage_{Scaled}(x,y) \times 1 + \left(\left(FullScreenImage_{Scaled}(x,y)\right)/LumWhite^2\right)}{1.0f + FullScreenImage_{Scaled}(x,y)}$$

Together with the scaling of the intensity shown in the previous section, tone mapping is done in the final rendering pass.

```
float4 PSScreen(float2 Tex : TEXCOORD0) : COLOR0
{
    float4 FullScreenImage = tex2D(FullResMapSampler, Tex);
    float4 BlurredImage = tex2D(RenderMapSampler, Tex);
    float AdaptedLum = tex2D(AdaptedLuminanceMapSampler, float2(0.5,
0.5));

    FullScreenImage.rgb *= MiddleGray / (AdaptedLum + 0.001f);
    FullScreenImage.rgb *= (1.0f + FullScreenImage/ 8.0f);
    FullScreenImage.rgb /= (1.0f + FullScreenImage);

    return FullScreenImage += (ExposureLevel/12) * BlurredImage;
}
```

The original image with the chosen exposure level is stored in `FullScreenImage` and the 1×1 texture resulting from the light adaptation process is stored in `AdaptedLum`. The result from the Gaussian blurs is stored in `BlurredImage`. This variable is not scaled or tone-mapped, because the value range was already scaled and tone-mapped in the bright-pass. To control the blurring level depending on the exposure level, these values are multiplied with a fraction of the exposure level.

Results

The example program accompanying this chapter in the directory Chapter 22 - Advanced Tone Mapping\Advanced Tone Mapping Reinhard offers a wide variety of variables that are controlled by the user. To control the results of all render steps involved, it shows the results from seven render targets as previews in the upper area of its window. All previews are ordered from left to right in the order shown in Figure 22.2.

The first preview shows the original image. To change the appearance of the Ashikhmin-Shirley reflectance model used here, the user can change the *mx* and *my* values of this model by pressing Page Up and Page Down. Furthermore, the ratio between the diffuse component and the specular component can be changed by pressing D and E.

The second preview shows the original image with a user-specified exposure value. This value can be set by pressing R and F. The third preview shows the surface

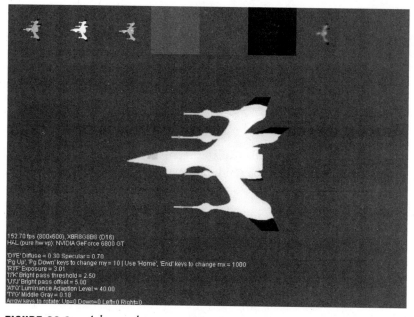

FIGURE 22.2   *Advanced tone mapping.*

of the 64×64 render target, which holds the luminance values from the first pass, that is used to measure luminance. The fourth preview shows the current luminance value stored in a 1×1 surface, and the fifth preview shows the adapted luminance value. To choose the level of deceleration of the light adaptation process, the keys Q and A are used to decelerate or accelerate this process. The sixth preview shows the content of the bright filter pass surface. To adjust the bright filter to different lighting conditions, the user can set the bright pass offset with U and J, the bright pass threshold with I and K and the middle gray value with T and G. The seventh preview shows the results of the two Gaussian blur passes.

As a starting point to play around with this example program, you might first choose a different exposure level. By raising or lowering this level, the effects of the light adaptation process are visible. This impression can be improved by raising the luminance adaptation value. Please note how the adaptation process is visible in the fourth preview, which shows the current luminance value, and the fifth preview, which shows the adapted luminance value.

Conclusion

This part of the book showed some basic techniques that covered a way to fake a high dynamic range of luminance values and some flexible ways to use a high dynamic range of luminance values on current graphics hardware. This chapter examines two different blurring techniques (Kawase bloom filter and Gaussian blur), several ways to map a high dynamic range image to a low dynamic range image, how to use a vignette to create a halo-like effect, and how to measure and adapt luminance to mimic the light adaptation behavior of the human visual system.

These techniques should be the basis for most of the high dynamic range effects used in current and future games. There is a lot of room for improvement by simplifying things and adjusting the technique to the hardware environment and the mood of the game (see [Kawase] and [Sousa]). Although imitating the human light adaptation process seems to be quite expensive, it is possible to implement this effect on recent hardware with suitable performance.

Projective Texture Mapping

Projective texture mapping allows the texture image to be projected onto the scene as if by a slide or video projector. Effects that can be created by using projective texturing are:

- Arbitrary projection of two-dimensional images onto geometry (Batman sign, Star Wars Hologram projector, etc.)
- Shadow mapping
- Spotlight effects

This part of the book will cover arbitrary projection of two-dimensional images onto geometry techniques. Shadow mapping will be covered in the next part.

23

Arbitrary Projection of Two-Dimensional Images onto Geometry

Quite popular effects can be achieved by projecting an image onto geometry. For example, a spinning fan on the ceiling, a Batman sign, or slide or video projections. All these effects are achieved with a technique called projective texture mapping, which will be covered in this chapter.

Background

Projective texture mapping refers both to the way texture coordinates are assigned to vertices, and the way they are computed during rasterization of primitives.

Assigning Texture Coordinates to Vertices

Texture coordinates are assigned to the vertices via a texture projection matrix. This matrix consists of a sequence of transformations, which maps from model space to texture space.

Consider that the texture is being projected onto the scene by a slide projector. This projector has most of the same properties that cameras have, such as a viewing transform (Look At) that transforms world space coordinates into projector space (or eye space) and a projection transform that maps the projector space view volume to clip coordinates. Finally, we have a scale and bias to apply a simple range mapping, because the transformed vertex values range from [−1..1], however, textures are indexed from [0..1]. This is done by multiplying the x, y, and z components of the results by 0.5f and then adding 0.5f/TextureSize. A single matrix multiplication accomplishes this mapping.

```
World Matrix->m_matWorld
*
Look At Matrix->D3DXMatrixLookAtLH->matView
*
Projection Matrix->D3DXMatrixOrthoLH ||
D3DXMatrixPerspectiveFovLH->matProj
*
Texture Space Matrix->matTextureAdj
```

This pseudo-code shows the matrices involved. The final matrix consists of the transpose of the product of a Look At matrix multiplied by a perspective projection matrix, multiplied by a scaling matrix that maps to the range [0..1] of texture space.

Computing Texture Coordinates During Rasterization

When performing projective texture mapping, we use homogeneous texture coordinates, or coordinates in projective space. For projective 2D texture mapping, the 3-component homogeneous coordinate (u, v, w) is interpolated over the primitive, and then at each fragment, the interpolated homogeneous coordinate is projected to a real 2D texture coordinate $(u/w, v/w)$ to index into the texture image.

For nonprojective 2D texture mapping, the two-component real coordinate (u, v) is interpolated over the primitive and used directly to index into the texture image.

Implementation

Implementing a projection matrix and projecting the interpolated homogenous texture coordinate to a 2D texture coordinate is a straightforward process. The latter is natively supported in graphics hardware.

Assigning Texture Coordinates to Vertices

Assigning texture coordinates to vertices is done by creating all the matrices mentioned earlier and multiplying them in the order World * View * Projection * TexAdjust. This is shown in the following source code snippet.

```
// Texture adjustment matrix
float dwOffsetX=0.5f + (0.5f / 350.0f);
float dwOffsetY=0.5f + (0.5f / 123.0f);

D3DXMATRIX matTextureAdj;
ZeroMemory(&matTextureAdj, sizeof(D3DXMATRIX));
matTextureAdj._11 = 0.5f; // scale by 0.5: from +/-1.0 to +/-0.5
matTextureAdj._22 = -0.5f; // same, but invert sense of y
matTextureAdj._41 = dwOffsetX;
// u: add 0.5 offset: from +/-0.5 to 0.0-1.0
matTextureAdj._42 = dwOffsetY; // same, for v
matTextureAdj._44 = 1.0f;
```

```
D3DXMATRIX matView, matProj, matTextureGen;
// starting point for the projection
D3DXVECTOR3 vProjector = D3DXVECTOR3(2.0f, 0.0f, -3.5f);
m_pEffect->SetVector("vecProjDir", &D3DXVECTOR4(vProjector.x,
vProjector.y, vProjector.z, 1.0));

// create view matrix
vEyePt = vLookatPt + vProjector * (1.0f /* model size*/  / 2.0f);
D3DXMatrixLookAtLH(&matView, &vEyePt, &vLookatPt, &vUpVec);

#define DEPTH_RANGE 5.0f

// Perspective Projection
FLOAT fAspect = ((FLOAT)m_d3dsdBackBuffer.Width) / m_d3dsdBackBuffer.Height;
D3DXMatrixPerspectiveFovLH( &matProj, D3DX_PI/4, fAspect, 0.09f,
                   DEPTH_RANGE);
m_pEffect->SetMatrix( "ProjTextureMatrix", &(m_matWorld * matView
* matProj * matTextureAdj));
```

`matView` holds the lefthanded Look At matrix of the light source, `matProj` holds the lights projection matrix, and `matTextureAdj` holds the scale and bias matrix to apply a simple range mapping.

```
0.5f,        0.0f,       0.0f, 0.0f,
0.0f,       -0.5f,       0.0f, 0.0f,
0.0f,        0.0f,       0.0f, 0.0f,
dwOffsetX, dwOffsetY,   0.0f, 1.0f
```

This matrix performs the scale and bias to map the u, v, and w components of the texture coordinate to the [0,1] range. The concatenated texture projection matrix is then sent to the vertex shader, and the position is multiplied with it.

```
...
Out.Tex = mul(Pos, ProjTextureMatrix);
// project texture coordinates
...
```

Computing Texture Coordinates During Rasterization

The projection of the interpolated homogenous coordinate to a real 2D texture coordinate is done by the `tex2Dproj` texture intrinsic.

```
...
tex2Dproj(ProjTexMapSampler, Tex);
...
```

Results/Notable Issues

Getting nice-looking projective texturing is quite straightforward at first glance. Depending on what you are trying to achieve, issues might arise that require some workarounds. Notably, there are two big issues with projective texturing: reverse projection and the missing of occlusion checks.

Reverse Projection

The first issue is reverse projection. Unlike a real projector, the math of projective texture mapping actually produces a dual projection: one along the projector's view direction and another in the opposite direction.

The sign of w becomes negative behind the projector, which inverts the texture image in the reverse projection.

On ps_2_0 and upwards capable hardware, we can check the value of w and if w is negative, ignore the projective texture computation and output black.

```
...
return Tex.w < 0.0 ? 0.0 : tex2Dproj(ProjTexMapSampler, Tex);
...
```

How to do this on ps_1_1 hardware: set D3DTTFF_PROJECTED in your texture state texture transformation flags and store the result of the dot-product between the texture projection matrix and the vertex position in a texture coordinate output register. Basically using D3DTTFF_PROJECTED in the texture transformation flags enables texture coordinates division by the last texture coordinate.

Solving the reverse projection issue is usually done with a so-called clipper texture on ps_1_1 hardware. You need a 1D texture, that is 2×1 with one black pixel and one white pixel. Set your texture u coordinate addressing to CLAMP. In your pixel shader (or in case of the fixed-function pipeline, in the texture stages), you now have to modulate your result color by the clipper texture. Basically what we are doing is, every time your results get negative, the u texture coordinate gets clamped and you use the black pixel from the clipper texture in the color modulation, thus correcting the inverse projection.

No Occlusion Checks

The second issue arises when there is no occlusion information available for projective textures. Therefore, the projective texture is applied to every triangle that is within the projector's frustum, without being able to care for occluded geometry. This is shown in Figure 23.1.

582.15 fps (800x600), X8R8G8B8 (D16)
HAL (pure hw vp): RADEON 9800 XT
W - Zoom In
S - Zoom Out
Home/End - Moves Light -z/+z
Up/Down - Moves Light -y/+y
Left/Right - Moves Light -x/+x
ShaderX
PROGRAMMING

FIGURE 23.1 *Projective texturing does not check for occlusion.*

The handle and the back of the teapot show the projected texture although they are located from the point of view of the projector behind the teapot. In other words, to mimic real-world experiences, the occluding geometry should prevent the texture from showing up on the handle and the back of the teapot.

There are several ways to solve this problem.

dot(P, N)

The first solution is calculating the dot-product between the projection vector and the normal. If the normal is facing away more than 90 degrees, the projective texture computation is ignored and the color black is sent to the output registers.

The drawback of this method is that on geometry that is occluded by other geometry but facing in the direction of the projection vector, the projected texture is still applied. This is shown in Figure 23.2.

Although the result is better than without occlusion checks, the texture is still projected onto the handle, as long as the vertex normal faces into the direction of the projector. This problem can be solved with the following approach.

Depth Map

To keep track of occlusion, a second texture is projected over the teapot in the same way the texture with the image is projected. This second texture only stores depth values and is used to restrict the areas where the depth map is applied. The result is shown in Figure 23.3.

FIGURE 23.2 *Projective texturing by checking for occlusion with dot(**P**, **N**).*

FIGURE 23.3 *Projective texturing combined with a depth map.*

Please note, that it should be possible to reuse the depth map to calculate the shadows of the teapot. How to implement depth maps and shadow maps is shown in the next chapter.

ON THE CD   This chapter is accompanied by two example programs, which can be found in the directory Chapter 23 - Projective Texturing. The names of the examples in the directory are:

- Projective Texturing + dot(P,N)
- Projective Texturing with Depth Map

The first example program uses the dot product between the normal and the projection vector to restrict the projected texture on vertices that face the projector, and the second example program shows how to use a depth map to restrict the projection of the texture on areas that are not occluded by geometry from the point of view of the projector.

Conclusion

Although projecting a texture onto geometry looks at first glance like a simple technique, it demands some clever tricks to overcome all its issues.

P A R T

VII

Shadows

As much as lighting can create a mood in a scene, it's often the rendered shadows that further define/refine that mood and give an object further lifelike qualities. Shadows are an important element in creating realistic images and in providing the user with visual cues about object placement. Furthermore, shadows can be a vital part of the game design. For example, the player might be a thief who has to move, stay, or crouch in the shadows to hide himself.

For as hard as it is to create and apply realistic and appropriate lighting to a scene, it can be equally challenging to render convincing shadows. There are several very different techniques to create shadows. They all have in common the description of the anatomy of a shadow. A shadowed scene needs a light source that is calculated per-vertex or per-pixel; an object that casts a shadow, called the occluder; and a surface onto which the shadow is being cast, called the receiver. Shadows themselves have two parts, called the umbra, which is the inner part of the shadow, and the penumbra, which is the outer and border portion of the shadow.

The shadow consists of the penumbra and the umbra. The penumbra creates the difference between hard and soft shadows. With hard shadows, the shadow ends abruptly, and looks unnatural, whereas with soft shadows, the penumbra transitions from the color of the shadow (usually black) to the adjacent pixel color, creating a more realistic shadow.

There are numerous ways to create shadows in a game. The following two chapters will feature a technique called shadow mapping and another called shadow volumes. The latter are available on DirectX 8 and in an optimized form on DirectX 9 graphics hardware. Shadow mapping is possible on all recent DirectX 9 hardware (RADEON 9500-X800, GeForce FX/6800), on a RADEON 8500-9200 with reduced precision, and on a GeForce 3/4 with a vendor specific extension that leads to good results.

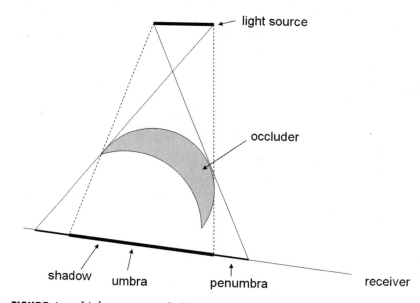

FIGURE 1.   *Light source, occluder, receiver, umbra, and penumbra.*

24

Shadow Mapping

Shadow mapping is an image space technique that can be used to shadow any object that can be rendered. The application does not have to have any knowledge of a scene's geometry. Thus, it is not necessary to find the silhouette of the shadowing object or clip the object being shadowed. Only a single texture is required to hold shadowing information for each light, and the stencil buffer is not used. Compared to shadow volumes, shadow mapping avoids high fill-rate requirements. (Read more in [Williams][Reeves][Segal].)

Shadow mapping was first described at SIGGRAPH 1978 by Lance Williams. It has been extensively used since, both in offline rendering and real-time graphics. Shadow mapping is used by Pixar's RenderMan and was used in major films such as *Toy Story*.

Background

Consider a simple scene lit by a single point light. How does a given point in the scene know whether it is lit or in shadow? Put simply, a point in the scene is lit if there is nothing blocking a straight line path between the light and that point. The key step in understanding shadow mapping is that these points are exactly those that would be visible (i.e., not occluded) to a viewer placed at the light source; in other words, a point is shadowed if something interrupts the straight line path between the light and that point.

Testing a point for occlusion takes two passes.

1. The scene is rendered from the light's point of view, while the depth of each pixel is recorded in a depth texture, called a shadow map.
2. Then the scene is rendered from the eye position but with the shadow map projected down from the light onto the scene using standard projective

texturing. At each pixel, the depth value from the shadow map is compared with the fragment's distance from the light. Letting the value in the saved depth texture be **D**, and the distance from the point to the light be **R**, we have:

R = D: There was nothing occluding this point when drawing from the light source, so this point is not occluded.

R > D: There must have been an object in front of this point when looking from the light's position. This point is thus in shadow.

Figure 24.1 illustrates the shadow map comparison.

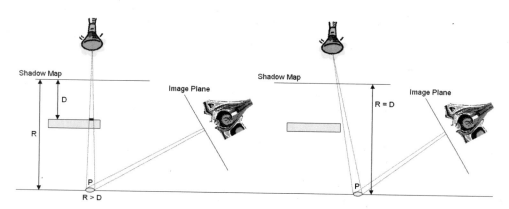

FIGURE 24.1   *The shadow depth comparison.*

On the left side of Figure 24.1, the point **P** that is being shaded is in shadow, because the point's depth **R** is greater than the depth **D** that is recorded in the shadow map. In contrast, the right side of this figure shows a case where the point **P** has the same depth as the recorded value in the shadow map.

Implementation

Shadow mapping requires two passes. In the first pass, the shadow map is created, and in the second pass, the shadow map is projected onto the geometry in a process similar to arbitrary projections of images, and its content is compared to the distance from the point to the light.

Overall, we use three concatenated matrices in the HLSL shader: one to transform the object, one to transform the light source, and one to project the texture.

```
// transform object
// mScale * mTransform * mRotate * m_mWorld * m_mView * m_mProj
...
// transform light source
// mScale * mTransform * mRotate * mView * mProj
...
// transform projected textures
// == mLightViewProj * texture adjustment matrix
// mScale * mTransform * mRotate * mView * mProj * mScaleBias
...
```

In the first rendering pass, the `mLightViewProj` matrix is used to render the scene as seen by the light source. This point of view is used to store the depth values in the shadow map.

In the second rendering pass, the `mWorldViewProj` matrix is used to transform the objects in the scene, and the `mLightViewProjTexAdj` matrix projects the shadow map onto the objects to compare the depth values in the shadow map with the depth values of the object.

Create Shadow Map

With the "camera" moved to the point of view of the light source, depth values are stored in the shadow map in the first rendering path. A common way to do this is to store the z value of the vertex divided by w (from the perspective of the light source) as shown in the following vertex shader.

```
VS_OUTPUTCREATESHADOWMAP VSCreateShadowMap(float4 Pos    :
                                  POSITION, float3 Normal : NORMAL)
{
    VS_OUTPUTCREATESHADOWMAP Out = (VS_OUTPUTCREATESHADOWMAP)0;

    // transform light source
    float4 Position = mul( Pos, mLightViewProj);

    // output position
    Out.Pos = Position;

    // perspective divide for depth value
    Out.Depth = Position.z / Position.w;

    return Out;
}
```

The depth value is then stored in the shadow map in the following pixel shader.

```
float4 PSCreateShadowMap(float Depth : TEXCOORD0) : COLOR
{
    return Depth;
}
```

Assigning Texture Coordinates to Vertices/ Computing Texture Coordinates During Rasterization

In the second rendering pass, texture coordinates are assigned to vertices to project the shadow map onto the scene in the vertex shader. This is done in the same way as shown in the previous chapter for projective texturing. A matrix formed by concatenation of the light's world view projection and a bias and scale matrix is used to map the shadow map onto the scene as seen by the light source.

Additionally, from the point of view of the light, depth values are retrieved in the same way as they were stored in the shadow map.

```
...
float4 uv = mul(Pos, mLightViewProj);
Out.Depth = uv.z / uv.w - 0.003;
...
```

It is common to subtract a depth bias value from the depth value to account for numerical precision errors. Biasing eliminates the Moiré patterns due to incorrect self-shadowing, but moves the shadow boundary away from its true position. Selecting a bias value large enough to eliminate self-shadowing artifacts, yet small enough to avoid any noticeable problems from the offset boundary positions, is done by seeing if a certain value fits to the scene.

The biased depth value is sent to the pixel shader and compared to the depth value stored in the shadow map. This is shown in the following pixel shader.

```
float4 PSScene(VS_OUTPUT In) : COLOR
{
    float4 Color = In.Ambient;
    float4 zero = {0,0,0,0};

    float  ShadowMap = tex2Dproj( ShadowMapSamp, In.ShadowMapUV ).x;

    // value of shadow_map bigger or equal than depth value: return
            diffuse
    Color += (ShadowMap < In.Depth.z) ? zero : In.Diffuse;

    return Color;
}
```

The depth value from the shadow map is fetched by the projective texture intrinsic `tex2Dproj()`. The texture coordinates provided to this intrinsic is the vertex position multiplied with the concatenated texture projection matrix. At the same time the depth value in `In.Depth` was fetched in exactly the same way as it was fetched in the first rendering pass for storage in the shadow map.

Results/Issues

Implementing the process of storing a depth value in the shadow map and retrieving a depth value in the second rendering path is simple at first glance, but does not necessarily lead to a satisfying visual quality, as shown in Figure 24.2.

FIGURE 24.2 *Shadow map aliasing.*

Figure 24.2 shows staircase effects on the floor and streaks of shadows on the model. Please note that the shadow map preview in Figure 24.2 in the top-left corner of the screenshot shows that the viewing frustum is much wider than would be necessary to catch the scene. Implementing better looking shadow mapping requires an understanding of the causes of the aliasing problems covered here. The most common reasons for aliasing in the shadow map algorithm are:

- The resolution/precision of the shadow map.
- Limited numerical precision used when performing the test between the depth value in the shadow map and the depth value retrieved in the second pass.

A shadow map with a low precision (e.g., a A8R8G8B8 texture) will lead to aliasing artifacts as well as a shadow map with a very small resolution. Choosing a 1024×1024 shadow map that can store depth values in a 32-bit floating-point format, should be good enough for most applications.

The second point mentioned in the previous list is more complex and is covered in numerous articles. We will focus on improving the numerical precision of the depth test by optimizing the following areas for precision:

- Distribution of depth values in the light's viewing frustum.
- Adjusting the viewing frustum of the light source, so that only visible areas of the scene are covered by the viewing frustum of the light.
- Percentage closer filtering and bilinear filtering.

Distribution of Depth Values in the Viewing Frustum of the Light Source

When rendering the scene from a given viewpoint, depth values are sampled non-uniformly ($1/z$) due to the perspective projection. This makes sense if we use the perspective projection for a camera, since objects near to the viewer are more important than those far away, and therefore sampled at a higher precision. For the light source position, this assumption is not true. Objects far away from the light source could be the actual main focus of the camera, so sampling those with less precision might introduce artifacts. Figure 24.3 illustrates the difference between linear and $1/z$ mapping.

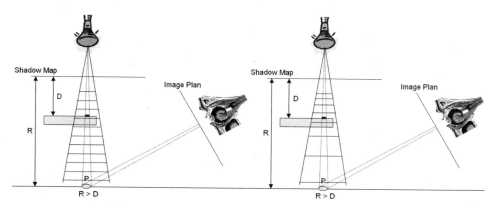

FIGURE 24.3   *Left: linear distribution of depth values/right: non-uniform distribution of depth values.*

On the right side, depth values are sampled using traditional perspective projection. Objects near to the light source obtain most of the available depth values, whereas objects far away (e.g., the ground plane) have less precision. The left side of Figure 24.3 shows the same setup using a linear distribution of depth values using a customized vertex transformation. Instead of transforming all components of a homogeneous point $P(x_e, y_e, z_e, w_e)$ by the perspective transformation matrix, e.g.,

$$\left(x_e, y_e, z_e, w_e\right) = Lightproj \times \mathbf{P}$$

we replace the z component of $\mathbf{P}$ with a new value

$$z' = z_l \times w$$

The linear depth value z_l corresponds to the view space value z_e mapped according to the light source near and far plane:

$$z_l = -\frac{z_e + near}{far - near}$$

To account for normalization, which takes place afterwards, we also premultiply z_l by w. This way the z component is not affected by the perspective division, and depth values are uniformly distributed between the near and far plane. The following source snippet demonstrates this:

```
...
float4 Position = mul( Pos, mLightViewProj);
...
Out.Depth = ((Position.z + fNear) / (fFar - fNear));
Out.Pos.z = Out.Depth * Position.w;
...
```

The effect of a linear distribution of depth values is visible in the shadow map preview window on the top left of Figure 24.4. Whereas the non-uniform distribution of depth values shows a different distribution for the object and the plane, the linear distribution does look much more unified (for more ideas on how to tweak a vertex's projected depth value see [Lengyel4].

Adjusting the Viewing Frustum of the Light Source

Another improvement of the shadow effect can be achieved by tightly fitting the light source's viewing frustum, from which the shadow map is generated, to the actual camera view [Brabec]. In other words, if the camera gets closer to the occluder and the shadow receiver, the light's viewing frustum should tightly fit to the visible parts of this scene by getting smaller. If the camera goes farther away, the viewing frustum of the light source should get bigger.

Adjusting the viewing frustum of the light source by hand and using a linear distribution of depth values in this viewing frustum leads to much better results, as shown in Figure 24.4.

FIGURE 24.4   *Hand-tuned viewing frustum of light source. Left: non-uniform distribution of depth values/right: linear distribution of depth values.*

The light's viewing frustum is tight-fitting around the object as shown in the preview of the shadow map. The visual quality of the shadow is therefore much better compared to Figure 24.2. It is interesting to note that the screenshot on the right is slightly worse, because compared to a non-uniform distribution of depth values in the viewing frustum, the linearly distributed depth values do not contain as much precision in the case where the object is very near to the light's camera. In a real-world situation, the light's viewing frustum won't fit so closely around the object. Then the linear distribution of depth values will be superior to the non-uniform distribution of depth values as shown by the example programs accompanying this chapter.

Despite the great results, adjusting the light's viewing frustum manually is only applicable in demos. Implementing this into a more flexible game engine requires the programmer to create an environment that can handle this restriction.

There are two ways to implement this:

- Using a shadow map per object
- Using one shadow map for all characters and adjusting the light's viewing frustum automatically to the camera view

Using a Shadow Map for Each Character

Because you use a shadow map for each character, the light's viewing frustum can probably be adjusted to this character with very good results. The disadvantage of this approach is the need for a high number of shadow maps. Let's assume we use, for example, 16 shadow maps, each with its own render target. This might kill graphics performance, because you're doing lots of mesh rendering, and switching render targets kills your parallelism between the CPU and GPU, because the render target switches may lead to hard stalls in graphics hardware. The solution to this is using one texture that holds several shadow maps. For example a 128×2048 texture can hold 16 128×128 shadow maps.

Another obvious optimization to this technique is to not generate all the shadows all the time. Only the player character shadow is generated every frame; other characters get their shadows updated every second frame or even less often.

To generate only the visible shadows, you need to cull the bounding volume of the area of effect of the shadow. This is just the frustum of the light that was used to generate the shadow map. This frustum has its near clip plane at the shadow map plane, and can have a far plane based on the distance fade-out of the shadow. This might be done by approximating the frustum with an oriented bounding box (OBB), and a sphere around it for acceleration. By testing the shadow bound against the real camera frustum, you only need to generate shadows whose bound is visible. (Read more in [Bloom].)

One Shadow Map for Everything

The most elegant solution is to use one shadow map for all objects in the visible area of the camera. This requires a mechanism that automatically adjusts the light's viewing frustum in such a way that it focuses on the area that is seen by the camera.

This means adjusting the near and far plane of the viewing frustum as well as its field of view. To adjust the near and far plane of the viewing frustum, Brabec et al. [Brabec] describe a method that uses a depth replace texture to hold depth values for objects that are outside the camera's frustum but cast a shadow on the object that is in the camera's viewing frustum.

To adjust the direction and the field of view, Brabec et al. use a control texture that contains color-coded information about the row-column position by projecting the scene from the light scene position into the texture. Then an axis-aligned bounding rectangle is computed to determine all relevant pixels. This is done by searching for the maximum and minimum row and column values. The x and y coordinates of this rectangle are then scaled and biased to apply them to the light's projection matrix. As an alternative, Brabec shows a more elegant method that uses a rotating caliper algorithm instead of the axis-aligned bounding rectangle technique to achieve this.

Percentage-Closer Filtering

To further antialias the staircase and Moiré effects visible in Figure 24.1, we use a technique called percentage closer filtering. This filtering method was presented by William T. Reeves, David H. Salesin, and Robert L. Cook in 1987 at SIGGRAPH [Reeves]. It is built on the fact that the result of the comparison between the depth value in the shadow map and the depth value retrieved in the second pass are binary; they are 1 or 0.

Comparing Texels to the Depth Value

With percentage closer filtering, a block of, for example, 3×3 texels is fetched from the shadow map and then compared to the depth value retrieved in the second pass. The result of this process is a 3×3 binary map consisting of 0s and 1s. Figure 24.5 illustrates this.

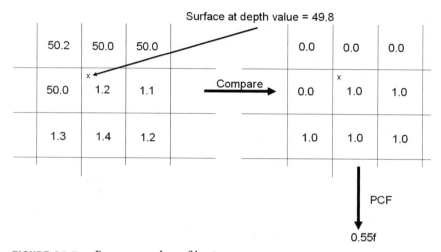

FIGURE 24.5   *Percentage closer filtering.*

Filtering by averaging the array of binary values leads to 0.55f, meaning that 55% of the surface is in shadow. This technique leads to a substantial improvement, but it can be improved even more by adding jitter sampling.

Jitter Sampling

To produce shadows that are even less noisy, a jitter value can be added to the texture coordinate. The jitter value is retrieved by approximating a Poisson disk distribution. With a Poisson disk distribution, you fetch a texel randomly and the next texel randomly, but you throw the next one out if it is too close to the first texel. This is modeled on the distribution of cells on the retina of the eye, which also have a seemingly random pattern but with a consistent minimum spacing. Because pixels cannot be left out on current hardware, the Poisson disk distribution needs to be approximated by using hardcoded texture coordinates, which are positioned as if they had been generated using the Poisson method (read more in [Mitchell]).

```
    . . .
    row.x = OffsetLookup(ShadowMapSamp, In.ShadowMapUV, float2(-
0.000692, -0.000868));
    row.y = OffsetLookup(ShadowMapSamp, In.ShadowMapUV,
float2(0.000450, -0.002347));
    row.z = OffsetLookup(ShadowMapSamp, In.ShadowMapUV,
float2(0.000773, -0.002042));
    row.w = OffsetLookup(ShadowMapSamp, In.ShadowMapUV,
float2(0.001880, -0.001592));
    . . .
    row2.x = OffsetLookup(ShadowMapSamp, In.ShadowMapUV, float2(-
0.001208, -0.001198));
    row2.y = OffsetLookup(ShadowMapSamp, In.ShadowMapUV, float2(-
0.000915, -0.000425));
    row2.z = OffsetLookup(ShadowMapSamp, In.ShadowMapUV, float2(-
0.000050, 0.000105));
    row2.w = OffsetLookup(ShadowMapSamp, In.ShadowMapUV,
float2(0.001719, -0.000753));

    . . .
    row3.x = OffsetLookup(ShadowMapSamp, In.ShadowMapUV, float2(-
0.001855, -0.000004));
    row3.y = OffsetLookup(ShadowMapSamp, In.ShadowMapUV, float2(-
0.001212, 0.001140));
    row3.z = OffsetLookup(ShadowMapSamp, In.ShadowMapUV,
float2(0.000684, 0.000273));
    row3.w = OffsetLookup(ShadowMapSamp, In.ShadowMapUV,
float2(0.000647, 0.000177));

    . . .
    row4.x = OffsetLookup(ShadowMapSamp, In.ShadowMapUV, float2(-
0.001448, 0.002095));
    row4.y = OffsetLookup(ShadowMapSamp, In.ShadowMapUV,
float2(0.000421, 0.000811));
    row4.z = OffsetLookup(ShadowMapSamp, In.ShadowMapUV,
float2(0.000542, 0.001491));
    row4.w = OffsetLookup(ShadowMapSamp, In.ShadowMapUV,
float2(0.002367, 0.000537));
    . . .
```

As you can see, jitter sampling is added by assigning jittered texture coordinates.

The screenshot in Figure 24.6 compares a 4×4 percentage closer filter with a 4×4 percentage closer filter with jitter sampling.

In the screenshot at the top of this figure is the implementation without jitter sampling, and at the bottom jitter sampling is added. The bottom image shows a much less noisy shadow compared to the top image.

Bilinear Filtering

To improve the visual quality of shadow maps even more, the values that are retrieved via percentage closer filtering can be bilinear filtered. Bilinear filtering is implemented in a similar way to that shown in Chapter 18. Figure 24.7 compares a percentage closer filter with a 2×2 kernel with and without bilinear filtering.

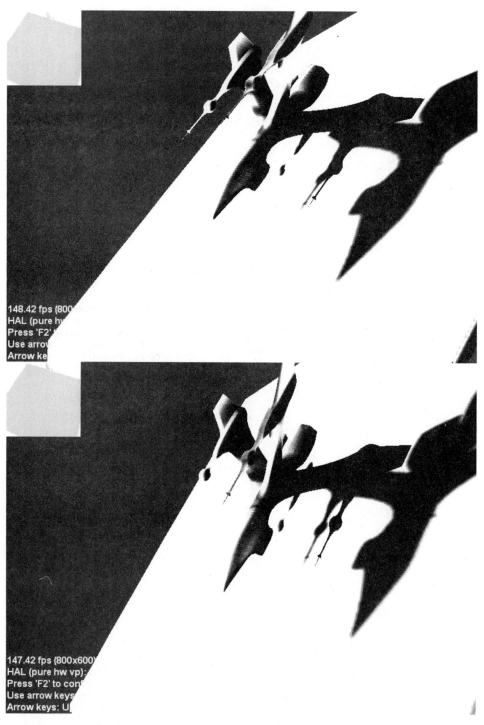

148.42 fps (800
HAL (pure h
Press 'F2' t
Use arrow
Arrow ke

147.42 fps (800x600)
HAL (pure hw vp):
Press 'F2' to con
Use arrow keys
Arrow keys: U

FIGURE 24.6 *Top: 4×4 percentage closer filtering/bottom: 4×4 percentage closer filtering with jitter sampling.*

FIGURE 24.7 *Top: 2×2 percentage closer filtering/bottom: 2×2 percentage closer filtering that is bilinear filtered.*

As can be seen, the difference between the bilinear filtered 2×2 percentage closer filter example shown in the screenshot at the bottom and the pure 2×2 percentage closer filter shown in the screenshot at the top is very noticeable. The screenshot in Figure 24.8 demonstrates that bilinear filtering of a percentage closer filter with a 3×3 kernel leads to even better results.

FIGURE 24.8   *Bilinear filtered 3×3 percentage closer filtering.*

Please note the nice self-shadowing on the top of the object. Additionally, the light's viewing frustum is big enough to cover nearly the whole plane, so adding more objects to the plane should lead to smooth shadows for each object.

Accompanying Examples

This chapter is accompanied by six example programs, which can be found in the directory Chapter 24 - Shadow Mapping. The names of the examples in the directory are as follows:

- Shadow Map shows the quality enhancement with a hand-tuned viewing frustum compared to Shadow Map Aliased.
- Shadow Map 2×2 PCF Linear Filtered demonstrates percentage closer filtering with a 2×2 kernel and bilinear filtering.
- Shadow Map 3×3 PCF Linear Filtered demonstrates percentage closer filtering with a 3×3 kernel and bilinear filtering.
- Shadow Map 4×4 PCF demonstrates the quality of 4x4 percentage closer filtering, and Shadow Map 4×4 PCF Jittered adds jitter sampling to reduce the noise.

Conclusion

This chapter has shown that shadow maps are difficult to implement with a high visual quality in a game engine environment. The main things to keep in mind are the use of a linear depth distribution in the light's viewing frustum and the adjustment of this viewing frustum to the cameras frustum. Additionally, percentage closer filtering in combination with adjacent bilinear filtering leads to good results.

The following list should further assist in implementing shadow maps more easily.

- Fading out shadows in the distance fakes the fact that in the distance other lights are contributing illumination. This can be done similarly to the attenuation technique for a point light.
- Running a Gaussian blur filter (as shown in Chapter 21) over the shadow map might lead to smoother shadows.
- On hardware that does not support floating point textures, the RGBE8 format or the RGB16 format might be used to store the shadow map.
- Another trick is to pack depth values into multiple channels of the depth texture, raising the depth resolution from 8-bit to 11-bit (read more at [ATISHAD-OWMAP]).
- To create shadows on walls in rooms, use a cube shadow map.
- Creating a second code path for NVIDIA cards by using their hardware shadow map approach improves the performance on these graphic cards remarkably. (Read more in [NVIDIASHADOWMAP]. NVIDIA provides a special depth texture format D3DFMT_D24S8 and D3DFMT_D16 for this. The hardware takes the interpolated depth from a texture coordinate, compares it to the 2×2 nearest samples in the depth map, and returns [0,.25,.5,.75] for percentage closer filtering.)

To further improve shadow mapping, you might look into *perspective shadow maps*. This approach was presented by Marc Stamminger and others at SIGGRAPH 2002. Its implementations issues are covered in [Stamminger] and by Simon Kozlow [Kozlow].

Another interesting approach was developed by Eric Chan and Frédo Durand and is named "Rendering Fake Soft Shadows with Smoothies" [Chan]. They attach geometric primitives that they call "smoothies" to the objects' silhouettes. The smoothies give rise to fake shadows that appear qualitatively like soft shadows, without the cost of densely sampling an area light source. The soft shadow edges hide objectionable aliasing artifacts that are noticeable with ordinary shadow maps.

25

Shadow Volumes

With the release of the first screenshots of DOOM III, shadow volumes became a very popular way to render shadows in games.

Frank Crow [Crow] first presented the idea of using shadow volumes for rendering shadows in 1977. Tim Heidmann [Heidmann] subsequently implemented Crow's shadow volume approach on IRIX GL by cunningly utilizing the stencil buffer commonly found in modern graphics hardware. In his implementation, he used the stencil buffer for counting the number of times that a ray from the eye enters and leaves the shadow volume. Further enhancements were made by John Carmack [Carmack], who uses a technique called depth-fail, which will be used in this chapter. A good overview of the recent developments has been written by Eric Lengyel [Lengyel3] and more recently by Cass Everitt and Mark J. Kilgard [Everitt]. There is also a very thorough overview by Hun Yen Kwoon [Kwoon].

Background

The basic concept of the stencil shadow algorithm is to use the stencil buffer as a masking mechanism to prevent pixels in shadow from being drawn during the rendering pass for a particular light source. This is accomplished by rendering an invisible shadow volume for each shadow-casting object in a scene using stencil operations that leave nonzero values in the stencil buffer wherever light is blocked. Once the stencil buffer has been filled with the appropriate mask, a lighting pass only illuminates pixels where the value in the stencil buffer is zero.

The volume of the shadow is constructed by finding the edges in the object's triangle mesh representing the boundary between lit triangles and unlit triangles (called the object's silhouette) and extruding those edges away from the light source. This is usually a pre-processing step. To render the shadow volume later, the altered triangle mesh is stored in an extra buffer. Usually this mesh has a higher number of vertices than the original mesh.

Object's Silhouette

To create an object's silhouette, the silhouette edges of the mesh need to be detected from the perspective of the light. A silhouette edge is an edge of the object where one polygon faces toward the light and the other faces away from it. To make such an edge detectable by the vertex shader, the source geometry must be pre-processed in a way that makes it possible to form a shadow volume in any direction, without the need to create new geometry on the fly. In this preprocessing step, shared edges of the objects are replaced by degenerate quads.

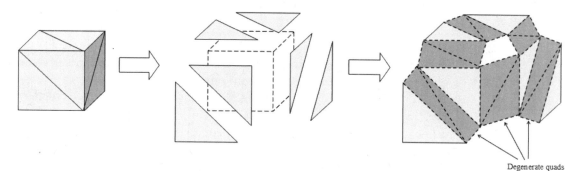

Degenerate quads

FIGURE 25.1   *Shared edges on flat surfaces need to be replaced by degenerate quads (courtesy of Hun Yen Kwoon).*

Figure 25.1 depicts the preprocessing of the source geometry that forms a cube; it shows only the front faces for simplicity. The shared edges of the faces are filtered out and a degenerate quad is inserted to replace the shared edge. The two edges that form the opposing sides of each degenerate quad have the same positional values but different face normals. Let us briefly run through the preprocessing algorithm we use in this:

1. Step through all faces in the source mesh
2. Compute face normals for each face
3. Step through the three edges of each face
   a. Insert edge into a list of checking
   b. If two vertices of the same two faces share one edge (shared edge found)
      i. If normals of faces sharing the edge are not parallel, change direction of face
      ii. Generate degenerated quad

First the face normals of all faces are calculated to see which direction each face points. Then vertices that share one edge are searched and in case of two vertices of one face sharing two vertices of one other face, a degenerated quad is inserted. This quad helps the vertex shader create the shadow volume independently of the location of the light source.

Note that we indiscriminately insert degenerate quads into every shared edge in the preprocessing step. The polygon count might be reduced by checking if a shared edge would have a good chance of becoming a silhouette edge. If a shared edge has almost zero chance of becoming a silhouette edge, there is really no need for the insertion of a degenerate quad to replace that edge. A simple way to determine the chances of an edge forming part of a silhouette is to test the parallelism of the normals of the faces that share it. If the two faces have normals that are almost parallel in the same direction, the shared edge lies in a flat surface and would have little chance of becoming part of a silhouette.

One other thing to note is that the source mesh should be a closed mesh. Any seams or holes, formed for example by T-junctions, would greatly complicate the silhouette determination algorithm in the vertex shader. Additionally, non-closed front faces would throw the stencil counting off-balance.

Rendering the Shadow Volumes

Now that we have the extended geometry, the question is, how is the shadow volume rendered? This is done with the help of the stencil buffer in the following way.

Just consider a single pixel. Assuming the camera is not in the shadow volume, there are four possibilities for the corresponding point in the scene. If the ray from the camera to the point does not intersect the shadow volume, no shadow polygons will have been drawn there and the stencil buffer is still zero. Otherwise, if the point lies in front of the shadow volume, the shadow polygons will be z-buffered out and the stencil again remains unchanged. If the point lies behind the shadow volume, the same number of front shadow faces as back faces will have been rendered and the stencil will be zero, having been incremented as many times as decremented. The final possibility is that the point lies inside the shadow volume. In this case, the back face of the shadow volume will be z-buffered out but not the front face, so the stencil buffer will be a nonzero value. The result is portions of the frame buffer lying in shadow have nonzero stencil values. To achieve this, the example program renders the following steps:

1. Clear render target, z-buffer, and stencil buffer
2. Render the scene into color and z-buffer
3. Disable color writes, z-buffer writes, activate stencil buffer, switch on flat shading mode
4. Pass stencil buffer when the stencil test pass or fails
5. Increment stencil buffer when the depth test fails

6. If two-sided stencil buffer is supported, switch it on
   a. Decrement the second side of the stencil buffer when the depth test fails
   b. Switch off backface culling
   c. Render Shadow volumes > filling up two-sided stencil buffer and go to step 8
7. Or else if two-sided stencil buffer is not supported
   a. Render front-facing polygons
   b. Reverse culling order so the back sides can be written to stencil buffer
   c. Decrement stencil buffer when depth tests fails
   d. Render back-facing polygons
8. Repeat steps 4-7 for every light source
9. Switch on Gouraud shading, color writes, z-buffer writes, de-activate the stencil buffer, and switch off z-buffer
10. Render your scene where the stencil value is greater than or equal to 1 into a shadow mask
11. Alpha blend 10 with 2 (optional)

The key to this and other volumetric stencil buffer effects is the interaction between the stencil buffer and the z-buffer. A scene with a shadow volume is rendered in three stages. First, the scene without the shadow is rendered as usual, using the z-buffer. Next, the shadow is marked out in the stencil buffer as follows. The front faces of the shadow volume are drawn using invisible polygons, with z-testing enabled but z-writes disabled and the stencil buffer incremented at every pixel passing the z-test. The back faces of the shadow volume are rendered similarly, but decrementing the stencil value instead.

The first render in steps 1 and 2 renders the scene into the color and z-buffer. Then the setup for the stencil buffer happens. We don't need Gouraud shading or to write color to fill up the stencil buffer with values, therefore, we go with the cheaper flat shading. Because we don't need to render geometry either, the z-buffer is switched off.

The value in the stencil buffer should be passed when the stencil buffer passes or fails, and it shoud be incremented when depth test fails. Depending on the support of two-sided stencil buffers, step 6 or step 7 is executed. If a two-sided stencil buffer is supported, the second side of the stencil buffer is decremented when the depth test fails. To render the shadow volumes according to the content of both sides of the stencil buffer, backface culling is switched off.

If a two-sided stencil buffer is not available, step 7 is executed. Because everything was set up for a stencil buffer write in steps 4 and 5, the stencil buffer values for the front-facing polygons can be rendered in step 7.a). Because the legacy stencil buffer has no back side, we need to reverse culling now and configure the stencil buffer so that it decrements when the depth test fails. Then we can fill up the stencil buffer a second time by rendering the back-facing values.

Steps 4-7 must be repeated as often as there are light sources.

Incremented values left in the stencil buffer correspond to pixels that are in the shadow. These remaining stencil buffer contents are used as a mask, to alpha-blend a large, all-encompassing black quad into the scene. With the stencil buffer as a mask, the result is to darken pixels that are in the shadows.

Rendering the Scene

The scene is rendered in the following steps:

1. Cast a light ray from the light source.
2. To check if a vertex of the extruded mesh is facing the light or is pointing away from the light, store the dot product of the light ray and the normal ($L \cdot N$).
3. Depending on the value of $L \cdot N$, store 0 or 1 in the variable scale.
4. Reduce the position value of the shadow geometry slightly, so that the shadow does not overlap the edges of the objects.
5. Scale the direction of the light ray and subtract it from the position value.

When the shadow volume geometry position is not extended in the direction of the light source (scale = = 0), it is hidden by the object, because it is smaller than the object.

Implementation

Implementing the shadow volumes in the example program follows the three steps covered earlier. First, we need a function that creates the object's silhouette and stores it in a global available variable. Then the rendering of the invisible shadow volumes with all the render state switches is done in the Render() function of the example program, and the visible shadows are rendered in the vertex shader.

Object's Silhouette

The object's silhouette is created in the CShadowVolume::Create() function in a pre-processing step.

```
    HRESULT CShadowVolume::Create( LPDIRECT3DDEVICE9 pd3dDevice,
LPD3DXMESH pSrcMesh )
    {
        HRESULT ret = S_OK;

        // local copy of the vertex buffer
        SHADOW_VOLUME_VERTEX* pVertices;

        // local copy of the index buffer
        WORD*       pIndices;
        DWORD i, j, k, l, face;
```

```
LPD3DXMESH pMesh;
if( FAILED( pSrcMesh->CloneMeshFVF(D3DXMESH_SYSTEMMEM,
                                   D3DFVF_XYZ | D3DFVF_NORMAL,
                                   pd3dDevice, &pMesh ) ) )
    return E_FAIL;

DWORD dwNumFaces    = pMesh->GetNumFaces();

// four times the number of faces and
// three times the number of vertices.
m_dwNumFaces = 4 * dwNumFaces;
m_pVertices = new SHADOW_VOLUME_VERTEX[3*m_dwNumFaces];

// lock buffers
pMesh->LockVertexBuffer( 0L, (LPVOID*)&pVertices );
pMesh->LockIndexBuffer ( 0L, (LPVOID*)&pIndices );

// allocate space for normal
D3DXVECTOR3 *vNormal = new D3DXVECTOR3[dwNumFaces];
if(NULL==vNormal)
{
   m_dwNumFaces = 0;
   ret = E_OUTOFMEMORY;
   goto end;
}

// compute face normals for each face
for( i=0; i < dwNumFaces; i++ )
{
    D3DXVECTOR3 v0 = pVertices[pIndices[3*i+0]].p;
    D3DXVECTOR3 v1 = pVertices[pIndices[3*i+1]].p;
    D3DXVECTOR3 v2 = pVertices[pIndices[3*i+2]].p;

    // calculate normal
    D3DXVECTOR3 vCross1(v1-v0);
    D3DXVECTOR3 vCross2(v2-v1);
    D3DXVec3Cross( &vNormal[i], &vCross1, &vCross2 );
     // store faces
     m_pVertices[3*i+0].p = v0;
     m_pVertices[3*i+1].p = v1;
     m_pVertices[3*i+2].p = v2;
     m_pVertices[3*i+0].n = vNormal[i];
     m_pVertices[3*i+1].n = vNormal[i];
     m_pVertices[3*i+2].n = vNormal[i];
}

// step through the three edges of each face
face = dwNumFaces;
for( i = 0  ; i < dwNumFaces; i++ )
{
  for( j = i + 1; j < dwNumFaces; j++ )
  {
   DWORD id[2][2]; // checklist
   DWORD cnt=0;
   for(k = 0; k < 3; k++)
```

```
{
 for(l = 0; l < 3; l++)
 {
  D3DXVECTOR3 dv;
  D3DXVec3Subtract( &dv, &pVertices[pIndices[3*i+k]].p,
                    &pVertices[pIndices[3*j+l]].p);

   // if two vertices from two different faces form one edge
   // put them into checklist and increment counter
   if( D3DXVec3LengthSq( &dv ) < 0.001f )
   {
      // cnt counts until two ...
      id[cnt][0] = 3*i+k;
      id[cnt][1] = 3*j+l;
      cnt++;
   }
 }
}

// if two times two vertices from two faces share one edge

...

if(2 == cnt)
{
 // if one face has a different direction than the other face

...

 // alternative: check if the face normals are parallel,
 // if not insert degenerate quad
 // else exit if statement
 if(id[1][0] - id[0][0]!=1)
 {
      // ... adjust direction of face
      DWORD tmp = id[0][0];
      id[0][0] = id[1][0];
      id[1][0] = tmp; // swap id[0][0] and id[1][0]
      tmp = id[0][1];
      id[0][1] = id[1][1];
      id[1][1] = tmp; // swap id[0][1] and id[1][1]
 }
 // insert degenerated quadrilateral
 // the face normals are used for the vertex normals
 m_pVertices[3*face+0].p = pVertices[pIndices[id[1][0]]].p;
 m_pVertices[3*face+2].p = pVertices[pIndices[id[0][1]]].p;
 m_pVertices[3*face+1].p = pVertices[pIndices[id[0][0]]].p;
 m_pVertices[3*face+0].n = vNormal[i];
 m_pVertices[3*face+2].n = vNormal[j];
 m_pVertices[3*face+1].n = vNormal[i];
 face++;
 m_pVertices[3*face+0].p = pVertices[pIndices[id[1][0]]].p;
 m_pVertices[3*face+2].p = pVertices[pIndices[id[1][1]]].p;
 m_pVertices[3*face+1].p = pVertices[pIndices[id[0][1]]].p;
 m_pVertices[3*face+0].n = vNormal[i];
 m_pVertices[3*face+2].n = vNormal[j];
 m_pVertices[3*face+1].n = vNormal[j];
 face++;
```

```
        }
       }
      }
      assert(face == m_dwNumFaces);
      delete[] vNormal;

end:
      // unlock buffers
      pMesh->UnlockVertexBuffer();
      pMesh->UnlockIndexBuffer();

   pMesh->Release();

   return ret;
   }
```

There is a local copy of the original geometry stored in pVertices and a global copy in m_ pVertices. The latter holds the shadow volume geometry at the end. After calculating the face normals, four vertices that share two edges from two triangles are searched for. If these two edges are found, the direction of the faces are checked and if one face has a different direction than the other face, a degenerated quadrilateral is inserted.

Rendering the Shadow Volumes

The invisible shadow volumes are rendered in the Render() function in the main file of the example program. The function checks for support of the two-sided stencil buffer. If it is not supported, the shadow geometry is drawn twice per light source, hence putting pressure on the vertex throughput of the GPU. If a two-sided stencil buffer is available, it reduces this process to one rendering pass.

Rendering the Scene

The scene is then rendered with the help of the following vertex shader.

```
VS_OUTPUT VS (float4 Pos: POSITION,  float3 Normal : NORMAL)
{
   VS_OUTPUT Out = (VS_OUTPUT)0;

   // light to vertex ray
   float4 dir = vLightPos - Pos;

   // dot ray and normal
   float LN = dot( Normal, dir );

   // scale is 0 for light facing or 1 for non-light facing
   float scale = (LN >=  0) ? 0.0f : 1.0f;
```

```
                    // reduce position slightly of shadow volume geometry
                    Pos.xyz -= 0.001f*Pos;
                    // reduced position - scale * light direction
                    Out.Pos = mul( Pos - scale * dir, matWorldViewProj );

                    return Out;
              }
```

By commenting out the line that starts with Pos.xyz, you can see the effect of the reduction of the position. There are several other ways to implement such a technique. Please consult [Kwoon] and [Lengyel] for further ideas.

Results

This chapter is accompanied by one example program in the directory Chapter 25 - Shadow Volume.

ON THE CD

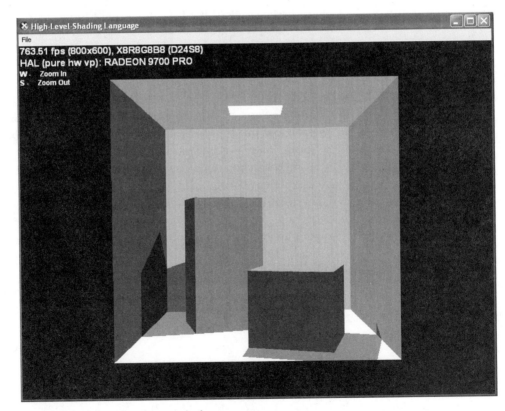

FIGURE 25.2 *Screenshot example program.*

Figure 25.2 shows the famous Cornell Box (*http://www.graphics.cornell.edu/online/box/*), which can be rotated by pressing the left mouse button in the applications window. The box can be moved to the camera or away by pressing W or S on the keyboard. The example program should work on all hardware that supports at least DirectX 8.

Here is a list of tips and tricks to consider, when improving this example program:

- This example could be further improved, by using Direct3D's depth biasing capabilities to overcome the reduced depth precision with increasing distance from the camera. This leads to a visible flickering when zooming in and out with W and S. DirectX 9.0 offers the D3DRS_DEPTHBIAS and D3DRS_SLOPESCALEDEPTH-BIAS render states for the calculation of an offset. This offset is used to position the front capping of the shadow volume behind the occluder's front facing geometries. This is done by adding the offset to the fragment's interpolated depth value that is used to create the final depth value that is used for depth testing. To check these new capabilities use the values of D3DPRASTERCAPS_DEPTHBIAS and D3DPRASTERCAPS_SLOPESCALEDEPTHBIAS. In case this functionality is not supported, the fallback path is to use the legacy D3DRS_DEPTHBIAS render state.

- Please note that the example application does not have to choose a specific light source out of several light sources, because there is only one light source. Additionally, a real-world application would determine the objects that should cast shadows in the visible region, to reduce the shadow generation only on the visible objects.

- Reducing the shadow geometry data set can be done by being more selective regarding the insertion of quads. This selection might be done by checking the direction of the normal more precisely. Additionally, a low polygon model of the occluder might be sufficient to compute the shadow volume geometry, but will decrease the visual experience of the shadow.

- One of the requirements of shadow volumes is the need for closed volume meshes. Otherwise, any gaps within the mesh would potentially throw the stencil counting off-balance and thus break the shadow volume implementation. Such a requirement mandates the need for modelers and designers to alter their work-flow and modeling style to avoid compromising the graphics engine.

- It is quite complicated to use shadow volumes together with a skinned mesh. [Brennan] describes a solution for this.

Conclusion

This part of the book covered the most popular dynamic shadow algorithms for games. Whereas shadow volumes raise the number of vertices that need to be processed due to the additional silhouette rendering path(s), the shadow map approach raises the fill rate requirements due to its usage of a big texture or several smaller textures.

Both techniques have their advantages and disadvantages. The biggest disadvantage of the shadow map approach is that it is not easy to implement on pre-DirectX 9 graphics hardware (with the exception of NVIDIA GeForce 3 and upwards), which would lead to the requirement to use another shadowing technique for older hardware. On the other side, shadow maps are independent of scene geometry and therefore do not rely on tweaked or changed geometry, which would need to be done by an artist. In other words, very high tessellated models are possible with shadow maps.

In the case of shadow volumes, a high tessellated model might lead to performance problems. The biggest disadvantage of shadow maps is the advantage of shadow volumes. Shadow volumes even run on DirectX 7 hardware and they are easier to scale throughout different versions of DirectX. Additionally, they always provide a perfectly sharp shadow without any flickering, Moiré effects, or aliasing.

Vertex Texturing

With the advent of vs_3_0 capable hardware, it is possible to sample textures in the vertex shader. This new capability opens the door to a world of new possibilities. Displacement mapping and geometry images are two techniques that store vertex values in a texture, and they are among the first techniques to be implemented with this new capability. Both will be covered in the following two chapters.

Other techniques store the position values of point sprites [Latta2] or vertices in textures, or the result of vertex transforms to re-use them on a copy of the model.

26 Displacement Mapping

Displacement mapping is a powerful technique for adding detail to objects and scenes. While bump mapping gives the appearance of increased surface complexity, displacement mapping actually adds surface complexity resulting in correct silhouettes and no parallax errors.

Displacement mapping can be used to add detail to a model but also to create the model itself. For example, you can add additional surface details to an already existing model, create terrain, or animate a water surface by applying a displacement map. Displacement mapping can be a method for geometry compression. A low polygon base mesh is tessellated in some way (e.g., by applying N-Patches). The vertices created by this tessellation are then displaced along a vector—usually the normal of the vertex. The distance that they are displaced is looked up in a displacement map.

Background

Displacement mapping was first mentioned by Robert L. Cook [Cook2] as a technique for adding surface detail to objects in a similar manner to texture mapping. A base surface can be defined by a function of two variables where the result is the position vector **P** that defines 3D points (x, y, z) on the surface. A corresponding scalar displacement map for that surface can be represented as **D**.

The normals on the base surface can be represented as **N**. Using this representation, the points on the new displaced surface **P'** are defined as:

$$\mathbf{P'} = \mathbf{P} + \mathbf{N'}$$

where

$$N' = D \times N \times S$$
$$D = d(u,v)$$

N is the unit surface normal, which is multiplied with the displacement scalar **D** from the displacement map and a user-defined scale factor **S** that scales the length of the resulting displacement vector **N'** and who should be constant for the whole surface. This vector is added to the position value of the vertex.

In other words, for each vertex, the GPU determines the height value from the displacement map at the provided 2D texture coordinate and uses this value together with a user-defined scale factor to displace the vertex position along the vertex normal.

A two-dimensional example of a displacement map is shown in Figure 26.1.

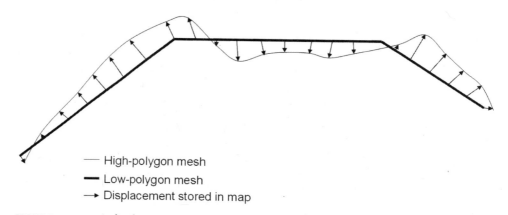

— High-polygon mesh
▬ Low-polygon mesh
➝ Displacement stored in map

FIGURE 26.1   *A displacement map applies scalar offsets along interpolated normals of a base mesh.*

The displacement map is authored by using a high-polygon model mesh and a low-polygon mesh. Each texel on the displacement and normal maps has a single position on the low-polygon mesh. A ray is cast from the position along the interpolated low-polygon normal and the intersection found with the high-polygon mesh. The normal of the high-polygon mesh is written into the normal map, and the distance along the ray to the point of intersection is written into the displacement map (read more in [Forsyth]).

Implementation

Implementing displacement mapping with a vs_3_0 capable graphics card is straight-forward. The displacement value is fetched from the displacement map in the vertex shader and added to the position value of the vertex as shown in the following source code.

```
VS_OUTPUT VS(float4 Pos : POSITION, float3 Normal : NORMAL,
                    float2 Tex: TEXCOORD0)
{
  VS_OUTPUT Out = (VS_OUTPUT) 0;

  float DisplacementScalar = tex2Dlod(s0,
                        float4(Tex.x, Tex.y, 0.0f, 0.0f));
  Out.TexCoordinate = Tex.xy;

  float3 DisplacementVector = Normal * scaleFactor.x;
  float3 ScaledDisplacementVector = DisplacementVector
                                * DisplacementScalar;
  float3 DisplacedVertexPos = Pos + ScaledDisplacementVector;
  Out.Pos = mul(float4(DisplacedVertexPos, 1.0f), matWorldViewProj);

  return Out;
}
```

To accentuate the effect of displacement mapping in the example program, a user-defined scalar is multiplied with the displacement value, so that the user can interactively raise or lower the displacement of the position values along the vertex normal.

Results and Conclusion

ON THE CD

This chapter is accompanied by an example program in the directory Chapter 26 - Displacement Mapping. It shows a very simplified earth texture on a sphere. The mountains can be raised by pressing the Down key on the keyboard and lowered by pressing the Up key.

Figure 26.2 shows how the vertices of the sphere are displaced in mountainous regions.

From the game programmer's point of view, the main challenge in providing objects with displaced vertices to a game engine is in the creation of the content tools that output displacement maps along with low-polygon models and normal maps. A good overview over this task is given by Tom Forsyth in [Forsyth].

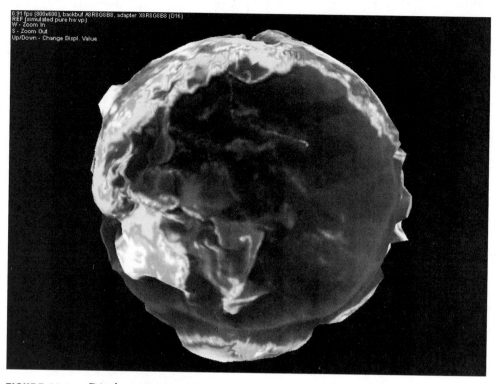

FIGURE 26.2   *Displacement mapping.*

27 First Steps to Geometry Images

Whereas displacement mapping can be used to compress geometry by storing for example a displacement value for a flat 2D plane in a texture map, geometry images go one step further. They store the whole position value and all other vertex attributes in a texture map. The advantages of using geometry images are:

- Easy compression.
- Quick and easy level-of-detail system by using mip-maps (constructing such a system is beyond trivial).
- Generating a normal map from geometry images should be easy.
- Blending between different geometry images to deform meshes. Blending between different level-of-detail levels should be easier than blending between different level-of-details in vertex buffers.

Geometry images were introduced by Xianfeng Gu, Steven J. Gortler and Hugues Hoppe at SIGGRAPH 2002 [Gu]. An improved parametrization algorithm and a hardware implementation using pixel shaders were presented at the Eurographics Symposium on Geometry Processing in 2003 by F. Losasso, H. Hoppe, S. Schaefer, and J. Warren [Losasso].

The idea of geometry images is that an arbitrary surface is remeshed onto a completely regular structure, called geometry image. It captures geometry as a simple $n \times n$ array of $[x, y, z]$ values. Other surface attributes, such as normals and colors, are stored as additional square images. To reduce the storage requirements even more, geometry images can be stored in DXTn compressed images.

The first two challenges to face when implementing geometry images are:

1. Remeshing an arbitrary surface onto a completely regular structure (= = Geometry Image). In other words, how to capture geometry as a simple 2D array of quantized points. In [Gu] this is done by cutting an arbitrary mesh along a network of edge paths and parameterizing the resulting single chart onto a square. In [Losasso], a scheme to represent an entire closed surface as a single uniform bicubic B-spline patch is presented.
2. How to fetch the 2D data with graphics hardware.

This chapter will only focus on challenge No. 2.

Background

Storing all the vertex attributes in texture maps requires a consistent way to access these values with the graphics card. Until the advent of vs_3_0 capable hardware, the only way to feed vertex data created by the pixel shader back into the vertex shader is via OpenGL prototype extensions (e.g., EXT_pixel_buffer_object). These extensions allowed the data to be written directly to the vertex buffer of the graphics card.

The vertex texturing capabilities available with vs_3_0 now offer a more efficient and elegant way for a texture created by the pixel shader to be read by the vertex shader. Texture coordinates used to access the vertex texture in the vertex shader can be stored in the vertex buffer, or an ID which is used to access a 1D texture in the vertex shader can be stored in a float variable in the vertex buffer. In both approaches, the vertices are grouped into an indexed list.

Implementation

To create a texture that stores the position values of a quad, we store the position values in a four channel 16-bit floating-point texture. This can be done as a 2×2 grid of pixels or a 1×4 grid of pixels. The vertex buffer layout for a 2×2 grid is shown in the following source code snippet.

```
VERTEX VertexBufferData[] =
{
  {  0.25,  0.25, 1.0f, 1.0f,}, // v0
  { -0.25,  0.25, 0.0f, 1.0f,}, // v1
  {  0.25, -0.25, 0.0f, 0.0f,}, // v2
  { -0.25, -0.25, 1.0f, 0.0f,}, // v3
};
```

Here the first two variables of each vertex are used to access the vertex texture in the vertex shader. To access a 1×4 grid of pixels in a vertex texture, the following vertex buffer is used.

```
inline float i2id(const float i, const float NumVertices)
{
 return (1.f / NumVertices) * i;
}
...
VERTEX VertexBufferData[dwNumVertices];
VertexBufferData[0].id = i2id(0, dwNumVertices);
VertexBufferData[0].tu = 1.0f;
VertexBufferData[0].tv = 1.0f;

VertexBufferData[1].id = i2id(1, dwNumVertices);
VertexBufferData[1].tu = 0.0f;
VertexBufferData[1].tv = 1.0f;

VertexBufferData[2].id = i2id(2, dwNumVertices);
VertexBufferData[2].tu = 0.0f;
VertexBufferData[2].tv = 0.0f;

VertexBufferData[3].id = i2id(3, dwNumVertices);
VertexBufferData[3].tu = 1.0f;
VertexBufferData[3].tv = 0.0f;
 ...
```

The id variable is used to access the vertex texture in the vertex shader. It is filled with the following values in this example: −0.75, −0.25, 0.25, and 0.75. The drawback of this technique is that there is a low maximum number of vertices that can be stored in a 1D texture. Other than this, it should be possible to store up to 4096 vertices (maximum texture size on common ps_3_0 cards) quite easily from a model in the same order they are stored in the mesh file.

Results

ON THE CD This chapter is accompanied by two example programs in the directory Chapter 27 - First Steps to Geometry Images that use a 1×4 pixel grid (in HLSL Geometry Images) and a 2×2 pixel grid (HLSL Geometry Images 2D Texture) in the vertex texture.

The simple example program shows a rotating quad, consisting of two indexed triangles in the form of a list. Additionally, this quad is textured in the pixel shader using the texture coordinates stored in the vertex buffer.

One obvious way to improve these example programs would be to use a separate texture for texture coordinates and other vertex attributes and to access this texture with the same argument that is used to access the texture that holds the position values. Another improvement would be to store the already rotated vertex positions in a texture and to access these in the vertex shader.

FIGURE 27.1 *Geometry image.*

Conclusion

Vertex textures offer a whole new world of capabilities. They move the workload for the graphics cards away from the pre-vertex shader states to the vertex shader. Additionally, they can offer a huge reduction in size by storing data in *.dds file format and using the DXTn compression scheme. Four vertices stored in a *.dds file, for example, are shown in Figure 27.1.

Using vertex textures to hold displacement values at first, and then using them to hold all kinds of vertex attributes, including vertex animation, we have redefined some of the common techniques for storing object data. Additionally, all kinds of mathematical formulas can be stored in a vertex texture. These mathematical equations can for example be used to transform the vertex data.

P A R T

IX Shaders as Part of a Graphics Engine

Shaders are a vital part of a game engine. One of the most important questions of game engine design is how to use shaders in a game engine in a way to impress the target group of the game and at the same time create an efficient shader workflow throughout the game development team.

This part will first cover how shaders can be used in a game production workflow, and then we will talk about how to build up a shader subsystem for a game engine that will satisfy the needs of a modern game.

28 Shaders as Part of a Game Engine

Before a game engine is designed, the required graphics hardware capabilities of the game must be defined. The required capabilities will be geared to the available hardware on the end-users market at the time of release of the game. This is a vital part of the business plan, which assures that the target group of the game is big enough to make some profit with the game.

Having a well-defined target group, a team will be built to develop the game. Optimizing the workflow in such a team is vital for the production costs. A lot of team members will work with shaders, and therefore, shader usage in such a team and the rights to create or change shaders need to be clarified before the team starts to work.

The planning of the team's shader workflow is accompanied with a first rough design of the game engine. One of the upcoming sections will cover some rules for engine design that help to optimize shader performance.

Let's start here at the beginning of the lifecycle of a game: evaluating the target group.

Target Group

The target group of a game is usually identified by the person or company who is responsible for the business plan. In most cases, this is someone working for the game publisher. Outlining such a target group will happen with respect to the game genre and for each title individually. In the PC market, the availability of specific graphics hardware is a factor to consider when defining the target group. In other words, the decision of whether a game supports ps_3_0 as the minimum specification is based on the number of graphics cards in the target group that support this pixel shader version at the time of the release of the game. Estimating the availability of certain graphics hardware in the future is not an easy task, but looking at past developments might help here. What follows is a case study on how to evaluate graphics hardware available in the target group of a first-person shooter game.

The majority of graphics cards are coming from ATI and NVIDIA while most graphics hardware is delivered by INTEL. According to Mercury Research on the fourth quarter 2003 graphics market [TheRegister], ATI's market share was 24.9 percent and NVIDIA's market share was 24.7 percent. Intel took 31.7 percent of the market, thanks to strong sales of its integrated-graphics chipsets. So for the beginning of 2004, it was safe to say that about 50% of all graphics hardware came from ATI and NVIDIA.

Having a rough picture of how many cards the main graphics card producers have sold is not enough, because the capabilities of these cards are very different as reflected in their prices, the key evaluator for the user group. The following list shows the currently known gamer graphics cards that are available at the time of this writing:

- fixed-function: DirectX7 (INTEL integrated chipsets, NVIDIA GeForce MX, ATI RADEON 7500) or earlier
- ps_1_1: NVIDIA GeForce 3
- ps_1_2-ps_1_3: NVIDIA GeForce 4/XBOX and others
- ps_1_4: ATI RADEON 8500-9200
- ps_2_0: ATI RADEON 9500+/XGI Volari/S3 Deltachrome
- ps_2_a: NVIDIA GeForce FX
- ps_2_b: ATI RADEON X800
- ps_3_0: NVIDIA GeForce 6800

The capabilities of these cards range from DirectX7 up to the most recent shader version, ps_3_0. All of the graphics cards that support the higher pixel shader versions are downward compatible (exception: a ps_2_b capable graphics card is not downward compatible to a ps_2_a capable graphics card but a ps_2_a graphics card is downward compatible to a card that supports ps_2_b), which means for example that all lower pixel shader versions must be supported by a graphics card that supports ps_3_0. Supporting more advanced hardware results in higher expectations from the target group and therefore there is a lot more work involved.

Estimating the amount of work necessary to target a specific group of games requires a more thorough understanding of the market share of specific cards. One source that is helpful here is the ongoing survey on VALVE's Web site [VALVE]. VALVE sells first person shooter games based on their Half Life engine. This engine is at the time of writing a little bit outdated, but the upcoming Half Life 2 engine seems to be much more demanding.

The online survey shows that at the end of April 2004, only about 26% of all graphics cards used by the users of this service supported ps_2_0, about 22% were cards that supported ps_1_1, and the rest of the cards were DirectX 7 compatible graphics cards or followed even lower standards. Assuming that the users of VALVE's online service invest above average into their graphics hardware, the numbers are disillusioning. That's why most games still focus on DirectX 7 support at the time of this writing, which means that in most cases, the art creation pipeline in these games targets DirectX 7 graphics cards, and some eye candy is added by using DirectX 8 (ps_1_1-ps_1_4) and DirectX 9 (ps_2_0-ps_3_0) class shaders, if supported (one obvious exception to that is XBOX titles, because they are developed for a DirectX 8 hardware environment).

Targeting a DirectX 8-capable graphics card as the minimum requirement of a game is the exception and not the rule these days, but this will change in the future. Based on the progression of the market in the last couple of years, one might assume that a game engine that should be available in two years should support second and third generation shaders and as a fallback, first generation shaders. Getting a more precise estimation requires a lot more data based on market studies, which is outside the scope of this book. The simple case study shown earlier should give you an idea of how a decision process happens and why a specific hardware feature is supported or not supported in a game. Having a clear picture of this, let us start to think about the requirements of such a game engine.

For the remainder of this chapter, we assume that the target platform of the game engine will be a ps_2_0 capable graphics.

Requirements of a Shader Subsystem

Focusing on the engine features that support the use of the hardware shader units of the graphics cards, the following list of features seems to form a common basis for a current shader subsystem.

- Art pipeline integration
- Support of industry standard formats
- Hardware-friendly design
- Data-driven support

Art Pipeline Integration

Shaders need to be created and handled in the game production workflow in the most efficient way to keep development costs at an optimal level. This is not an easy task because of the sheer number of expected shaders.

Assuming that the game will target only graphics hardware that supports programmable shaders, the game programmers might end up creating-depending on the genre of the game-perhaps 300 different effects, each consisting of a vertex and a pixel shader. This number might then be tripled by the artists, because they want to mix up effects or tune effects. (Gary McTaggart reported at GDC 2004 that Half-Life 2 uses 1,920 different pixel shaders [McTaggart].)

Therefore having a clear picture of how shaders are handled in the game production workflow is vital for a calculation of the necessary effort for a game. Figure 28.1 shows a simplified overview of the workflow in a game development team with respect to shaders, which might help as a starting point for your own planning.

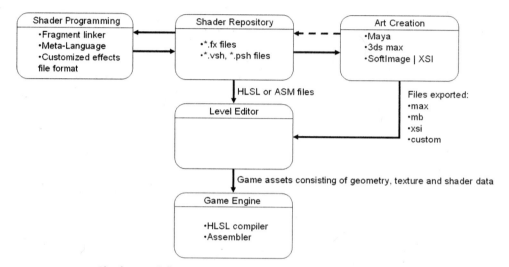

FIGURE 28.1   *Shader workflow in a game development unit.*

Shaders are created by a low-level Direct3D programmer, as shown in the top left of Figure 28.1. They are stored in a shader repository, where the artist can access the shaders to attach them to the models. The level designer will access the shader repository and will get all the geometry data from the artist in a file format created by the art tools or a customized format that is used for the game engine (this might be a package consisting of geometry and shader data). Finally, the game assets will be provided to the game engine. Shaders will be compiled or assembled in the game engine.

The critical path is the dashed line. Depending on the knowledge of the artist, it is possible to allow him to change or build shaders from other shader fragments. This will lead to a much higher number of shaders and perhaps decrease performance. On the other hand, controlling the diversification of shaders by only allowing the programmer to change shaders seems to be quite common, but it reduces the creative input of the artists.

To help the artist to change or create shaders, tools like RT/shader (*www.rtzen.com*) need to be bought or created, so that he can build a large amount of shaders with the least amount of work. Integrating real-time shaders that run on the underlying graphics hardware into all the popular DCC tools is possible with plug-ins, but even if these plug-ins allow changes to the shader code, most artists will not know C/C++ or HLSL well enough to alter these shaders. Therefore most of these plug-ins have graphical user interfaces to alter specific constants of one shader. Unfortunately, this is not enough to utilize the creativity of artists.

To solve this situation, in-house tools are developed nowadays. One approach is to expose a metalanguage similar to the metalanguage used in Quake III and the new DirectX Standard Annotation and Semantics script language. Such a metalanguage has a higher level of abstraction than HLSL and should be easier for the art department to learn. The capabilities of this language can be reduced so that the possible number of different shaders stays low.

Another approach is to build fragments of HLSL shaders, which are put together by the programmer or artist and then compiled in the game engine or put together on the fly. This approach reduces the complexity of the available shader fragments and allows a high-level of creativity. It might even be combined with the first approach.

The shader creation process can be abstracted even further by using a shader metalanguage that describes the ideal shader with fallback paths provided by the metalanguage compiler for different platforms [Forsyth2].

Creating these tools and integrating their output with the shader engine is made easier by following existing industry standards.

Support of Industry Standard Formats

Using existing tools like ATI's RenderMonkey or NVIDIA's FX Composer should be considered. They can not only be used in prototyping shaders, but they can also be integrated into the production flow shown earlier. These tools are getting more and more customizable and are able to import standards like Microsoft's *.fx file format or NVIDIA's Cgfx file format. Staying compatible with these formats reduces time to train people with the proper tools and reduces development costs of tools, because they are frequently updated for free. This is why the shader repository in Figure 28.1 stores *.fx or assembly files as an intermediate format.

Having shown some guidelines for how to integrate shaders into the art pipeline, it is time to move on to the scope of this book by talking about shader-friendly game engine design.

Hardware-Friendly Design

Optimizing the graphics engine design for a heavy shader workload should be considered already in the design stage. Balancing the exchange of game assets like textures, render states, texture states, and vertex and pixel shaders is one of the challenges in game engine design. The following list shows the performance impact of exchanging game assets and possible solutions.

1. Options for reducing or eliminating shader changes:
   -Sort
   -Use fewer shaders
   -Use longer shaders
2. Options for reducing or eliminating constant and texture changes:
   -Sort
   -Change fewer constants
   -Use more shaders that don't require constant changes
3. Options for reducing or eliminating vertex declaration changes:
   -Sort
   -Use fewer vertex declaration
4. Options for increasing z-rejects:
   -Sort
   -Generally categorize your geometry (entities, architectural occluders, portals, etc.)

Switching shaders is one of the most expensive things on current graphics hardware. As you can see, sorting is an option in every case, but it potentially increases the administrative overhead of the application and memory footprint, especially in the case of multipass rendering.

One option that should be considered before implementing specific sorting mechanisms is reducing changes by caching geometry, shaders, textures, and render states.

It is not publicly known if and which hardware caches vertex and/or pixel shaders. At the least caching can be implemented with Microsoft's effect file format, so that SetVertexShader() or its pixel equivalent are only called if the vertex or pixel shader changes. A simple caching system with SetVertexShader() calls is to check the handle that is provided to the function, and if it is not the same as in the previous call, the function is called again. A simple mechanism to ensure that the texture is set only once is shown by the following line of code.

```
if(md3Model->md3Meshes[iCurrMesh].iNumTextures > 0)
{
  for (i = 0; i < md3Model->md3Meshes[iCurrMesh].iNumTextures; i++)
  {
    if( pMiniTextureCache[i] != md3Model->
                    md3Meshes[iCurrMesh].pTexturesInterfaces[i])
    {
      pMiniTextureCache[i] = md3Model->md3Meshes[iCurrMesh]
                        .pTexturesInterfaces[i];
      m_pDevice->SetTexture(i, pMiniTextureCache[i] );
    }
  }
}
```

This code snippet assumes that all textures with a specific functionality are always loaded in the same texture stages. For example, the normal map is always loaded in texture stage 1. Some rules for this will be discussed later in this chapter. Texture stages can be cached even more by storing smaller textures in one big texture and setting this big texture once and fetching the different smaller textures from it frequently.

To cache render states, the state block mechanism is provided by the Direct3D API.

If your application is not CPU-limited and you have already implemented all other options, you might implement sorting following the previous overview. That means that meshes with the same shaders are drawn first, then meshes with different shaders but the same constants, then meshes with different shaders and different constants but the same vertex declarations. To achieve early z-rejects, a rough front-to-back order can be helpful. This can be done first. Categorizing geometry in "good" and "bad" occluders might help to increase z-rejects even more.

> *There is no rule without exceptions: one exception is that alpha-blended objects need to be sorted back to front.*

It is important to note that the order of rules is not necessarily set in stone. Having a system that can change this order and measure the results is a good investment to account for different hardware environments and overall performance of the game. As usual, measuring what you do is crucial.

These rules just reflect the needs of the underlying graphics hardware. A more general engine design approach is shown in Figure 28.2.

The scene graph is used to organize the scene content hierarchically. Each object in the scene graph can be referenced using a unique value (such as a string name). After the world is composed of the scene objects, the visibility determination system is involved. This system is composed of several stages that accomplish different optimizations in the view cone for the current camera. It is concerned with hidden surface determination and hidden object determination and culling. This system can create arbitrary frustum databases containing only the visible objects. This is crucial for example for multipass rendering, because multiple rendering passes should use the smallest possible number of vertices. The frustum processor references existing meshes, textures, and effects. It is also responsible for proper sorting, as mentioned in this section. Meshes are stored in one large vertex buffer, which is the most efficient case, or in several vertex buffers, depending on mesh type and size.

The resource system consists of a material system, which manages the effects and the textures for meshes. It ensures that effects can be combined over arbitrary texture passes and supports multipass techniques. It should also be able to handle level-of-material systems to account for distance in games that allow a wide viewing distance.

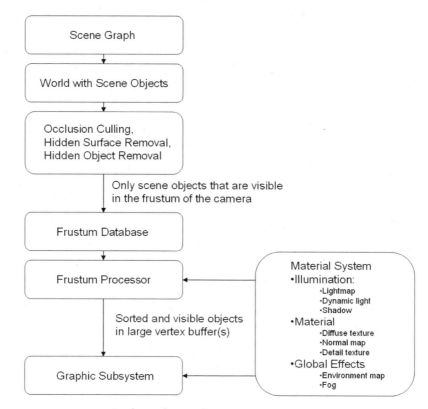

FIGURE 28.2   *Outline of a graphics engine.*

The material system differentiates between three kinds of materials (this approach is used in the CodeCreatures Engine [Hoeller] and the Krass Engine [Frick]): the illumination stage is responsible for all lighting activities and is repeated in multipass environments, the material stage is always applied once, and the global effects stage handles effects that influence the whole scene.

Balancing such a system is an extremely complex process. There are numerous articles targeting this challenge. Read more in [ATI] and [Rege]. An easier to realize improvement to your graphics engine is to keep all effect related data separate from the compiled application code.

Data-Driven Support

Data-driven support allows a shader to be utilized with no source code compilation required. This target is easy to achieve by using the Direct3D effect file format, which stores all data including render states for the shader in one ASCII file. This ASCII file can be exchanged easily without compiling any code. If the Direct3D effect file format is not used, a similar functionality needs to be created in the game engine.

A Simple Data-Driven Level-of-Shading System

As a case study, we look at a simple data-driven shader system, which supports level-of-shading functionality. The example program accompanying this chapter is a character engine that uses an enhanced Quake III model format. This model format can store more than one mesh in one *.md3 model file and usually uses up to four *.md3 files to construct a model.

Having a model that consists of several meshes (some consist of up to 14), allows setting a different texture or effect for each mesh.

The level-of-shading (LOS) system can change each shader used by a mesh interactively. This is done by defining a so-called shader level for each mesh in a shader profile (in the file with the postfix *.profiles) like this.

```
shaderprofile0
head01,shaderlevel1
lower_mesh01,shaderlevel0
lower_mesh02,shaderlevel0
l_legs01,shaderlevel0
upper_mesh01,shaderlevel1

shaderprofile1
head01,shaderlevel1
lower_mesh01,shaderlevel0
lower_mesh02,shaderlevel0
l_legs01,shaderlevel1
upper_mesh01,shaderlevel1

shaderprofile2
head01,shaderlevel1
lower_mesh01,shaderlevel0
lower_mesh02,shaderlevel1
l_legs01,shaderlevel1
upper_mesh01,shaderlevel1
```

This model consists of five meshes and it uses three different shader profiles. Each shader profile defines a shader level for each mesh. The shader level attaches a specific vertex or pixel shader to the specific mesh with the help of the shader file (files with the postfix *.sha).

```
lower_mesh01,shaders/diffuse.vsh,shaderlevel0
lower_mesh02,shaders/diffuse.vsh,shaderlevel0
l_legs01,shaders/diffuse.vsh,shaderlevel0
lower_mesh01,shaders/diffuse.psh,shaderlevel0
lower_mesh02,shaders/diffuse.psh,shaderlevel0
l_legs01,shaders/diffuse.psh,shaderlevel0
lower_mesh01,shaders/diffuse.vsh,shaderlevel1
lower_mesh02,shaders/diffuse.vsh,shaderlevel1
l_legs01,shaders/diffuse.vsh,shaderlevel1
lower_mesh01,shaders/diffuse.psh,shaderlevel1
lower_mesh02,shaders/diffuse.psh,shaderlevel1
l_legs01,shaders/diffuse.psh,shaderlevel1
```

```
lower_mesh01,shaders/diffspec.vsh,shaderlevel2
lower_mesh02,shaders/diffspec.vsh,shaderlevel2
l_legs01,shaders/diffspec.vsh,shaderlevel2
lower_mesh01,shaders/diffspec.psh,shaderlevel2
lower_mesh02,shaders/diffspec.psh,shaderlevel2
l_legs01,shaders/diffspec.psh,shaderlevel2
```

Here, you can see three different shader levels. The number of shader levels and shader profiles is unlimited. A different set of shaders can be set by choosing a different shader profile. This system offers the flexibility to change each mesh individually for each shader profile without having any dependencies.

All these files are ASCII files that are stored in the same folder as all model files. This folder also holds a skin file, which follows conventions similar to those used in the original *.md3 file format. It attaches one or more textures to a mesh. The number of textures that can be attached to one mesh is unlimited, but the example program is limited by the number of textures that can be attached in one pass, because it does not expose multipass capabilities.

```
lower_mesh01,models/players/dragon/Deranged_Crowley.dds
lower_mesh02,models/players/dragon/Deranged_Crowley.dds
lower_mesh01,models/players/dragon/normal.dds
lower_mesh02,models/players/dragon/normal.dds
l_legs01,models/players/dragon/Deranged_Sir_Bruin.dds
l_legs01,models/players/dragon/Deranged_Sir_BruinNormal.dds
tag_torso,
```

Other shaders or different textures can be attached by altering the ASCII files in a text editor, without recompiling any code.

Results

The following three screenshots in Figure 28.3 show three different shader profiles. Please note that the railgun model is provided courtesy of Lee David Ash (available at *http://www.planetquake.com/polycount*), and the dragon model was created by Michael "Magarnigal" Mellor (available at *http://www.planetquake.com/polycount*).

The first profile shown in the top screenshot uses a combination of Phong and Cook-Torrance shaders. The second profile uses diffuse shaders, and the third profile at the bottom only uses shaders that output the texture colors. Mixing up the shaders in any way is possible. Using the shader profile system to make the character engine scalable according to the underlying hardware is easy. You might define for example shader profiles 1-8 for ps_1_1 hardware, shader profiles 9-16 for ps_2_0 capable hardware, and shader profiles 17-19 for ps_3_0 capable hardware. For each type of hardware, you might define different levels of shading profiles. For example, shader profile 1 is used if the model is very near with Cook-Torrance, Phong, and environment map shaders; shader profile 2 is used if the model is in a medium distance and

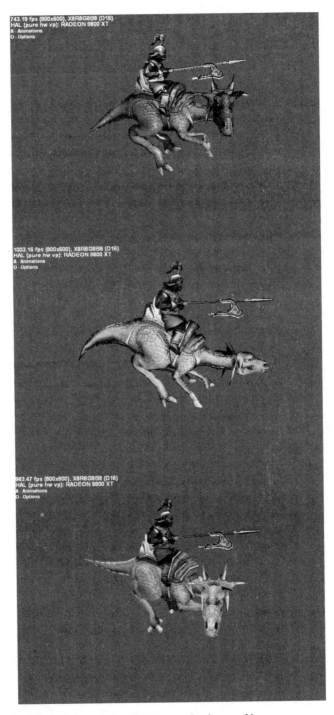

FIGURE 28.3 *Three different shader profiles.*

switches off environment mapping, reduces specular lighting to a cheaper effect, and does not use the Cook-Torrance shader; shader profile 3 uses shaders that just show the color of the textures; and shader profile 4 uses color only shaders that just colorize everything.

This might go hand-in-hand with a level-of-detail system that reduces the geometrical detail based on distance.

ON THE CD This chapter is accompanied by two example programs, which can be found in the directory Chapter 28 - Shaders as Part of a Graphics Engine. The example in the directory CharacterEngine uses three different shader profiles to cover ps_2_0 shaders. These three shader profiles are shown in Figure 28.3. The example in the directory ps_1_1 CharacterEngine covers seven shader profiles with different combinations of ps_1_1 compatible shaders.

Summary

This chapter gave a short overview on the inconveniences that may be caused by designing a game engine in shader-friendly way. All this should not hide the fact that most games end up CPU-limited and that therefore the capabilities of the graphics cards cannot be fully used. In all non-CPU-limited cases, it is important to develop strategies to use graphics hardware in the most efficient way.

Some engine design requirements come from the fact that the art pipeline needs to be involved in the most efficient way, and others come from the importance of support of industry standards in increasing efficiency and reducing development costs.

Storing shaders in an easy to edit format in separate files helps to follow the paradigm of a data-driven graphics engine, which does not need to be recompiled if shaders are altered.

Afterword

If you've followed me this far, you might agree that we've come through some rough country. Having seen some ways to create mind-blowing visual effects, you might resist heading toward the next new graphics feature available nowadays in three-month cycles, just relax and look at the photos in a book written by Ansel Adams or a classic black-and-white movie directed by Alfred Hitchcock from the 50s or 60s. Take your time and think about the reasons that make these photos or movies visually so impressive.

I think it is something more substantial than colors or effects; it is mood and imagination.

Appendix

A

vs_3_0/ps_3_0 Assembly

This appendix of the book covers how to program shaders with the vs_3_0 and ps_3_0 assembly versions. Using these assembly versions instead of using the HLSL compiler has its advantages and disadvantages.

The advantage of using assembly is direct control on what is provided to the hardware drivers.

The disadvantages include the following:

- HLSL encourages thinking on a more algorithmic level, because the C-like language is more abstracted.
- It is easier to program in C than in assembly.
- The HLSL compiler can optimize code for specific hardware before running the application. Being able to link together a HLSL source code snippet and compiling this during runtime, or up-front with the optimizing HLSL compiler, reduces the amount of shaders necessary to target different hardware substantially compared to a similar assembly functionality.

Although the advantages of using HLSL to program shaders are intriguing from a business perspective, learning how to program shaders in assembly is still necessary to understand how hardware uses shaders and to be able to control the HLSL compiler output, and if the HLSL compiler does not support all features exposed by assembly shaders, to use these features.

This book focuses on the third generation shader versions, because these versions are already very consistent and powerful, whereas previous versions were more difficult to learn and had a lot more restrictions.

The next section will cover how vertex data is manipulated with an assembly vertex shader.

Assembly Vertex Shader Programming Fundamentals

The vertex shader is used to manipulate data that is part of a structure that describes a vertex. Figure A.1 shows the data flow in the graphics pipeline; the programmer has to take care of the circled portion when programming vertex shaders.

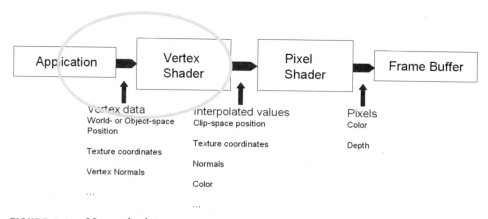

FIGURE A.1   *Vertex shader stream processing.*

The vertex shader expects data from the application, and the Direct3D runtime needs to be informed about the structure of this data. Usually the data is provided in a so-called vertex structure through a vertex buffer. The steps necessary to input this data are as follows:

- Create a structure that shows the segmentation of the data.
- Create a vertex declaration that describes this structure.
- Create a vertex buffer object and an index buffer object (if indexed primitives are used).
- Input vertex data into the vertex and index buffer (as shown in the vertex structure and described in the vertex declaration).
- Create a vertex shader and compile it.
- Set render states for the non-programmable parts of the pipeline.
- Set vertex and index buffer as the input stream for the draw primitive functions.
- Set vertex shader to modify the vertex data.
- Execute stream(s) by calling the DrawIndexedPrimitive() function.

The creation of the vertex structure, the vertex declaration, and a vertex buffer and index buffer were already covered in Chapter 3, because they are the same for assembly shaders as for HLSL shaders.

Assembly shaders are compiled differently than HLSL shaders. In fact, they are assembled instead of compiled. After declaring the vertex layout and setting up the vertex stream processing capabilities requested from hardware, we need to assemble and create (i.e., allocate resources) the already written vertex shader. The following functions assemble and create a vertex shader:

```
TCHAR strVertexShaderPath[512];
LPD3DXBUFFER pCode;

DXUtil_FindMediaFileCb(strVertexShaderPath, sizeof(strVer-
texShaderPath), _T("vertex.vsh"));
D3DXAssembleShaderFromFile(strVertexShaderPath, NULL, NULL,
dwFlags, &pCode, NULL);
m_pd3dDevice->CreateVertexShader((DWORD*)pCode->GetBuffer-
Pointer(), &vsVertexShader);
```

The first function, `DXUtil_FindMediaFileCb()`, returns the path of the ASCII file that holds the shader. This file is assembled by the function `D3DXAssembleShader-FromFile()`, which stores a buffer that contains the compiled shader code in its fifth parameter, as well as any embedded debug and symbol table information. `Create VertexShader()` uses the compiled shader code (sent in the first parameter) to produce a vertex shader object, returned in its last parameter.

To hand the vertex shader object over to the Direct3D runtime, it has to be set before every call to `DrawIndexedPrimitive()` with the following function.

```
HRESULT SetVertexShader(IDirect3DVertexShader9* pShader);
```

After executing the vertex streams with a `DrawIndexedPrimitive()` function, the vertex shader is called as often as there are vertices sent to the hardware processor.

So far, we have seen an overview of the whole vertex stream processing flow as related to the vertex shader. The following section will show how to program one part of this flow—the vertex shader—by starting with an explanation of the data format that is used in a vertex shader.

Vertex Shader Data Format

The main data format used in vertex shaders is represented by 128-bit quad floats (4 × 32-bit) as shown in Figure A.2.

The hardware processor that handles vertices and that is "driven" by a vertex shader can be seen as a typical SIMD (Single Instruction Multiple Data) processor. One instruction affects up to four 32-bit variables. This data format is useful, because most of the transformation and lighting calculations are performed using 4×4 matrices or a quaternion.

Additionally, a 32-bit integer data format and a Boolean data format are supported.

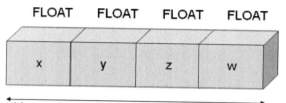

FLOAT FLOAT FLOAT FLOAT

| x | y | z | w |

4 byte = 32 bits leads to 4 x 32 bits = 128 bits

FIGURE A.2 *128-bit quad float.*

All data in a vertex shader are held by registers (registers are similar to variables) and modified by instructions. Following the data flow, one might differentiate between input registers, temporary registers, indexing registers, sampler registers, and output registers.

Input Registers

The vertex shader processor receives data via input registers and constant registers. A vs_3_0 vertex shader uses up to 16 input registers, named *v0–v15*, to receive vertex input data. The vertex data for the input registers is provided by the vertex buffer to the vertex shader in the layout described in the vertex declaration (semantic mapping) and the vertex structure.

Following the example vertex structure used earlier, the vertex shader input might be declared like this:

```
; declare input
dcl_position0   v0.xyzw
dcl_normal0     v3.xyz
dcl_texcoord0   v7.xy
dcl_tangent0    v8.xyz
```

The four position values are retrieved through v0, the normal through v3, and the texture coordinate and tangent through v7 or v8. As you can see, the declaration with dcl_ maps the data to the vn registers. The number at the end of the declaration represents the index used in the vertex declaration. Please consult the documentation for further available dcl_* declarations.

Figure A.3 shows the relationship between the vertex structure, the vertex buffer, the vertex declaration, and dcl_*:

To retrieve data for a second texture coordinate, one might use the following declaration:

```
dcl_texcoord1   v9.xy
```

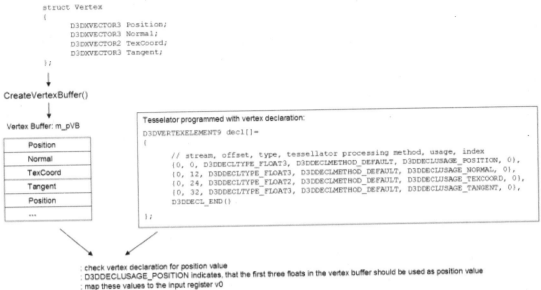

```
struct Vertex
{
    D3DXVECTOR3 Position;
    D3DXVECTOR3 Normal;
    D3DXVECTOR2 TexCoord;
    D3DXVECTOR3 Tangent;
};
```

CreateVertexBuffer()

Vertex Buffer: m_pVB

| Position |
| Normal |
| TexCoord |
| Tangent |
| Position |
| ... |

```
Tesselator programmed with vertex declaration:
D3DVERTEXELEMENT9 decl[]=
{
    // stream, offset, type, tessellator processing method, usage, index
    {0, 0, D3DDECLTYPE_FLOAT3, D3DDECLMETHOD_DEFAULT, D3DDECLUSAGE_POSITION, 0},
    {0, 12, D3DDECLTYPE_FLOAT3, D3DDECLMETHOD_DEFAULT, D3DDECLUSAGE_NORMAL, 0},
    {0, 24, D3DDECLTYPE_FLOAT2, D3DDECLMETHOD_DEFAULT, D3DDECLUSAGE_TEXCOORD, 0},
    {0, 32, D3DDECLTYPE_FLOAT3, D3DDECLMETHOD_DEFAULT, D3DDECLUSAGE_TANGENT, 0},
    D3DDECL_END()
};
```

```
; check vertex declaration for position value
; D3DDECLUSAGE_POSITION indicates, that the first three floats in the vertex buffer should be used as position value
; map these values to the input register v0
dcl_position v0
```

FIGURE A.3   *Map data to vertex input register.*

Upcoming hardware might pack inputs together into registers during the declaration phase of the shader. In other words, the hardware compresses the data, so that it fits into the 16 input registers. As an example, a vertex shader 3.0 declaration could accept position, normal, tangent, binormal, two colors, eight blending weights, eight blending indices, and 14 2D texture coordinates by optimal use of input registers packing. With the vs_2_0 model, such a declaration would only be possible by pre-packing all this data in the vertex structure using 16 total inputs [Thibieroz].

All the vn registers are fed by the tessellator with data from the vertex buffer in the order and format specified in the vertex declaration. Other data can be fed to the hardware via constant registers directly, without using the vertex buffer. To differentiate this data from the data that is fed via the vn registers, it is called constant data or short constants. There are float, integer, and Boolean constant registers. In vs_3_0, there are 256 floating-point constant registers (c0–c255), each one 128-bit long, 16 integer constant registers (i0–i15), each one 128-bit long, and 16 Boolean registers (b0–b15), each one a bool data type long (undocumented: might be 32-bit).

Constant registers can be used in two ways: in the vertex shader via def (float constants), defi (integer constants), and defb (Boolean constants) instructions and from inside the application via SetVertexShaderConstantF() (float constants),

SetVertexShaderConstantI() (integer constants), SetVertexShaderConstantB() (Boolean constants).

They are set within the vertex shader like this:

```
def c0, 1.0, 0.0, 0.0, 1.0  ; float constant register c0
defi i0, 1, 0, 0, 1         ; integer constant register i0
defb b0, TRUE               ; bool constant register b0
```

From within the application, constant registers are set like this:

```
// four floats (128-bit) in c8
m_pd3dDevice->SetVertexShaderConstantF(8, -m_LightDir, 1);
// four integers (128-bit) in i8
m_pd3dDevice->SetVertexShaderConstantI(8, iCounter, 1);
// one bool in b8
m_pd3dDevice->SetVertexShaderConstantB(8, bSwitch, 1);
```

For example, providing the concatenated world, view, and projection matrix to the vertex shader can be done as follows:

```
D3DXMATRIXA16 matTemp;
D3DXMatrixTranspose(&matTemp,&(m_matWorld * m_matView * m_mat-
Proj));
    m_pd3dDevice->SetVertexShaderConstantF(0, (FLOAT*)&matTemp, 4);
// four vectors in c0 - c3
```

The last parameter indicates that we're using four 128-bit floating-point vectors that occupy floating-point constant registers c0 through c3.

All input registers can only be used to load data from within the vertex shader (read-only). Any single instruction can access only one vn register, but this register can be used up to three times as a source register in one instruction. The following example demonstrates this concept:

```
add r0.xyz, v0, v1 ; error X5751: 2 different input registers (v#)
read by instruction.
...
add r0.xyz, v0, v0 ; valid
```

Any single instruction can only access one cn, in, bn register (the constant float, integer, and Boolean registers).

A typical use of the constant registers is shown in the following code snippet:

```
dp4 o0.x, v0, c0    ; position in clip space
dp4 o0.y, v0, c1
dp4 o0.z, v0, c2
dp4 o0.w, v0, c3
```

The four dot-product instructions map from concatenated world, view, and projection matrix to clip space. The four component dot-product performs the following calculation:

```
        o0.x = (v0.x * c0.x) + (v0.y * c0.y) + (v0.z * c0.z) + (v0.w *
   c0.w)
```

Given that we use unit length (normalized) vectors, it is known that the dot product of two vectors will always fall between [-1..1]. Therefore, o0 will always fall within this range.

Alternatively, you can replace the dp4 instructions by a complex instruction like this:

```
   m4x4 o0, v0, c0
```

Although the assembler might expand this instruction to four dp4 instructions in some situations, this might not necessarily be a 1:1 replacement for the four dp4 instructions. Vertex shaders might return different results for an m4x4 instruction and four dp4 instructions, since the graphics hardware/software vertex shader implementation treats them differently (we'll expand on this later).

Temporary Registers

The temporary registers can be used to store intermediate results, because they can load and store data (read/write), in contrast to the input registers, which can only be used to load data. The 32 temporary registers in vs_3_0 are named r0–r31. Each temporary register has single-write and triple-read access. The following example is taken from a Cook-Torrance shader.

```
   . . .
   mul        r2.a, r10.g, r10.g   // N.H^2
   sub        r4.r, c1.a, r2.a     // 1 - N.H^2
   mul        r4.a, c1.r, r2.a     // m^2 * N.H^2
   rcp        r2.r, r4.a           // 1 / m^2 * N.H^2
   // r3.r = 1 - N.H^2 * 1 / m^2 * N.H^2
   mul        r3, r4, r2
                                   // r3.a = m^2 * N.H^2 * N.H^2
   // r3.r = (1 - N.H^2) * (1 / m^2 * N.H^2) * -1.4427
   mul        r3.r, r3.r, c4.r
   rcp        r4.a, r3.a           // 1 / m^2 * N.H^2 * N.H^2
   exp        r5.r, r3.r
   mul        r1.a, r5.r, r4.a     // D
   . . .
```

It is a nice example of how the read/write access to the temporary register can be used to juggle data. Please note that in the fifth row, the mul instruction is used to multiply two independent values with each other in the r4.r, r2.r and the r4.a and r2.a components of the respective registers.

Indexing Registers

There are two indexing registers in vs_3_0: the address register a0 and the loop counter register aL. They use an integer data type as the index value. During the conversion from floating point to integer, a round to nearest happens. The indexing registers can be used to relatively address the c0–c255 floating-point constant registers. The aL register can additionally be used to relatively address the output registers. To address a register absolute, you use for example:

```
mov r0, c0
```

To relatively address a register, you use the indexing registers in brackets.

```
mov r1, c[a0]      // or ...
mov r1, c[a0 + 1]  // or ...
mov o0[aL + 2], c0
```

Any instruction can only access one of these registers at a time. Please note that the a0 register can only be modified with the mova instruction. Both registers offer an integer data type.

Sampler Register

The four sampler registers s0–s3 are input pseudo-registers for a vertex shader, which are used to identify the texture sampling stage. In other words, in vs_3_0, it is possible to fetch textures in the vertex shader. This is called vertex texturing.

The following source snippet is used in the displacement mapping example explained later in this book:

```
vs_3_0
dcl_2d s0 ; declare sampler

; declare input
dcl_position0 v0.xyzw
...
dcl_texcoord0 v7.xy

; declare output
...
texldl r0, v7.xy, s0 ; sample displacement scalar from texture
```

The sampler stages for the first texture stage can be set like this:

```
// displacement map
   m_pd3dDevice->SetSamplerState( D3DVERTEXTEXTURESAMPLER0,
D3DSAMP_MINFILTER, D3DTEXF_LINEAR);
   m_pd3dDevice->SetSamplerState( D3DVERTEXTEXTURESAMPLER0,
D3DSAMP_MAGFILTER, D3DTEXF_LINEAR);
   m_pd3dDevice->SetSamplerState( D3DVERTEXTEXTURESAMPLER0,
D3DSAMP_MIPFILTER, D3DTEXF_LINEAR);
   m_pd3dDevice->SetSamplerState( D3DVERTEXTEXTURESAMPLER0,
D3DSAMP_ADDRESSU,  D3DTADDRESS_WRAP );
   m_pd3dDevice->SetSamplerState( D3DVERTEXTEXTURESAMPLER0,
D3DSAMP_ADDRESSV,  D3DTADDRESS_WRAP );
```

and the vertex texture can be set with the following call:

```
m_pd3dDevice->SetTexture(D3DVERTEXTEXTURESAMPLER0, m_pDispMap);
```

Please note that similar to render targets used together with pixel shader textures, a vertex texture should not be simultaneously set as a render target and a vertex texture at any given stage (a solution to this might be to flip two textures each frame).

Predicate Register

For hardware that supports ps_2_x and higher, a special register that is useful for predication is available. This predication register is essentially a destination write mask. Its content is computed per component (component: one of the four components) and it enables shader instructions to be performed on a per-component basis based on results of previous calculations. The flags in the predicate register are set with the setp_* instruction, which makes a per-channel comparison between the two source registers and saves the Boolean result of this comparison operation in p0. For example, the following code will set the predicate register components to (True, False, False, True):

```
def c0, 0.0f, 2.0f, -4.0f, 1.0f
def c1, -1.0f, 2.0f, -2.0f, 0.0f

mov r0, c0
setp_gt p0, r0, c1
```

The _gt postfix of the setp_* instruction means that when the content of the first component of register r0 is greater than the content of the first component of register c1, a TRUE is stored in the first component of p0.

Once p0 is set, its content can be used to allow or prevent per-component operations from being carried out. For example, based on the predicate register contents as defined in the previous code, only the .x and .w components of the destination register r0 will be affected by the result of the following instruction:

```
(p0)mul r0, r1.x, c1
```

A negative modifer ! and single-component replicate swizzle (covered in the section "Source Register Swizzling" later) can also be used with the predicate register. In the following source line based on the previous predicate content, none of the components of r0 will receive the multiplication results:

```
(!p0.x)mul r0, r1.x, c1
```

In the next example, all the components of r0 will receive the multiplication results:

```
(!p0.y)mul r0, r1.x, c1
```

The register p0 should be used for very short branching sequences instead of dynamic branching instructions like if_comp, because it uses fewer temporary registers compared to the equivalent non-predicated sequence of instructions.

The instruction slot count for instructions that use a predication register differ depending on the type of instruction. In the following group of instructions, the fact that these instructions use p0 does not affect their instruction slot count.

- if pred
- callnz pred
- break pred
- setp

All arithmetic and texture instructions can be optionally predicated by prefixing ([!]p0) . For example:

```
(p0.x) texld r0, t0, s0
(!p0) rsq r2, r4.x
(!p0.z) add r1, r2, r3
```

In all these cases, the instruction slot count is increased by one, in addition to the original slot count.

Output Registers

There are 12 output registers in vs_3_0, named o0–o11. These write-only registers can be used for anything the user wants to interpolate for the pixel shader: texture coordinates, colors, fog, etc.

Similar to the input registers, the output registers need to be declared at the beginning of the vertex shader.

```
; declare input
dcl_position0 v0.xyzw
dcl_normal0 v3.xyz
dcl_texcoord0 v7.xy
dcl_tangent0 v8.xyz

; declare output
dcl_position0 o0.xyzw  ; position
dcl_texcoord0 o1.xy    ; texture coordinate
dcl_texcoord1 o2.xyz   ; eye vector
dcl_texcoord2 o3.xyzw  ; light vector
dcl_texcoord3 o4.xyzw  ; light2 vector
dcl_texcoord4 o5.xyzw  ; light3 vector
dcl_texcoord5 o6.xyzw  ; light4 vector
```

This source snippet shows first the declaration of the input registers and then the declaration of the output register. The output registers can be used for any data, but two registers are dedicated to specific tasks. One register must be used for position data and one is reserved for a scalar pointsize value (e.g. dcl_psize o0.x).

Note that the output registers can be indexed with aL.

A typical example for the use of output registers is shown in the following lines:

```
vs_3_0

; declare input
dcl_position0 v0.xyzw
dcl_normal0 v3.xyzw

; declare output
dcl_position0 o0.xyzw
dcl_texcoord0 o1.xyzw
dcl_texcoord1 o2.xyzw

m4x4 o0, v0, c0     ; position in clip space
m4x4 o1, v3, c4     ; normal in world space
mov o2, c8          ; send light vector to pixel shader
```

Here, the complex instruction m4x4 maps from object space to clip space using a concatenated world, view, and projection matrix. It gets the position data of the vertex via the input register v0, and outputs the result of the four dot-products to the output register o0. The second m4x4 instruction gets the position data of the vertex normal in v3, and outputs the transformed normal in o1. The light vector in c8 is sent directly to the interpolators via o2.

As you can see, all output registers o0–o11 are mapped via the vertex shader output decl_* declarations to the input registers of the pixel shader.

Source Register Swizzling

Before an instruction runs, the data in a source register is copied to an internal temporary register (not accessible by the programmer). Swizzling refers to the ability to copy any source register component to any internal temporary register component (see Figure A.4). Swizzling does not affect the source register data.

Swizzling is very useful in case the source registers need to be rotated. Another use is converting constants such as (0.5, 0.0, 1.0, 0.6) into other forms such as (0.0, 0.0, 1.0, 0.0) or (0.6, 1.0, 0.5, 0.6).

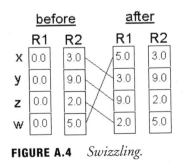

FIGURE A.4 *Swizzling.*

All registers that are used in instructions as source registers can be swizzled. For example:

```
mov R1, R2.wxyz;
```

Figure A.5 shows R1 as the destination register, where R could be a write-enabled register like the output (on) or any of the temporary registers (rn). The source register is R2, where R could be an input (vn), constant (cn, in, bn) or temporary register (source registers are located on the right side of the destination register in the instruction syntax).

The following instruction copies the negation of R2.x into R1.x, the negation of R2.y into R1.y and R1.z, and the negation of R2.z into R1.w. As shown, all source registers can be negated and swizzled at the same time:

```
mov R1, -R2.xyyz
```

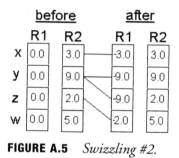

FIGURE A.5 *Swizzling #2.*

A good demonstration of swizzling is shown in the following two instructions. They calculate the cross product of two 3D vectors.

```
; Cross product
mul r0, r1.zxyw, -r2.yzxw;      ; z1 * y2, x1 * z2, y1 * x2, w1 * w2
 mad r6, r1.yzxw, -r2.zxyw,-r0;  ; -(y1 * z2, z1 * x2, x1 * y2, w1 *
w2) -
```

This source also shows how to negate a source register (the r7 register) with the negate modifier.

Write Masking

A destination register can mask which components are written to it. If you use R1 as the destination register (actually any write-enabled registers: on, rn), all the components are written from R2 to R1. If you choose, for example:

```
mov R1.x, R2
```

only the x component is written to R1, whereas

```
mov R1.xw, R2
```

writes only the .x and .w components of R2 to R1. Negation is not supported on the destination registers.

Other Register Modifiers

The _abs source modifier forces the absolute value of a source register to be used in an instruction. It takes precedence over the negate modifier so that a negative value can always be guaranteed. Here is an example:

```
add r0, r7_abs.x, c11
```

If one or more constant float registers (cn) are used in an instruction, one of the following must be true:

- All of the constant floating-point registers must use _abs.
- None of the constant floating-point registers can use _abs.

Vertex Shader Instructions

One might differentiate between three groups of instructions. There are instructions that perform arithmetic operations (arithmetic instructions), flow control instructions, and texture instructions.

The syntax for all these instructions is:

```
OpName dest, s1 [,s2 [,s3]] ;comment
e.g.
mov r1, r2
mad r1, r2, -r3, r4 ; content of r3 is negated
```

Vertex Shader Arithmetic Instructions

In vs_3_0, there are 37 arithmetic instructions. The following text groups these instructions in logical groups and shows them in alphabetical order, together with the number of instruction slots they occupy:

abs dest, src (1 slot)

The abs instruction computes the absolute value (it strips the sign) of src and stores the result in dest.

add dest, src1, src2   (1 slot)

This instruction adds `src1` and `src2`. It can be used to subtract these registers from each other by using the negation modifier. Here is an example:

```
add r1, r2, -r3
```

crs dest, src1, src2   (2 slot)

This instruction computes a cross product from the two vectors in `src1` and `src2` using the righthand rule. This is equivalent to the following pseudo-code:

```
dest.x = src1.y * src2.z - src1.z * src2.y;
dest.y = src1.z * src2.x - src1.x * src2.z;
dest.z = src1.x * src2.y - src1.y * src2.x;
```

dp3 dest, src1, src2 | dp4 dest, src1, src2   (1 slot)

`dp3` and `dp4` perform a dot-product between `src1` and `src2`. This is equivalent to the following pseudo-code:

```
    dest.w = (src1.x * src2.x) + (src1.y * src2.y) + (src1.z * src2.z);
// dp3
    dest.w = (src1.x * src2.x) + (src1.y * src2.y) + (src1.z * src2.z)
+ (src1.w * src2.w); // dp4
    dest.x = dest.y = dest.z = dest.w;
```

dst dest, src1, src2   (1 slot)

The instruction `dst` is useful in calculating standard attenuation. Its functionality is equivalent to the following pseudo-code:

```
dest.x = 1;
dest.y = src1.y * src2.y;
dest.z = src1.z;
dest.w = src2.w;
```

This instruction is useful for implementing attenuation formulas. A typical attenuation formula looks like this:

$$A = \frac{1}{k_c + k_l \times d + k_q \times d^2}$$

In this formula, d is the distance, k_c is the constant attenuation constant, k_l is the linear attenuation constant, and k_q is the quadratic attenuation constant.

```
// c9 (kc, kq, kl, undefined)
// c10 (1.0, d, d, 1.0)
// d = distance
// kc = constant attenuation
// kl = linear attenuation constant
// kq = quadratic attenuation constant
dst r2, c10, c10       // r2 (1, d^2, d, 1.0)
dp3 r3.x, c9, r2       // r3.x (kc + d^2 * kq + d * kl)
rcp r4.x, r3.x         // 1 / r3.x
```

exp dest, src | expp dest, src   (1 slot each)

The exp instruction provides full precision (at least 21-bit precision) exponential $2x$, whereas the expp instruction only provides partial precision (10-bit precision) exponential $2x$, and both instructions occupy one instruction slot. The exponential functions are useful for fog effects, procedural noise generation, behavior of particles in a particle system, and for implementing a damage control system. You will also use them in any case when a fast changing function is necessary. For vertex shader versions vs_2_0 and higher, the following pseudo-code shows the operations performed by exp and expp:

```
dest.x = dest.y = dest.z = dest.w = (float)pow(2,
    src.replicateSwizzleComponent);
```

The following source code snippet simulates the pow instruction with the exp instruction:

```
// Original version
def c0, 2.7182818284f, // e
      3.1415926535f, // pi
      5.0f, // useful constants
      2.5f  // Ii * dw
pow r5.r, c0.r, -r4.r
...
// Optimized version
def c4, -1.4427, 0.9, 0.1, 0.0 // pow -> exp, 0.9, 0.1, unused

mul r3.r, r4.r, c4.x
exp r5.r, r3.r
```

The optimized version occupies two instructions, whereas the pow version occupies three instruction slots. Additionally, single-slot instructions have a higher chance of getting optimized by hardware that can do this.

The optimization comes from the fact, that pow can be replaced by exp(src2 * log(src1)) and the result of the log instruction is stored in a constant.

frc dest, src   (1 slot)

The instruction frc computes the fractional portion of each component of src, and stores the result in dest. The following code fragment shows conceptually how the instruction operates.

```
dest.x = src.x - (float)floor(src.x);
dest.y = src.y - (float)floor(src.y);
dest.z = src.z - (float)floor(src.z);
dest.w = src.w - (float)floor(src.w);
```

lit dest, src   (3 slots)

The `lit` instruction calculates the diffuse and specular lighting component and the specular power value. The source vector is assumed to contain the values shown in the following pseudo-code.

```
src.x = N*L        ; The dot product between normal and direction
to light
src.y = N*H        ; The dot product between normal and half vector
src.z = ignored    ; This value is ignored
src.w = exponent   ; The value must be between -128.0 and 128.0
```

The following code fragment shows the operations performed.

```
dest.x = 1;
dest.y = 0;
dest.z = 0;
dest.w = 1;
float power = src.w;
const float MAXPOWER = 127.9961f;
if (power < -MAXPOWER)
    power = -MAXPOWER;              // Fits into 8.8 fixed point format
else if (power > MAXPOWER)
    power = -MAXPOWER;              // Fits into 8.8 fixed point format
if (src.x > 0)
{
    dest.y = src.x;
    if (src.y > 0)
    {
        // Allowed approximation is EXP(power * LOG(src.y))
        dest.z = (float)(pow(src.y, power));
    }
}
```

Please note, that the dot-product of the light and normal vector is used to do self-shadowing. If N.L is less than 0, the specular term will also be 0. lit only supports a precision of 8-bit.

Here is an example of how the `lit` instruction calculates a per-vertex diffuse and specular reflection:

```
def c10, 5.0f, 0.0f, 0.0f, 1.0f
...
dp3 r0.x, r7, c8 ; N.L
dp3 r0.y, r7, c9 ; N.H
mov r0.w c10.x     ; move power to r0.w
lit r0, r0         ; diffuse in r0.y | specular in r0.z
```

The following code snippet shows another version of a specular lighting calculation:

```
def c10, 5.0f, -1.4427f, 0.0f, 1.0f
...
dp3 r0.x, r7.r, c8   ; N.L
dp3 r0.y, r7.r, c9   ; N.H
setp_gt p0.x, r0.x, c10.z
(p0.x)pow r0.y, r0.y, c10.x ; diffuse in r0.x | specular in r0.y
(!p0.x)mov r0.y, c10.z
```

The second version offers higher precision and a higher power value range. The next version offers this higher precision and higher power value range with fewer instructions compared to the previous version.

```
def c10, 5.0f, -1.4427f, 0.0f, 1.0f
...
dp3 r0.x, r7.r, c8   ; N.L
dp3 r0.y, r7.r, c9   ; N.H
setp_gt p0.x, r0.x, c10.z
(p0.x)mul r0.y, c0.x, r0.x
(p0.x)exp r0.y, r0.y ; diffuse in r0.x | specular in r0.y
(!p0.x)mov r0.y, c10.z
```

Although this version won't necessarily execute faster (depends on underlying hardware) than the `lit` instruction, it offers higher power value range and a higher precision.

Please note that the HLSL compiler in the version available at the time of this writing, does not use `lit`.

log dest, src | logp dest, src (1 slot each)

The `log` instruction calculates the logarithmic function with at least 21-bits of precision, whereas the `logp` instruction calculates this function with 10-bits of precision, and both instructions occupy one instruction slot. In contrast to the `exp/expp` instructions, the `log/logp` instructions are useful if an extremely slow growth is necessary (although they grow pretty fast at the beginning). A `log` instruction can be the inverse of the `exp` instruction, meaning it undoes the operation of the `exp` instruction.

The following pseudo-code shows the operations performed by these instructions:

```
float f = abs(src);
if (f != 0)
    dest.x = dest.y = dest.z = dest.w = (float)(log(f)/log(2));
else
    dest.x = dest.y = dest.z = dest.w = -FLT_MAX;
```

lrp dest, src1, src2, src3 (2 slots)

The `lrp` instruction interpolates linearly between the second and third source register by the proportion specified in the first source register. The following pseudo-code shows the operations performed by this instruction:

```
dest.x = src1.x * (src2.x - src3.x) + src3.x;
dest.y = src1.y * (src2.y - src3.y) + src3.y;
dest.z = src1.z * (src2.z - src3.z) + src3.z;
dest.w = src1.w * (src2.w - src3.w) + src3.w;
```

lrp can be used to blend between two textures based on the *z*-component of the normal of the ground plane [Vlachos]. For example, this is useful for showing a different vegetation at different heights on a mountain.

The vertex and pixel shader source code snippets might look like this:

```
vs_3_0
;——————————————-
; c0 - WorldViewProj matrix
;——————————————-
; declare input
dcl_position0 v0.xyzw
dcl_normal0 v3.xyz
dcl_texcoord0 v7.xy

; declare output
dcl_position0 o0.xyzw ; position
dcl_texcoord0 o1.xy   ; texture coordinate
dcl_texcoord1 o2.xyz  ; n.z^3

m4x4 o0, v0, c0       ; position in clip space

mov o1.xy, v7
mul r0, v3.z, v3.z    ; z^2
mul o2.xyz, r0, v3.z  ; z^3
——————
ps_3_0
def c2, 0.0f, 2.0f, 3.0f, 1.0f ; useful constants

dcl_2d s0 ; color map
dcl_2d s1 ; normal map

dcl_texcoord0 v1.xy ; load light vector
dcl_texcoord1 v2.xyz ; load n.z^3

texld r0, v1.xy, s0 ; fetch color map
texld r1, v1.xy, s1 ; fetch second color map

lrp oC0, v2.xyz, r0, r1
```

For example, blending between two textures can be used to simulate snow falling from a given direction and sticking to the side of a mountain. Over time, the intensity of the blend value could be increased to show the accumulation of snow.

m3x2 | m3x3 | m3x4 | m4x3 | m4x4 dest, src1, src2   (2 | 3 | 4 | 3 | 4 slots)
The matrix multiplication instructions multiply a 3×2, 3×3, 3×4, 4×3 or 4×4 matrix with a 2D, 3D, or 4D vector. These instructions behave similarly to a series of dp3

and `dp4` instructions. For example, the following pseudo-code shows the operations performed by the `m4x4` instruction:

```
dest.x = (src1.x * src2.x) + (src1.y * src2.y) + (src1.z * src2.z)
+ (src1.w * src2.w);
    dest.y = (src1.x * src3.x) + (src1.y * src3.y) + (src1.z * src3.z)
+ (src1.w * src3.w);
    dest.z = (src1.x * src4.x) + (src1.y * src4.y) + (src1.z * src4.z)
+ (src1.w * src4.w);
    dest.w = (src1.x * src5.x) + (src1.y * src5.y) + (src1.z * src5.z)
+ (src1.w * src5.w);
```

Looking only at this pseudo-code, one might think, that `m4x4` outputs exactly the same result as delivered by four `dp4` instructions, but this is not the case. `m4x4` and four `dp4` instructions can deliver slightly different results on the software implementations (vs_1_1, vs_2_sw, and vs_3_sw), because the software implementations optimize `m4x4` instructions. It is good programming practice to stay with a `dp4` or `m4x4` approach throughout a project.

mad dest, src1, src2, src3 (1 slot)

The `mad` instruction is useful for replacing a `mul` and an `add` instruction. It multiplies `src1` and `src2` and then adds `src3`. The instruction behaves similarly to the following pseudo-code:

```
dest = (src1 * src2) + src3;
```

max | min dest, src1, src2 (1 slot each)

The `max` and the `min` instructions compare the channels of the sources separately and move the maximum or minimum into the equivalent destination register channel. The following pseudo-code shows the operations performed by the `max` instruction:

```
dest.x=(src1.x >= src2.x) ? src1.x : src2.x;
dest.y=(src1.y >= src2.y) ? src1.y : src2.y;
dest.z=(src1.z >= src2.z) ? src1.z : src2.z;
dest.w=(src1.w >= src2.w) ? src1.w : src2.w;
```

The following pseudo-code shows the operations performed by the `min` instruction:

```
dest.x=(src1.x < src2.x) ? src1.x : src2.x;
dest.y=(src1.y < src2.y) ? src1.y : src2.y;
dest.z=(src1.z < src2.z) ? src1.z : src2.z;
dest.w=(src1.w < src2.w) ? src1.w : src2.w;
```

The following code snippet mimics the `abs` instruction and returns an absolute value [Wloka]:

```
; r0 = | r1|
max r0, r1, -r1
```

Like pixel shaders, the vs_3_0 model now supports a _sat modifier. In earlier vertex shader versions, max and min can be used to clamp to the range [0..1].

```
; r0 = (r0 < 0) ? 0 : (r0 > 1) ? 1 : 0
def c0, 0.0f, 1.0f, 0.0f, 0.0f
max r0, r0, c0.x
min r0, r0, c0.y
```

mov | mova dest, src   (1 slot)

The mov and the mova instruction copy data from src to dest. The mova instruction is a specialized version of mov that is used to copy data into the address register a0. Question every use of mov, because there might be methods that perform the desired operations directly from the source register or accept the required output register as the destination.

mul dest, src1, src2   (1 slot)

The mul instruction multiplies each channel of src with the corresponding channels of dest. The following pseudo-code shows the operations performed by this instruction:

```
dest.x = src1.x * src2.x;
dest.y = src1.y * src2.y;
dest.z = src1.z * src2.z;
dest.w = src1.w * src2.w;
```

nop   (1 slot)

The nop instruction does nothing.

nrm dest, src   (3 slots)

The nrm instruction normalizes a 3D-vector. A normalized vector is a unit vector. To calculate a unit vector, divide the vector by its magnitude or length. The magnitude of a vector is calculated by using the Pythagorean Theorem, as follows:

$$x^2 + y^2 + z^2 = m^2$$

The length of the vector is retrieved by

$$\|\mathbf{A}\| = sqrt\left(x^2 + y^2 + z^2\right)$$

The magnitude of a vector has a special symbol in mathematics. It is a capital letter designated with two vertical bars: $\|\mathbf{A}\|$. So dividing the vector by its magnitude is accomplished as follows:

$$UnitVector = Vector \: / \: sqrt\left(x^2 + y^2 + z^2\right)$$

Instead of using the complex instruction nrm, which needs three instruction slots to perform, you can use a dp3, rsq, and mul instruction. This makes sense if one of the intermediate results is needed later in the vertex shaders. This technique is illustrated as follows:

```
; normalize it
; (src1.x * src2.x) + (src1.y * src2.y) + (src1.z * src2.z)
dp3 r1.w, r1, r1
; if (v != 0 && v != 1) v = (float)(1.0f / sqrt(v))
rsq r1.w, r1.w
; r1 * r1.w
mul r1, r1, r1.w
```

The instruction dp3 squares the x, y, and z components of the temporary register r1, adds them, and returns the result in r1.w. The instruction rsq divides 1 by the square root of r1.w and stores the result in r1.w. The instruction mul multiplies all components of r1 by r1.w.

The underlying calculation of these three instructions can be represented by the following formula, which is almost identical to the formula presented previously:

$$UnitVector = Vector \times 1 / sqrt\left(x^2 + y^2 + z^2\right)$$

pow dest, src1, src2   (3 slots)

This instruction performs a full precision *abs(src1)src2*. Each source register requires an explicit use of one replicate swizzle. This instruction works as follows:

```
dest.x = dest.y = dest.z = dest.w = abs(src1)src2;
```

rcp dest, src   (1 slot)

This instruction computes the reciprocal from one of the components of src. The following pseudo-code shows the operations performed.

```
float f = src;
if(f == 0.0f)
    f = FLT_MAX;
else
{
    if(f != 1.0)
    {
        f = 1/f;
    }
}
dest = f;
```

If no component is explicitly chosen from the src register, the instruction uses the src.x component. This instruction is useful for doing a division:

```
; scalar r0.x = r1.x/r2.x
rcp r0.x, r2.x
mul r0.x, r1.x, r0.x
```

rsq dest, src   (1 slot)

The `rsq` instruction calculates a reciprocal square root of `src`. Its functionality is equivalent to the following pseudo-code.

```
float f = abs(src);
if (f == 0)
    f = FLT_MAX
else
{
    if (f != 1.0)
        f = 1.0/(float)sqrt(f);
}
dest.z = dest.y = dest.z = dest.w = f;
```

`rsq` can be used to calculate a square root with the following code snippet:

```
; scalar r0.x = sqrt(r1.x)
rsq r0.x, r1.x
mul r0.x, r0.x, r1.x
```

sge | sgn | slt dest, src1, src2   (1 | 3 | 1 slot(s))

`sge` returns 1 if `src1.component` is greater than or equal to `src2.component`, otherwise 0. `sgn` (shortcut for signum function) returns 0, 1, or -1 depending on whether `src1.component` is smaller than 0, equal to 0 or bigger than 0. `slt` returns 1 if `src1.component` is smaller than `src2.component`, otherwise 0.

Here is pseudo-code that mimics the functionality of each:

sge:

```
dest.x = (src1.x >= src2.x) ? 1.0f : 0.0f;
dest.y = (src1.y >= src2.y) ? 1.0f : 0.0f;
dest.z = (src1.z >= src2.z) ? 1.0f : 0.0f;
dest.w = (src1.w >= src2.w) ? 1.0f : 0.0f;
```

sgn (signum function):

```
for each component in src0
{
    if (src1.component <  0)
        dest.component = -1;
    else
        if (src1.component == 0)
            dest.component = 0;
        else
            dest.component = 1;
}
```

```
slt:
```

```
dest.x = (src1.x < src2.x) ? 1.0f : 0.0f;
dest.y = (src1.y < src2.y) ? 1.0f : 0.0f;
dest.z = (src1.z < src2.z) ? 1.0f : 0.0f;
dest.w = (src1.w < src2.w) ? 1.0f : 0.0f;
```

Please note that you can use sge to evaluate if a component of src1 is less than or equal compared to a component of src2 [Wloka].

```
; r0 = (r1 <= r2) ? 1 : 0
sge r0, -r1, -r2
```

slt can be used to evaluate if a component of src1 is greater than a component of src2.

```
; r0 = (r1 > r2) ? 1 : 0
slt r0, -r1, -r2
```

Furthermore, sge can also help to identify if two registers have the same content.

```
; r0 = (r1 == r2) ? 1 : 0
sge r0, -r1, -r2
sge r2, r1, r2
mul r0, r0, r2
```

slt helps to identify if components of src1 and src2 are not equal.

```
; r0 = ( r1 != r2) ? 1 : 0
slt r0, r1, r2
slt rw, -r1, -r2
add r0, r0, r2
```

sincos dest, src (< vs_3_0: ,src2, src3) (8 slots; ps_3_0: 2 slots)
The instruction sincos computes sine and cosine, in radians. Only one component of the src register can be specified.

```
dest.x = cos(src.x|y|z|w)
dest.y = sin(src.x|y|z|w)
```

Providing a fast sincos function to vertex shaders or pixel shaders prior to *s_2_0 can be done by using Taylor-series expansion [Wloka] or a lookup table [Wenzel].

sub dest, src1, src2 (1 slot)
This function subtracts src2 component-wise from src1.

All these instructions are guaranteed to occupy the number of instruction slots that are defined by the DirectX 9 documentation. Nevertheless, some hardware might execute instructions even faster. Please check out the section "Optimizing Assembly Shaders" for a discussion on how to optimize assembly shaders.

Arithmetic Instruction Modifier

The _sat modifier is an instruction modifier that clamps the result to the [0..1] range:

```
mad_sat r0, r1, r2, -v2
```

Texture Instructions

One of the revolutionary features of vs_3_0 is vertex texturing. The possibility of reading textures in the vertex shader makes it possible to store, for example, lookup tables, displacement maps, or geometry images in a texture and to use them in the vertex shader. There is only one texture instruction, texldl, that fetches textures in the vertex shader.

texldl dest, src1, src2

The texldl instruction allows you to fetch a texture in the vertex shader by specifying the mip-map in the fourth component of src1.w, which is to be sampled using up to three channels the texture coordinates. This value can be negative, in which case the LOD selected is the zeroeth one (biggest map) with the magnification filter MAGFIL-TER. Because src1.w is a floating-point value, the fractional value is used to interpolate (if the mip-map filter used during minification (MIPFILTER) is set to LINEAR) between two mip levels.

src2 identifies the source sampler register (s#), where # specifies which texture sampler number to sample. The sampler has an associated texture and a control state defined by the D3DSAMPLERSTATETYPE enumeration (for example, D3DSAMP_MINFILTER).

The following rough algorithm, which is followed by the reference device, has been provided for reference.

```
LOD = src0.w + LODBIAS;
if (LOD <= 0 )
{
   LOD = 0;
   Filter = MagFilter;
   tex = Lookup( MAX(MAXMIPLEVEL, LOD), Filter );
}
else
{
   Filter = MinFilter;
   LOD = MAX( MAXMIPLEVEL, LOD);
   tex = Lookup( Floor(LOD), Filter );
   if( MipFilter == LINEAR )
   {
      tex1 = Lookup( Ceil(LOD), Filter );
      tex = (1 - frac(src0.w))*tex + frac(src0.w)*tex1;
   }
}
```

The instruction `texld1` looks up the texture set at the sampler stage referenced by `src2`. The functionality is identical to that in the pixel shader texture units.

The instruction `texld1` uses two instruction slots for 2D textures and two and three instruction slots for cube maps.

Similar to ps_3_0, there is no texture dependent read limit in the vertex shader (all lower pixel shader versions have a texture dependent read limit). A dependent read is a read from a texture map using a texture coordinate that was calculated earlier in the pixel shader.

Vertex texturing has an impact on performance, because all texture accesses come with high latencies, meaning that the period between fetching a value from a texture and being able to use the result can be quite long. There will be a lot of clock cycles spent moving the data from external memory into the chip (on a cache miss), through the cache, through a texture filtering calculation, and eventually into the vertex shader. For this reason, throughput when using vertex texturing can potentially be quite low, but it also means that if the shader has instructions that do not rely on the result of the texture fetch, the texture fetch can be free since non-dependent instructions can be executed while waiting for the texture data to arrive (read more in [Beets]).

Flow Control Instructions

There are 18 flow control instructions supported in vs_3_0. Their syntax is similar to the flow controls used in C. Using them makes the code more readable and loops offer ways to use a higher number of vertex shader slots than available without using loops.

call I callnz_bool I callnz_pred I label I ret   (2 / 3 / 3 / 0 / 1 slots)

The `call*` instructions call a subroutine named by the specified label. Whereas call calls a subroutine without depending on a condition, the `callnz_bool` or `callnz_pred` instructions call a subroutine if a bool or predicate register is not zero.

Only forward calls are allowed. This means that the label inside the vertex shader should be after the call instruction referencing it. The following example shows two function calls:

```
vs_3_0
...
rep i0
...
   call 10
...
endrep
...
ret // end of main
```

```
label 10
...
   callnz 11, b0
...
ret // end of subroutine 10


label 11
...
ret // end of subroutine 11
```

The label instruction defines a label that starts with the next shader instruction. A label is an integer between 0 and 16. The ret instruction marks the end of a subroutine.

if_bool | if_comp | if_pred | else | endif   (3 / 3 / 3 / 1 / 1 slots)

The branching instructions if* begin an if block. Whereas if_bool begins an if block depending on a Boolean condition, the if_comp and if_pred instructions begin an if block depending on a comparison or a predication.

The if_comp compares its two source registers. It can be one of the following:

- _gt Greater than
- _lt Less than
- _ge Greater than or equal
- _le Less than or equal
- _eq Equal to
- _ne Not equal to

This instruction is used to skip a block of code, based on a condition. It is equivalent to the following pseudo-code:

```
if (src0 comparison src1)
   jump to the corresponding else or endif
   instruction;
```

Here are two examples:

```
if_ne r3.x, c0.x
...
endif

if_gt r4.r, c13.x
...
else
...
endif
```

The if_pred instruction begins an if...endif block with a predicate. The contents of the if block are executed if the expression evaluates to true.

Example:

```
if [!]p0.z
...
endif
```

The `endif` instruction ends an `if` block, and the `else` instruction begins an `else` block in an `if`/`endif` block.

loop / endloop | rep / endrep | break | break_comp | breakp *(3 / 2 | 3 / 2 | 1 / 3 / 3 slots)*
There are two kind of loops in vs_3_0. Loops with the `loop` instruction and loops with the `rep` instruction.

The `loop` instruction begins a `loop...endloop` block whose parameters are specified by a four-component integer. This integer's first three components—n1, n2, and n3—have the following meaning:

- The loop cycles for n1 iterations
- The loop variable starts at n2
- The loop increments by n3

The parameter aL is the loop variable. Following is an example:

```
defi i0, 4, 2, 1, 0 ; loop four times,
                       starting from 2,
                       increment by 1
...
loop aL, i0 ; loop through lights
...
endloop
```

The `rep` instruction begins a `rep...endrep` block. This `endrep` instruction is used to mark the end of a repeat block. A repeat block is allowed to be either completely inside an `if` block or completely surrounding it.

`rep` consumes one vertex shader instruction slot but must be used with `endrep`, which consumes another.

The maximum loop iteration count is 255.

This instruction works as shown here:

```
LoopInterationCount = LoopIterationCount - 1;
if (LoopIterationCount > 0)
    Continue execution at
    the StartLoopOffset
```

Here is an example:

```
rep i0
...
endrep
```

The break, break_comp, and breakp instructions break out from a loop. break breaks out without any further condition. break_comp leaves a loop depending on the result of a comparison of its two source registers src1 and src2.

The modifier _comp can be one of the following:

- _gt Greater than
- _lt Less than
- _ge Greater than or equal
- _le Less than or equal
- _eq Equal to
- _ne Not equal to

This is equivalent to the following pseudo-code:

```
if (src0 comparison src1)
   jump to the corresponding
   endloop or endrep instruction;
```

The breakp instruction evaluates the Boolean expression predicate, breaking the loop only if the expression evaluates to true. Use one of the components of the predicate register as a condition to determine whether to perform the instruction.

Example:

```
break [!]p0.z
```

setp_comp (1 slot)

The setp_comp instruction sets the predicate register. The modifier _comp is a per-channel comparison between the two source registers. It can be one of the following values:

- _gt Greater than
- _lt Less than
- _ge Greater than or equal
- _le Less than or equal
- _eq Equal to
- _ne Not equal to

Example:

```
setp_gt p0, r11.r, c223
(p0.z) mov r14, c129
(p0.y) mov r14, c130
(p0.x) mov r14, c131
```

All flow control instructions can be grouped regarding their ability to execute code based on static or dynamic data.

Static and Dynamic Branching

The most common branching support in current graphics hardware is static branching with the if...endif flow control instruction. Static branching is a capability in a shader model that allows for blocks of code to be switched on or off based on a Boolean shader constant. This is a convenient method for enabling or disabling code paths based on the type of object currently being rendered. Between rendering calls, you can decide which features you want to support with the current shader and then set the Boolean flags required to get that behavior.

With dynamic branching, the comparison condition resides in a register that is writeable in the vertex shader, which means that the comparison is done on a per-vertex level and not on a per-vertex-shader runtime level. This incurs a performance hit, because the branch must be checked on a per-vertex level. So every flow control branch instruction that uses registers that are writeable can do dynamic branching. These are the if_comp and if_pred flow control instructions.

A typical application of dynamic branching is the common N.L calculation used in diffuse lighting. Depending on the result of the dot product, the rest of the lighting equation may or may not be performed, improving performance in the process. Here is an example of how N.L can direct the lighting calculation in a Phong lighting implementation:

```
if_gt r3.x, c2.x ; no calculation if N.L < 0

    ; reflect = normalize(2 * diffuse * normal - lightDir);
    mul r4, r3, r0                  ; diffuse * normal
    mad r5, r4, c2.y, -r1           ; * 2 - lightDir
    nrm r6, r5                      ; normalize(reflect)

    ; specular = pow(saturate(dot(reflect, eye vector)), 3);
    dp3_sat r7, r6, r2              ; saturate(dot(R, V)) == specular
    pow r1, r7.x, c2.z              ; power

    ; ((color * diff + spec) * Attenuation)) + previous result;
    mad r10, r8, r3, r1             ; color * diffuse + specular
    ; * attenuation + previous result
    mad r11, r10, v[aL].w, r11
endif
```

The same principle can be applied to shadows (in or out of shadow), light attenuation (distance from the light exceeds maximum range), etc.

Static and Dynamic Looping

Static loops can be changed on a per-vertex-shader basis, because they are controlled by registers that cannot be altered in the vertex shader. The loop and rep flow control instructions are controlled by integer constant registers, which are read-only.

A dynamic loop can be built with the loop and rep instructions together with break_comp and break_pred control flow instructions.

Static and Dynamic Subroutine Calls

Subroutines can be called on a static basis, by using `call` and `callnz_bool`, whereas the dynamic version can be specified with the `callnz_pred` instructions.

Nesting

The nesting depth defines how many flow control instructions can be called inside of each other. Each type of instruction has one or more nesting limits:

Table A.1   Nesting Depth

Instruction Type	Maximum
Static nesting	24
Dynamic nesting	24
Loop/rep nesting	4
Call nesting	4
Static flow count	no limit

Maximum Number of Instructions

Each vs_3_0 vertex shader is allowed a number of instructions anywhere from 512 up to the number of slots in the `MaxVertexShader30InstructionSlots` member of `D3DCAPS9`, although the number of instructions can be much higher because of looping support.

Guidelines for Writing Vertex Shaders

The most important rules you should remember when writing vertex shaders are the following:

- Do not switch vertex shaders until it is absolutely necessary.
- The vertex shader must write at least one component of a `dcl_position` declared output register.
- There is an instruction limit of at least 512, which can be exceeded because of looping support.
- Every instruction can access no more than one input register.
- Try to set all constant data with as few `SetVertexShaderConstant*()` functions as possible, since these functions incur overhead.
- Pause and think hard before using a `mov` instruction.
- Choose instructions that perform multiple operations over instructions that perform single operations.
- A rule of thumb for load-balancing between the CPU/GPU: many calculations in shaders can be pulled outside and reformulated per-object instead of per-vertex and put into constant registers. If you are doing some calculation that is per-

object rather than per-vertex, do it on the CPU and upload it to the vertex shader as a constant, rather than doing it on the GPU.

- One of the most interesting methods to optimize your vertex throughput, is using compressed vertex data [Calver][Calver2].

Assembly Pixel Shader Programming Fundamentals

Figure A.6 illustrates pixel shader stream processing.

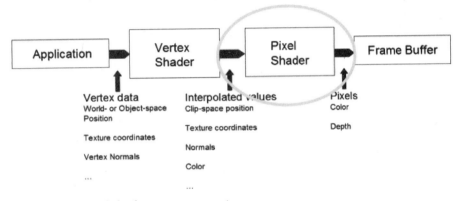

FIGURE A.6   *Pixel shader stream processing.*

The nonprogrammable part of the pipeline between the vertex and the pixel shader is controlled by setting render states. The pixel shader retrieves interpolated position values, texture coordinates, normals, and—if needed—color values. Additionally, it will fetch data from textures.

Modification of this data is done via registers.

There are input, temporary, output, and other registers. We will examine each class of register in sections that follow.

Input Registers

The pixel shader version ps_3_0 has 10 floating point input registers named v0–v9 (compared to eight float and two integer input registers in ps_2_0). Thus, interpolated colors from the vertex shader can be passed as float, increasing their precision in the process. The input registers v0–v9 can contain any kind of data that is sent via the

Direct3D pipeline to the pixel shader. The semantic mapping declares what kind of data is stored in the input registers.

In the following example, five vectors and one pair of texture coordinates are sent from the vertex shader to the pixel shader. The output declaration of the vertex shader looks like this:

```
; declare output
dcl_position0 o0.xyzw    ; position
dcl_texcoord0 o1.xy      ; texture coordinate
dcl_texcoord1 o2.xyz     ; eye vector
dcl_texcoord2 o3.xyzw    ; light vector
dcl_texcoord3 o4.xyzw    ; light2 vector
dcl_texcoord4 o5.xyzw    ; light3 vector
dcl_texcoord5 o6.xyzw    ; light4 vector
```

The input to the pixel shader is mapped to the v0 to v5 registers via declarations:

```
; declare input
dcl_texcoord0 v0.xy      ; texture coordinate
dcl_texcoord1 v1.xyz     ; load eye vector
dcl_texcoord2 v2.xyzw    ; load light vector
dcl_texcoord3 v3.xyzw    ; load light2 vector
dcl_texcoord4 v4.xyzw    ; load light3 vector
dcl_texcoord5 v5.xyzw    ; load light4 vector
```

This is also called semantic mapping and it is the way to map the vertex shader output registers to the pixel shader input registers. This is illustrated in the following figure:

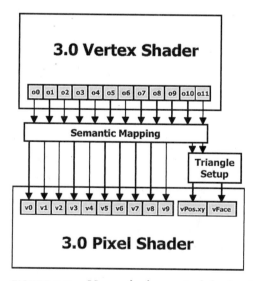

FIGURE A.7 *Vertex shader to pixel shader data flow.*

Additionally, there are constant input registers, which are set in the application and that are sent directly to the pixel shader (not through the Direct3D pipeline). The pixel shader version ps_3_0 supports 224 floating-point constant registers, 16 integer constant registers, and 16 Boolean constant registers. The constant registers, like vertex shader constant registers, are set by using the def, defi, and defb instructions, as shown:

```
def c0, 1.0, 0.0, 0.0, 1.0  ; float constant register c0
defi i0, 1, 0, 0, 1         ; integer constant register i0
defb b0, TRUE               ; bool constant register b0
```

The constant registers can also be set in the application source by using the following functions:

```
// four floats in c8
m_pd3dDevice->SetPixelShaderConstantF(8, -m_LightDir, 1);
// four integers in i8
m_pd3dDevice->SetPixelShaderConstantI(8, iCounter, 1);
// one bool in b8
m_pd3dDevice->SetPixelShaderConstantB(8, bSwitch, 1);
```

All input registers can only be used to load data from within the pixel shader (read-only). Any single instruction can only access one vn register, but this can be used up to three times as a source register in one instruction. The following code snippet illustrates valid and invalid ways of using an input register:

```
add r0.xyz, v0, v1 ; error X5751: 2 different input registers (v#)
read by instruction.
...
add r0.xyz, v0, v0 ; valid
```

Any single instruction can only access one cn, in, or bn register, but this register can be used up to two times as a source register in one instruction, as shown below:

```
mad r0, r0, c2.y, -c2.w ; scale with 2.0 and bias with -1.0
```

Temporary Registers

ps_3_0 supports 32 temporary registers named r0–r31. The temporary registers can be used to store intermediate results, because they can load and store data (read/write), in contrast to the input registers which can only be used to load data. Each temporary register has single-write and triple-read access.

Indexing Register

There is one indexing register in ps_3_0: the loop counter register aL. It can be used to relatively address in the ps_3_0 pixel shader the input registers v0–v9 in ps_3_0 pixel shaders. aL uses an integer data type, which is rounded to nearest when the conversion from floating point to integer happens. To address a register absolutely you use for example:

```
mov o0, v0
```

To relatively address an output register with aL, the following source snippet may be used:

```
mov oC0, v[aL]
```

The aL register can be used up to two times as a source register in one instruction.

Sampler Registers

There are 16 sampler registers s0–s15, which are used to identify the sampling stage. Each sampler uniquely identifies a single texture surface, which is set to the corresponding sampler using SetTexture(). However, the same texture surface can be set at multiple samplers. Up to 16 texture surfaces can be read in a single shader pass. Sampler registers must be declared in advance with dcl_*.

```
ps_3_0
...
dcl_2d s0     ; color map
dcl_2d s1     ; normal map
```

To declare a 2D sampler stage, dcl_2d needs to be used. In case of a cube map or a volume texture, dcl_cube and dcl_volume would be necessary.

Samplers are pseudo-registers, because the pixel shader cannot directly read or write to them. However, you can read and write particular elements in the texture surfaces identified by the registers. This is done with the texld instruction, as shown in the following snippet.

```
...
texld r8, v0.xy, s0        ; fetch color map
texld r0, v0.xy, s1        ; fetch normal map
mad r0, r0, c2.y, -c2.w    ; scale with 2.0 and bias with -1.0
...
```

The pixel shader version ps_3_0 completely removes any and all texture-read limits that exist in previous pixel shader versions (ps_2_0: 32 texture instructions and 4 dependent reads; if the cap bit D3DPS20CAPS_NODEPENDENTREADLIMIT is set, there is no dependent read limit). Shaders can now read from a texture any number of times, with coordinates calculated from any source and with unlimited complexity. These new abilities make iterative/recursive algorithms possible. For example, it is now possible to write a pixel shader that performs ray-tracing operations through a volume texture [Burton] or that uses single pass blur filters or spatial convolution each with unlimited kernel size.

Predicate Register

A predicate register is available in ps_3_0 with the same functionality as the predicate register already covered in vs_3_0.

vFace Register

A face register is now available in ps_3_0, which is used to indicate whether the incoming pixel is part of a front- or back-facing triangle. If the vFace value is less than zero, the primitive is a back face.

Typical uses of this register include two-sided lighting and volume algorithms. The following example sets front faces to red and back faces to green:

```
ps_3_0

; declare face register
dcl vFace

def c0, 0, 0, 0, 1

; set p0.x to TRUE if front-facing
setp_gt p0.x, vFace, c0.x

; if p0.x == TRUE -> red
(p0.x) mov oC0, c0.wxx
; if p0.x == FALSE -> green
(!p0.x) mov oC0, c0.xwx
```

This pixel shader belongs to a small example program in the directory X - Appendix A - s_3_0 Assembly Shaders\ps_3_0 vFace register. This program shows a rotating quad with a green backside and a red frontside.

The vFace register requires declaration, so undeclared use will be flagged with warnings. The face register can only be used with the setp, if_break, and if_comp instructions and it is not set for lines and point primitives.

vPos Register

The new position register vPos holds the current pixel position in screen coordinates. As such only the .x and .y components of vPos are valid. This register might be used in deferred lighting to retrieve the current pixel position in a screen-aligned texture. The following example program renders every second horizontal line with a different color:

```
ps_3_0

def c0, 0.5, 0, 1, 0
dcl vPos.y

mul r0.w, vPos.y, c0.x // multiply with 0.5f
frc r0.w, r0.w        // fraction is 0 or 1
cmp_pp oC0, -r0.w, c0.yzyz, c0.zyyz
```

ON THE CD The instruction `frc` returns a floating-point value for the y component representing the largest integer that is less than or equal to its source register. In this example, the return value of this instruction can only be 0.0f or 1.0f. The comparison with `cmp` returns the red color, if the fraction is greater than 0, otherwise, the green color. The result of the pixel shader shown in the screenshot in Figure A.8 belongs to a small example program in the directory X - Appendix A - s_3_0 Assembly Shaders\ ps_3_0 vPos register.

FIGURE A.8   *vPos example.*

Please note that the vPos register must have one of the following masks: .x, .y, or .xy.

Output Registers

The main output registers for a pixel shader is oC0. If the graphics hardware supports a multiple-render target (MRT) or multi-element textures (MET), there are also additionally the registers oC1–oC3.

Additionally, there is an output register oDepth, which is a write-only scalar register. It returns a new depth value for a depth test against the depth-stencil buffer. Please note that in ps_3_0 shaders, you should avoid varying the set of output registers (oCn, oDepth) across dynamic flow control, static flow control, or predication. This would lead to undefined results, because the shader is always assumed to write out all output registers appearing in the shader.

There is one exception to this rule, which only applies to static flow control. This is the case where the user masks different render targets with the D3DRS_COLOR-WRITEENABLE* render states according to the way the static flow control chooses its path.

Source Register Swizzling/Write Masking

Arbitrary source register swizzling and destination write masking are supported in ps_3_0 in the same way as in vs_3_0. Please consult the section "Assembly Vertex Shader Programming Fundamentals" on page 342 for examples and further explanation.

Compared to previous pixel shader versions, ps_3_0 can also use destination write masks on the texture instructions. For example:

```
texld r0.zw, v0, s0.abrg ; sample the .r and .g channel data into
r0.zw
```

For example, sampling two 32-bit textures of D3DFMT_R16G16F format containing the xy values in s0 and zw values in s1 can be achieved with the following code snippet:

```
texld r0.xy, v0, s0       ; samples data from first R16G16F tex-
ture
texld r0.zw, v0, s1.abrg  ; samples data from second R16G16F tex-
ture
```

 The predicate register p0 can also be used to specify dynamic write masks on a texture sampling instruction.

Pixel Shader Arithmetic Instructions

The vertex shader and pixel shader programming models are becoming more and more similar in syntax and functionality. Therefore, most of the instructions are used in the ps_3_0 model in exactly the same way as in the vs_3_0 vertex shader model. ps_3_0 offers all the arithmetic instructions available in the vs_3_0 model with the exception of dst, expp, lit, logp, mova (ps_3_0 has no address register), sge, sgn, and slt and offers the following additional arithmetic instructions.

cmp dest, src1, src2, src3 (1 slot)

The cmp instruction conditionally chooses between src2 and src3, based on a per-channel comparison src1 >= 0.

```
def c0, -0.6, 0.6, 0, 0.6
def c1  0,0,0,0
def c2  1,1,1,1

mov r1, c1
mov r2, c2
cmp r0, c0, r1, r2
```

```
// r0 is assigned 1,0,0,0 based
// on the following:
// r0.x = c2.x because c0.x <  0
// r0.y = c1.y because c0.y >= 0
// r0.z = c1.z because c0.z >= 0
// r0.w = c1.w because c0.w >= 0
```

dp2add dest, src1, src2, src3   (2 slot)

The dp2add instruction performs a 2D dot-product followed by addition. It is equivalent to the following pseudo-code:

```
// The scalar result is replicated
// to write mask components
dest = src1.r * src2.r + src1.g * src2.g + src3.selected_component
```

The scalar value for the addition is chosen by the replicate swizzle on src3.

```
// t0 == x and y position
// c1.w == 0.5f
dp2add r0, t0, t0, c1.w // x^2 + y^2 + 0.5
```

dsx | dsy dest, src   (2 slots)

The dsx and dsy instructions compute gradients on the current contents of registers in pixels in the render target's *x*- or *y*-direction, storing the result in dest.

The gradient instructions dsx, dsy are used to detect the rate of change of a given register across adjacent pixels in horizontal (dsx) and vertical directions (dsy). This could be useful in a number of cases where information about adjacent texels is required (e.g., on-the-fly computation of normals from height data). The texldd can be used to sample a pixel according to the horizontal and vertical rates of changes retrieved by the instructions dsx and dsy. Gradient instructions are generally used to determine the mip-map levels applied to a sampled texel, so that custom filtering can be applied.

ON THE CD   The following screenshot is taken from the example in the directory X - Appendix A - s_3_0 Assembly Shaders\ps_3_0 gradient instructions and shows a simple edge detection shader.

The following pixel shader shows how the edge detection filter is implemented with the ddx / ddy instruction pair.

```
ps_3_0
def c0, 4.0, 1.0, 1.0, 1.0

dcl_2d s0
dcl_texcoord0 v0.xy

texld r0, v0, s0
```

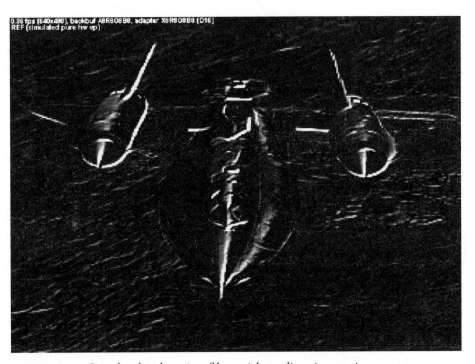

FIGURE A.9 *Simple edge detection filter with gradient instructions.*

```
; find horizontal and vertical rates of changes
; of sampled texel
dsx r1, r0
dsy r2, r0

; add them together
add r0, r1, r2

; multiply by four
mul oC0, r0, c0.x
```

The aim of an edge detection filter is to determine the edge of shapes in a picture and, for example, to enable drawing of a result bitmap where edges are in white on black ground or vice versa (see Figure A.9). This can be done by going through the image pixel by pixel and comparing the color of each pixel to its right neighbor, and to its bottom neighbor. If one of these comparisons results in a big difference, the pixel studied is part of an edge.

In the example program, the dsx instruction sets r1 the rate of change of the color value fetched by the texld instruction compared to its adjacent pixels in the *x*-axis. It quantifies the "difference" between colors. The dsy instruction does the same for the y-axis. The two values are added to be sure that pixels that differ from their neighbors in both directions are more highlighted than pixels that differ only from neighbors that are located in one direction. The result is multiplied by four to amplify the visibility of the edge.

The dsx and dsy instructions cannot be used in flow controls, because the result of a gradient calculation on a computed value (i.e., not an input such as a texture coordinate) inside dynamic flow control is ambiguous when adjacent pixels may go down separate paths.

Texture Instructions

In contrast to all previous pixel shader versions, the texture instructions in ps_2_a and ps_3_0 have no dependent read-limit and no maximum usage limit. There can be as many texture instructions as there are instruction slots. Sampling unsigned RGB textures will result in float values between 0.0 and 1.0. Sampling signed textures will result in float values between −1.0 and 1.0.

texkill src   (2 slots)

The texkill instruction cancels rendering of the current pixel if any of the first three components (UVW) of the texture coordinates is less than zero. This is used to simulate user clip planes on hardware that has no native support.

Please note that you should not use texkill for user clip planes, if clipping can be done on the vertex level. Additionally, texkill can influence the performance by interfering with the automatic occlusion culling mechanism implemented in modern hardware.

texld dest, src1, src2   (2-D Texture: 1 slot; Cube maps: 4 slots)

The texld instruction retrieves the texture coordinates in src1 and the sampler stage in src2.

Example:

```
ps_3_0
dcl_2d          s0
dcl_texcoord0 v0.xy
...
texld r0, v0.xy, s0
...
```

texldb dest, src1, src2   (6 slots)

This instruction loads and biases a texture. It uses the fourth element (.a or .w) of src1 to bias the texture-sampling level of detail (LOD). In ps_3_0, bias values can be in the range [−16.0 .. 15.0]. Values outside this range produce undefined results. Positive bias values will result in smaller mip-maps selected and negative values in bigger mip-maps selected.

After `texldb` is executed, the contents of src1 are unaffected (unless dest is the same register).

texldl dest, src1, src2   (2D-Texture: 2 slots; Cube maps: 5 slots)

See description of `texldl` in vs_3_0.

texldd dest, src1, src2, src3, src4   (3 slots)

This instruction samples a texture with additional gradient inputs. src1 is an input source register containing texture coordinates.

src2 is an input source register that specifies the sampler register. See "Sampler Register." The sampler states supported are D3DSAMP_MAXMIPLEVEL and D3DSAMP_MIPMAPLODBIAS. src3 is an input source register that specifies the *x* gradient retrieved with the instruction dsx. src4 is an input source register that specifies the *y* gradient retrieved with the instruction dsy.

texldp dest, src1, src2   (2-D Texture: 3 slots; Cube map: 4 slots)

This instruction performs texture sampling with projective divide by src1.w. This is useful for projective texturing and shadow mapping.

Instruction Modifiers

The `_centroid` modifier can be appended to texture instructions. It used to adjust the texture sampling location when multisampling is used. This is used to avoid artifacts when a multisampled triangle edge does not cover the center of a pixel but does cover the center of at least one subpixel of the multisampled mask (see the explanation of the `_CENTROID` modifer in Chapter 3 for an example):

```
texld_centroid r0, v0, s0
```

The partial precision hint `_pp` can be used by the application to indicate to the device that the operation can be performed and the result stored at a lower precision (at least s10e5). This is a hint implementations are free to follow or ignore it as they see fit. For example NVIDIA's GeForce FX hardware supports 16-bit rendering with the half data type, whereas ATI's RADEON 9500 and upwards always uses its default precision. This hint will lead to the use of 16-bit precision and, on some graphics cards, therefore to a higher performance (at the cost of precision).

The `_sat` modifier is an instruction modifier that clamps the result to the [0..1] range. The usage is:

```
mad_sat r0, r1, r2, -v2
```

Flow Control

The flow controls in ps_3_0 are identical to the flow controls in vs_3_0. This is a result of unifying the vertex and pixel shader models. The flow control instructions can be grouped according to their ability to execute code based on static or dynamic data. Here is a ps_3_0 shader that shows a Mandelbrot.

```
ps_3_0
defi i0, 255, 0, 1, 0  ; loop variable
def c1, 2,0.00390625,0.5,0 ;2,1/256,0.5,0
def c2, 1,1,-3,-1
def c3, 2,1,2,0
def c4, 0,0,-1,0

; inputs
dcl_texcoord0 v0.xy  ; texcoord 0
mov r0, c1.wwww

; c_x and c_y is the pixel position
; r2 = (c_x/2, c_y/2, unused , colour )
mul r2.xyw, c1.zzw, v0.xyy

; for aL = 0 to 255 step 1
loop aL, i0
   ; x and y are the real and imaginary components of Z
   ; r0 = ( x, y, -y, x*x+y*y )
   ; r1 = ( x*x + c_x/2, x*y + c_y/2, -y*y + c_x/2, unused )
   mad r1.xyz, r0.xxy, r0.xyz, r2.xyx

   ; r0 = ( r1.x*1+r1.z, r1.y*1+r1.y, r1.y*-3+r1.y, r1.z*-1+r1.x )
;      = ( x*x-y*y+c_x, 2*x*y+c_y, -2*x*y-c_y, y*y+x*x )
   ; c2 = ( 1,1,-3,-1 )
   mad r0.xyzw, r1.xyyz, c2.xyzw, r1.zyyx
   break_gt r0.w, c1.x

   ; increment the colour (r2.w)
   add r2.w, r2.w, c1.y
endloop

; create colour
mul r2, r2.wwww, c3
add_sat oC0, r2, c4
```

The Direct3D runtime restricts the usage of texture instructions in flow controls to the texldd and texldl instructions. Only these texture instructions are allowed in a flow control, because the calculation of the derivatives can then happen outside the flow control.

Static and Dynamic Branching, Static and Dynamic Looping, and Static and Dynamic Subroutine Calls

ps_3_0 has the same control flow instructions as vs_3_0. Therefore, the same static and dynamic branching, looping, and calls are possible. Please check out the examples in the vertex shader section for more information.

Maximum Number of Instructions

Each ps_3_0 pixel shader is allowed a number of instruction slots anywhere from 512 up to the number of slots in the `MaxPixelShader30InstructionSlots` member of `D3DCAPS9`. The number of instructions run can be much higher because of the looping support.

Guidelines for Writing Pixel Shaders

The most important rules you should remember when writing pixel shaders are the following:

- The pixel shader must write four components to the output register oC0.
- There is an instruction limit of at least 512, which can be crossed by using loops.
- Every instruction can source no more than one input register.
- Try to set all constant data with as few `SetPixelShaderConstant*()` functions as possible, since these functions incur extra overhead.
- Pause and think about using a `mov` instruction. Choose instructions that perform multiple operations over instructions that perform single operations.
- Most calculations can be made in the vertex or in the pixel shader. A rule of thumb for load-balancing between the vertex and pixel shader is: performing calculations in the vertex shader is more efficient than performing them in the pixel shader. However, if you perform them at the vertex level and send the linearly interpolated results to the pixel shader, the results may not look as good.
- Having writing guidelines for pixel shaders makes sense (e.g., putting the color map always in s0, etc.). In this way, you can write one vertex shader that sends data to several different pixel shaders, thus optimizing performance by reducing vertex shader switching.

Optimizing Assembly Shaders

Optimizing assembly shaders can be a tough task, because the hardware vendors do not publish many details of their hardware architecture, meaning that optimizing for specific hardware is partly guess work. Additionally, different hardware architectures will need specifically optimized assembly implementations, and changing drivers will be a constantly moving target.

Nevertheless, knowledge of how different instructions perform on various types of hardware will help you to strive for the best possible source code. Although the following rules should help you with that, the safest way to get optimized code is by measuring its speed.

At the time of this writing, there are two ps_2_0 graphics cards series on the market with some substantial market share: the NVIDIA GeForce FX and the ATI RADEON 9500+. To read more about this topic, please check out the presentations published by ATI [ATI] and NVIDIA [Dominé].

The following rules are true for both cards.

Fewer Instructions Are Better

This is the most trivial rule, because it is obvious. Nevertheless it seems that older NVIDIA driver versions sometimes performed better with more instructions.

You should pre-bake constants or move the calculation onto the CPU. For example, multiplying the material color with the light color can be done on the GPU or pre-baked. You might also move linear computations out of the pixel shader and into the vertex shader. For example, the attenuation might be computed in the vertex shader, and the moving of vectors into the tangent space usually belongs into the vertex shader.

The reflection vector used to access cube maps does not need to be normalized, because its length does not matter. You might further optimize the reflection function in the following manner:

$$R = 2 \times N \times (N \cdot V / N \cdot N) - V$$

to

$$R = 2 \times N \times N \cdot V - N \cdot N \times V$$

If **N** is already normalized, this leads to:

$$R = 2 \times N \times N \cdot V - V$$

Leave normal/bump map lookups and the light vector unnormalized for diffuse per-pixel bump mapping. The normal/bump maps should have stored unit vectors, and in case of diffuse per-pixel bump mapping, an unnormalized vector looks good enough.

Use texture lookups instead of arithmetic instructions. Texture lookups can be faster than math in many cases. Additionally, you get free clamping and free filtering. On pre-ps_2_0 hardware, the following texture lookups were helpful:

- Normalization cube map (A8R8G8B8)
- $N \cdot L$, $N \cdot H$ in 2D texture (A8L8)
- $N \cdot L$, $N \cdot H$, $N \cdot H$ in 3D texture
- Attenuation values in texture

It is a different story on ps_2_0 hardware. On ps_2_0 hardware, it is safe to say as a rule of thumb that saving more than three instructions by doing a texture lookup might be worth doing.

Use signed textures on ps_2_0 and higher hardware, because ps_2_0 does not know the _bx2 modifier and it takes a mad instruction to bias and scale unsigned textures.

Vectorization of all data is important on all hardware. The simplest example is combining four add instructions into one dp4, as shown in the following pseudo-code.

```
float a, b, c, d;
a + b + c + d                      // four add instructions
a * 1 + b * 1 + c * 1 + d * 1      // one dp4 instruction
```

This way, it is possible to perform four operations by using one instruction slot. The following example shows how to vectorize the distribution function of the Cook-Torrance reflection model, which determines how the light is distributed over the surface of an object (more in Chapter 12). The unoptimized version uses instructions that might use 13 instructions slots.

```
dp3_sat    r7, r11, r8         // N.H
mul        r0, r7.r, r7.r      // N.H^2
mul        r3, c1.x, c1.x      // m^2
mul        r3, r3.r, r0.r      // m^2 * N.H^2
sub        r4, c1.w, r0.r      // 1 - N.H^2
rcp        r2, r3.r            // 1 / m^2 * N.H^2
mul        r4, r4.r, r2.r      // (1 - N.H^2) * (1 / m^2 * N.H^2)
// pow(e, -(1 - N.H^2) * (1 / m^2 * N.H^2))
pow        r5, c0.r, -r4.r
mul        r3, r3.r, r0.r      // (m^2 * N.H^2) * N.H^2
rcp        r4, r3.r            // 1 / (m^2 * N.H^2) * N.H^2
mul        r0, r5.r, r4.r      // D
```

The optimized distribution function uses instructions that might use 10 instruction slots or less, depending on the underlying hardware.

```
dp3_sat    r10.g, r8, r11      // N.H
mul        r2.a, r10.g, r10.g  // N.H^2
sub        r4.r, c1.w, r2.a    // 1 - N.H^2
mul        r4.a, c1.x, r2.a    // m^2 * N.H^2
rcp        r2.r, r4.a          // 1 / m^2 * N.H^2
mul        r3, r4, r2          // r3.r = 1 - N.H^2 * 1 / m^2 * N.H^2
                               // r3.a = m^2 * N.H^2 * N.H^2
// r3.r = (1 - N.H^2) * (1 / m^2 * N.H^2) * -1.4427
mul        r3.r, r3.r, c4.x
rcp        r4.a, r3.a          // 1 / m^2 * N.H^2 * N.H^2
exp        r5.r, r3.r
mul        r1.a, r5.r, r4.a    // D
```

Please note how the optimized version uses the same two channels of two registers to store values like this.

```
r2.r - 1 / m^2 * N.H^2
r2.a - N.H2
r4.r - 1 - N.H^2
r4.a - m^2 * N.H^2
```

This way, only one `mul` instruction is necessary to multiply the value in r2.r with the value in r4.r and the value in r2.a with the value in r4.a, which saves one instruction. By using all four channels, you might save up to three instructions by vectorizing data this way.

ATI RADEON 9500+

It helps to think of the RADEON 9500+ graphic cards as a ps_1_4 card on steroids. Output vertex position as early as possible. This allows the optimizer to do his job better. Reuse texture coordinates with ps_1_4 and ps_2_0 and output from the vertex shader only necessary information.

The vertex shader on ATI RADEON 9500+ can execute an instruction that results in a 4D vector and an instruction that results in a 1D vector in one cycle. This is called vertex shader co-issuing. The rules of thumb are:

- The results should not be dependent on each other.
- Use the write mask .w with pow, exp, log, rcp, and rsq.

As with the ps_1_4 capabilites of the RADEON 8500–9200 graphics cards, the pixel shader in the RADEON 9500+ can execute an instruction that results in a 3D vector and an instruction that results in a 1D vector in one cycle. Although the + sign used in ps_1_4 is not supported in ps_2_0, it is still capable of pixel shader co-issuing. This is done by using the .rgb and .a write masks. The same rules of thumb apply here as for vertex shader co-issuing.

Dependent texture reads on RADEON 9500+ are not free. The first and second levels are executed at top performance, but the third and fourth levels are executed slower, but performance is still reasonable for practical use. Here is an example of making unnecessary dependent texture reads.

```
ps_2_0
dcl_2d s0
dcl t0.xy

add r0.xy, t0, c0

texld r0, r0, s0
mul r1, r0, c8
add r0.xy, t0, c1

texld r0,r0, s0
mad r1, r0, c0, r1
add r0.xy, t0, c2

texld r0, r0, s0
mad r1, r0, c10, r1
mov oC0, r1
```

The optimized version looks like this:

```
ps_2_0
dcl_2d s0
dcl t0.xy

add r0.xy, t0, c0
add r1.xy, t0, c1
add r2.xy, t0, c2
```

```
texld r0, r0, s0
mul r3, r0, c8
texld r1, r1, s0
mad r3, r1, c9, r3
texld r2, r2, s0
mad r3, r2, c10, r3
mov oC0, r3
```

Avoid using texkill whenever possible on RADEON 9500+. Use clip planes for clipping of geometry on the vertex level instead. texkill affects the automatic occlusion culling mechanism and therefore the performance of the whole graphics pipeline. Additionally, it creates an additional level of dependency.

Limit cases where the depth value is output via the oDepth register in ps_2_0 and the texdepth instruction in ps_1_4. It affects the automatic occlusion culling mechanism and it interferes with top of the pipe z-rejects.

The RADEON 9500+ can simultaneously read textures and perform ALU operations. As long as texture bandwidth is not a bottleneck, try to keep numbers of texture instructions close to the number of arithmetic instructions.

Use ps_1_4 shaders where possible, because ps_2_0 does not expose all the instruction modifiers and operand modifiers available on RADEON 9500+.

Using half as a data type or using the _pp modifier for half precision has no effect on RADEON 9500+, because all pixel calculations happen in 24-bit float format. half and _pp are just ignored here.

NVIDIA GeForce FX

It helps to think of the GeForce FX as of a ps_1_1–ps_1_3 card on steroids.

Using a normalization cube map (creating normalization cube maps was shown in Chapter 16) on GeForce FX hardware is faster in some cases than using a nrm or any other trick that involves arithmetic instructions [Harris]. A cube map fetch of a 16-bit signed cube map takes only one instruction slot here. The DirectX 9 SDK documentation states that in the worst case it takes three instruction slots.

If you use one dot product of two normalized vectors in the pixel shader, you might optimize the instruction sequence on NVIDIA hardware in the following way:

```
N / |N| dot (L / |L|)
// two dp3, rsq, mul sequences + dp3: 7 instructions
```

changes this to:

```
N.L / (|N| * |L|)
```

which leads to:

```
N.L * rsq(N.N * L.L)
// three dp3, rsq + two mul: 6 instructions
```

This optimization technique gains an advantage only if the vectors that are normalized are not reused in different dot products. Additionally, only an rsq instruction is saved in this case, which needs two cycles on NVIDIA hardware.

The unoptimized version in ps_2_x might look like this:

```
ps_2_x
def c0, 1, 0, 0.1, 0

dcl t0.xyz              ; load normal vector
dcl t1.xyz              ; load light vector
nrm r0, t0.xyz          ; normalize normal vector
nrm r1, t1.xyz          ; normalize light vector
dp3_sat r0.w, r0, r1
; diffuse intensity(1.0f, 0.0, 0.0, 1.0f)
mad r2, r0.w, c0.xyyx, c0.zyyx
                        ; ambient(0.1f, 0.0, 0.0, 1.0f)
mov oC0, r2
```

The optimized version saves one instruction slot, assuming that rsq takes two instructions.

```
ps_2_x
def c0, 1, 0, 0.1, 0
dcl t0.xyz                      ; load normal vector
dcl t1.xyz                      ; load light vector
dp3 r0.r, t0.xyz, t0.xyz        ; N.N
dp3 r1.a, t1.xyz, t1.xyz        ; L.L
mov r6, t0.xyz
dp3 r2.r, r6, t1.xyz            ; dot(N.N, L.L)
mul r3.a, r0.x, r1.a            ; N.N * L.L
rsq r4.r, r3.a                  ; rsq(N.N * L.L)
; saturate(dot(N.N, L.L) * rsq(N.N * L.L))
mul_sat r5.a, r2.r, r4.r
; diffuse intensity(1.0f, 0.0, 0.0, 1.0f)
mad r6, r5.a, c0.xyyx, c0.zyyx
                         ;ambient(0.1f, 0.0, 0.0, 1.0f)
mov oC0, r6
```

Another optimization strategy matters in case of not-power-of-two textures (NP2) on NVIDIA hardware. Here a separate texture coordinate pair for each NP2 texture should be used. Otherwise, the NVIDIA driver must insert a scale into pixel shader, even if all NP2 textures that use one texture coordinate are of the same size.

One reason different hardware might perform differently is that the instruction set implemented in hardware is not identical to the instructions exposed by DirectX 9. For example, the NVIDIA GeForce CineFX architecture exposes a lit instruction by the driver [NVIDIA], but it is not clear if this instruction maps directly to the lit instruction exposed by DirectX. If it does, there is a good chance that the lit instruction is executed on a GeForce FX in one cycle, whereas the DirectX documentation states that it takes three instruction slots. The lrp instruction is more expensive than other blending operations on GeForce FX. Look for opportunities to simplify or remove it.

Using the half data type and the _pp instruction modifier leads to higher performance on GeForce FX. But when using these features, the internal precision will be reduced to 16-bit precision, which might lead on the other side to visual artifacts.

NVIDIA GeForce 6800 (NV4x)

Compared to the GeForce FX, the half data type is still faster on NV4x, although the delta from fp32 is much less. This data type is useful for texture fetches and especially for normalizing on this graphics card. All NV4x parts have a free half-precision nrm. It actually uses ~20 bits for the input values (i.e., you can use fp32 inputs to it), and as long as you declare the result to be half3, it is almost always scheduled for free. The only time it's a problem is where lighting is performed in a space with a large range, such as world space.

The new vertex texture fetches are slow. They are useful for displacement geometry but not for storing large number of vertex constants. All NV4x cards cannot hide texture latency with instructions (either vertex or pixel).

The new branching functionality seems to break even about 12–16 cycles. So if the branch is capable of skipping 12–16 cycles, it saves cycles. The key to branches is that it will be a win as long as you can skip a good chunk of instructions in a screen-space coherent way. For instance, a pixel sized checkerboard pattern of red squares going over the branch and black squares going in the branch would be a horrible branching case. The left half of the screen going into the branch and the right half skipping it would be the best case.

The NV4x supports all kind of texture instructions in branches, whereas the Direct3D runtime restricts the usage of texture instructions on texldl and texldd.

All these optimization rules also apply to the assembly code created by the HLSL compiler.

Example Programs

This appendix is accompanied by numerous example programs in the directory X - Appendix A - s_3_0 Assembly Shaders.

ON THE CD The examples in ps_3_0 vPos register, ps_3_0 vFace register, and ps_3_0 gradient instructions cover the usage of the vPos, vFace, and ddx/ddy registers.

The examples in Assembly Versions of Chapter 4 - 9 and Assembly Versions of Chapters 26 + 27 are assembly implementations of the HLSL examples covered in these chapters.

Conclusion

This appendix covered shader assembly programming. Although the recent HLSL compiler creates well-optimized code, it is still a good practice to learn shader assembly programming to be able to see how the compiler creates assembly code for the different target profiles. By reading the assembly code generated by the HLSL compiler, the HLSL code can be optimized or debugged.

The CD-ROM contains the example programs with source accompanying the applicable chapters. The directory structure closely follows the book structure by using the chapter number as the name of the subdirectories.

- Each chapter subdirectory contains the source code for the example programs that accompany each chapter.
- The directory Framework Files contains the framework files from the latest DirectX SDK.
- The directory Media contains all the art assets for the example programs.
- As a bonus, the directory X-Appendix A contains some vs_3_0 and ps_3_0 assembly versions of the HLSL examples covered in previous chapters.
- The directory DirectX SDK contains the—at the time of this writing—latest available DirectX SDK.
- All of the figures from the book are also provided in a zip file and set up by chapter.

System Requirements

To compile and execute this code you need the following equipment:

- Latest DirectX 9 System Development Kit (SDK) (*http://msdn.microsoft.com/directx*)
- Windows XP Professional with the newest service pack (Windows XP Home does not support debug runtimes)
- Visual C++.NET 2003 (the DirectX shader debugger requires at least Visual C++.NET 2002)
- At least 512 MB RAM
- At least 500 MB of free space on your hard drive

- A Pentium IV/ATHLON with more than 1.5 GHZ
- A graphics card that supports pixel shader versions 2 or 3

All examples were tested on a NVIDIA GeForce FX, NVIDIA 6800 and several ATI RADEON with a 9500+ chipset. At the time of testing, the GeForce FX cards did not support floating-point textures. So all examples that require floating-point texture support did not run in hardware. This support should be available with future drivers.

Updates

Updates of the example programs will be available on *www.wolfgang-engel.info* and on *www.charlesriver.com*.

Visual C++.NET Settings

Please include the directory <Framework Files> in your include path of the Visual C++.NET IDE.

COMMENTS/SUGGESTIONS

Please send any comments or suggestions to *wolf@shaderx.com*.

Have fun!

—Wolfgang Engel

Bibliography

[Ashikhmin] Ashikhmin, Michael, Peter Shirley, "An Anisotropic Phong BRDF Model." *Journal of Graphics Tools*: JGT, Vol. 5, No. 2, 2000: pp. 25–32.

[ATI] ATI, "Dark Secrets of Shader Development." *www.ati.com/developer*.

[ATISHADOWMAP] ATI, "Shadow Map." *http://mirror.ati.com/developer/samples/shadowmap.html*.

[Beaudoin/Guardado01] Philippe Beaudoin, Juan Guardado, "A Non-Integer Power Function on the Pixel Shader." *http://www.gamasutra.com/features/20020801/beaudoin_01.htm*.

[Beckmann] Petr Beckmann, Andre Spizzichino, *Scattering of Electromagnetic Waves from Rough Surfaces.* Artech House, 1987.

[Beets] Kristof Beets, "Cloth Animation with Pixel and Vertex Shader 3.0." *ShaderX² - Shader Programming Tips and Tricks with DirectX 9,* Wordware Inc., pp. 40–58.

[Blinn] James F. Blinn, "Models of Light Reflection for Computer Synthesized Pictures." SIGGRAPH 77, pp. 192–198.

[Blinn2] James F. Blinn, "Simulation of Wrinkled Surfaces." SIGGRAPH 78, pp. 286–292.

[Bloom] Charles Bloom, Phil Teschner, "Advanced Techniques in Shadow Mapping." *http://www.cbloom.com/3d/techdocs/shadowmap_advanced.txt*.

[Boyd] Chas. Boyd, "Distributed Area Lighting." MSDN Web site: *http://www.microsoft.com/corpevents/gdc2002/slides2002/DistributedAreaLighting.ppt*.

[Brabec] Stefan Brabec, Thomas Annen, Hans-Peter Seidel, "Practical Shadow Mapping." *Journal of Graphics Tools,* 7(4):9–18, 2002.

[Brennan] Chris Brennan, "Shadow Volume Extrusion Using a Vertex Shader." *Direct3D ShaderX - Vertex and Pixel Shader Programming Tips and Tricks,* Wordware Inc., pp. 188–192, 2002.

[Brennan2] Chris Brennan, "Accurate Reflections and Refractions by Adjusting for Object Distance." *Direct3D ShaderX - Vertex and Pixel Shader Programming Tips and Tricks,* Wordware Inc., pp. 290–294, 2002.

[Burton] Aaron Burton, "Rendering Voxel Objects with ps_3_0." *ShaderX² - Shader Programming Tips and Tricks with DirectX 9,* Wordware Inc., pp. 161–172.

[Calver] Dean Calver, "Vertex Decompression in a Shader." *Direct3D ShaderX - Vertex and Pixel Shader Programming Tips and Tricks,* Wordware Inc., pp. 172–187, 2002.

[Calver2] Dean Calver, "Using Vertex Shaders for Geometry Compression." *ShaderX² - Shader Programming Tips and Tricks with DirectX 9,* Wordware Inc., pp. 3–13.

[Card/Mitchell] Drew Card, Jason L. Mitchell, "Non-Photorealistic Rendering with Pixel and Vertex Shaders." *Direct3D ShaderX - Vertex and Pixel Shader Programming Tips and Tricks,* Wordware Inc., pp. 319–333, 2002.

[Carmack] John Carmack in an E-mail Exchange with Mark Kilgard, *http://developer.nvidia.com/attach/5628.*

[Caruzzi] Francesco Carucci, "Simulating Blending Operations on Floating Point Render Targets." *ShaderX² - Shader Programming Tips and Tricks with DirectX 9,* Wordware Inc., pp. 172–177.

[Chan] Eric Chan, Frédo Durand, "Rendering Fake Soft Shadows with Smoothies." *http://graphics.csail.mit.edu/~ericchan/papers/smoothie/.*

[Cook] Robert L. Cook, Kenneth E. Torrance, "A Reflectance Model for Computer Graphics." *Computer Graphics* (SIGGRAPH '81 Proceedings), Vol.15, No.3, July 1981, pp. 301–316.

[Cook2] Robert L. Cook, "Shade Trees." *Computer Graphics* (SIGGRAPH '84), Vol. 18, No. 3, July 1984, pp. 223–231.

[Crow] Frank Crow, "Shadow Algorithms for Computer Graphics." *Computer Graphics,* Vol. 11:3, SIGGRAPH '77, July 1977.

[Dempski] Kelly Dempski, *Real-Time Rendering Tricks and Techniques in DirectX.* Premier Press, Inc., pp. 578–585, 2002.

[Dempski2] Kelly Dempski, *Real-Time Rendering Tricks and Techniques in DirectX,* Premier Press, Inc., pp. 485–486, 2002.

[Dietrich] Sim Dietrich, "Guard Band Clipping in Direct3D." NVIDIA Web site (*http://developer.nvidia.com*).

[Dietrich2] Sim Dietrich, "Attenuation Maps." *Game Programming Gems.* Charles River Media Inc., pp. 543–548, 2000.

[Dominé] Sébastien Dominé, "Canonical Shaders for Optimal Performance." NVIDIA developer Web site (*http://developer.nvidia.com*).

[Elias] Hugo Elias, "Exposure." *http://freespace.virgin.net/hugo.elias/graphics/x_posure.htm.*

[Everitt] Cass Everitt and Mark J. Kilgard, "Practical and Robust Stenciled Shadow Volumes for Hardware-Acclerated Rendering," (*http://developer.nvidia.com/object/robust_shadow_volumes.html*).

[Fernando/Kilgard] Randima Fernando, Mark J. Kilgar, *The Cg Tutorial.* Addison Wesley, pp. 188–195, 2003.

[Foley] James D. Foley, Andries van Dam, Steven K. Feiner, John F. Hughes, *Computer Graphics - Principles and Practice, Second Edition in C.* pp. 729–731, Addison Wesley.

[Foley2] James D. Foley, Andries van Dam, Steven K. Feiner, John F. Hughes, *Computer Graphics - Principles and Practice, Second Edition in C.* p. 730, Addison Wesley.

[Foley3] James D. Foley, Andries van Dam, Steven K. Feiner, John F. Hughes, *Computer Graphics - Principles and Practice, Second Edition in C.* p. 760, Addison Wesley.

[Forsyth] Tom Forsyth, "Displacement Mapping." *ShaderX² - Shader Programming Tips and Tricks with DirectX 9.* Wordware Inc., pp. 73–85.

[Forsyth2] Tom Forsyth, "Shader Abstraction." *ShaderX² - Shader Programming Tips and Tricks with DirectX 9.* Wordware Inc., pp. 597–613.

[Fosner] Ron Fosner, *Real-Time Shader Programming.* Morgan Kauffmann, pp. 54–58, 2003.

[Frazier] Ronald Frazier, "Advanced Real-Time Per-Pixel Lighting in OpenGL." *http://www.ronfrazier.net/apparition/index.asp?appmain=research/advanced_per_pixel_lighting.html.*

[Frick] Ingo Frick, "Visualization with the Krass Game Engine." *Direct3D ShaderX - Vertex and Pixel Shader Programming Tips and Tricks.* Wordware Inc., pp. 453–461, 2002.

[Ginsburg] Dan Ginsburg/Dave Gosselin, "Dynamic Per-Pixel Lighting Techniques." *Game Programming Gems 2.* Charles River Media Inc., pp. 452–462, 2001.

[Green] Ned Green, "Environment Mapping and Other Applications of World Projections." *IEEE Computer Graphics and Applications*, Vol. 6, No.11, pp. 21–29, November 1986.

[Gu] Xianfeng Gu, Steven J. Gortler, Hugues Hoppe, "Geometry Images." SIGGRAPH 2002, pp. 355–361.

[Halpin] Matthew Halpin, "Specular Bump Mapping." *ShaderX² - Shader Programming Tips and Tricks with DirectX 9.* Wordware Inc., pp. 149–160.

[Hargreaves] Shawn Hargreaves, "Hemisphere Lighting with Radiosity Maps." *ShaderX² - Shader Programming Tips and Tricks with DirectX 9.* Wordware Inc., pp. 107–122.

[Harris] Mark Harris, "Normalization Heuristics." *http://developer.nvidia.com/object/normalization_heuristics.html.*

[Heidmann] Tim Heidmann. "Real shadows, real time." Iris Universe, 18:28–31, 1991. Silicon Graphics, Inc. (*http://developer.nvidia.com/attach/6833*).

[Heidrich] Wolfgang Heidrich, Hans-Peter Seidel, "Realistic, Hardware-accelerated Shading and Lighting." SIGGRAPH 99, pp. 171–178.

[Hoeller] Oliver Hoeller, "Shaders under Control (Codecreatures Engine)." *ShaderX² - Shader Programming Tips and Tricks with DirectX 9.* Wordware Inc., pp. 625–630.

[Hurley] Ken Hurley, "Photo Realistic Faces with Vertex and Pixel Shaders." *Direct3D ShaderX - Vertex and Pixel Shader Programming Tips and Tricks.* Wordware Inc., pp. 296–317, 2002.

[Kaneko] Tomomichi Kaneko, Toshiyuki Takahei, Masahiko Inami, Naoki Kawakami, Yasuyuki Yanagida, Taro Maeda and Susumu Tachi, "Detailed Shape Representation with Parallax Mapping." ICAT, 2001, pp. 205–209.

[Kawase] Masaki Kawase, "Frame Buffer Postprocessing Effects in DOUBLE-S.T.E.A.L (Wreckless)." *http://www.daionet.gr.jp/~masa/.*

[Kawase2] Masumi Nagaya, Masaki Kawase, Interview on WRECKLESS: The Yakuza Missions (Japanese Version Title: "DOUBLE-S.T.E.A.L"), *http://spin.s2c.ne.jp/dsteal/wreckless.html.*

[Kozlow] Simon Kozlow, "Perspective Shadow Maps: Care and Feeding." *GPU Gems*, Addison Wesley, pp. 217–244.

[Kwoon] Hun Yen Kwoon, "The Theory of Stencil Shadow Volumes." *ShaderX² - Introduction and Tutorials with DirectX 9*. Wordware Inc., pp. 197–278.

[Lambert] J. H. Lambert, "Photometria sive de mensure de gratibus luminis colorum umbrae." Eberhard Klett, 1760.

[Latta] Lutz Latta, Andreas Kolb, "Homomorphic Factorization of BRDF-based Lighting Computation." SIGGRAPH 2002, pp. 509–516.

[Latta2] Lutz Latta, "Building a Million Particle System." GDC 2004, *http://www. 2ld.de/gdc2004/*.

[Le Grand] Scott Le Grand, "Some Overlooked Tricks for Vertex Shaders." *Direct3D ShaderX - Vertex and Pixel Shader Programming Tips and Tricks*. Wordware Inc., pp. 228–231, 2002.

[Lengyel] Eric Lengyel, *Mathematics for 3D Game Programming & Computer Graphics - Second Edition*. Charles River Media, pp. 194–210, 2003.

[Lengyel2] Eric Lengyel, *Mathematics for 3D Game Programming & Computer Graphics - Second Edition*. Charles River Media, pp. 184–189, 2003.

[Lengyel3] Eric Lengyel, "The Mechanics of Robust Stencil Shadows." *http://www.gamasutra.com/features/20021011/lengyel_01.htm*.

[Lengyel4] Eric Lengyel, "Tweaking a Vertex's Projected Depth Value." *Game Programming Gems*. Charles River Media, Inc., 2000, pp. 361–365.

[Losasso] F. Losasso, H. Hoppe, S. Schaefer, J. Warren, "Smooth Geometry Images." *Eurographics Symposium on Geometry Processing* (2003), pp. 138–145.

[Maughan] Chris Maughan, Daniel Horowitz, "FX Composer 1.5 – Standardization." *ShaderX³: Advanced Rendering With DirectX And OpenGL*, Charles River Media 2004.

[McCool] Michael D. McCool, Jason Ang, Anis Ahmad , "Homomorphic Factorization of BRDFs for High-performance Rendering." SIGGRAPH 2001, pp. 171–178.

[McTaggart] Gary McTaggart, "Half-Live 2/Valve Source Shading." GDC 2004, *http://www.ati.com/developer/gdc/D3DTutorial10_Half-Life2_Shading.pdf*.

[Mitchell] Jason L. Mitchell, "Poisson Shadow Blur." *ShaderX³: Advanced Rendering With DirectX And OpenGL*. Charles River Media 2004.

[NVIDIA] NVIDIA, "NVIDIA CineFX Shaders - Cinematic Programmability for Amazing Visual Effects." Technical Brief, *http://developer.nvidia.com*.

[NVIDIASHADOWMAP] NVIDIA, "Hardware Shadow Mapping." *http://developer.nvidia.com/object/hwshadowmap_paper.html*.

[Olano] Marc Olano, Trey Greer, "Triangle Scan Conversion using 2D Homogeneous Coordinates." *http://www.cs.unc.edu/~olano/papers/2dh-tri/*.

[Oren] Michael Oren, Shree K. Nayar, "Generalization of Lambert's Reflectance Model." SIGGRAPH 1994, pp. 239–246.

[ParallaxThread] *http://www.opengl.org/discussion_boards/ubb/Forum3/HTML/011292. html*.

[Peeper/Mitchell] Craig Peeper, Jason L. Mitchell, "Introduction to the DirectX High Level Shading Language." *ShaderX² - Introduction and Tutorials with DirectX 9*, Wordware Inc., pp. 1–62.

[Persson] Emil Persson, "Fragment level Phong Illumination." *ShaderX² - Shader Programming Tips and Tricks with DirectX 9*, Wordware Inc., pp. 131–149.

[Pharr] Matt Pharr, "Fast Filter-Width Estimates with Texture Maps." *GPU Gems*, Addison Wesley, pp. 417–424.

[Phong] Bui Tuong Phong, "Illumination for Computer Generated Pictures." *Communications of the ACM Archive*, Vol. 18, Issue 6 (June 1975), pp. 311–317.

[Reeves] William Reeves, David Salesin, and Robert Cook (Pixar), "Rendering Antialiased Shadows with Depth Maps." SIGGRAPH 87, pp. 283–291.

[Rege] Ashu Rege, "Optimization for DirectX9 Optimization for DirectX9 Graphics." *http://download.nvidia.com/developer/presentations/GDC_2004/Dx9Optimization_AshuRege.pdf.*

[Reinhard] Erik Reinhard, Michael Stark, Peter Shirley, James Ferwerda, "Photographic Tone Reproduction for Digital Images." *http://www.cs.utah.edu/~reinhard/cdrom/.*

[Rost] Randi J. Rost, *OpenGL Shading Language*. Addison Wesley, pp. 341–345, 2004.

[RTR] Tomas Möller, Eric Haines, *Real-Time Rendering (Second Edition)*. A K Peters, Ltd., p. 73, 2002.

[RTR2] Tomas Möller, Eric Haines, *Real-Time Rendering (Second Edition)*. A K Peters, Ltd., pp. 35–36, 2002.

[Savchenko] Sergei Savchenko, "3D Graphics Programming Games and Beyond." SAMS, Seite 266, 2000.

[Schlick] Christophe Schlick, "An Inexpensive BRDF Model for Physically-based Rendering." Proceedings Eurographics 1994, Computer Graphics Forum, v13, n3, pp. 233–246, 1994.

[Sekulic] Dean Sekulic, "Efficient Occlusion Culling." *GPU Gems*, Addison-Wesley, pp. 487–503.

[Segal] Mark Segal, et. al. (SGI), "Fast Shadows and Lighting Effects Using Texture Mapping." SIGGRAPH 92, pp. 249–252.

[Smith] Bruce G., Smith, "Geometrical Shadowing of a Random Rough Surface." IEEE Transactions on Antennas and Propagation, AP-15(5), September 1967, pp. 668–671.

[Sousa] Tiago Sousa, "Adaptive Glare." *ShaderX³: Advanced Rendering With DirectX And OpenGL*, Charles River Media 2004.

[Stamminger] Mark Stamminger, George Drettakis, Carsten Dachsbacher, "Perspective Shadow Maps." *Game Programming Gems 4*, Charles River Media 2004, pp. 399–410.

[Steigleder] Mauro Steigleder, Michael McCool, "Factorization of the Ashikhmin BRDF for Real-Time Rendering." *Journal of Graphics Tools: JGT*, Vol. 7, No. 4, pp. 61–68, 2002.

[TheRegister] The Register, "ATI Q4 Market Share Beats Nvidia – Just." *http://www.theregister.co.uk/2004/01/30/ati_q4_market_share_beats/*.

[Thibieroz] Nicolas Thibieroz, Kristof Beets and Aaron Burton, "Introduction to the vs_3_0 and ps_3_0 Shader Models." *ShaderX² - Introduction and Tutorials with DirectX 9*, Wordware Inc., pp. 63–82.

[Torrance] K.E. Torrance and E.M. Sparrow, "Theory for Off-Specular Reflection from Roughened Surfaces." *Journal of the Optical Society of America*, Vol. 57, No. 9, 1967, pp. 1105–1114.

[Turkowski] Ken Turkowski, "Properties of Surface-Normal Transformations." in Andrew Glassner (editor), *Graphics Gems*, Academic Press, Inc., pp. 539–547, 1990 or on his Web site at *http:/www.worldserver.com/turk/computergraphics/index.html*.

[Upstill] Steve Upstill, "The RenderMan Companion." Addison Wesley 1990, pp. 340–341.

[Valient] Michal Valient, "Advanced Lighting and Shading with DirectX 9." *ShaderX² - Introduction and Tutorials with DirectX 9*, Wordware Inc., pp. 83–150.

[VALVE] VALVE, Online Survey, *http://www.steampowered.com/status/survey.html*.

[Vlachos] Alex Vlachos, "Blending Textures for Terrain." *Direct3D ShaderX - Vertex and Pixel Shader Programming Tips and Tricks*, Wordware Inc., pp. 256–257, 2002.

[Waliszewski] Arkadiusz Waliszewski, "Floating-point Cube Maps." *ShaderX² - Shader Programming Tips and Tricks with DirectX 9*, Wordware Inc., pp. 319–323.

[Ward] Gregory J. Ward, "Measuring Modeling Anisotropic Reflection." SIGGRAPH 1992, pp. 265–272.

[WardG] Greg Ward, "Real Pixels." *Graphic Gems II*, Ed. by J. Arvo, Academic Press, 1992.

[Watt] Alan Watt, Mark Watt, *Advanced Animation and Rendering Techniques*. Addison Wesley, 1992.

[Weisstein] Eric Weisstein's World of Physics, *http://scienceworld.wolfram.com/physics/SnellsLaw.html*.

[Welsh] Terry Welsh, "Parallax Mapping." *ShaderX³: Advanced Rendering With DirectX And OpenGL*, Charles River Media 2004.

[Wenzel] Carsten Wenzel, "Using Lookup Tables in Vertex Shaders." *ShaderX² - Shader Programming Tips and Tricks with DirectX 9*, Wordware Inc., pp. 13–17.

[Williams] Lance Williams, "Casting Curved Shadows on Curved Surfaces." SIGGRAPH 78, pp. 270–274.

[Wloka] Matthias Wloka, "Where is That Instruction ? - How to Implement 'Missing' Vertex Shader Instructions." *http://developer.nvidia.com*.

[Wloka2] Matthias Wloka, "Fresnel Reflection." NVIDIA Technical Report, *http://developer.nvidia.com*.

[Wloka3] Matthias Wloka, "GPU GPU-Assisted Assisted Rendering Techniques." GDC 2004, *http://developer.nvidia.com*.

[Wynn] Chris Wynn, "Real-Time BRDF-based Lighting Using Cube-Maps." *http://developer.nvidia.com*.

Glossary

Anisotropic: Exhibiting different properties when measured from different directions. Directional dependence. For instance, anisotropic lighting takes into account direction with respect to the surface of incoming and/or outgoing light when illuminating a surface.

Anisotropic Filtering: With 2D textures, anisotropic filtering is thought of as a filter along a line across the texture with a width of two, and length up to the maximum degree of anisotropy. In three dimensions, this increases to a slab with width two extending in the other two dimensions up to the maximum degree of anisotropy. 3D anisotropy is not supported by current accelerators.

Anisotropic Lighting: See Anisotropic.

Bilerping/Bilinear Filtering: An image interpolation technique that is based on the averaging of the four nearest pixels in a digital image. First computes a texel address, which is usually not an integer address. Then finds the texel whose integer address is closest to the computed address. After that, computes a weighted average of the texels that are immediately above, below, to the left of, and to the right of the nearest sample point.

Binormal: To realize per-pixel tangent space lighting, a texture space coordinate system is established at each vertex of a mesh. With the help of this texture space coordinate system, a light vector or any other vector can be transformed into texture space. The axes of the texture space coordinate system are called tangent, binormal, and normal.

BRDF: Bidirectional Reflectance Distribution Functions. The BRDF is a generalization of all shading models, such as Lambert, Blinn, or Phong. A shading model is an analytic approximation of a surface's reflective properties. It describes how incoming light is reflected by a surface. The simplest shading model, Lambert shading, says that a surface reflects incoming light equally in all directions. Phong lighting, on the other hand, has an additional additive specular term, which permits a surface to reflect different amounts of light in different directions. Thus, each model is a formula, which computes for a given incoming and outgoing light direction the portion of incoming light that gets reflected in the outgoing direction. Such functions are called BRDFs.

Bump Map: Bump mapping adds the illusion of surface detail (bumpiness) to objects in 3D scenes, without adding more geometry than already exists. It does so by varying the lighting of each pixel according to values in a bump map texture. As each pixel of a triangle is rendered, a lookup is done into a texture depicting the surface relief (a.k.a. the bump map). The values in the bump map are then used to perturb the normals for that pixel. The new bumped-and-wiggled normal is then used during the subsequent color calculation, and the end result is a flat surface that looks like it has bumps or depressions in it. Usually a normal map (see normal map) contains the already perturbed normals. In this case, an additional bump map is not necessary.

C

Cartoon Shading: Cartoon shading (or *toon shading*) is properly only applied to shading in a cartoon style; the wider variety of shading in styles such as pen-and-ink, etc. falls under the category of NPR (Non-Photorealistic Rendering), which includes cartoon shading as a special case.

Cube Map: Cube mapping has becoming a common environment mapping technique for reflective objects. Typically, a reflection vector is calculated either per-vertex or per-pixel and is then used to index into a cube map that contains a picture of the world surrounding the object being drawn. Cube maps are made up of six square textures of the same size, representing a cube centered at the origin. Each cube face represents a set of directions along each major axis +X, -X, +Y, -Y, +Z, -Z. Think of a unit cube centered about the origin. Each texel on the cube represents what can be seen from the origin in that direction. The cube map is accessed via vectors expressed as 3D texture coordinates (S, T, R or U, V, W). The greatest magnitude component, U, V, or W, is used to select the cube face. The other two components are used to select a texel from that face. Cube mapping is also commonly used on ps_1_1 hardware for vector normalization with the light vector placed in the texture coordinates.

D

Dependent Read: A read from a texture map using a texture coordinate that was calculated earlier in the pixel shader, often by looking up the coordinate in another texture. This concept is fundamental to many of the advanced effects which use textures as transfer functions or complex functions like power functions.

Diffuse Lighting: Diffuse lighting simulates the light reflected by an object due to a particular light source. Therefore, you are able to see that light falls onto the surface of an object from a particular direction by using the diffuse lighting model. It is based on the assumption that light is reflected equally well in all directions, so the appearance of the reflection does not depend on the position of the observer. The intensity of the light reflected in any direction depends only on how much light falls onto the surface. If the surface of the object is facing the light source, which means it is perpendicular to the direction of the light, the density of the incident light is the highest. If the surface is facing the light source under some angle smaller than 90 degrees, the density is proportionally smaller. The diffuse reflection model is based on a law of physics called Lambert's law, which states that for ideally diffuse (totally matte) surfaces, the reflected light is determined by the cosine between the surface normal $\mathbf{N}$ and the light vector $\mathbf{L}$.

Directional Light: A directional light is a light source in an infinite distance. This simulates the long distance the light beams have to travel from the sun. In game programming, these light beams are treated as being parallel.

Displacement Map: A texture that store a single value at every texel, representing the distance to move the surface point along the surface normal.

E

Edge Detection: A type of filter that has a strong response at edges in the input image and a weak response in areas of the image with little change. This kind of filter is often used as the first step in machine vision tasks that must segment an image to identify its contents.

EMBM: Environment Mapped Bump Mapping. Introduced with DirectX6, this is a specific kind of dependent lookup (see Dependent Read) allowing values of texels in one texture to offset the fetching of texels in another texture, often an environment map. There are spherical, dual paraboloid, and cubic environment mapping (see Cube Map).

F

Fillrate Limited: One can generally differentiate between three kinds of possible limitations. CPU limited, vertex throughput limited, and fillrate limited. Whereas CPU limited and vertex throughput limited are self-explanatory, fillrate limited means that the application causes a bottleneck in the area between the rasterization stage and the end of the Direct3D pipeline.

Flux: Flux is the rate at which light energy is emitted.

Fresnel Term: Common real-time environment mapping reflection techniques reflect the same amout of light no matter how the surface is oriented relative to the viewer, much like a mirror or chrome. Many real materials such as water, skin, plastic, and ceramics do not behave in this way. Due to their particular physical properties, these materials appear to be much more reflective edge-on than when they are when viewed head-on. The change in reflectance as a function of the viewing angle is called the Fresnel effect. This effect is exhibited by all materials, not just glass and ceramic. It just happens to be less noticeable in metals due to the fact that they have higher reflectivity at normal incidence, so the Fresnel effect causes a less dramatic change in reflectance than in non-metals.

G

Graham-Schmidt Orthonormalization: Given a set of vectors making up a vector space, Graham-Schmidt Orthonormalization creates a new set of vectors that span the same vector space, but are unit length and orthogonal to each other.

I

Interreflection: Interreflection means the effect of indirect illumination; the light is not falling directly from any light source but being reflected from other surfaces of the world.

Irradiance: The term irradiance is the radiometric terminology for the energy of the incident light. It is expressed as energy per unit time and per unit area of the reflecting surface and is measured in W / m2 (Watt is the unit to measure flux, which is the rate at which light energy is emitted).

Isotropic: Exhibiting the same properties when measured from different directions. Directional independence.

L

Lambert Model: See Diffuse Lighting.

Light Reflection Vector: A vector that is usually called **R** that describes the direction of the reflected light.

Light Vector: A vector that describes the light direction.

LUT, Lookup Table: A pre-computed array of values used to replace a function evaluation often for the sake of performance. Many pixel shader techniques use 1D and 2D textures as lookup tables to calculate functions that are prohibitive or even impossible to calculate given the limited size and scope of the pixel shader instruction set.

Lux: Standard unit for illuminance is Lux (lx) which is lumens per square meter (lm/m^2).

M

Mip-Mapping: Mip-maps consist of a series of textures, each containing a progressively lower resolution of an image that represents the texture. Each level in the mip-map sequence has a height and a width that is half of the height and width of the previous level. The levels could be either square or rectangular. Using mip-maps ensures that textures retain their realism and quality as you move closer or farther away.

Multielement Texture: Multielement textures enable applications to write out to multiple elements of a texture, simultaneously, from the pixel shader. The result in the next rendering pass is that an application can use one or more of the elements as a single-element texture—that is, as inputs to the pixel shader. The main difference to multirender targets is that METs are contiguous. We have done some work with METs internally and with several developers. Because METs are implemented on graphics hardware via pack/unpack instructions, the performance curves are different than with MRT.

Multiple-Render Target: Up to four render-targets are supported by some graphics hardware. The advantage of using a multiple-render target (MRT) is that the pixel shader can write to the four render targets in one pass. The alternative and slightly different approach to MRT is the multielement texture (see Multielement Texture).

N

Normal Map: A normal map stores vectors that represent the direction in which the normal vector (see Normal Vector) points. A normal map is typically constructed by extracting normal vectors (see Normal Vector) from a height map whose contents represent the height of a flat surface at each pixel. A special case of a normal map is a bump map.

Normal Vector: Normals are vectors that define the direction a face or vertex is pointing, or the visible side of a face.

O

Orthogonal: A pair of vectors is orthogonal when the angle is PI/2 radians (90°) between them.

Orthonormal: Two vectors are considered to be orthonormal if both vectors are unit length, and have a dot product of 0 between them; i.e., the angle between them must be PI/2 radians (90°).

P

Photometry: Photometry is like radiometry except that it weights everything by the sensitivity of the human eye. Therefore, photometry deals with only the visible spectrum, also called the visible band, a wavelength range of about 380 to 780 nanometers (nm). A wavelength of 450 nm is blue, 540 nm is green, and 650 nm is red. However, photometry does not deal with the perception of color itself, but rather the perceived strength of various wavelengths. For example, green light appears considerably brighter to the eye than red or blue light.

Power of 2 Texture: A texture that has dimensions that fall into the set 1, 2, 4, 8, 16, 32, 64, 128, 256, 512, 1024, 2048, 4096. Some hardware is limited to textures of these dimensions, while other hardware may be more efficient at manipulating textures with these dimensions.

R

Radiance: Radiance is the term used to describe the flux density of radiation per unit solid angle and is measured in watts per square meter per steradian (W/m^2 sr).

Radiometry: Radiometry deals with the measurement of radiation throughout the electromagnetic spectrum. Historically, the field of radiometry has be concerned with optical radiation in the frequency range between $3 * 10^{11}$ and $3 * 10^{16}$ Hertz, which corresponds to wavelengths from 1000 to 0.01 micrometers. This range includes the infrared, visible, and ultraviolet regions of the electromagnetic spectrum.

Reflection: Is the return of light from a surface.

Reflection Vector: The mirror of a vector around a surface normal.

Refraction: Refraction is a phenomenon that simulates the bending of light rays through semi-transparent objects. There are several properties defined with refraction, Snell's law, and the critical angle. Snell's law states that for a light ray going from a less dense medium to a higher dense medium, the light ray will bend in one direction and going from a higher density medium to a lower density medium, it will bend in the other direction. These properties are known as the refraction index, and it is a ratio of the speed of light through one medium divided by the speed of light through the other medium.

Render Target: The buffer in memory to which a graphics processor writes pixels. A render target may be a displayable surface in memory like the front or back buffer or the render target may be a texture.

Renderable Texture: The render target (see render target) is a texture.

S

Sampling: Sampling means looking up a value in a texture at the specified up to four coordinates (u, v, w, q) while taking into account the texture stage attributes.

Shadow Volume: The volume of space that forms a shadow for a given object and light. Objects inside this volume of space are in shadow. Rapidly determining whether something is in shadow can be done by using the stencil buffer and a vertex shader.

Skinning: A technique for blending several bone matrices at a vertex level to produce a smooth animation.

Solid Angle: The unit solid angle is measured in terms of the area on a sphere intercepted by a cone whose apex is the sphere's center. Solid angles are measured in steradians (sr). The solid angle is the concept of a two-dimensional angle extended to three dimensions. In two dimensions, an angle of 2PI radians covers the whole unit circle. Extending this to three dimensions, a solid angle of 4PI steradians would cover the whole area of a unit sphere.

Spotlight: A light source in which all light rays illuminate in the shape of a cone. The falloff (the attenuation in the intensity of a light source as the distance increases), spread (the parameter that controls the width of the cone of light produced by the spotlight), and dropoff (the parameter that controls the way the light intensity fades based on its distance from the center of the light cone) of a spotlight are adjustable.

Steradian: Solid angles are measured in steradians.

T

Tangent Space: Tangent space is a 3D coordinate system defined for every vertex on the surface of an object. It can be used to transform from object or world-space into texture space. The x and y axes are tangent to the surface at the vertex, and are equal to the u and v directions of the texture coordinates respectively. The z axis is equal to the surface normal. Tangent space is used for a variety of per-pixel shaders due to the fact that most bump maps and other types of maps are defined in tangent space. Tangent space is sometimes called the Frenet Frame or a Surface Normal Coordinate Frame.

Tap: Each sample that contributes to a filter result is called a tap.

Taylor Series: A Taylor series allows one to generate approximate sine and cosine values without being computationally as expensive as the sine and cosine functions.

Texels: Abbreviation for texture elements, usually meaning 1 RGB or ARGB component of the texture.

Texture Space: See Tangent Space.

Topology: The arrangement in which the nodes of a 3D object are connected to each other.

Transfer Function: A function (often 1-dimensional) which is used to enhance or segment an input image. Transfer functions are often used in scientific visualization to enhance the understanding of complex datasets. A transfer function might map a scalar such as heat, pressure, or density to a color to aid in understanding the phenomenon being drawn. In games, transfer functions can be used on images to stylize them or to simulate effects like night-vision goggles or heat-sensitive displays. In volume graphics this is the mapping of a number to an RGBA tuple; it is used in volume visualization and volume graphics to assign colors to numeric data.

Trilinear Filtering: In case of 2D textures, that means that multiple linear filtered mip-maps are being blended together. In case of a 3D texture, trilinear filtering performs a linear filtering along all three axes of the texture, sampling colors from eight different texels. The filtering method that is called trilinear filtering in conjunction with 2D textures is called quadrilinear filtering for 3D textures.

Tweening: A technique for interpolating between two or more key frames to produce a smooth animation.

U

Unit Vector: A unit vector is a vector with the length 1. To calculate a unit vector, divide the vector by its magnitude or length.

W

Watt: Watt is the unit to measure flux.

Wavelength: Wavelength is the distance between identical points in the adjacent cycles of a waveform signal propagated in space or along a wire. In the case of infrared, visible light, ultraviolet, and gamma radiation, the wavelength is more often specified in nanometers (units of 10-9 meter) or Angstrom units (units of 10-10 meter).Wavelength is inversely related to frequency. The higher the frequency of the signal, the shorter the wavelength. If f is the frequency of the signal as measured in megahertz, and w is the wavelength as measured in meters, then $w = 300/f$ and conversely $f = 300/w$. Wavelength is sometimes represented by the Greek letter lambda.

Index